Charting the Course

of the University of Michigan
over Half of a Century

James and Anne Duderstadt

Preface

When the University of Michigan celebrates its Bicentennial year in 2017-2018, the Duderstadts will also be completing our 50th year at the University, surpassing all other Michigan presidents in the number of years of service to the University (including Presidents Angell and Ruthven). Furthermore, 35 of these years have been spent as members of the Michigan faculty community, including two decades after the presidency, yet another first for former presidents.

Over our half-century as members of the University community, we have had the opportunity to serve the University of Michigan in almost every faculty role. We began our service when Jim was recruited as a young faculty member in the Department of Nuclear Science and Engineering while Anne joined and later assumed leadership of the Faculty Women's Club (while earning her graduate degree). Next we were recruited into a sequence of University leadership roles that were very much two-person jobs: Dean and "Deanette", Provost and "Provostess", and President and First Lady of the University. After returning to the faculty and the University family in the late 1990s, we have both continued to work in a variety of roles for the University, creating new academic programs, launching dozens of projects to capture and illustrate its remarkable history through the use of rapidly evolving technologies, and working hard to advance the interests of the University through both roles and projects at the national and international level. Furthermore we have had the experience of being Michigan parents when both of our daughters earned their graduate degrees (a PhD and MD) at the University.

Hence we have had a front row seat in both observing and experiencing many of the events and changes that have occurred during this half-century of the University of Michigan and the Ann Arbor community, and also within the context of the extraordinary changes characterizing our state, the nation, and the world.

Hence it occurred to us that it might be interesting to share this unusual perspective of what has changed and what has stayed the same, the ups and downs, and what our University has gained and what it has lost over these many years. In fact, by charting the course of the University over the past half-century, perhaps we might be able to suggest some of the most important characteristics, principles, and values that could guide Michigan as it enters its third century in 2017.

Of course, over such an extended period, most characteristics of the University tend to fluctuate rather than exhibit a secular trend (except for the downward path of state support). For example, when we first arrived in Ann Arbor in the 1960s, the campus was alive with student activism and protest concerning important social issues such as civil rights, the Vietnam War, and the draft. President Fleming's wise leadership and the shifting priorities of society calmed the campus during the 1970s, but activism flared up once again in the 1980s and 1990s on both old issues (the lack of University progress in achieving racial diversity) and new (the creation of a campus police department). The late 1990s and early 21st century were again a time of calm, but both student and faculty activism have flared up once again during the 2010s over the administration's awkward efforts to impose a corporate style of centralized management onto a highly decentralized academic institution. The cyclic nature of many of these issues is important to recognize, since what is up today is likely to be down tomorrow, and vice versa.

There is also considerable variation in how one would measure the changing nature of various university activities. Some of these can be easily quantified, at least if one can pry the data out of the bureaucratic complexity of a $7 billion/year enterprise. For example, it is straightforward to demonstrate the University's rise and fall in racial diversity over this period. African American student enrollments rose from 4% during the 1960s up to over 9% in the 1990s due to the Michigan Mandate effort, only to collapse back to the 4% range over the past 15 years due both to state policy (a constitutional ban on affirmative action) and the lack of a strategic commitment to social diversity and inclusion.

However it requires a more subjective assessment to determine how many other characteristics have fared. For example, the Michigan saga as a pathfinder was in high gear during the 1960s, challenging the flaws of our society through student organizations such as the Students for a Democratic Society and academic activities such as Teach-ins. However the 1970s were a relatively placid time, without great impact on broader society. Michigan resumed its leadership role in the 1980s and 1990s, changing the world yet again through its role in building and managing the Internet and then developing the paradigm of massive digitization of scholarly materials. However this was followed by yet another inactive decade as the University focused on internal issues such as enrollment growth, cost-containment, and private fund-raising, while shifting both attention and priorities from resource-strained academic activities to the opportunities presented by prosperous auxiliary activities (e.g., hospitals, housing, and football).

To identify and analyze such trends requires not only a breadth of experience across the University, but also immersion in its activities over a considerable period of time. Since both happen to characterize our many years at Michigan, we have set out to provide just such a perspective as the University approaches its 200th birthday in 2017.

There are several important caveats we need to stress at the outset of this book. First our effort to chart the course of the University of Michigan over the past five decades is a highly personal one, based on experiences we have had, how we understood them, and, in limited instances, how we attempted to deal with what we found. Put another way, this is certainly not intended as either a comprehensive history of the University (a la Peckham's *The Making of the University of Michigan*),

or a data-driven analysis of the University at different points in its history (a la the *Michigan Almanac*).

A second caveat: This is an attempt to utilize the perspective gained through highly personal experiences to chart the course of the University of Michigan over its past half-century. Although we have concluded each chapter with several suggestions–some obvious, some on the radical fringe–about paths one might explore for Michigan's future, the University's third century will be shaped and led by new generations of faculty, students, staff, and leaders.

Finally, we have sprinkled throughout occasional observations and stories of a more humorous nature, accompanied from time to time with a few "zingers", both to reawaken the reader and to avoid any interpretation that this book is intended as an accurate history of the past half-century of the University of Michigan. Instead it is simply the perspective of two loyal members of the University community who have regarded serving the University of Michigan as our highest calling to public service.

James and Anne Duderstadt
Ann Arbor, Michigan
2016

Table of Contents

iv

Chapter 1

The University of Michigan, Circa 1960s

In December of 1968, the Duderstadts moved from Southern California to Ann Arbor, Michigan, following four years in sunny (rather, smoggy) Pasadena, Jim's graduate education, Anne's job as a department manager, and the birth of our two daughters, Susan and Kathy. It was a hot, sunny day in Pasadena–a Santa Ana condition, in fact–when we loaded our furniture moving van and took a taxi to LAX to fly to Detroit. We packed up our kids, who had never even seen snow, much less Michigan, and flew to Detroit, arriving in subzero cold and heavy snow.

We checked into the Ann Arbor Holiday Inn and awaited the arrival of our furniture–and our VW, which was also on the moving van–before we could move into our bare apartment in Northwood IV married student housing on the University's North Campus. Here we would note that during the 1960s, few of the new young faculty families could afford to purchase a house, so the University kindly allowed us to rent an apartment in married student housing until we earned enough to purchase our own home.

Christmas was approaching. Michigan Bell was on strike, so we had no telephone, no house, no friends, and little money. No wonder we felt rather alone in this strange, cold place, so different from the house we had been living in in Pasadena, surrounded by avocado trees and adjacent to the Caltech Campus.

Yet Ann Arbor during the 1960s was a very exciting place, with the University in a building boom that was rapidly changing the campus, student activism at fever pitch, and the arrival of a new football coach (Bo Schembechler)–ironically arriving the same week we did–kindling a new spirit of optimism about the Wolverines.

Hence, perhaps the best place to begin this narrative concerning our perspective of the past half-century of the University of Michigan is to describe our first impressions of the institution, its campus, and the Ann Arbor community.

The University of Michigan 1950s

The University of Michigan had long been regarded as one of the leading public universities in the nation, both in terms of the quality of its academic programs and the scale of its activities. For much of its early history it had been the largest university in the nation, both in terms of enrollment and the scale of its campus (and its football stadium, of course). Its medical center was similarly renown for the quality of its clinical care, its scale, and the medical research of its faculty. Following WWII, the federal commitment to funding campus-based research transformed the University into one of the world's leading research universities, with particularly strong programs in the social sciences, engineering, and the professions. Of note were major national research centers such as the Institute for Social Research, the Willow Run Laboratories, and the Michigan Memorial Phoenix Project, the nation's first university effort to develop peaceful applications of atomic energy. In fact, it was the latter effort that attracted us to Michigan, since the University had the world's leading programs in nuclear science and engineering, Jim's particular interests following graduation from Caltech with a PhD in engineering science and physics.

As described in more detail in Appendix A, the University's unusual degree of autonomy provided by the state constitution and its early establishment in 1817 as a territorial university some two decades before Michigan attained statehood gave it a broader character as both a national and international institution, in contrast to those public universities created much later by the states in response to the Morrill (Land-Grant) Act. Although state support was sufficient to sustain both the quality and growth of the institution during the first two decades following WWII, by the time we arrived in the late 1960s there were already early signs that this was beginning to deteriorate. Fortunately, the University had launched a successful fund-raising campaign during the 1960s (the first among public universities), and optimism was high that growth would continue, even if state support were to fluctuate.

The strong support of the Regents during the post-war decades, coupled with the strong leadership of President Harlan Hatcher and key deans such as Roger Heyns, William Haber, G. G. Brown, and Thomas Francis, along with unusually able administrators such as Wilbur Pierpont, had built both the quality and capacity of the University to the point where it rivaled not only leading public universities such as the University of California at Berkeley but also private universities such as Harvard, Yale, and MIT. Yet there were new challenges to the campus that required new leadership, and the year before we arrived, the Regents had selected a new president, Robben Fleming, from the chancellorship of the University of Wisconsin Madison, who had the skills to address both the activism developing on college campuses and the new challenges presented by the state and the federal government. President Fleming and his wife Sally were to become both our mentors and friends as we later followed them into leadership roles ourselves.

The Michigan Campus, Circa 1960s

When we first arrived in Ann Arbor, in 1968, the Central Campus of the University looked much as it does today, with the major Albert Kahn buildings already several decades old (including the great Hill Auditorium). Both the towering Hatcher Library and the Mondrian-designed Administration building had recently opened, although the most majestic new building on the Central Campus was the new Dental School, rumored to be the most expensive building in the University's history.

The Medical Campus included not only a bewildering complex of clinical buildings surrounding the "Old Main" University Hospital, but several blocks to the west was St. Joseph's Mercy Hospital, a clinical facility comparable in both size and activity to the University's medical campus.

Further to the North and across the Huron River was the University's North Campus, still largely a vacant area of rolling hills and forests, inhabited only by research facilities such as the Phoenix Memorial Laboratory, the Cooley Electronics Laboratory, several engineering research buildings, and Jim's Department of Nuclear Science and Engineering (because of the use of the Ford Nuclear Reactor and other nuclear research laboratories on the North Campus). There had been some recent efforts to begin to populate the new campus, including the Eero Saarinen designed School of Music and the tower of the Institute of Science and Technology, but in the 1960s the North Campus had few students or instructional activities.

There was a long-standing promise to move the entire College of Engineering (and perhaps as well the School of Education) out to the campus, but these remained only dreams, although the College encouraged its faculty members to purchase homes near the North Campus. We ignored this advice, primarily since we could not afford the housing in the northern Ann Arbor subdivisions. We eventually ended up purchasing a home on the south side of Ann Arbor, close to the public schools.

The South Campus was dominated by Michigan Stadium and the new Crisler Arena, nicknamed "the House that Cazzie built" because of the Michigan basketball team's 1960's success led by its star, Cazzie Russell. The great size of Michigan Stadium, even then one of the largest stadiums in the nation, was hidden by its location in an excavated bowl with only a small pressbox and entrance tunnels visible from ground level, until one walked into the massive stadium itself.

The rapid growth of the campus began to slow in the late 1960s, both because of the weakening of state appropriations, but even more so because of action by the State Legislature to allocate all monies for planning and constructing university buildings through the state controller, including planning and letting contracts. Unfortunately this conflicted directly with the University of Michigan's constitutional autonomy, and the institution wisely refused to put this at risk by

The University of Michigan Central Campus in the 1960s

accepting state-funded projects with this restriction for the next decade. Although the constraint eventually was withdrawn, by that time the impact of the energy crisis on the state's economy, coupled with the growing pressure of the Japanese automobile industry on Detroit, triggered the beginning of a more permanent erosion of state support that would continue for decades to come.

Academic Activities

The 1960s were a time of unusual experimentation for the University. A Residential College for undergraduates was launched in the East Quad Residence Halls (although the original plan called for a new set of residence halls along Fuller Road between Center and North Campus). The Pilot Program, the Inteflex program (a joint-B.S./M.D. program), and the Honors programs were other examples of important academic innovations in student living-learning environments

With the Cold War following closely on the heals of WWII, it was natural that the engineering and physical science programs of the University would continue to be heavily involved in defense research, including the efforts of the Willow Run Laboratories (Project Wolverine) in remote sensing, Aerospace Engineering's involvement in guided missile and space flight technology (including astronaut training), and Computer Science and Engineering, with the co-development with IBM of the first time-sharing system (MTS). The University launched the world's first university program in the peaceful uses of atomic energy with the Michigan Memorial Phoenix Project as its WWII memorial to the University's war casualties. The Phoenix Project began to contribute major scientific breakthroughs such as Donald Glaser's development of the bubble chamber for high-energy physics and William Beierwaltes's use of I-131 to launch the field of nuclear medicine. The social sciences also rapidly gained strength and national leadership with the Survey Research Center, the Institute for Social Research, and the Center for Research on Learning and Teaching. In

4

Our daughters provide a tour of the University, circa 1969, including our VW, Northwood Housing, the Central Campus "dinosaur museum", the "cube", Jim's North Campus lab, ..and their future home (20 years later).

fact, by the 1960s, 21 of the University's departments were ranked in the top 10, a number exceeded only by Harvard, Yale, and UC-Berkeley.

As it has often been, the University's academic priorities were heavily influenced by national rather than state needs. There was a strong emphasis on science and engineering associated with the defense needs of the nation in the Cold War years along with the space program. Similarly, the latter years of the 1960s were characterized by the priorities of the Great Society, with major investments in programs in education, social sciences, and public health. Although the energy crisis of the 1970s shocked the national economy, there were already signs that the aging baby boomers where shifting national priorities toward health care, perhaps best illustrated on the UM campus by the investment in the new Dental School complex and the massive Replacement Hospital Project. The weakening of the Michigan economy brought economic competitiveness onto the table with major investments in Engineering (including the move to the North Campus) and Business Administration. Although the "dot-com" explosion during the 1990s and the end of the Cold War suggested that a "peace dividend " would boost investment once again in technology, instead an aging population continued to place health care and hence biomedical research as the nation's highest priority, at least in terms of investment in higher education, with strong growth across all of the health sciences.

The Protest Generation

In the early 1960s a new generation of students, largely pampered by "the Greatest Generation" of their parents, who had not only saved the nation in WWII but invested heavily in their children's future, had arrived on campus with a new spirit of activism. While much of their agenda was concerned with significant national issues such as civil rights and the Vietnam War, they were also intent with challenging the establishment. The Free Speech Movement at UC-Berkeley spawned student rebellion against not only the student policies of American universities, but also challenged the full spectrum of student traditions such as *in loco parentis*, student disciplinary policies, fraternities and sororities, and other traditional aspects of student life.

Demonstrating their new freedoms, they dropped out and turned on, embracing the drug culture and hippie movement of Haight-Ashbury on many campuses. The youth culture of the 1960s were anti-establishment, anti-war, anti-elitism, anti-materialism, and were instead for free love, free sex, and free pot! Michigan not only was a part of this new student culture, but the University's students actually led it with more radical groups such as the Students for Democratic Society and the Port Huron Manifesto.

The "protest generation" of students not only pushed the universities out of student lives, but in many ways the new spirit of rebellion and rejection of tradition severed much of the University from its past. Students refused to attend not only commencements but even athletic events–although they would use these for highly visible protest movements from time to time. Old traditions such as the J-Hop, freshman hazing, class plays, and other long-standing student activities disappeared. Even the Greeks were on hard times and had to take in boarders, dropping from 12% to 5 % of the student body.

Students took to the streets to protest national causes such as the war in Vietnam, energized in part by the threat of the draft for most male college students by the late 1960s. A particularly volatile issue concerned Michigan's low minority enrollments, triggering the formation of the Black Action Movement that demanded commitment to achieving 10% black enrollment by the early 1970s, and using both sit-ins and University-wide strikes to push their agenda.

Our memories of the University and Ann Arbor of the late 1960s are filled with images that are more amusing that threatening today: The liberation of South University as a "free love" zone. The John Lennon concert to free John Sinclair, jailed for smoking pot. Hacking a Ford car to death on the Diag to demonstrate the damage cars do to the environment. A counter-culture version of a University Homecoming parade. A rock concert in an Ann Arbor park by the rock group, the MC-5, "kicking out the jams". Candidates of the Rainbow People's Party running for City Council.

Of course, all was not fun and peaceful demonstrations. University buildings were taken over. The Black Action Movement threatened the University with several strikes against classes. Fortunately, the

Rallies on the Diag against the Viet Nam War

Students led the battle against "isms"!

It was a time for protest...even during the Homecoming parade.
Even our daughters joined in with friend to protest a protest!

University's president, Robben Fleming, was an experienced labor negotiator and understood how to keep such demonstrations from boiling over into violence and personal injury. He skillfully kept the agenda of a few radical agitators from provoking larger crowds into serious disruption of the campus. In fact, President Fleming succeeded in earning the respect of both the University community and those who were challenging its policies and commitments. He was clearly the right leader for these difficult times.

The Faculty Family

Fortunately, within a few weeks after our arrival, Anne encountered the first signs of the strong social network that had developed within the University through the wives of faculty members. She was contacted by the leaders of the Newcomers Section of the Faculty Women's Club and invited both to join and to meet other new arrivals at a series of social get-togethers for the over 700 new faculty wives joining the University that year.

Here it is important to stress just how important such faculty organizations were to new faculty families. The University is a very diverse and complex organization, broken up into smaller social groups usually aligned with academic departments or work areas. One can image the differences among academic units such as Law, Medicine, Engineering, and LS&A, or among the diverse departments and programs in each of these

Back in those days, Michigan football was a "community event", with $2 tickets
for children and a special day to honor the State's high school bands.

units. While most of these academic departments made some effort to welcome and orient their new faculty members, their families were generally ignored.

In contrast, the Faculty Women's Club spanned the entire university, hosting an unusually broad set of activities and interest groups both for faculty wives and more broadly their families. In fact, since being launched by President Burton's wife, Nina Burton, in the 1920s, it had become the primary social organization for pulling together faculty members and their families across the University. While many of the women in the Faculty Women's Club would remain active throughout their lives (including many of the wives of senior university leaders such as presidents and deans), the FWC Newcomers group played a particularly important role both in welcoming new arrivals to the University and providing them with opportunities to become engaged in its broad range of activities, both as members and as families.

Although there were many other opportunities for faculty to come together, such as family events (school programs, summer activities), cultural events (performing arts), or "cosmic athletic events" (UM football and basketball), these usually appealed to particular interests or periods in family life (e.g., school-age children). It was also a time when academic programs such as departments and research institutes hosted frequent events to pull together faculty members and their families to create a sense of community.

The City of Ann Arbor

Part of our attraction to the University of Michigan was the city of Ann Arbor itself. We remember an observation made by Robben Fleming during the 1970s when he suggested that the three universities that were the most difficult to raid for faculty were: i) Harvard, because of its tradition and reputation, ii) Indiana University, because of the strange role Bloomington plays in symbolizing the best of the state's culture, and iii) Ann Arbor, in large measure because of the quality of life characterizing our community.

Esquire magazine once called cities such as Ann Arbor as "academic womb" communities, a small city whose culture is dominated by a great university. After a few years at Michigan, one might be tempted to go to another institution, but it would be difficult indeed to leave the "academic womb" of communities such as Madison, Chapel Hill, Champaign-Urbana, or Berkeley. These are cities with a vast array of world-class cultural opportunities, intellectual excitement, and (at least until recently priced beyond most of our citizens) big-time college sports and all within a few minutes drive, if you can find the parking.

Ann Arbor is an exciting, cosmopolitan, richly diverse, and wonderful place to live and work. Not to say that there are not some drawbacks: the crowds during football game days, the amount of property taken off the tax roles by the University, occasional

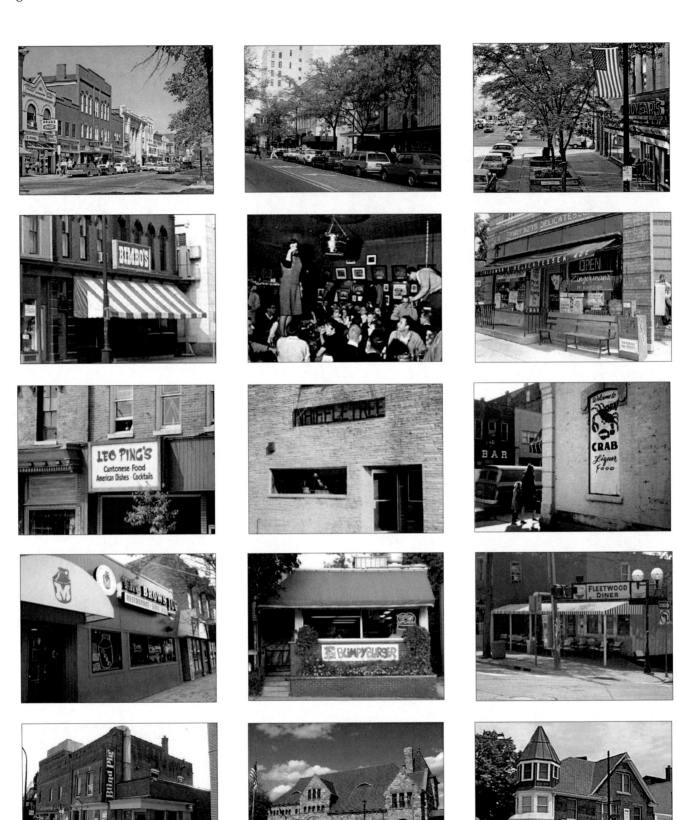

Ann Arbor memories from the 1960s and 1970s

Ann Arbor memories from the 1960s and 1970s

The Ann Arbor community today

student rowdy behavior, and, of course, never enough parking. Yet the presence of one of the nation's largest universities in the relatively small city of Ann Arbor provided an unusual array of world-class community events, affordable, easily attended, and important for pulling together a diverse communities of students, faculty, staff, and townspeople.

Of course, the premier activity in the fall was Michigan football. Although the team was good, Michigan Stadium was so large that it was rarely sold out during the 1960s (except for Ohio State and Michigan State), typically averaging 80,000 fans. Hence it was both easy and affordable for groups of faculty couples and even families to arrange to sit together (children's tickets were only $2), so that the games became an important social event. In fact, in an effort to build attendance, each fall the University would invite dozens of high school bands to participate in the halftime performance, and invite all of the Boy Scouts in the area to serve as ushers for a game. This social role of Michigan football provided a very important opportunity for gathering the diverse town-gown community together in a common activity (either to cheer on Michigan Wolverines or the Michigan Marching Band, depending on one's proclivities).

The second world-class activity involved the University Musical Society, which attracted many of the world's leading symphonies and musical performers to Hill Auditorium, again priced attractively enough that this became a community event ($15 to $30 for a season ticket to the entire Choral Union Series). The highlight of each year was the May Festival, four nights of performances by the Philadelphia Orchestra led by Eugene Ormandy, which capped off the academic year with guest performers such as Vladimir Horowitz and Van Cliburn.

Of course there are many other more relaxed memories of Ann Arbor and the University from those early days. The Pretzel Bell and Village Bell restaurants were still the places where students would celebrate reaching their 21st birthdays and "drinking age". New hangouts such the Gandy Dancer and the Whiffletree became popular eating establishments. And who could ever forget Bimbos, with peanut shells on the floor and a great Dixieland band or the Blind Pig with a more progressive taste in avant guarde music.

Charting a Course to the Future

Both the University of Michigan and the City of Ann Arbor in the 1960s provide several benchmarks, in the energy, excitement, and impact of these communities, against which we might measure the subsequent evolution of the University over the next half-century. Ann Arbor was still very much a small town, but with extraordinary cultural resources. The University was highly regarded as one of the great universities of the world. And University students and faculty were unusually active, engaged, and influential in addressing some of the importance challenges of this era, although their energy and concerns frequently challenged the authority and patience of University leadership and governance.

Today a rapidly changing world demands new commitments from leading universities such as Michigan–a new level of knowledge, skills, and abilities on the part of its students, research of both basic and applied nature to address the future challenges facing our world, and deep engagement with our society, deploying the unique assets of great public research universities to address their needs and concerns. Perhaps these should frame the discussion of the future of the University of Michigan as it approaches its third century. It certainly provides the context for considering the evolution of the University of Michigan, its ups and its downs, over the past half century.

Appendix

Some Timelines of the Past 50 Years

National and World Events

1950 McCarthy
1950 Korean War
1955 Salk Vaccine
1957 Little Rock School Desegregation
1958 National Defense Education Act
1958 Integrated Circuit
1961 Bay of Pigs
1961 Vietnam War
1962 Cuban Missile Crisis
1962 SDS
1963 MLK March
1963 JFK Assassination
1965 Lyndon Johnson's Great Society speech
1965 Voting Rights Act
1965 Medicaid and Medicare
1965 Higher Education Act
1967 Detroit Riots
1968 Tet Offensive
1968 Nuclear Nonproliferation Treaty
1969 Neal Armstrong on Moon
1969 Woodstock
1970 Kent State
1970 Earth Day
1970 EPA
1972 Nixon to China
1972 Watergate
1972 Apollo 17
1973 Roe vs. Wade
1973 OPEC Oil Crisis
1974 Nixon resigns; Ford becomes president
1975 Bill Gates founds Microsoft
1977 First personal computer (Commodore)
1979 Three Mile Island nuclear accident
1979 Chrysler loan guarantees
1981 Reagan becomes president
1986 Gramm-Rudman
1987 Berlin: Tear down this wall
1989 End of Cold War
1990 Gulf War

1991 USSR dissolved
1992 Major weather events begin
1998 Lewinsky scandal
1999 Y2 Bug
2001 Bush Tax Cuts
2001 Patriot Act
2002 No Child Left Behind Act
2002 Department of Homeland Security
2002 Invasion of Iraq
2004 Hurricane Katrina
2008 Great Recession
2009 Barack Obama
2010 Patient Protection and Affordable Care Act
2010 Deepwater Horizon Spill
2011 Dodd Frank Bill
2012 Fragmentation of political collaboration

National Higher Education

1950s
Massification
NSF-NIH-DOD created
Cold War-Sputnik
National Defense Education Act

1960s
Formation of state university systems
California Master Plan
Publics overtake privates as national priority
Research universities begin to appear
R&D focus on defense and space
Protest generation (Free Speech, SDS)
Racial unrest, civil rights

1970s
Baby boomer student surge
Pell Grants signal federal involvement
Mansfield Amendment changes fellowships into RAs
Affirmative action
Cal Prop 13 signals decline of priority of K-12

1980s
Baby boom ceases, HS graduate dip
Federal grants replaced by loans
Private wealth swamps publics

Research priorities: Cold War ends, guns to pills
Bayh-Dole Act and tech transfer
USN&WR launch rankings game

1990s
For profits appear
Internet and Dot-Com bubble
Prop 209 challenge to affirmative action
Tidal Wave 2 on horizon with baby boomer kids

2000s
State funding collapses (-35%)
Immigration surge
Social networking (Facebook, Twitter,…)
Open knowledge: OCW, Google, Wikipedia…
No Child Left Behind…worry about K-12

2010s
States no longer support research universities
Both privates and publics approach tuition ceilings
Faculty retirement challenges
China passes US both in economy and HE
New technologies (MOOCs, big data, analytics)

U Michigan Timeline

1950s
UMAA doubles in size (GI Bill)
Willow Run defense research (Project Michigan)
Defense and space research
Strong state support for operations and facilities
North Campus expansion
Strength in the quantitative sciences

1960s
UM Expansion as a "system": UM Flint, UM Dear-
born, North Campus
Survey Research Center, Institute for Social Research
Student protests, SDS
Black Action Movement (Detroit riots)
In loco parentis ends
Some academic innovation: RC, Pilot, Inteflex, etc.
Shift from UG focus to professional school focus
State constitutional convention extends UM's consisti-
tutal autonomy to all state universities

1970s
Robben Fleming calms the storm
Labor takes over Regents; major unionization of UM
Expansion of state higher education as community
colleges become 4-year institutons
Spinoff of Willow Run (and classified research)
Early preparation for anticipated financial storm
by Provost Harold Shapiro (e.g., Budget Priorities
Committee)

1980s
Automobile industry collapses (Japan competition)
State support collapses (drops 30% over 2 years)
State support of facilities ceases (never restored)
Shapiro Three-Point plan: costs down, tuition up,
fund-raising up
"Smaller but better" strategy --> focus on excellence
Massive growth in Medical Center: RHP, CMHC, …
Research incentives drives UM R&D $ to #1 in nation
UM joins with IBM to create Internet

1990s

VP Womack establishes central "bank" increasing UM
reserves from $200 M to a $2.5 B endowment during
decentralization strategy: RCM, TQM, placing power
with deans
$1.4 billion campaign, endowment up x10, R&D $
doubles
Diversity becomes priority: Michigan Mandate,
Agenda for Women, Gay rights leading to highest UM
diversity in history (9.4% AA, doubling AA faculty)
Innovation: Media Union, JSTOR, School of
Information
Renewal of most academic facilities
Focus on Leadership, Vision, Transformation
Duderstadt --> Bollinger ("back to the future")

2000s
Replace tuition increases with enrollment increases
Preoccupation with whims: Royal Shakespeare
Theater, Life Sciences Institution, Michigan Stadium
"halo"
Resources flat (no fund-raising, no tuition increases)
State support drops another 50%

Enrollment increases begin; diversity begins to drop
  2003 Supreme Court case; diversity continues to drop,
      erasing all the gains of the 1990s and dropping
      below levels of the 1960s
Attempts to recentralize by weakening deans through
external appointments
Major fund-raising $3.3 B fund-raising campaign
Expansion of PR efforts ("global" communications,
branding, Athletic Director Brand-on)

2010s
State support continues to deteriorate
Huge enrollment growth (+10,000 students, +25%,
most out-of-state)
Tuition revenue increases to $1.2 B, R&D up to $1.3 B,
Endowment: $10 B
Shift to part-time faculty for UG instruction
University priorities shift from academic to auxiliary
(hospitals, housing, athletics
Loss of community
Loss of public purpose (a university for "the common
man" becomes a university for "the 1%"
Efforts to re-centralize ("shared services")
Athletics out of control (sold to the highest bidder)
Modest academic innovation (mostly "me-too-isms")

2020 and beyond
Third Century Goals:
    Reflection: Restore the Michigan Saga
    Renaissance: Stress creativity, innovation
    Enlightment: Provide the light of knowledge and
        learning to the world
    "A more perfect union": Restore UM as a learning
        community!

Chapter 2

Growth

Throughout its history, the University of Michigan has been one of the nation's largest universities, vying with the largest private universities such as Harvard and Columbia during the 19th and early 20th centuries, and then holding this position of national leadership until the emergence of the statewide public university systems (e.g., the University of California and the University of Texas) in the post-WWII years. Perhaps this addiction to growth was best explained by Michigan President Marion Leroy Burton during the 1920s, when he concluded "A state university must accept happily the conclusion that it is destined to be large. If its state grows and prosper, it will naturally reflect those conditions." (Peckham, 1963)

During our early years at Michigan, we really did not sense the immense size of the University except on Saturday afternoons in the fall. After several years living in Pasadena and the Los Angeles metroplex, Ann Arbor seemed quite small–indeed, even quaint. But the scale of the University became more apparent with the amount of construction that began to appear on the University campus in the early 1980s with the Replacement Hospital Project and then on the North Campus with the construction of the new Engineering facilities. Throughout the late 1980s and 1990s, the University campuses continued to be dotted with new construction, stimulating the suggestion that perhaps Michigan should trade its wolverine mascot for the crane (the construction crane, that is).

By the mid-1990s in the roles of dean, provost, and president, we had accumulated considerable experience with all of the University's campuses: Central Campus, North Campus, Medical Campus, Athletic Campus, and to some extent even the Flint and Dearborn Campuses. In these roles we became aware of the growth of the University in other areas such as sponsored research activity (a national leader), the rapid expansion of the University health system (growing larger than the University itself), and, fortunately, the endowment created by our financial teams, led by Farris Womack, which grew from \$200 M to \$2.5 B during the 1990s. Such growth in resources was fortunate, since state support continued to decline during the 1980s and 1990s and then even more rapidly after 2000, dropping to less than 8% of the academic budget and 4% of the total budget of the Ann Arbor campus by 2015.

In contrast to the growth in facilities and endowment, the enrollments of the University remained stable at roughly 35,000 students during the 1980s and 1990s. However enrollments began to grow rapidly in the 2000s with the decision of a new administration to attract more out-of-state students capable of paying much higher tuition (e.g., \$40,000/y compared to \$14,000/y for instate students). The addition of another 10,000 students to the University's Ann Arbor campus, while compensating for the loss of state support, seriously strained both the faculty and physical capacity of the University, raising serious questions about whether this unbridled growth had changed the fundamental character of the institution.

Growth of the University

It can be argued that it was in the Midwest, in frontier towns such as Ann Arbor and Madison, that true universities first appeared in America. By augmenting the traditional mission of educating the young with faculty scholarship and public service to society, the emerging public state universities created a uniquely American university capable of responding to the needs of a rapidly changing nation in the 19th Century and that still dominates higher education today.

The University of Michigan campus (1855, Cropsey)

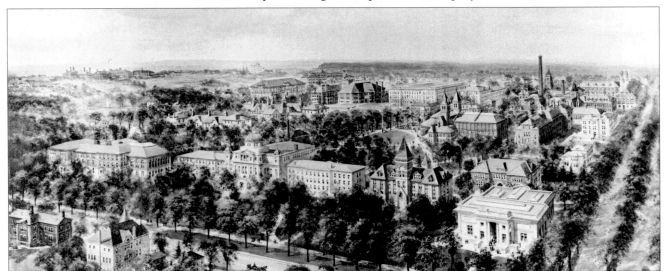

The University of Michigan campus (1910, Rummell)

The University of Michigan campus (1930)

The University of Michigan campus (1970)

The University of Michigan campus (2000)

The University of Michigan campus (2010)

The University of Michigan was established in 1817 in the village of Detroit by an act of the Northwest Territorial government and financed through the sale of Indian lands granted by the United States Congress. However it was only after the State of Michigan entered the Union in 1837 that a new plan was adopted to focus the University on higher education, establishing it as a "state" university after the Prussian system, with programs in literature, science and arts; medicine; and law–the first three academic departments of the new university. The new Michigan State Legislature authorized funds to purchase a campus for the University, and an enterprising group of citizens from Ann Arbor offered a 40 acre site in their community, now known as the University's Central Campus. (Actually, the group first wanted to attract the state capital, but that went to Lansing. Then they considered going after the state prison before finally offering the site for a university.)

Campus Growth

The Ann Arbor campus expanded rapidly through the latter 19th and into the 20th century, as shown by the sequence of campus illustrations, broadening beyond the confines of the original 40 acres and then expanding northward toward the Huron River to accommodate the expansion of the University hospital and related medical facilities.

Although growth was relatively modest during the early 20th Century through the Depression years, following WWII the returning veterans doubled enrollments, followed by the baby boom of the 1960s and 1970s that doubled the size again. To accommodate anticipated further growth, the Regents acquired farm property north of the city of Ann Arbor for both academic programs and student residences. During the 1950s the University began to build new laboratory facilities and student apartments on its North Campus. There were even plans to build additional student residence halls along the Huron River between the Central Campus and the North Campus with estimates of future enrollments ranging as high as 100,000 students.

In the post WWII years, the federal government adopted policies that funded much of the nation's basic research on university campuses, thereby transforming leading institutions such as Michigan into research universities, and expanding their public purpose to include contributions to the security, public health, and prosperity of the nation in addition to their responsibilities to their states. The University's commitment to serve the needs of the state also continued to expand with the growth of clinical care facilities by the University Medical Center, the creation of extension services to provide instruction throughout the state through instructional television, strong collaboration with Michigan industry, and, of course, providing high quality educational opportunities at the undergraduate, graduate, and professional level for Michigan citizens. Hence the expanding missions of the University in teaching, research, and service (particularly in the Medical Center) have led to continued growth of the institution in all its characteristics–people, facilities, budget, and impact–over the past half century, despite the decline in state support.

The history of the growth of the University from its move to Ann Arbor to the late 1960s when we arrived in Ann Arbor is shown in a detailed map developed by Myron Mortenson of the UM Plant Department (and known as "Mort's Map" and available at: http://umhistory.dc.umich.edu/mort/). The dramatic growth since that time can be seen by detailed 3D maps of the Central, Medical, and North Campuses in Chapter 9.

Enrollment Growth

Although University enrollments stabilized at 9,000 during the Depression years of the 1930s, they exploded following World War II, as the returning veterans supported by the G.I. Bill arrived on campus, taking enrollments to over 20,000 by 1950 (of whom 11,000 were veterans). The enrollments on the Ann Arbor campus declined following the post WWII surge, slipping back to 17,000 in 1956. However they began to grow again during the 1960s as both faculties and campuses expanded rapidly to accommodate the children of the post-war families (the "baby boomers") reaching college age in the 1960s, swelling the University to 22,000 in 1960 and 30,000 in 1970. Federal research funding increased dramatically. National priorities such as the Cold War and the space program and the

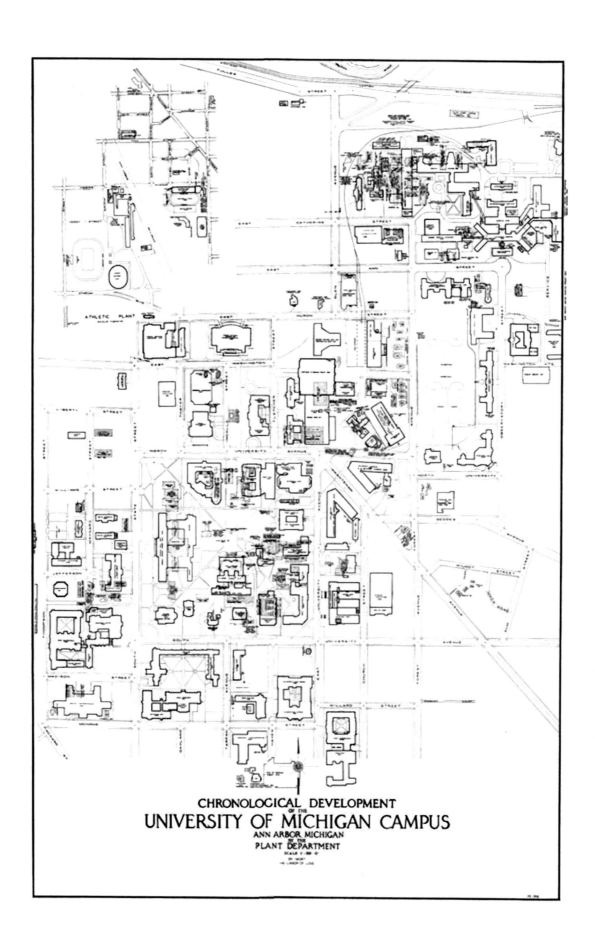

CHRONOLOGICAL DEVELOPMENT
OF THE
UNIVERSITY OF MICHIGAN CAMPUS
ANN ARBOR MICHIGAN
BY THE
PLANT DEPARTMENT

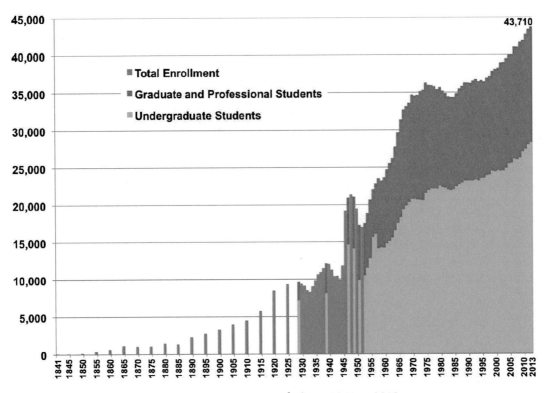

UM Enrollment Growth from 1841 to 2013

social priorities of the Great Society fueled dramatic growth in graduate education and professional schools such as education, social work, and public health.

In 1956 the Flint Board of Education asked UM to establish a Flint branch of an upper-class college coupled to Flint Community College, while the Ford family presented the Fairlane estate along with a $6.5M gift to encourage a similar upper-class college in Dearborn. The assumption was that these upper-class colleges would be discontinued as the post War II enrollments subsided, and both programs began to flounder in the late 1960s, stagnating with enrollments of less than 2,000. However once launched, universities campuses are rarely abandoned, and with the help of the Mott and Ford Foundations and a state commitment of appropriations, the Regents approved upgrading these upper-class colleges into viable 4-year campuses, UM-Flint and UM-Dearborn.

During the 1960s and 1970s there were similar examples of "mission creep" throughout Michigan as the community colleges at Grand Valley and Saginaw Valley successfully convinced the State Legislature to allow them to evolve into 4-year "universities".

Several of the state's undergraduate colleges began to add graduate programs, thereby creating increasing pressure for additional state support. Wayne State University joined Michigan and Michigan State as a "constitutional" university in 1956. This growth and competition of public colleges and universities in the state would soon put pressure on the traditionally strong state support of the University of Michigan.

Enrollments on the Ann Arbor campus stabilized at 35,000 during the 1980s and 1990s. However, in an effort to counter the decline in state appropriations by admitting more out-of-state students paying high tuition, in 1998 the University began to increase enrollments once again. By 2014, enrollments had reached 44,000, a 25% increase from the 1980s and 1990s. While this generated a very significant increase in tuition revenue (rising to $1.2 billion per year and far exceeding the University's state support), it not only strained facilities but also dramatically increased instructional loads on the existing faculty, which had to be augmented by large increases in non-tenure track and part-time instructors, particularly at the undergraduate level.

Another demonstration of enrollment growth.

Growth of student high-rise apartments in Ann Arbor.

Faculty and Staff Growth

Ann Arbor Growth

With a relatively stable enrollment during the 1980s and 1990s, there was little growth in the size of the faculty, particularly since the rapid growth in enrollment of baby-boomer children during the 1960s had stimulated significant faculty hiring at that time. Furthermore, the decline in state funding during the 1980s and 1990s also limited staff growth, at least in numbers.

Yet in recent years there has been significant change in the faculty and staff population. Rather than accommodating the rapid growth in enrollments during the past two decades (from 34,500 to 44,000 students) with comparable growth in the permanent faculty, the University chose instead to rapidly increase the number of part-time lecturers and non-tenure track faculty, now providing over 50% of the instruction at the undergraduate level.

Furthermore, while the staffing has been relatively constant across most of the University, there has been a very significant growth in the number of administrative staff, particularly in areas such as fund-raising, public relations, and university marketing. While this has been most evident at the level of the central administration, many schools and colleges also have seen very significant growth in staff size. For example, the administration of the College of Engineering, which had only 30 staff in the 1980s, now has over 240 staff members reporting to the deans and department chairs, many of whom are compensated at levels significantly higher than the core faculty of the College.

The City of Ann Arbor grew with the University of Michigan's enrollment, in part because over 30,000 of its employees live among the 117,000 population of the city (including 12,000 from the Medical Center). To this one must add the 44,000 students, only one-third of whom live in University housing. The surge both in enrollments and in the relative wealth of students has driven an apartment boom in the city, as evidenced by the larger number of high rise buildings dotting the city center. Indeed, when we first arrived in Ann Arbor during the late 1960s, there were only three buildings above 10 stories in height. Today hardly a year goes by without several new high-rise buildings proposed by real estate developers with the purpose of housing the growing number of affluent students.

While the actual population of the city appears to be growing gradually, the urbanization of the city in terms of new construction and traffic flow driven by the University seems quite pronounced.

Michigan Today: "The Biggest in the Land"!

Today the University of Michigan's Ann Arbor campus has become one of the largest in the nation, while not in terms of enrollment (44,000 students), but rather in budget ($7.1 B/y), research activity ($1.3 B/y), campus facilities (36 million net-square-feet)...and, of course, Michigan Stadium (110,000). It is instructive to consider each of these measures in more detail:

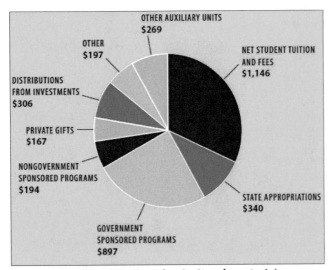

UM Total Budget (including hospitals)

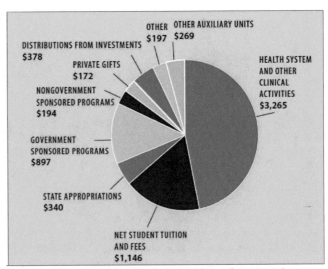

UM Academic Budget (without hospitals)

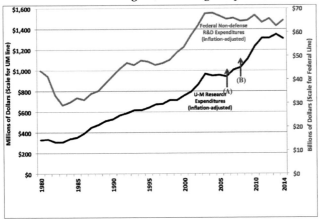

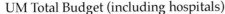

Growth in UM research expenditures

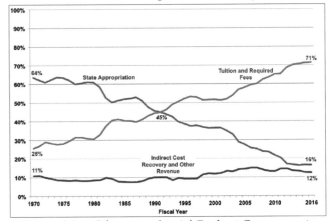

General Fund (core academic) Budget Components

Financial Resources

Today the University of Michigan leads the nation in the size of the budget for its Ann Arbor campus ($7 B for FY2015) and its academic (non-hospital) activities ($2.8 B).

Of course, while these characteristics are impressive, so too are the challenges facing the University. Over the past several decades, state support of the University has dropped to less than 8% of its academic budget. Fortunately, the University managed to dramatically increase its endowment during the past two decades (from $200 million to $10 billion), so that the endowment now generates more support for the University than the state appropriation ($450 M/y vs $300 M/y). Nevertheless, the sustainability of adequate support to maintain the quality of research and teaching for a public university of this scale with state support

declining to less than 4% of the total University budget is a matter of great concern.

As a consequence of the dramatic growth in student enrollments, research activity, clinical care, campus construction, and budgets over the past two decades, today the University has reached an extraordinary scale. With a total budget now exceeding $7 billion/year, a campus continuing to expand both with new buildings and the acquisition of the 200 acre site and facilities of the adjacent Pfizer Global Research Laboratories, and a research budget now in excess of $1.32 billion/year, one could well claim that the Ann Arbor campus of the University of Michigan has become the largest, most comprehensive, and most complex university campus in the world. In fact, the population of 65,362 students, faculty, and staff on the Michigan campus is comparable to the population of 117,000 for its host city, Ann Arbor (which is nearly exceeded on Saturday afternoons by

Undergraduate Students	28,395
Graduate Students	8,238
Professional Students	6,992
Tenured/Tenure-Track Faculty	3,051
Lecturers	842
Clinical Faculty	1,565
Research Faculty	874
Other Academic	429
Research Fellows	1,145
Staff	14,003
Ann Arbor Campus Total[1]	65,625

UMAA Population in 2015

the attendance at Michigan Stadium!)

Enrollment

Of particular note here has been the growth in student enrollments, from 34,500 in the 1990s to almost 44,000 today, a 25% growth occurring mostly at the undergraduate level with a particular emphasis on out-of-state students paying private tuition levels capable of increasing tuition revenue to compensate for the loss of state support. Yet this growth has also changed the character of the University, shifting somewhat the balance between graduate/professional education to undergraduate education, demanding a significant increase in the number of non-tenure track lecturers (who now provide over 50% of undergraduate instruction), driving a major expansion of student housing (on the part of both the University and private developers), and threatening to overload other academic infrastructure such as libraries, study space, course availability, and computer access. Teaching loads, as measured by students per full-time faculty member, are now the highest in the University's history. It is also clear that the demand of affluent students for high quality living environments is distorting even the character of Ann Arbor as it becomes dotted with high-rise apartment buildings.

Unfortunately, the rapid increase in the number of out-of-state students capable of paying private tuition levels has also seriously distorted the economic diversity of the student body. As the University has become increasingly dependent on the high tuition paid by out-of-state students from affluent backgrounds, it has seen a decline in the percentage of low income and under represented minority students enrolling in the University. Michigan's long-stated public purpose of "providing an uncommon education for the common man" has become at serious risk. The increasing number of students from wealthy families (recruiting for their tuition revenue) has not only shifted the income diversity of the University (with the percentage of low-income Pell Grant students dropping below 12%, the lowest among major public universities), but also attracted many students who distort the student culture with a "paying for the party" attitude. (Armstrong, 2012)

Campus

Campus Facilities

36 M nsf of buildings and core infrastructure
601 buildings, 2,125 classrooms and labs
900 study rooms, and 6,300 labs
7 miles of utility tunnels
150 miles of fiber optic cables
137,200 networked desktop computers
660 elevators and escalators
25 miles or roads
4.7 M sf of sidewalks, steps, and plazas
280 acres of parking lots and decks
16,100 trees and 13 M sf of turf

The University of Michigan campus has continued to evolve over the past 15 years, despite the disappearance of state support for major capital facilities. New buildings have appeared across the campus–Weill Hall, the Ross School of Business Administration, North Quad, the Law School expansion, the gigantic Mott Pediatrics Hospital, and of course, the "new" Michigan Stadium. The two major complexes designed by architect Robert Stern, Weill Hall (for the Ford School) and North Quad, provided elegant entrances to the Central Campus. While Venturi's Life Sciences complex was actually a somewhat smaller version of buildings he designed for Yale and UCLA, the biomedical research complex on Huron and Observatory was important for the continued expansion of research activity in the life sciences, as was the acquisition of the former Pfizer Global Research campus for the site of North Campus

Research Center. Furthermore the massive biological sciences facilities for LS&A programs launched in 2014 will further expand these part of the campus.

Of course, much of this growth was highly opportunistic. Low interest rates and the University's high credit rating enabled it to launch a massive series of renovations of student residence halls ($650 million), felt to be necessary not only to house growing enrollments but also attracting high quality (and high tuition paying) students. The addition of skyboxes and club facilities coupled with aggressive increases in ticket prices (now among the highest in the nation) brought in the additional revenue to enable growth in facilities (and compensation) for Michigan athletics. The University Medical Center continued its rapid expansion with a Cardiovascular Center, a major expansion of the East Medical Campus, and the massive new Mott Pediatrics Hospital, along with planned expansion of the Medical School. In addition there was further capital facilities growth fueled by philanthropy including a $150 million expansion of the Ross Business School, a $100 million gift for expansion of the Athletic Campus, and a $110 million gift toward a $180 million project to build a graduate residence hall.

Of course, with the disappearance of state funding of university buildings during the 1990s, campus growth has depended increasingly on alternative funding mechanisms characterized not only by greater risk but in some cases controversy. For example, the financing of the construction of new research facilities as additions in the schools of Medicine, Public Health, and Engineering have become heavily dependent upon sponsored research support. As such, they have faced the risk of declining federal research budgets, such as that which occurred in 2010 with the budget sequestration actions of a conservative Congress.

Furthermore, while private giving stimulated further campus construction, donors tended to give to their own priorities rather than the University's needs (e.g., the Munger graduate residence that was roundly panned by graduate students for its "dormitory-like character"). Furthermore such projects require substantial University contributions because of the nature of the gift (e.g., through pledges and bequests that led to present worth values that fell far short of the proclaimed size of the gift) and the requirement of further cost sharing by the University for both the construction of the facility and its eventual operation. Here the lesson overlooked was that large donors usually give money for what they want rather than what universities need, hence all too frequently imposing sizeable additional university expenses for resources only peripheral to academic priorities. In retrospect, it quickly became clear that the University had failed to adequately look many of these gift horses in the mouth, resulting in considerable additional expenses.

There were also more general concerns. Most of the recent campus growth (75%), at least in terms of investment, occurred in auxiliary units (i.e., clinical activities, housing, athletics) and were funded by auxiliary revenue streams, albeit with debt secured by student fee revenues. Those buildings responding to academic needs have generally depended upon anticipated federal research support (e.g., Public Health Annex) or private funding (Ross Business School, Weill Hall). This raised a serious question as to just how, in the absence of state support, the University could meet the future capital facilities needs of those academic units that had no donors or other external revenue sources (e.g., federal R&D).

Of course, with such growth came both risk and controversy. The large scale of the new Mott Pediatrics Hospital ($750 million) quickly drove the budget of the University Hospitals into the red, with operating losses in excess of $200 million per year. The aggressive ticket pricing program of the Athletics Department, with ticket prices (including "seat licenses") averaging $230 per game in Michigan Stadium, drove many long-time faculty, staff, and townspeople season ticket-holders away, while student ticket prices (at $290 per season, the highest in the nation) and policies (open seating requiring queuing hours before game-time) quickly eroded student attendance.

Limits to Growth?

In recent years faculty surveys suggest growing concerns about whether the current financial strategy of the University is capable of sustaining both the quality and the public purpose of the institution.

An aerial photograph of the University of Michigan campus (2014)

The University's Central Campus (2014)

The University's Medical Campus (2014)

The University's North Campus (2014)

While private support–and particularly endowment– is also important, frequently these funds are heavily constrained by donor intent and frequently unavailable to meet the highest priorities of the University. While research expenditures have continued to grow, maintaining the University's position as the nation's leader by this measure, the fact that over 30% of UM research expenditures are now provided from University funds such as tuition revenue and clinical fees suggest that plugging the hole in eroding federal sponsorship of research with University funds may also be distorting institutional priorities. Yet it is also clear that the financial dependence on such growth creates a dependence that makes it hard to reverse.

The rapid growth in student enrollments coupled with the unbridled expansion of auxiliary activities (hospitals, housing, and athletics) has triggered concern that the University is on a determined path toward become big, bigger, and biggest at the expense of both quality of its academic programs and the quality of life both on campus and beyond. Comparisons with the size of the highest rated public research universities (UC-Berkeley at 35,000, UC-Virginia at 21,000, and UNC-Chapel Hill at 30,000) and private universities (Harvard at 21,000, Stanford at 23,000, and Yale at 12,000) does indeed suggest that as the size of Michigan swells to 45,000 or greater, it will begin to count among its peers larger campuses such as MSU, OSU, and U Texas rather than the elite public and private institutions that have sustained a commitment to focus resources to achieve excellence rather than disperse them to drive scale. A related scale issue concerns the relative balance between undergraduate and graduate/professional enrollments. Leading private universities (Harvard, Stanford) typically have a majority of graduate and professional students. Michigan's balance today is 65% undergraduate and 35% graduate/professional.), a significant shift from its peers.

A similar phase transition may occur when a university becomes sufficiently large to not only be ungovernable but also unleadable. In anticipation of such management challenges in the early 1980s, the University of Michigan began a decade-long effort to decentralize both authority and responsibility to the level of its academic and auxiliary operating units, with the deans and directors assuming the role of distributed management responsibility for both revenue generation and expenditure controls. This system, known more generally as "responsibility center management", has allowed the University not only to adapt and maintain academic priorities during the 1980s and 1990s as it became larger, but its loosely coupled adaptive system structure has enabled it to withstand stresses that might cripple smaller institutions. Of course, this decentralization places a high premium on the selection of outstanding deans and directors

Unfortunately as the University entered a new century, a new trend to recruit deans and senior administrators from universities with more centralized cultures has stimulated efforts to recentralize the institution, while leading to major growth in both the numbers and compensation of administrators. It also resulted in efforts to apply corporate management styles, complete with the demands to centralize and standardize services, bonus-based compensation systems, and excessive investment in corporate-like functions (e.g., marketing, branding, advertising, and other forms of "institutional advancement"). Such attempts to recentralize the institution's management have encountered strong faculty opposition because of the threat of damage to the core academic mission by such a corporate-style central administration.

Beyond these signals of possible problems, a more careful assessment suggests that Michigan is clearly facing many of the challenges currently experienced by the rest of higher education, e.g., the unsustainability of its traditional sources of financial support, the increasing competition for the best students and faculty, and mission creep that dilutes the priority given to the academic core of the university. Cracks are beginning to appear in our façade of confidence. There is a growing fear we may be whistling through the graveyard, ignoring serious issues and concerns that could threaten our most fundamental goals of quality, public purpose, leadership, and even our institutional saga as a pathfinder for American higher education.

During the first serious encounter with the decline in state appropriations in the early 1980s, President Harold Shapiro once suggested that in facing financial pressures, the University should consider a strategy of becoming "smaller but better". Although seriously misinterpreted by many in the campus community at the time, since there was the fear of program discontinuance in the face of budget exigency, the intended meaning was that the institution's size should be adjusted to sustain or even enhance its quality. Yet during the 1980s the University continued to grow, just as it does today.

While growth brings opportunities (and pride), it also brings challenges such as financing and managing such a gigantic complex. While overwhelming size commands respect, we have many disturbing examples of how size and complexity can lead to disaster, e.g., the dinosaurs and General Motors. On a more positive note, we also have some excellent examples of organizations that have managed to transform themselves to achieve agility and innovation despite their immense scale, e.g., IBM and China! Growth demands serious thought be given to how one organizes and manages such scale.

The Road Ahead

It is critical that the University develop a more strategic approach to growth. One of the problems with a loosely coupled adaptive ecosystem is how to control growth, e.g., to prevent explosive growth in some components at the expense of others or even the entire organism. A key is communication among components and across the institution. When such communication is artificially limited or distorted (whether intentional or not), instabilities can set in.

Hence it is important to use a multiplicity of networks both to monitor growth and subject it to assessments of its relationship to University priorities such as quality, financial sustainability, and impact. Bigger is not always better!

Here an excellent example is enrollment growth. Although this allows the University to serve more students, the dramatic growth over the past two decades (over 10,000 students) was clearly driven not by a desire to broaden the University's impact but rather to increase tuition revenue to compensate, in part, for the loss of state support. However in the process enrollment growth has clearly overloaded both faculty and facilities resources, shifting much of instruction to the use of part-time or non-tenure-track faculty and driving the priorities for capital facilities. It has also driven a major private construction boom of high-cost apartment complexes designed for the expanding student population. And it has clearly had a negative impact on student behavior.

Hence any strategy for enrollment growth must take into account the impact on faculty, staff, facilities, campus infrastuctucture, and the city of Ann Arbor, itself, in addition to priorities such as quality and mission. The desire for additional tuition revenue through enrollment growth should also consider other options such as year-round operation, distance learning (e.g., MOOCs and MOORs), and other forms of Internet-based academic organizations such as collaboratories and virtual organizations.

Finally, careful consideration should be given to strategic issues of institutional balance and priorities. While the relative scale of different academic programs such as schools and colleges is an important issue for University leadership and governance, perhaps even more so is the balance among academic and auxiliary activities. For example, auxiliary activities such as clinical services, student housing, and intercollegiate athletics have increased in scale (by any measure–financial, personnel, visibility) at rates considerably larger than those characterizing the core academic activities of the University. While such auxiliary activities certainly are responding to demand, they also have been benefiting from lucrative markets that are relatively price insensitive, thereby fueling substantial growth.

Here the University needs to address in a more strategic fashion whether it is appropriate for an academic institution to be responsibile for a health system comparable in size to the academic institution itself (e.g., $3.5 billion/year compared to $3.1 billion/year) or an intercollegiate athletic program that has clearly evolved into a $150 million/year commercial enterprise rather than a student activity, with an alarming tendency to exploit student academic opportunities and health to generate coaching salaries at truly obscene levels.

Perhaps the time is approaching for a serious consideration of exploring a different organizational structures (e.g., a holding company) to govern and manage such rapidly growing auxiliary enterprises so different in character to the academic core of the University.

Tables on University Size

The World's Largest Campus

Facilities (36 million nsf)
Budget ($7.1 billion per year)
Research volume ($1.32 billion per year)
Federal research ($800 million per year)
Medical center (2 million patient visits per year)
Alumni (560,000)
Michigan Stadium (114,000)

UMAA Budget

State support: $300 M
Fed support: $905 M
Foundation Support: $220 M
Tuition Revenue: $916 M
Gifts for Op: $128 M
Endowment: $10 B; Payout: $340 M/y
UM Hospitals: $2.9 B
Other Aux: $341 M

$7.1 B Total; $3.1 B Academic

Quality and Breadth

Offers all academic and professional disciplines
Most programs are ranked in the top 10 nationally
Particular strengths
Social sciences (anthropology, psychology)
Biomedical sciences
Engineering (nuclear, aerospace, industrial)
Professional schools (law, business, medicine, music, public health, social work, information)

The Physical Plant

36 M nsf of buildings and core infrastructure
601 buildings, 2,125 clasrooms and labs
900 study rooms, and 6,300 labs
7 miles of utility tunnels
150 miles of fiber optic cables
137,200 networked desktop coputers
660 elevators and escalators
25 miles or roads

4.7 M sf of sidewalks, steps, and plazas
280 acres of parking lots and decks
16,100 trees and 13 M sf of turf

2014 Rankings

National Universities
USN&WR: 29th all (4rd public)
World QS: 23th (1st public)
London Times: 19th
Shanghai Jiao Tong: 22th

Research

1st nationally in total research ($1.3 B/y)
1st nationally in federally sponsored research

Doctorate production
2nd in PhDs (841 in 2011)

Enrollments

13th total (43,426)
7th international students (6,100)
1st alumni (560,000)

Financial

1st in total budget ($7.1 billion)
7th in endowment ($10 billion)
21st in annual private giving
Last in state appropriations (only 4% of total budget)

Ann Arbor
2nd in intellectual life (USN&WR)
2nd in economic vitality (Forbes

Diversity

Enrollments (2015)
African American: 4.4% UG, 5.3% grad
Asian American: 13.6% UG, 11.9% grad
European American: 65% UG, 48 % grad
Hispanic American: 4.9% UG, 6.6% grad
International: 5.7% UG, 30.9% grad
Gender: Women: 47%, Men: 53%

Chapter 3

Leaders and Best

The University of Michigan clearly qualifies for inclusion in the small group of institutions that have shaped American higher education. Although premature for a frontier state, Tappan's vision for the University of Michigan in the 1850s and 1860s provided the first American model of a modern university, adapting the European model of rigorous seminars and advanced scholarship based on the tradition of high intellectual standards in the arts and sciences. Michigan was also among the first universities to develop strong professional schools (the Medical School, for example, had established its distinction even before the Civil War). From its founding, the University of Michigan has always been identified with the most progressive forces in American higher education.

Michigan has long defined the model of the large, comprehensive, public research university, with a serious commitment to scholarship and service. It has been distinguished by unusual breadth, a rich diversity of academic disciplines and professional schools, social and cultural activities, and intellectual pluralism. This unrelenting commitment to academic excellence, broad student access, and public service continues today. In virtually all national and international surveys, the university's programs rank among the very best, with most of its schools, colleges, and departments ranking in quality among the top ten nationally and with several regarded as the leading programs in the nation. The late Clark Kerr, the president of the University of California, once referred to the University of Michigan as "the mother of state universities," noting it was the first to prove that a high-quality education could be delivered at a publicly funded institution of higher learning. (Kerr, 1963)

Although most new arrivals to the campus sense that the University of Michigan is a large public university with unusually strong quality, they would not necessarily conclude that this was a place where the practice was to attempt to change the world. Of course, from time to time a newcomer arrives with the hope of harnessing this gigantic academic beast to do just that! In fact, we came to Michigan with just that objective, since in our areas of interest, the University was then (and remains today) a world leader.

A Tradition of Leadership through Pathfinding and Trailblazing

Beyond academic excellence and unusually broad educational opportunities, one more element of the Michigan character seems particularly appropriate during these times of challenge and change in higher education. It is certainly true that the vast wealth of several of the nation's elite private universities–e.g., Harvard, Yale, Princeton, and Stanford–also allows them to focus investments in particular academic areas far beyond anything that Michigan or almost any other university in the nation can achieve. They are capable of attracting faculty and students of extraordinary quality and supporting them with vast resources.

Yet Michigan has one asset that these universities are rarely able to match: its unique combination of quality, breadth, and scale. This enables Michigan to take risks far beyond anything that could be matched by a private university. Indeed, because of their relatively modest size, most elite private universities tend to take a rather conservative approach to academic programs and appointments, since a mistake could seriously damage a small academic unit. In contrast, Michigan's vast size and breadth allows it to experiment and innovate on a scale far beyond that tolerated by most institutions, as evidenced by its long history of leadership in higher education. It can easily recover from any failures it encounters on its journeys along high-risk paths.

This ability to take risks, to experiment and innovate, to explore various new directions in teaching, research, and service, defines Michigan's unique role in American higher education. In fact, beyond academic leadership, from time to time the University actually does something that changes the world! For example, it was the first university to own and operate its own hospital, thereby combining the medical research conducted by its faculty with the clinical care offered by its hospitals. It introduced the new discipline of aeronautical engineering within a decade after the Wright Brothers' flight and nuclear engineering only a few years after the Manhattan project. In the 1950s Michigan conducted the clinical trials to verify the success of the Salk Vaccine. Astronauts trained at the University led NASA missions to the moon in the 1960s. And in the 1980s, Michigan joined with IBM and MCI to build and manage the Internet, a role it continued to play into the 1990s.

Put another way, throughout its history, both the University of Michigan–through, of course, its students, faculty, staff, and alumni–does BIG Things! In fact, every once in awhile, it does something that truly changes the world! Some of these achievements are listed in the appendix to this chapter.

In fact, one might well make the case that in an era of great change in society, Michigan's most important role has been that of a *pathfinder* and a *trailblazer*, building on its tradition of leadership and relying on its unusual combination of quality, capacity, and breadth, to reinvent the university, again and again, for new times, new needs, and new worlds. (For more background on this character of the Michigan "saga", we have provided a brief historical background in the Appendix.)

Whether in academic innovation (e.g., the quantitative social sciences), social responsiveness (e.g., its early admission of women, minorities, and international students), or its willingness to challenge the status quo (e.g., teach-ins, Earth Day, and the Michigan Mandate), Michigan's history reveals this pathfinding and trailblazing character time and time again. When Michigan won the 2003 Supreme Court case concerning the use of race in college admissions,

the general reaction of other colleges and universities was "Well, that's what we expect of Michigan. They carry the water for us on these issues." When Michigan, together with IBM and MCI, built NSFnet during the 1980s and then expanded it into the Internet, this again was the type of leadership the nation expected from the university.

However, continuing with the frontier analogy, while Michigan has a long history of success as a pathfinder, trailblazer, and occasional pioneer, it has usually stumbled as a settler, that is, in attempting to follow the paths blazed by others. All too often this leads to complacency and even stagnation at an institution like Michigan. The University almost never makes progress by simply trying to catch up with others.

Michigan travelers in Europe and Asia usually encounter great interest in what is happening in Ann Arbor, in part because universities around the world see the University of Michigan as a possible model for their own future. Certainly they respect—indeed, envy— distinguished private universities, such as Harvard and Stanford. But as public institutions themselves, they realize that they will never be able to amass the wealth of these elite private institutions. Instead, they see Michigan as the model of an innovative university, straddling the characteristics of leading public and private universities.

Time and time again colleagues mention the "Michigan model" or the "Michigan mystique." Of course, people mean many different things by these phrases: the university's unusually strong and successful commitment to diversity; its hybrid funding model combining the best of both public and private universities; its strong autonomy from government interference; or perhaps the unusual combination of quality, breadth, and capacity that gives Michigan the capacity to be innovative, to take risks. Of course, all these multiple perspectives illustrate particular facets of what it means to be "the leaders and best."

It is instructive to trace the University's success in fulfilling this heritage as a pathfinder over the past half-century, since there have been periods of strong leadership as a pathfinder, and other times when the University has taken a more conservative approach to its teaching, research, and service activities. We need to understand better just what has led to these bursts of unusual creativity and impact, as well as the forces that sometimes cause Michigan to take a more conservative path that tends to follow rather than lead.

1950s and 1960s

The 1950s were a time of rapid growth of the University with the returning veterans supported by the G.I. Bill and the rapid increase of federally sponsored research associated with the science policies developed by Vannevar Bush (i.e., his report *Science, the Endless Frontier*) and new federal science agencies such as the National Science Foundation and the National Institutes of Health. The University of Michigan rapidly evolved into not only one of the world's leading research universities, but also one of its most innovative.

For example, a leading team of social scientists from the Department of Agriculture relocated to the University to build the Survey Research Center and later the Institute for Social Research, which was later to become the nation's leading center for quantitative social science research.

The presence of one of the nation's first aeronautical engineering programs and graduates such as Kelly Johnson, the leading engineer for Lockheed (and creator of the Lockheed Skunkworks for advanced aircraft design), enabled Michigan to rapidly became a leader in rocket and missile technology, later becoming NASA's leading research university and a leader in astronaut training. Many astronauts attending Michigan played major leadership roles in the nation's space program, including the entire crew of Apollo 15 (that, appropriately enough, took a car to the moon)

The wartime effort in remote sensing and radar through Project Michigan at the Willow Run Laboratories led to the development of the ruby maser and holography. This later led to developments in advanced radar and stealth technology. In the 1960s this expertise in remote sensing was extended to surveillance satellite technology.

The University's School of Public Health conducted the clinical trials that established the efficacy of the Salk Vaccine for preventing polio, appropriate since Jonas Salk had spent his early career at Michigan. Furthermore, the Medical school developed the treatments for diseases such as sickle cell anemia.

And following WWII, the University established through the Michigan Memorial Phoenix Project, the first university research efforts addressing the peaceful uses of atomic energy. Interestingly enough, it was a student committee of WWII veterans that pressed the Regents to commemorate the memory of those students, faculty, staff, and alumni who had given their lives to the nation in the war effort by attempting to develop a research institute, using the symbolism of the Phoenix bird rising from the ashes, with the mission of transforming the nuclear weapons technology that had ended the war into peaceful applications. The University launched its first major fund-raising effort to raise $6.5 for the Phoenix Laboratory, and the Ford Motor Company contributed $1 million to build one of the first nuclear reactors on a university campus. Not only was this one of the first effort in the peaceful uses of atomic energy in the world, but the work of its scientists soon enabled discoveries such as the bubble chamber for physics detection (Don Glaser) and the use of I-131 to establish the field of nuclear medicine (William Beierwaltes).

The leadership of the University during the decades immediately following WWII was truly stunning:

1st program in computer science and engineering
1st program in nuclear science and engineering
1st program in nuclear medicine
1st program in atmospheric science
1st courses in thermonuclear fusion
Development of time-sharing computing
Development of quantitative social sciences
Development of laser holography
Development of synthetic aperture radar
Development of medical endoscopy
Clinical trials for Salk vaccine
Highway Safety Research Institute
The Center for Research on Learning, the first research center on teaching in higher education.
The Kresge Hearing Research Institute, the first research institute on hearing and deafness
The Center for Education of Women (CEW), the first center focused on enabling the continuing education of women

Michigan led in many other ways during these

Announcing the success of the Salk polio vaccine

Kennedy's Peace Corps speech at Michigan

The world's first academic programs in atomic energy

Apollo 15, the All-Michigan mission to the moon

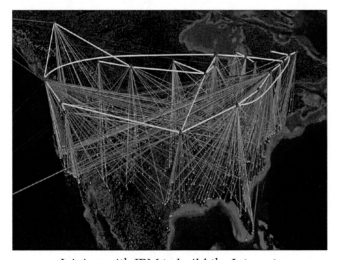

Joining with IBM to build the Internet

Creating the world's largest digital library

Michigan is one of the few universities capable of changing the world.

years. The University had long attracted an activist student body and faculty that have driven not only much of the agenda of the University, but beyond that, have frequently become the social conscience of the nation on important issues. While occasionally disruptive, if well intentioned, such activism has had a very positive effect in raising issues of great importance: e.g., the Vietnam War in the 1960s, the environmental movement in the 1970s, and social justice and the plight of underrepresented minority communities through the latter half of the 20th century.

We noted in Chapter 1 that the 1960s was such a period of campus activism and protests at the University of Michigan, with important social causes such as the international development (i.e., Kennedy's 1960 speech announcing the concept of the Peace Corps), the Vietnam war (i.e., the Teach-Ins of 1965), civil rights and racial diversity (i.e., the Black Action Movement of 1969), and environmental issues (i.e., Earth Day in 1972). To be sure, these were issues of great importance, and the voices of Michigan students and faculty were important both to the institution and to the nation.

The 1970s and 1980s

After the spectacular leadership of the University during the 1950s and 1960s, as it became what many regarded as the leading public research university in the nation, it was only natural that this momentum would be hard to sustain during the 1970s. To be sure, the decade started off with the work of atmospheric scientists Ralph Cicerone and James Anderson who discovered that CFCs were causing the ozone hole opening up every year over the Antarctic and threatening global sustainability. Beyond this important discovery, this led to the first global agreement to implement measures to protect the planet.

The University played a major role in the effort to build the Merit Computer Network, led by computer engineer Eric Aupperle, which connected the state's public research universities. The technology used in building this network and the experience gained by engineers at UM, MSU, and WSU would later position Michigan to play a major role in building the Internet during the 1980s.

Just as with the announcement of the Peace Corps

in the 1960s, the University played a major role in the establishment of Earth Day and the announcement of Americorps during the 1970s.

And high on the agenda was the planning for a new adult general hospital, which would require strong University leadership and creative financing.

In summary, however, the 1970s were a rather quiet period, with both the erosion of state appropriations, a state policy that hindered the construction of state funded buildings at the University, and the energy crisis triggered by the Arab Oil Embargo largely preoccupying the University.

The 1980s brought a new round of leadership activities, as the University, led by President Harold Shapiro, reconfigured itself to adapt to declining state support, making hard decisions to become "smaller but better", launching new fund-raising efforts, and implementing new policies that provided strong incentives to faculty members to attract sponsored research grants. Of most importance was the stress that both President Shapiro and Provost Billy Frye placed on academic excellence that positioned the University for the 1980s and beyond.

Shapiro understood the longer term implications of weakening state support (dropping from 65% to less than 30% of the academic budget during his tenure). He moved in the 1980s to put in place a series of major financial measures to sustain the quality and capacity of the University. First a more conservative financial management and investment strategy was implemented, making tough decisions to set priorities, focusing resources to achieve excellence, and beginning a major decentralization of authority and responsibility for resource decisions that was better aligned with both revenue generation and cost containment. As the state subsidy of the costs of educational programs declined, it was necessary to compensate with major increases in tuition, highly differentiated between Michigan resident and out-of-state students. Finally, aggressive fund-raising efforts were launched with campaigns raising over $300 million during the 1980s.

The decade of the 1980s began with the final commitment to build the new Replacement Hospital Project, a $300 million effort jointly funded by state government and the University, which anchored a medical center that would become a national leader in clinical care and research.

The University was successful in recruiting a new chief information officer, Douglas van Houweling, who led an effort in which the Merit Computer Network joined with IBM and MCI to submit a successful proposal to build NSFnet, the first of the major national networks to link together scientists. The effort was so successful that other federal agencies broadened the Michigan effort to include their own networks, creating a national "Internetwork", managed by the University and IBM, that later would be renamed the Internet. The University continued to manage the new national resource until 1993 when commercial traffic grew to the point where it needed to be spun off to private industry. However van Houweling followed quickly to create Internet2, a consortium of universities that built and managed a new ultra-high-speed network for scientific research.

Led by Richard Phillips and Daniel Atkins, the UM College of Engineering built one of the world's most sophisticated campus network, the Computer Aided Engineering Network (CAEN), in partnership with IBM, Apple, and other computer manufacturers.

The University also attracted Gerard Morou to build and direct the Center for Ultra-Fast Optics, containing several of the world's most powerful lasers.

The School of Public Health, led by faculty member Ken Warner, played a major role in addressing the health implications of tobacco and stimulating new federal regulation of smoking.

1990s

The University continued a series of strategic transformations to prepare it for leadership in a new century. The challenges to this vision of leadership were great. Throughout the 1970s and 1980s, state support of the University had deteriorated to the point where it provided less than 20% of the University's resource base. The Ann Arbor campus, ranking as the nation's largest with over 26 million square feet of space, was in desperate need of extensive renovation or replacement of inadequate facilities. Although the fund-raising efforts of the 1980s had been impressive, the University still lagged far behind most of its peers, with an endowment of only $200 M, clearly inadequate for the

size and scope of the institution. There were an array of other concerns, including the representation and role of women and minorities in the University community, campus safety, and student rights and responsibilities. So, too, the relationships between the University and its various external constituencies–state government, federal government, the Ann Arbor community, the media, and the public-at-large–needed strengthening. And all of these challenges would have to be met while addressing an unusually broad and deep turnover

The new leadership team formed in the late 1980s continued to embrace the strategy that Harold Shapiro had developed to address the erosion of state support during the 1970s and 1980s. Aggressive efforts were taken to actively manage the University's endowment, increasing it from a modest $200 million during the 1980s to over $2.5 billion by the late 1990s. Michigan launched the largest fund-raising campaign in the history of public higher education, raising over $1.4 billion (comparable in constant dollars to the $3 and $4 billion campaigns of recent years). The focus on cost-containment and total quality management continued in all parts of the University.

But there was one more key step in the strategy. Beginning with Harold Shapiro and intensified by the administration during the 1990s, steps were taken to radically decentralize the University, transferring control of resources and accountability for the expenditures to the deans and directors of academic units. In part this was in recognition of the fact that as state support declined, the academic units themselves would become the source of most University resources, through student tuition revenue, sponsored research grants, and private fund-raising. Since the deans and directors understood best the operations and resource needs of their units, it seemed appropriate to give them both control of the resources they were generating and hold them accountable for their wisdom of their expenditures.

This transformation of the management structure of the University during the 1980s and 1990s into a loosely coupled adaptive ecosystem was carefully crafted to create an institution with the powerful capacity to continually adapt to the rapid and profound changes likely to occur in the world it would face in future years. While not well understood by many, including

36

Time-sharing and MTS

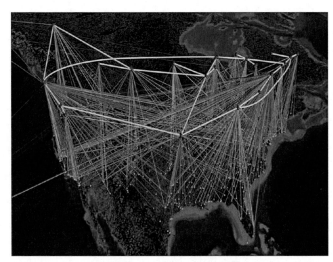

NSFnet and the Internet

The Industrial Technology Institute

The Media Union

The Molecular Medicine Institute

The School of Information

the University administrations of the early 2000s, it would be key in sustaining the quality of the University during difficult times by responding rapidly to address new challenges and opportunities.

Leadership initiatives continued into the 1990s, with the discovery of the gene for cystic fibrosis and the early development of human gene therapy led by Francis Collins, James Wilson, and William Kelley. The School of Public Health developed a Flumist nasal vaccine for flu virus (Hunein "John" Maassab).

With the support of the Mellon Foundation and the National Science Foundation, the University launched through the JSTOR project important leadership efforts in the massive digitization and provision of access to scholarly materials and data.

Through the leadership of Daniel Atkins, the University transformed its library science program into the nation's first School of Information, creating a new discipline in the use of knowledge. Associated with the effort was the construction of a bold new facility on the University's North Campus, the Media Union that provided a collaborative environment supported by state-of-the-art technology, which brought together the Schools of Engineering, Architecture, Art, and Music to merge their creative activities.

The University continued its leadership in the level of its research activities, surpassing in research expenditures all other universities, both public and private. In this sense, Michigan had become the leading research university in the world.

There was also leadership on other fronts, with important policy efforts such as the Michigan Mandate, that doubled the presence of underrepresented minorities among the University's students, faculty, and leadership; the Michigan Agenda for Women, that broke through the glass ceiling constraining the progress of women in leadership roles; and broadened University policies to include the rights of gay and lesbian students and staff.

Achieving the goals of excellence and leadership while facing the financial challenges of declining state support required more than simply determination and dedication. It required a major strategic planning process through which the University community at large could ask the most important, although difficult, questions: What kind of an institution was the University

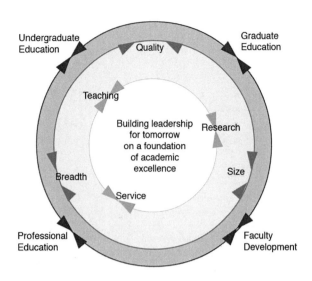

The 1990s Vision: Quality and Leadership

of Michigan? What kind of an institution did we wish to become? What were our values and goals, our priorities and objectives? Working first with small groups of faculty, students, and administrators, the University tackled these fundamental issues and then propagated this dialog to involve larger and larger elements of the University community. These discussions rapidly converged on the themes of excellence and leadership as foundations for the planning effort. These themes were woven together in the earliest attempt to define an appropriate mission and vision for the University.

Rather than viewing the quality, breadth, and scale of the University as competing objectives–or possibly even as constraints on what it could accomplish within a world of limited resources–instead these characteristics, when linked together creatively, could provide an unusual opportunity. By building leadership in an environment that demands commitment to all three characteristics, with a particular stress on academic excellence, it can distinguish the University from other institutions that tend to focus on only one of these factors.

However, perhaps the most important contribution of these years was the recognition that to serve a rapidly changing world, the University itself would have to change dramatically. As its strategies shifted from building a great 20th Century university to transforming Michigan into a leadership role in defining a 21st Century institution, a series of key

Quality and reputation of the University
   Quality of academic programs at highest level in history
   Reputation of university as a leader, an innovator
Leadership
   National leader in amount of research activity
   Most successful academic health center in nation
   Financially strongest public university in nation
   Leadership in key areas such as information technology
   Intercollegiate athletics
Financial Strength
   $1.4 billion Campaign for Michigan
   $2.0 billion endowment
   Tuition up to $450 M/y
   Private support to $160 M (gifts) + $90 M (endow
Campus Environment
   Rebuilt all four campuses ($2 billion of construction)
   Redesigned master landscaping plans
   Enhanced campus safety
   Created campus police
   Achieved a new level of pride in campus appearance
Diversity
   The Michigan Mandate
   The Michigan Agenda for Women
   Diversity highest in UM history
   Prohibited discrimination against gays and lesbians
People
   Faculty (ability to attract and retain outstanding faculty)
   EO Team (strongest in nation)
   Deans (exceptionally strong)
   Staff (exceptionally strong)

Leadership achievements of the 1990s

initiatives were launched that were intended as seeds for a university of the future. Certainly highly visible efforts such as the Michigan Mandate and financial restructuring were components of this effort. However, beyond these were a series of visionary experiments such as the Media Union, the School of Information, the Institute of Humanities, the Global Change Institute, and the Office of Academic Outreach—all of which were designed to explore new paradigms for higher education.

The strategy designed for this leadership vision was successful by any measure. As a consequence of this decade-long effort, by the late-1990s the University of Michigan had become a better, stronger, more diverse, and more exciting institution. Hence as the 21st Century arrived, it was clear that the University of Michigan had not only become one of the leading universities in America, but that it was challenged by only a handful of distinguished private and public universities in the world in the quality, breadth, capacity, and impact of its many programs and activities. This progress was not serendipitous. It resulted from a carefully designed and executed strategy, created and sustained by remarkable teams of faculty, students, and staff throughout the University.

2000s

While the University of Michigan continued to provide strong leadership for higher education along with occasional path-breaking efforts, most of the accomplishments during the first decade of the new century had antecedents from earlier eras. For example, Paul Courant and John Price-Wilkins led the effort to build the world's largest digital library, the HathiTrust, providing links to over 15 million digitized volumes from 80 major university libraries. In a sense, this initiative has become a contemporary version of the great Library of Alexandria, except that its goal is to open up as many volumes as possible for full public access (currently over 4 million). The seeds for this effort were planted at Michigan during the 1990s the University's management of the JSTOR Project to provide broad electronic access to publications in the social sciences and NSF grants to develop the technology for digital libraries. This latter project later stimulated the work of a former Michigan computer science student, Larry Page, who with Stanford colleague, Serge Brin, founded Google, which launched its own digital books project at Michigan in 2004.

Similarly, John Greden, the long-standing chair of the UM Department of Psychiatry, pulled together his colleagues to found the nation's first National Depression Center at Michigan in 2002, a model that he would later use to build a national network of such centers for both research and clinical care in mental illness.

The University launched several major efforts in the areas of technology transfer, creating several new programs in entrepreneurial activities, hiring new staff experienced in high-tech startups, and launching instructional efforts (including a new effort that promises to provide courses in entrepreneurism for every student). There was a major effort to develop new models of instruction that augment the usual classroom paradigms with broader experiences (such as public service, team building, and project-based learning) and technologies (such as MOOCs participation through established organizations such as Coursera and launching new efforts such as Unizen). But, again while substantial investments of resources and faculty effort have occurred, the University would not yet be characterized as a leader in such instructional paradigms.

There were other attempts at University leadership in the 2000s that missed the mark. For example, the University spent $3 million a year to attract the Royal Shakespeare Theatre to Ann Arbor, but after several years this week-long visit was discontinued. A leading architect, Robert Venturi, was named as the new master planner for the University, but his first project, adding a "halo" about Michigan Stadium to celebrate the circus nature of college football with 10 foot high words of the "Hail to the Victors" fight song was a particularly embarrassing failure, infuriating Michigan fans. His firm later was given the architectural design work for the new Life Sciences Institute, but this yielded only a smaller copy of similar Venturi-designed biomedical research facilities at Yale and UCLA. In fact, even the Life Sciences Institute itself, designed to attract Nobel Laureate quality faculty to Michigan and funded with $200 million from UM Hospital reserves, was only marginally successful, staffed during its early years with postdocs and faculty from the discontinued Pfizer research center in Ann Arbor.

Unfortunately, the University lost its leadership in other important areas. Despite the willingness of the U.S. Department of Energy to provide sustained funding, the leadership of the University insisted on shutting down the Ford Nuclear Reactor, one of the nation's most valuable campus-based resources for nuclear research. The decision to rapidly expand enrollments of wealthy students paying out-of-state tuition decimated the economic diversity of the institution. And long-standing traditions such as the Big Ten Conference and the community aspects of Michigan athletics have been eroded by the greed of conference commissioners, athletic directors, and coaches seeking ever higher revenues and, of course, salaries.

To be sure, the University managed to sustain its reputation and academic quality in the face of losing another 50% of its state support during the first decade of the new century. But this was in part due to earlier fundamental steps taken in the 1980s and 1990s, including decentralizing financial authority and accountability to deans and directors, stressing more aggressive investments of University resources including endowment, and placing a premium on the appointment of strong academic leadership that was intentionally biased toward internal appointments to those who understood and were capable of sustaining the Michigan character.

There were also new concerns that the University may have walked out on a limb with efforts such as expanding enrollments by 25% to generate more tuition revenue, but also overloading instructional faculty and facilities and sacrificing much of the economic diversity of our students; making massive investments in debt-financed auxiliary enterprises such as the Mott Children's Hospital, student residence halls, and intercollegiate athletics (particularly Michigan Stadium and a new complex for olympic sports), and rapidly expanding staffing in both unit and central administration areas only marginally related to its academic mission such as marketing and communications. Only time will tell.

Lessons Learned

So how might we explain the unusual level of innovation and University leadership during the 1980s and 1990s and the relative absence of such efforts in the 1970s and 2000s? In part this has to do with the ability of the institution to build on its long history as a pathfinder. It is this very unique history that defines not only the character and strengths of the University but also how it functions. Michigan's character as leader through its pathfinding and trailblazing required it to build spires of excellence in key fields, rather than trying to achieve a uniform level of lesser quality across all of its activities. Only by attempting to be the best in these fields can we develop in our students, faculty, and staff the necessary intensity and commitment to excellence. Furthermore, only by competing with the best can Michigan establish appropriate levels of expectation and achievement.

The University culture has traditionally operated by placing very large bets in high-risk ventures involving our very best people at the grass roots level. Few of these have been top-down from the University's

Venturi's "Halo" on Michigan Stadium

Expansion of Michigan Stadium

Life Sciences Institute

Mott Children's Hospital

North Quad

Munger Graduate Residence Hall

leadership but rather from the willingness to work hard to prospect, identify, and support major opportunities among its faculty, students, and staff.

A particular warning flag should be raised about the use of initiatives at the presidential or executive officer level to lead or steer the university, since Michigan throughout its history has been very much a bottom-up driven institution. It is not just that most top-down initiatives are soon rejected by the Michigan grassroots culture and fade away into obscurity, but more important, the true creativity, wisdom, and drive flourishes best at the grass-roots level with outstanding faculty members, students, and staff rather than administrators.

One might point to the limited success of the presidential initiatives launched during the past two decades such as the repertory theater planned to be originally sited next to the Power Center, the Venturi-Scott-Brown master plan for the campus, the brief (and expensive) tenure of the Royal Shakespeare Theatre group, the "Halo" design of Michigan Stadium, and even the Life Sciences Institute. Some sank beneath the waves, some were ridiculed into oblivion, and some have been bailed out and still float (at considerable expense), but none was a dramatic success.

Furthermore, efforts to climb on the bandwagon by launching high visibility efforts in areas prospected by other institutions such as "sustainability", "entrepreneurship", and interdisciplinary research again do not align well with Michigan's strength as a pathfinder. Contrast these with initiatives such as the Institute for Social Research, NSFnet (later to become the Internet), the Molecular Medicine Institute (a precursor to the Human Genome Project), the School of Information, and the Digital Library Project (leading eventually to the PageRank algorithm, Google, and the HathiTrust). In the past the University has achieved institutional leadership by placing very large bets on high risk ventures involving our very best people where we have established strengths.

The deans and department chairs are the key players in such pathfinding ventures. They are the ones who understand best both the quality of their faculty and the unusual nature of the Michigan culture. Hence throughout the history of the University, the deans have been given extraordinary authority, accompanied by responsibility, in providing the leadership necessary to build and sustain outstanding programs. Fortunately, this has long been recognized by most in the central administration, including the president, provost, and other Executive Officer, and supported and sustained by the Board of Regents.

Yet here the experience of the past five decades provides a warning. The University gets into trouble when it loses contact with its past. An example was the disruption of the 1960s, which decoupled UM from its history and traditions and led essentially to a lost decade of the 1970s, which was later reenergized by Shapiro and then reconnected with UM's history by the subsequent administration in the 1990s.

Equally important has been a long University tradition of making certain that the University's distributed academic leadership is well balanced between long-time members of the University faculty who understand the unique Michigan culture of pathfinding and innovation and those newcomers to the University who may not understand its culture initially but bring in new ideas and insights. Such a balance is able to preserve the University's long role as a pathfinder, not a follower. Of particular importance is the appointment of a series of powerful deans with long experiences at Michigan.

Fortunately, institutions characterized by the longevity, scale, and impact of major research universities such as Michigan are analogous to large ocean liners in their resistance to attempts to make rapid steering adjustments. As Peter Steiner, one of the most prominent of LS&A deans serving under Harold Shapiro, once observed when referring to administrative micromanagement, "This too shall pass…" There is ample evidence that most attempts to redirect the University away from its heritage, its institutional saga as a pathfinder, tend to bounce off without making much of a dent, although they can lead for a time to only marginal progress, as they did during the "lost" decades of the 1970s and the 2000s…

The Road Ahead

Spires of Excellence

Michigan's character as leader through its pathfinding and trailblazing requires it to build "spires of excellence" in key fields, rather than trying to settle for a uniform level of simply good quality across all of its activities. Only by attempting to be the very best in these fields can we develop in our students, faculty, and staff the necessary intensity and commitment to excellence. Furthermore, only by competing with the best can it establish appropriate levels of expectation and achievement.

It must be stressed here that it should not be the University's goal to build a few isolated spires of excellence in the manner of smaller private universities. Rather, it should seek to achieve within each of its academic units–its schools, departments, centers, and institutes–a number of spires of focused excellence. In other words, the general level of quality in each of our academic units can be achieved through the development of a series of sharply focused peaks of excellence within the units. Thus, even for those programs where the University is unable to provide the resources to be national leaders, it aspires to achieve some peaks of extraordinary excellence through the focusing of resources. It is determined to make every effort to avoid mediocrity, but constrained resources suggest that it will inevitably have some areas that were very good as opposed to excellent.

The theme of pathfinding leadership influences the focus of emphasis within Michigan's traditional endeavors of education, scholarship, and service. For example, it requires that the University become even more committed to the concept of a liberal education for its students. The development of leaders among its students demands challenging intellectual experiences, both in formal instruction and in the extracurricular environment.

In order to develop leaders among its faculties, at least some fraction of its scholarship needs to be devoted to venturesome intellectual activities at the cutting edge of inquiry. Some of the University's faculty should be encouraged to work in seminal, cross-disciplinary areas where extraordinary insight and intellectual breadth can lead to the creation of entirely new fields of knowledge.

The University continues to have important service roles. Leadership requires that such activities be justified as important experiences for its students and faculty, as models to be propagated to other institutions, and as sources of important questions for basic investigation.

The Link Between Quality, Breadth, and Scale

The quality of the University of Michigan academic programs is the most fundamental determinant of its ability to develop and maintain leadership. However, a comprehensive and diverse array of intellectual, social, and cultural experiences is also important for its leadership role in higher education. And, the scale of our programs not only contributes to the richness and quality of the University (e.g., the size and quality of central resources such as libraries, computing networks, and athletic facilities), but it also determines its potential impact on society.

Rather than viewing the quality, breadth, and scale of the University as competing objectives–or possibly even as constraints on what it can accomplish within a world of limited resources–instead these characteristics, when linked together creatively, can provide an unusual opportunity. By building leadership in an environment that demands commitment to all three characteristics, with a particular stress on academic excellence, it can distinguish the University from other institutions that tend to focus on only one of these factors.

For example, highly selective private institutions sometimes sacrifice breadth and size in an effort to achieve absolute excellence in a small number of fields. This results in institutions highly focused in an intellectual sense, which while certainly capable of conducting distinguished academic programs, are nevertheless unable to provide the rich array of opportunities and diverse experiences of "multiversities" such as Michigan. At the other end of the spectrum, the University can also set itself apart from many other large, comprehensive public universities by the degree to which it chooses to focus its resources on academic quality.

UM Does Big Things!

Ways in which the University of Michigan
has changed the world

(1817) Catholepistimead or University of Michigania (in Detroit with Michigan Territorial Land Grant)

(1837) University moves to Ann Arbor; Michigan achieves statehood.

(1845) Alpha Epsilon chapter of Chi Psi Fraternity: first fraternity house in the nation.

(1850s) First effort to build true university in America similar to those emerging in Europe (von Humboldt), secular in character with a balance between teaching and research, as evidenced by the construction of the Detroit Observatory, the third largest observatory in the world (Tappan)

(1856) First university building designed and equipped solely as a chemical laboratory

(1859) First university to introduce moot courts in law curriculum

(1860s) First university to own and operate its own hospital

(1868) Alumnus Joseph Beal Steere, naturalist, explorer, educator; set off in 1870 on a five-year exploration around the world, particularly on the Amazon River and later in the Philippines, where he discovered many previously unknown species of flora and fauna

(1869) Alumnus Charles F. Brush earned recognition as the "Father of the Arc Electric Lighting Industry" for his many inventions

(1870s) Created secondary school system (Henry Frieze)

(1870) The first large university to admit women.

(1871) Introduced the seminar method of teaching

(1873) Alumnus John Harvey Kellogg developed and advocated the eating of a dry breakfast cereal, from which came the flaked cereal product that led his brother to found the famed Kellogg cereal brand in 1906

(1870s-1890s) Developed and taught the first courses in new disciplines such as bacteriology, forestry, meteorology, sociology, modern history, journalism, and American literature, modern languages, pharmacy, speech, forest administration, sanitary science, science and art of teaching

(1880s) One of a handful of early leaders in the reform of U.S. medical education

(1880s) Leadership in introducing new disciplines of engineering: naval architecture, marine engineering (1881), aeronautical engineering (1916), automotive engineering (1913), transportation engineering (1922)

(1893) Alumna Alice Hamilton , a specialist in lead poisoning and industrial diseases, was known as the "Mother of Industrial Health." Her work led to a state law requiring medical examinations and various safety procedures in the workplace

(1900) Moses Gomberg, U-M professor of chemistry, discovered organic free radicals

1900s: Microbiology: development of culture techniques for parasites and spirochetes (Frederick George Novy)

(1905) Built the first naval architecture towing tank and model basin.

(1915) First degrees in public health (together with Harvard)

(1915) Alumni E. C. Sullivan and H. W. Hess, invented in 1915 several new forms of glass, including Pyrex, "Daylight Glass" and chemical-resistant glassware, which helped relieve shortage of German-made glassware during Word War I

(1919) The first student union (the Michigan Union)

(1924) Development of iodized salt to wipe out endemic goiter (David Cowie)

(1929) First courses in data processing

(1920s and 1930s) Summer physics conferences on quantum mechanics

(1930s) Development of electrocardiogram or EKG (Frank N. Wilson)

(1931) Created the first Alumni University

(1934) First Bureau of Industrial Relations

(1939) Development of plan for voluntary health insurance (Nathan Sinai)

(1940s) William Dow led Allied scientists in the design and construction of a 125-ton jamming device used to disable German and Japanese radar systems.

(1944) Development of influenza vaccine for U.S. Army (Thomas Francis, Jr.)

(1945) Bureau of Public Health Economics established in UM School of Public Health as primary source of archival information on medical care

(1940s) Alumnus Kelly Johnson, working for Lockheed, he established the legendary Lockheed Skunk Works and created the P-38, the F-104, the U-2 and the SR-71 Blackbird during a remarkable 40-year career.

(1940s) James V. Neal discovery that defective genes cause sickle cell anemia

(1947) Own and operate a large commercial airport (Willow Run Airport)

(1950s) First university program in peaceful uses of atomic energy (Phoenix Project)

(1950s) First degree program in nuclear science and engineering

(1950s) Developed first major programs in quantitative social sciences (Survey Research Center)

(1958) Built and operated the largest nuclear reactor on college campus (1 MW Ford Nuclear Reactor)

(1960s) Lawrence Klein develops econometric models (Nobel Prize)

(1950s) William Beierwaltes develops the use of I-131 in nuclear medicine using UM's Ford Nuclear Reactor

(1950s and 1960s) Developed the first university-based programs in rocketry and guided missile technology for the Air Force

(1960s) Became a major astronaut training center

(1960s) The Apollo 15 mission had an all Michigan crew (and a car) on the moon

(1950s) Developed first degree program in computer engineering

(1953) Jonas Salk, research associate and fellow in the U-M School of Public Health from 1940-44, developed in 1953 the polio vaccine.

(1954) Donald Glaser, developed in 1954 the world's first liquid bubble chamber to study high-energy subatomic particles and won the Nobel Prize in physics for his invention in 1960

(1955) Clinical trials for Salk vaccine for polio (Thomas Francis)

(1957) Chihiro Kikuchi, professor of nuclear engineering, developed in 1957 the ruby maser, a device for amplifying electrical impulses by stimulated emission of radiation

(1957) Alumnus John Sheehan, pioneered in 1957 development of synthetic penicillin, the life-saving antibiotic discovered in 1928 and developed ampicillin, a semi-synthetic penicillin taken orally.

(1958) Faculty member C. Wilbur Peters and Lawrence E. Curtis developed in 1958 a fiberoptic technique leading to medical endoscopy technology.

(1959) First program in engineering meteorology and later atmospheric science

(1960) First program in computer and communications science

(1964) Alumnus Jerome Horwitz, an organic chemist at Michigan Cancer Foundation, synthesized in 1964 the drug AZT, which is used to fight AIDS.

(1960s, 1980s) Peace Corps and later Americorps announced at UM

(1960s) Developed time-sharing computing (MTS with IBM)

(1960) First courses in thermonuclear fusion for AEC

(1962s) Developed laser holography (Emmett Leith and Juris Urpatnieks)

(1962) Center for Research on Learning and Teaching is first research center on university teaching.

(1963) First university research institute on hearing and deafness (Kresge Hearing Research Institute)

(1964) Center for Education of Women (CEW), the first center focused on enabling the continuing education of women (Jean Campbell and Louise Cain)

(1960s-1970s) Willow Run Labs development of satellite remote sensing

(1968) Alumnus Marshall Nirenberg shared the 1968 Nobel Prize in medicine and physiology for cracking the genetic code

(1968) John G. Wagner, professor of pharmacy, began to develop pharmacokinetics, a field that uses mathematical models to study the body's metabolism of drugs, and to determine safe dosage levels

(1969) Richard C. Schneider, professor of neurosurgery, co-patented a football helmet with an inflatable inner lining that is designed to reduce head injuries

(1970s) MERIT Computer Network (Eric Aupperle)

(1970s) Discovery that CFCs cause Ozone Hole (Ralph Cicerone)

(1972) Founding of the nation's first Anxiety Disorders Program (George Curtis)

(1976) Alumnus Samuel C. C. Ting shared the 1976 Nobel Prize in physics for co-discovering a subatomic structure called the J particle

(1982) Discovery that Venus seas were lost to greenhouse gases (Thomas Donahue)

(1980s) Computer-Aided Engineering Network (Richard Phillips, Daniel Atkins)

(1985) Key Study and Senate testimony on health implications of tobacco (Kenneth Warner); Tobacco Research Network established in 1999

(1985) Alumnus Richard Smalley , along with two other scientists, won 1996 Nobel Prize in chemistry for the 1985 discovery of a form of the carbon element in the faceted shape of a soccer ball called fullerene

(1986) Alumnus Stanley Cohen was co-winner of the 1986 Nobel Prize in medicine for discovering growth factors (proteins regulating cell growth) in human and animal tissue.

(1987) Development of high-power chirped-pulsed lasers (Gerard Mourou)

(1987) Douglas Richstone, professor of astronomy, discovered in 1987 evidence for massive black holes in the Andromeda Galaxy and its satellite galaxy M32

(1988) Art Rich and James Van House develop positron microscope

(1980s) NSFnet and the Internet (with IBM and MCI) (Doug Van Houweling, Eric Aupperle)

(1980s) Development of Photoshop and software for digital photography (Tom and John Knoll)

(1990) Donabedian Paradigm statistical model for ranking hospitals and health care facilities (Avedis Donabedian)

(1990s) Francis Collins identifies gene for cystic fibrosis and neurofibromatisis

(1990s) Developed JSTOR project for the Mellon Foundation (Randy Frank, Daniel Atkins)

(1990s) NSF Digital Library Project

(1990s) First School of Information (and informatics program) (Dan Atkins)

(1996) Created the Media Union (aka Duderstadt Center) to explore paradigms for the future of higher education.

(1997) Developed technology for operating research nuclear reators on low-enrichment (non-weapons-grade) uranium to secure nonproliferation (John Lee)

(1998) Mark Burns headed 1998 multidisciplinary team that created miniature "laboratory on a chip" for the analysis of DNA samples

(1999) Alumnis Tony Fadell creates the iPod (and subsequent mobile devices such as the iPhone).

(2003) FDA approves FluMist nasal flu vaccine developed at the School of Public Health (Hunein "John" Maassab)

(2000s) Alumnus Larry Page creates Google, the nation's leading search engine

(2004) UM Libraries as leader in Google Book project

(2006) Created first University National Depression Center (John Greden)

(2008) Created and managed the HathiTrust (world's largest digital library)

(2010s) Involvement of SPH on Genome Wide Association Studies identifying key (druggable) targets for widespread and orphan disease (Goncalo Abecasis and Mike Boehnke)

(2010s) SPH and UM Cancer work on understanding responses to chemotherapies.

Chapter 4

Academic Programs

There is an old saying, particularly among college presidents, that the academic programs of the contemporary university are, in reality, a very fragile enterprise, precariously balanced between the football stadium on one end of the campus and the university medical center on the other. From our experience with the Michigan presidency, we can certainly attest to the dangers presented by these two "auxiliary" activities, since while misdeeds in the Athletics Department are usually sprayed across the front page, above the fold, of the newspapers, the mismanagement of the university hospital can sink the institution financially.

Yet the core missions of the university, its teaching and its research, are the responsibility of its academic programs. They determine not only the quality but moreover the reputation of the institution. Hence, it is important that we understand how these have evolved over the past several decades if we are to understand both the current status and the future challenges and opportunities faced by the University of Michigan.

The University of Michigan, Inc.

The late University of California President Clark Kerr once coined the term "multiversity" to describe today's comprehensive university, a loosely coupled adaptive system that mutates and evolves with ever-greater complexity to respond to the ever-greater knowledge needs and opportunities posed by society. One can certainly understand this viewpoint when considering the current organization of the University of Michigan. In fact, one might depict U of M, Inc., as essentially a holding company of knowledge-intensive services. This would include the traditional components of a university: undergraduate colleges, graduate programs, and professional schools, all clustered about an intellectual core of faculty masters and advanced student scholars (in medieval terms, a *universitas magistrorum et scholarium*). But it also includes an array of auxiliary enterprises, largely operated on a self-financing basis, including sponsored research institutes, laboratories, and projects; clinical activities such as hospitals and health systems; student housing and services; and, of course, public entertainment venues such as intercollegiate athletics. Furthermore, a major university such as Michigan is always launching new ventures such as international programs, not-for-profit knowledge services such as digital libraries, and possibly even activities that draw on the "brand name" of the university to establish new institutions through

An academic institution delicately balanced between the football stadium on one end of the campus and the University hospital on the other end.

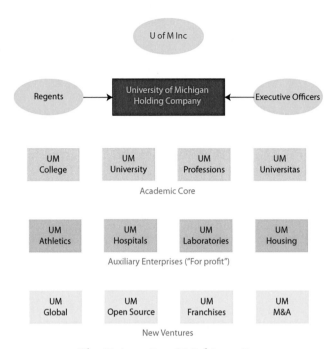

The University of Michigan, Inc.

The academic core of the university

franchising or mergers and acquisition.

Yet, even as the university continues to grow and diversify as it evolves, one must always remember that at its core are its academic programs. The usual Copernican view of the solar system of the university would place the liberal arts college and its core academic disciplines as the sun, the four inner planets as the most powerful professional schools—Medicine, Engineering, Law, and Business—and then a series of elliptical orbits for the remaining professional schools, depending upon their quality and priority within a particular institution. (Actually, some universities have evolved almost into a binary star system in which the medical center has assumed a size and financial importance almost comparable to that of the rest of the university. Some of our liberal arts colleagues suggest that a more appropriate astronomical metaphor would be that of the university as a star orbiting about a gigantic black hole created by the gravitational collapse of the University Hospital and the Athletic Department).

However it is useful to consider a somewhat different model: At the center of the university solar system would be the University Library and the Graduate School (posed strategically on either end of Ingalls Mall running through the core our Central Campus). This, of course, is the contemporary remnant of the medieval university, the *Universitas Magistrorum*

et Scholarium, the union of scholars and masters both mastering and extending knowledge. Then the nearest four planets, where one at least has a chance of finding life, would be the liberal arts...the humanities, the arts, the natural sciences, and most recently the social sciences. Still farther out are the gas giants, the four large professional schools: medicine, law, engineering, and business. Finally, there are a range of other planet-like disciplines...some very similar to the liberal arts (e.g., the performing and visual arts), some that behave like comets (e.g., public policy, information sciences), and some that appear to be remnants of ancient university activities (e.g., Kinesiology as the remnant of Physical Education).

One might also describe the academic programs of the university in terms of the flow of students, first entering the university as undergraduates at the lower division (freshman, sophomore) level with the primary early objectives of socializing young adults, providing foundational learning, and enabling students to sample an array of disciplines for possible majors. Although lower division programs comprise a primary mission of community colleges and four-year liberal arts colleges, most public research universities today assign both instruction and student counseling to non-tenure track faculty (lecturers and instructors) and professional staff, with only occasional student

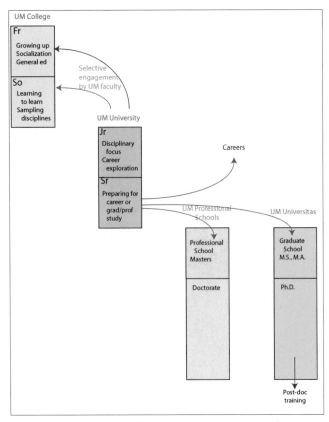

The flow of students

Schools and Colleges Profile					Degrees Granted
(Fall 2008)	Under-graduate	Graduate	First Professional	Gen Fund FTE	
Architecture and Urban Planning	244	365	0	34.4	227
Art & Design	470	25	0	32.6	95
Business	1,060	1,882	0	91.9	1,159
Dentistry	101	110	442	37.7	155
Education	206	329	0	34.9	276
Engineering	5,217	2,603	0	256.1	2,163
Graduate Studies, Rackham	0	682	0	0.0	52
Information	0	391	0	21.2	127
Kinesiology	808	49	0	19.0	239
Law	0	12	1,206	32.2	429
Literature, Science, and the Arts	16,309	1,977	0	722.5	4,454
Medicine	0	410	1,832	95.6	274
Music, Theatre & Dance	777	261	0	102.8	295
Natural Resources & Environment	0	283	0	19.5	96
Nursing	647	259	0	28.2	243
Pharmacy	51	88	247	21.5	78
Public Health	0	866	0	59.3	308
Public Policy	104	161	0	14.1	81
Social Work	0	554	0	35.4	328
Total	25,994	11,307	3,727	1,658.8	11,079

UMAA Schools and Colleges

interaction with senior faculty in survey courses. There is a much greater involvement of senior faculty with undergraduate education at the upper division level, where students select to concentrate in an academic discipline and begin to prepare either for careers or further study at the graduate or professional level.

In fact, many students at leading research universities such as Michigan will continue their studies in professional schools at the graduate level in fields such as law, medicine, business administration, or education. These studies generally lead to graduate professional degrees at the masters level (MBA, M.Arch, MAT) or doctorate level (M.D., LL.D.).

A select few undergraduates will choose instead to enter the graduate programs of the university to prepare for careers in research or as college faculty. These graduate programs of the university are the closest analog to the structure of ancient universities since learning and scholarship occurs through unions or communities of masters (the faculty) and scholars (the students) leading to graduate degrees such as the M.S. or M.A. and the Ph.D. In fact, in many fields such

as the physical and biomedical sciences, even further education at the postdoctoral level has become the norm for students wishing to enter the academy.

From a more fundamental perspective, these graduate programs (and their associated graduate schools in many universities), along with knowledge resources such as the university libraries, comprise the true academic core of the research university. They determine the intellectual vitality and reputation of the university and its various undergraduate and graduate programs. At Michigan, this academic core also has an important physical presence on the university campus, with the Rackham School of Graduate Studies and the University Library at either ends of the Ingalls Mall, about which are distributed not only the various schools and colleges but as well key cultural resources for the performing arts (e.g., Hill Auditorium and the Power Center) and museums (e.g., Museum of Art, Kelsey Museum, Ruthven Museum of Natural Sciences). Moving beyond this academic core, one finds first the University's many professional schools (e.g., Law, Business Administration, Education, Social Work, Public Policy), then moving still further those professional schools associated with major research and clinical activities (e.g., the health sciences and the University Hospital, the North Campus with the creative disciplines such as Art, Music, Architecture, and Engineering) and finally to the many research institutes and laboratories scattered about Ann Arbor. Many American research universities have a similar structure, with a clearly identifiable academic core surrounded by an array of schools, colleges, cultural institutions, and research activities.

The quality of the University of Michigan academic programs is the most fundamental determinant of its ability both to serve and to lead. However, a comprehensive and diverse array of intellectual, social, and cultural experiences is also important for its leadership role in higher education. And, the scale of our programs not only contributes to the richness and quality of the University (e.g., the size and quality of central resources such as libraries, computing networks, and athletic facilities), but it also determines its potential impact on society.

Rather than viewing the quality, breadth, and scale of the University as competing objectives–or possibly even as constraints on what it can accomplish within a world of limited resources–instead these characteristics, when linked together creatively, can provide an unusual opportunity. By building leadership in an environment that demands commitment to all three characteristics, with a particular stress on academic excellence, it can distinguish the University from other institutions that tend to focus on only one of these factors.

1960s -1970s

Much of the evolution of the University's academic programs during the 1950s and 1960s was driven by enrollment growth, first the impact of returning WWII veterans funded by the GI Bill, and then a decade later, the post-WWII baby boom. Academic programs were challenged to expand their faculties and facilities to handle this enormous influx of new students. It was fortunate that the nation was willing to invest heavily both in higher education and research to enable this rapid growth of the campuses, particularly among public universities.

State support was strong, and there were sufficient resources for significant academic experimentation at the University with the Inteflex program, a joint and compressed B.S./M.D. program; the Pilot Program, a living-learning program based on writing and the arts; the Residential College, a major living-learning effort located in East Quad and patterned after the colleges at Yale and Oxbridge; and the Honors Program, an interdisciplinary major for outstanding students.

In the early 1960s, enrollment pressures motivated the Regents to consider opening the University for year-round operation, based on a "trimester" calendar with shortened four-month terms. Unfortunately, although a trial effort was a success, the University was never able to persuade Lansing to provide the necessary appropriations for spring-summer instruction, and the plan was abandoned, although, interestingly enough, the "trimester calendar" continued, only with the trimesters renamed "semesters" with little spring-summer enrollment. This four-month term calendar not only remains today at the University, but it has been adopted by many other universities with shortened semesters.

While Michigan's undergraduate programs in LS&A and Engineering grew rapidly during this period, there were also changes in the relative priorities among its professional schools and colleges, as shifting public priorities were reflected in the ebb and flow of University activities. During the 1950s, American priorities remained national defense (the Cold War) and getting the economy back on stable peacetime growth, stimulating the campuses to place high priority on building engineering and the physical sciences.

These priorities shifted to social themes during the 1960s, with emphasis on the social sciences and professional schools such as Education, Social Work, and Law. The 1970s saw major emphasis on the health sciences, with major investments in Medicine, Dentistry, Nursing, Public Health, and Pharmacy–culminating in the commitment to a major new University Hospital in 1978. As both the state and the nation became concerned with issues such as economic competitiveness and industrial productivity in the early 1980s, the University once again shifted priorities to focus on Engineering and Business Administration.

Michigan entered the 1960s with 21 of its departments rated in the top 10, exceeded only by Harvard, UC-Berkeley, and Yale. But with the emergence of disruptive student activism and then later the erosion of state support, the University had other priorities during the latter years of the 1960s and the 1970s, and the innovation in academic programs languished. The erosion of state support, particularly for new buildings, coupled with the pressures of the energy crisis, restricted opportunities that required major additional resources. Engineering remained largely trapped in old buildings on the Central Campus, with any opportunity to build new facilities on the North Campus only a pipe-dream. Medicine anxiously awaited a new adult general hospital accompanied by modern research facilities, but again while planning proceeded, the absence of adequate funding constrained academic programs.

In summary, the 1970s were largely a status quo time for the academic programs, just as they were for other characteristics such as major initiatives and institutional leadership. Yet although surveys suggested that the stature of most of the University's academic programs was maintained throughout these years in its traditional areas of strength, the social and behavioral sciences, warning signs did appear in some areas such as the physical science and medicine. It was clear that without improvement of existing facilities and strong initiatives at faculty hiring in the next decade, the stature of the University would clearly diminish.

1980s

The University faced even greater financial challenges during the 1980s as the weakening of the American automobile industry in the face of competition from Japan led to serious erosion in state support that would continue to decline throughout the decade. With the loss of over one-third of its state support during the first years of his presidency, Harold Shapiro realized it was necessary to adapt the University to a future of declining state support. While it was clear that a major cost-cutting effort was necessary to bring expenditures into line with resources, Shapiro recognized that a far more strategic approach would be necessary to sustain the quality of the institution. To this end, Shapiro created a University-wide Budget Priorities Committee comprised of faculty and academic leaders (deans and executive officers) reporting to the provost to determine both University priorities and targets for possible cuts. Although most budget reductions were in administrative areas, several academic units (Art, Education, Natural Resources) were proposed for major budget reductions or possible

even program discontinuance. Here the "holy trinity" of quality, centrality, and cost were used to make these determinations.

While Shapiro and his provost, Billy Frye, were successful in adapting the University to reduced state support through cost reductions, increased tuition rates, and fund-raising, they did so with their intense and unrelenting commitment to academic excellence. Indeed, it is no exaggeration to state that during Harold Shapiro's tenure as provost and president, the University intensified its commitment to serious academic excellence and developed a determination to compete with the finest universities in America for the very best faculty, students, and programs.

While the quality of the various academic programs of the University is determined by many factors such as resource commitments and capital facilities, there is nothing more critical to the quality of faculty and the standards applied in promotion and tenure. As provost and then president, Shapiro personally reviewed carefully each faculty casebook for promotion and tenure and frequently challenged academic units if he believed these cases fell short of the University's aspiration for excellence. To be sure, this was challenging in an institution of Michigan's unusually broad intellectual span, ranging from the liberal arts to professional schools such as medicine and law to the performing and visual arts. By working closely with senior colleagues with experience in many of these areas, including in particular John D'Arms, a classicist who was then Dean of the Graduate School, and George Zuidema, Executive Vice President of the Medical Center, he was able to raise the bar for faculty promotion. This effort required not only thoughtful review but also considerable courage, such as when tenure was denied for the first time to a junior faculty member in the Law School, challenging their long standing contention that since every faculty member they hired was outstanding, all should be promoted.

The commitment set by Shapiro was continued by his successors, drawing on the assessment of colleagues to help review each case and frequently challenging academic programs when the case seemed insufficient for positive action. The basic philosophy was rarely to deny directly a promotion or tenure recommendation, but instead to return the casebook with the explanation that more was needed to make a strong case. On one occasion over 50% of the recommendations from the Medical School were returned without approval, noting that they all looked like they had been prepared from the same word-processor template (they had). The philosophy was summarized in a communication to the school's dean and executive committee: "Put yourself in our shoes for a moment. In the course of a year we are asked to evaluate and rule on hundreds of appointments for all conceivable academic and professional appointments. This year we received 70 tenure recommendations from your school. The decision to offer tenure is the most important decision we make in this university. It is also our most important responsibility, since these decisions affect the institution for decades to come. The burden must be on the unit to demonstrate that the candidate has the degree of excellence, of achievement, necessary to merit tenure. You have not done so on many of these recommendations, and until that case has been made, we are unable to support tenure for these individuals."

1990s

By the late 1980s it had become apparent that the College of Literature, Science, and Arts and, in particular, its undergraduate programs, had suffered the most from the erosion of public support and the shifting priorities of the University. In part this was due to the shear size of LS&A. Whenever budget cuts were necessary, LS&A had to take a major cut since it had the largest share of resources. But, in part, this was also due to the trend in most large public universities in the post-war years to stress professional education–Business, Law, Engineering, and Medicine–rather than undergraduate education.

Hence, during the 1990s it was important to set firm priorities on restoring core support for both LS&A and improving the quality of undergraduate education. During the early years this was done both through the provision of additional operating funds as well as special initiatives which benefited LS&A, e.g., the priority given to rebuilding the natural sciences, additional funding designed to improve the quality of first year undergraduate education, and special salary programs for outstanding faculty. However,

in later years, the University went beyond this to launch an ambitious program to renovate or rebuild all of the buildings housing LS&A programs, which had deteriorated during the 1970s and 1980s as the University had addressed other capital priorities such as the Hospital. In the decade from 1985 to 1996, the University invested more than $350 million in capital facilities for LS&A, essentially rebuilding the entire Central Campus area.

During the 1990s the focus on improving the quality of the undergraduate experience was also a clear priority. The Undergraduate Initiative Fund was created to provide over $1 million per year of grants to projects aimed at improving undergraduate education. The common thread throughout these initiatives was grassroots involvement. By seeking proposals, ideas, and participation in defining programs from faculty, students, and staff, the University sought to invest resources in a way that would motivate our most creative people to become involved and to become committed. The first awards in this program created an interesting portfolio of new initiatives. A new series of core curriculum courses in the liberal arts was developed. Instruction in science and mathematics for the first two undergraduate years underwent major revisions. New initiatives to better integrate the arts such as theater, dance, and music into the undergraduate curriculum. The University funded pedagogical needs such as teaching assistant training and took substantive action to improve counseling and sensitivity to pluralism in the University. It also funded a number of student proposals, ranging from undergraduate colloquia to faculty fellow programs in the residence halls, to on-line counseling and information services on our campus computer network, to an alternative career center. A series of named professorships, the Thurnau Professors, were established to honor faculty with extraordinary achievements in undergraduate education.

Similar steps were taken to improve undergraduate education in other schools including Engineering, Music, Art, Nursing, and Business Administration, including major new facilities such as the Angell-Haven Center and the Media Union on the North Campus to provide undergraduates with state-of-the-art computing resources. A series of renovations and new construction projects were launched to improve the quality of instructional space on campus, including renovation of the Undergraduate Library. As part of this effort, $500,000 per year base budget line was committed to renovate over time every classroom on the Central Campus.

Similar efforts were launched to improve the quality of graduate and professional education. The School of Medicine completely restructured the medical curriculum to provide students early on with clinical experience. Business Administration redesigned its MBA program to stress teamwork and community service. Engineering introduced new professional degrees at the masters and doctorate level to respond to the needs of industry for practice-oriented professionals. The School of Dentistry underwent a particularly profound restructuring of its educational, research, and service programs. The Institute for Public Policy Studies was restructured into a new School of Public Policy. The School of Library Science evolved into a new School of Information, developing entirely new academic programs in the management of knowledge resources.

International education was also given high priority. Following planning efforts of the 1980s, a series of steps were taken to broaden and coordinate the University's international activities. Michigan joined its Big Ten colleagues as a member of the Midwestern University Consortium for International Activities (MUCIA), the leading university organization for international development. The University created a new International Institute to coordinate international programs. It continued to expand its relationship with academic institutions abroad, with particular emphasis on Asia and Europe. Of particular note were the distance learning efforts of the Business School, which used computer and telecommunications technology, along with corporate partnerships, to establish overseas campuses in Hong Kong, Seoul, Paris, and London.

National rankings of the various academic and professional programs continued their upward climb. By the mid-1990s, Michigan had achieved rankings across the full range of undergraduate, graduate, and professional programs that were matched in academic quality by only a handful of peer institutions–notably Harvard, Stanford, and the University of California. During the 1990s, the University of Michigan completed

the ascension in academic quality launched years earlier by Harold Shapiro. Its quality and impact across all academic disciplines and professional programs ranked it not only among the most distinguished universities in the world but tied with the University of California Berkeley as the nation's leading public university.

2000s – 2010s

While Michigan's deans continued to play key roles in the fortunes of the academic programs of schools and colleges as the new century commenced, their power began to be challenged by a new University administration. Major projects such as the renovation of Hill Auditorium and a Master Plan for the University's North Campus were halted and replaced by new presidential initiatives such as the Life Sciences Institute, funded from $200 million from UM Hospital reserves, that would compete with the needs of the biological sciences, which continued to struggle with inadequate space in the shadow of the new Institute designed by Robert Venturi.

Ironically, however, one such presidential initiative inadvertently had a very positive impact on the North Campus academic programs. The new administration diverted a $10 million gift originally intended for LS&A by alumnus Charles Walgreen to fund a new repertory theater proposed for a Central Campus location adjacent to the Power Center. This site was soon determined to be inappropriate, as was the original intent of using the new theater for a professional repertory company rather than for student-related performances. Eventually the School of Music was able to persuade a subsequent administration both to repurpose the complex for its academic programs in theater and relocate it to a central location on the North Campus, adjacent to the Media Union (aka Duderstadt Center) with its sound stages and recording studios. This new location and purpose for the Walgreen Center (and its experimental theater, named after Arthur Miller) fit in well with the other creative disciplines evolving on the North Campus in Art and Design, Architecture, and Engineering.

There was further expansion of research space, with the acquisition of the Pfizer global research center (although the University fumbled an offer from Pfizer to provide this large complex as a gift and later had to pay

$105 million for the property). Engineering also missed the opportunity to acquire the Industrial Technology Institute, a research facility built for robotics research during the 1980s, and instead allowed the University Hospitals to acquire it for the storage of Hospital records (ironically placed in the high-bay laboratories originally designed for automated manufacturing research).

Although the University managed to maintain its rankings in various international "league tables", a more definitive analysis of the change in the US News & World Report graduate rankings for UM programs suggests there was some erosion in many programs over the past decade. In fact, many of the University concerns arising over the past decade trace their origin to the changing culture of the university as it became larger, more extended, more complex, and less driven by academic priorities.

New Challenges to Academic Priorities

Although the academic activities of the University remain key to its reputation and impact, the attention of recent University administrations and Regents has increasingly been focused on nonacademic opportunities. During the first decades of the new century there has been a growing faculty concern that the rapid growth of the Michigan's auxiliary activities (hospitals, housing, and athletics), now comprising almost 50% of the University's budget, has driven an increased focus on these activities by the leadership and governance of the institution to the neglect of academic programs.

This was certainly the case in areas such as the University's investment in capital facilities–e.g., the new $750 million pediatrics hospital, the $650 million investment in renovation of residence halls, and the $500 million additions to Michigan Stadium and the Crisler Center–in comparison to the modest investments in the academic core limited to the $150 M Business school complex, a $100 M Law addition, a $50 million building for Nursing, and a limited investment in LS&A facilities. To be sure, the auxiliary units operate in markets that are relatively insensitive to pricing compared to the tuition constraints and limited public support of academic units. But there is

growing concern that this rapid growth is also driven by unusually aggressive leadership of auxiliary units as well as the priority given by the University's leadership and governance.

There is also the related issue as to whether the aggressive growth of the auxiliary units actually competes with and draws resources away from the academic core. To be sure, the strong influence of the clinical units in the Medical Center on fund raising is understandable and usually beneficial to the Medical School. However the aggressive fund-raising of the Athletics Department through devices such as skyboxes and seat taxes clearly draws away private giving that in the past has benefited academic units. So too, the recent aggressive fundraising activities of the University Musical Society is almost certainly at the expense of the School of Music, particularly as UMS has expanded its programs beyond musical performance to include theater and dance. While there is disagreement about how damaging this has been to academic priorities, it is certainly appropriate to raise the policy issue of the priority given auxiliary unit fund-raising activities relative to that given academic units.

This concern about academic priorities applies not only to resource allocation but also to the attention of governance (the Regents), leadership (the Executive Officers), and management (central administration functions such as development and communications). Too many universities have seen the quality of their academic programs deteriorate through the distraction of important but clearly secondary activities such as fund-raising (e.g., donor cultivation and influence), the management of billion-dollar enterprises such as health systems, the public visibility of intercollegiate athletics, and the misguided efforts to force upon universities many of the inappropriate practices of business and commerce (e.g., "shared services").

While much of this is driven both by the differing financial opportunities and challenges facing academic, auxiliary, and administrative activities, it is also due to an erosion of the academic voice in University leadership. For example, there has been a decided shift away from long tradition of appointing senior administrators (including the Executive Officers of the University) with significant faculty experience. During the 1980s and 1990s, the majority of the Executive

University (Privates in italics)	2009	2010	2011	2012	2013 All	2013 Public
Princeton University	1	2	1	1	1	--
Harvard University	1	1	1	1	2	--
Yale University	3	3	3	3	3	--
Columbia University	8	4	4	4	4	--
University of Chicago	8	9	5	4	5	--
Stanford University	4	5	5	6	5	--
University of Pennsylvania	4	5	5	8	7	--
Northwestern University	12	12	12	12	12	--
Cornell University	15	15	15	15	16	--
University of California-Berkeley	21	22	21	21	20	1
University of California-Los Angeles	24	25	25	24	23	2
University of Virginia	24	25	25	24	23	2
MICHIGAN	27	29	28	29	28	4
University of North Carolina	28	30	29	30	30	5
University of Wisconsin	39	45	42	41	41	11
University of Illinois	39	47	45	46	41	11
University of Washington	42	41	42	46	52	16
University of Minnesota	61	64	68	68	69	24
Indiana University	71	75	75	83	75	30

USN&WR Rankings of Undergraduate Programs

University (Privates in italics)	Number of Programs Ranked	Percent of Programs where best S (survey) Ranking was in — Top half	Top quartile	Percent of Programs where best R (Direct) Ranking was in — Top half	Top quartile
University of Wisconsin	78	90%	77%	95%	74%
University of Minnesota	69	77%	51%	80%	55%
MICHIGAN	65	98%	82%	100%	92%
Cornell University	61	90%	69%	95%	80%
University of California-Los Angeles	59	93%	76%	93%	85%
University of Washington	59	93%	76%	95%	75%
University of Illinois	58	91%	62%	91%	79%
Harvard University	52	100%	100%	100%	100%
University of California-Berkeley	52	100%	94%	100%	98%
University of North Carolina	51	86%	67%	100%	76%
Yale University	49	100%	80%	100%	82%
Columbia University	47	94%	81%	96%	74%
Stanford University	47	100%	94%	100%	91%
Indiana University	44	80%	48%	91%	57%
Average of All AAU Institutions	42	86%	61%	89%	64%
University of Pennsylvania	41	100%	90%	100%	85%
University of Virginia	38	76%	42%	95%	55%
University of Chicago	37	95%	78%	95%	86%
Princeton University	35	100%	91%	97%	94%
Northwestern University	31	97%	84%	97%	90%

NRC Rankings of Graduate Programs

University (Privates in italics)	2011	2012	2013	2014
Harvard University	1	1	1	1
Stanford University	5	4	6	3
University of California Berkeley	4	5	5	6
Princeton University	7	7	7	7
Yale University	9	10	10	8
University of California Los Angeles	12	9	8	10
Columbia University	23	15	13	12
University of Chicago	15	14	14	14
University of Michigan	13	12	12	15
Cornell University	16	16	17	17
University of Pennsylvania	22	19	18	22
University of Illinois	21	23	24	23
University of Wisconsin	--	27	30	28
University of Washington	26	28	27	31
Northwestern University	40	35	37	37
University of Minnesota	43	47	51-60	51-60
University of North Carolina	41	46	51-60	61-70
Indiana University	--	--	--	71-80
University of Virginia	--	--	--	--

London Times (THE) Rankings (U.S. Only)

University (Privates in italics)	2012	2013
Harvard University	1	1
Stanford University	2	2
Columbia University	9	6
University of California-Berkeley	10	7
Princeton University	6	8
University of Chicago	11	9
Yale University	8	10
University of Pennsylvania	13	12
Cornell University	12	13
University of California-Los Angeles	19	16
University of Wisconsin	25	23
University of Illinois	26	24
Northwestern University	33	28
University of Washington	39	31
MICHIGAN	34	32
University of North Carolina	36	34
University of Minnesota	49	44
University of Virginia	84	71
Indiana University	-	85

CWUR Rankings (U.S. Only)

University (Privates in italics)	2009	2010	2011	2012	2013
Harvard University	1	2	2	3	2
Stanford University	16	13	11	15	7
Yale University	3	3	4	7	8
University of Chicago	7	8	8	8	9
Princeton University	8	10	13	9	10
University of Pennsylvania	12	12	9	12	13
Columbia University	11	11	10	11	14
Cornell University	15	16	15	14	15
MICHIGAN	19	15	14	17	22
University of California-Berkeley	39	28	21	22	25
Northwestern University	32	26	24	27	29
University of Wisconsin	61	48	41	38	37
University of California-Los Angeles	32	35	34	31	40
University of North Carolina	78	57	55	57	54
University of Illinois	63	63	61	56	56
University of Washington	80	55	56	59	59
University of Minnesota	105	96	102	104	102
University of Virginia	128	130	126	123	132
Indiana University	193	227	216	210	240

Quacquarelli Symonds (QS) Rankings (U.S. Only)

University (Privates in italics)					
Harvard University	1	1	1	1	1
Stanford University	2	3	3	2	2
University of California-Berkeley	3	2	2	4	4
Princeton University	8	7	7	7	7
Columbia University	7	8	8	8	8
University of Chicago	9	9	9	9	9
Yale University	11	11	11	11	11
University of California-Los Angeles	13	13	13	12	12
Cornell University	12	12	12	13	12
University of Pennsylvania	15	15	15	14	15
University of Washington	16	16	16	16	16
University of Wisconsin	17	17	17	19	19
MICHIGAN	22	22	22	22	23
University of Illinois	25	25	25	25	25
University of Minnesota	28	28	28	29	29
Northwestern University	30	29	29	30	30
University of North Carolina	39	41	41	41	43
Indiana University	93	90	90	84	85
University of Virginia	91	96	96	101-150	101-150

Shanghai Jiao Tong Rankings (U.S. Only)

1	Program	2004	2005	2006	2007	2008	2009	2010	2011	2012	2013	2014	2015	Abs. Change	Norm. Change
2	Business	13	10	11	11	11	12	13	12	14	13	14	11	-1.33	-6%
3	Public Policy	7	8			8	7	7	7	7					
4	Education	8	10	9	9	6	9	14	14	9	12	11	8	-1.33	-7%
5	Engineering	6	8	6	6	9	9	9	8	9	8	9	8	-1.67	-11%
6	Medicine	8	7	11	11	10	11	11	6	10	10	8	12	-1.33	-7%
7	Nursing	3	3	3	3	5	5	5	5	6	6	6	6	-3	-33%
8	Pharmacy	4	4	4	4	4	5	5	5	5	7	7	7	-3	-27%
9	Public Health	5	5	5	5	5	5	5	5	4	4	4	4	1	11%
10	Social Work	1	1	1	1	1	2	2	2	2	1	1	1	0	0%
11	Law	7	7	8	8	8	9	9	9	7	10	9	10	-2.33	-14%
12	Economics	11	11	11	11	11	11	12	12	12	12	13	13	-1.67	-7%
13	English	11	11	11	12	12	12	13	13	13	13	13	13	-2	-8%
14	History	5	5	6	7	7	7	7	7	7	7	7	7	-1.67	-14%
15	Pol. Sci.	2	2	2	3	3	3	4	4	4	4	4	4	-2	-33%
16	Psychology	2	2	2	2	2	2	3	3	3	3	4	4	-1.67	-29%
17	Sociology	3	3	3	3	3	3	3	3	3	3	4	4	-0.67	-10%
18	Biol. Sci.	14	14	13	12	15	15	15	20	20	20	20	19	-6	-18%
19	Chemistry	21	21	19	17	16	16	16	16	16	16	16	15	4.67	13%
20	Comp. Sci.	14	14	14	15	15	13	13	13	13	13	13	13	1	4%
21	Earth Sci.	5	5	5	5	5	5	5	9	9	9	9	8	-3.67	-27%
22	Math	8	8	8	7	7	9	9	8	8	8	8	9	-0.33	-2%
23	Physics	13	13	13	13	13	13	13	11	11	11	11	11	2	8%

C1=Average ranking over 2004 to 2006. C2=Average ranking over 2013 to 2015.
AC=Absolute Change=C1-C2. NC=Normalized Change=(C1-C2)/(C1+C2).

USN&WR Rankings of UM Graduate Programs (Courtesy of F. Ulaby)

Officers had sufficient academic backgrounds to merit faculty appointments. In recent years, however, only the president, provost, and vice-president for research have had backgrounds that merit academic appointments.

So, too, the long-standing practice of achieving a balance between the appointment of internal and external candidates for senior leadership positions such as deans in an effort to balance both the continuity provided by long-standing University employees with new viewpoints from outside seems to have been abandoned, with a decided preference toward external candidates in recent years. During the 1970s through the 1990s, the majority of the deans came from internal appointments of outstanding faculty. In recent years there has been a very significant preference for external candidates, now comprising over two-thirds of the deans and the majority of the executive officers.

But perhaps the most worrisome trend has been the weakening of the voice and influence of the University's deans and faculty executive committees in recent years. The University of Michigan has long been known as a "deans' university", in which the authority and responsibility of deans as academic leaders is unusually strong, working closely with elected executive committees generally populated with many of the University's most outstanding faculty members. Deans are the key academic leaders most responsible for the priority, quality, and integrity of the University's academic programs. They select department chairs, recruit and evaluate faculty, seek resources for their school both within the university (arguing for their share of university resources) and beyond the campus (through private fundraising or research grantsmanship). As the key line officers for the faculty of the university, they have rather considerable authority that usually aligns well with their great responsibilities. Good things happen in the University's academic programs because of good deans, at least over the long term–and vice-versa, of course.

Yet, despite this dispersal of power, Michigan is also an institution where team building and cooperation is greatly valued. Deans come together quite easily as teams, particularly if encouraged by the provost and president, and willingly work together on university-wide priorities. Although technically the deans report to the provost, the wise provost will join the deans' team as a member and captain rather than as its coach–and certainly not as its owner!

Since the influence of faculty governance at the University is primarily concentrated in powerful elected faculty executive committees at the school, college, and department level rather than with a University-wide faculty senate, the deans also have primary responsibility for making certain that academic priorities dominate the attention of the University administration and governing board. To weaken the

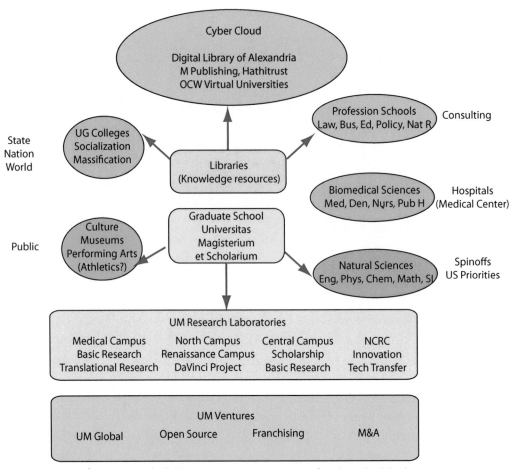

At the center of all University activities: academic priorities!

access and influence of the deans relative to both the Executive Officers and Regents of the University is tantamount to weakening the academic priorities of the institution.

The Road Ahead

So, how does one sustain the quality and leadership of academic programs in an unusually large and complex institution such as the University of Michigan that is continually challenged to balance rapidly changing challenges, responsibilities, and opportunities? For example, highly selective private institutions sometimes sacrifice breadth and size in an effort to achieve absolute excellence in a small number of fields. This results in institutions highly focused in an intellectual sense, which while certainly capable of conducting distinguished academic programs, are nevertheless unable to provide the rich array of opportunities and diverse experiences of "multiversities" such as Michigan. At the other end of the spectrum, the University can also set itself apart from many other large, comprehensive public universities by the degree to which it chooses to focus its resources on academic quality. As the diagram above suggests, not only the reputation but also the impact of the University is driven by its deep commitment to the priority given the quality of its academic activities.

Once again we must stress the importance of understanding the history of the University, the nature of our past achievements of academic quality and leadership, and our unique institutional culture. The University's unusual combination of quality, breadth, spirit, and scale not only allow it but actually compel it to provide leadership for higher education through risk taking, path finding, and trail blazing. To this leadership character, one must add the importance of recognizing that the true source of Michigan's excellence and leadership rests with the quality, spirit, and innovation of its people–its faculty, students, and staff–and decidedly not with its administrative leadership or governance. It thrives as a loosely coupled, adaptive organization, drawing its strength, innovation, and vision from the grass roots, from the faculty, students, and staff who embrace deep commitments to academic priorities.

Of course, this character is quite unusual in higher education (although certainly present in several other great universities such as Harvard, Caltech, and Stanford). While clearly ingrained in the culture of the institution and shaping the perspective and achievements of its people, it can be a threatening characteristic to those new to the University–particularly to those recruited into leadership positions as deans or executive officers or elected to serve on the University's Board of Regents. Hence the challenge is both to make certain that the selection of University leadership at all levels is balanced among insiders both knowledgeable and committed to the unique history and culture of the University, and those recruited from outside into leadership positions adequately informed and committed to sustaining this culture and its academic priorities.

People

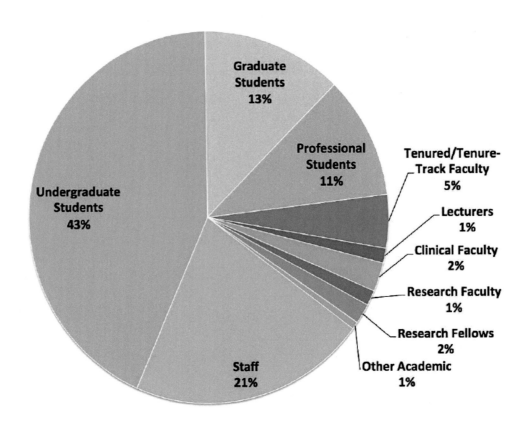

The people of the University: students, faculty, and staff

Chapter 5

Students

Despite what the faculty, administrators, alumni, and football fans may think, students are the most important participants on a university campus. Yet there is as much diversity in this community–rather communities–as in higher education itself, distinguished by degree programs (undergraduate, graduate, professional, postdoctoral), academic majors (from Art to Zoology), extracurricular interests (sports, politics, parties, etc.), sociodemographics, and so on. Hence it is useful to begin first by considering the general characteristics of the University student body over the past fifty years.

As we have noted earlier in Chapter 2, for much of its history, the University's enrollment was among the largest in the nation. Although growth was slow and relatively stable during most of its early history, enrollments expanded rapidly following WWII with the GI Bill and returning veterans. A second wave of enrollment increases occurred with the baby boomers, the children of the "greatest generation", who swelled college enrollments in the 1960s and 1970s. But in sharp contrast to their parents, these comprised the protest generation, challenging not only the values of their parents, but of the university more generally. In the 1960s students wanted to change the world. Parties were out (except for street efforts like the MC5). Fraternities and sororities almost disappeared. To be sure, many of their causes such as civil rights and war protests were just, but their rejection of "the establishment" not only challenged many of the traditions of higher education but severed the long-standing relationship of the University of Michigan with its past.

After a lull between generations, a second surge in enrollments began in the late 1980s with "tidal wave II", the children of the boomers, who were more career focused, regarding their education as a stepping stone

to employment and prosperity. After modest increases, enrollments stabilized once again throughout the 1990s. Although there was a brief period of student activism during the late 1980s and early 1990s, student interest began to shift to preparing for an increasingly competitive job market, with majors such as business administration rising to the top of the list in student interest.

But there was another important change during the past two decades. Throughout much of the last half of the 20th Century, the University had attracted a broad spectrum of students, many from low-income families in the cities, factories, and farms, and as the first college students in their families. They came to Michigan, determined to work hard to take advantage of its opportunities, and striving for leadership roles in society. This character was reflected in their work ethic, whether working to pay their way through college or to achieve academic competence in tough majors like medicine and engineering; in their competitiveness, whether in the classroom, on the field, or later in life; and in their activism, challenging the flaws in our society and proposing new paths to the future, and in their competitiveness. The majority of Michigan students were indeed "the common man" seeking "an uncommon education", in Angell's words, to become the "leaders and best".

Yet in the late 1990s and continuing today, many public universities began to increase their undergraduate enrollments dramatically, with a strong bias given to out-of-state students capable of paying much higher tuition in an effort to compensate for the loss of state support. Since most of these students came from families (or nations such as China) capable of paying the high costs of private universities, the socioeconomic mix of students began to shift toward

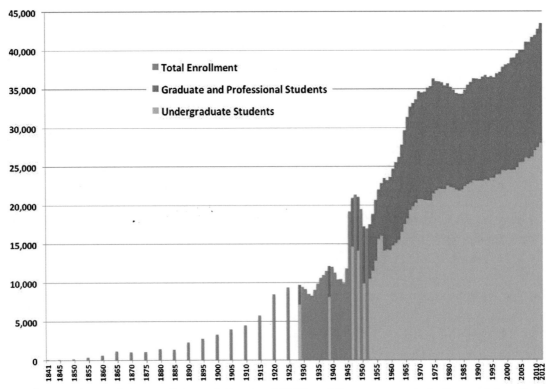

The rapid growth in enrollments following WWII and then once again in the past decade.

higher incomes, leaving behind those from low-income backgrounds and underrepresented minorities. This has raised the great concern that the shift toward high income students to compensate for weakening state support threatened to erode the public purpose of universities such as Michigan, committed in early eras to providing "an uncommon education for the common man."

1950s

The growth of the University following WWII surged with the returning veterans to over 20,000, then stabilized and slipped back briefly to 17,000 students in the mid-1950s, then began to grow again, reaching 22,180 students in 1960. The veterans added maturity to the student body as they returned from war seriously committed to their education. In fact, many senior faculty remember these times as the most intellectually exciting of their careers, challenged as they were by the maturity and commitment of the returning veterans. However eventually as the veterans graduated, the campus student body once again returned to the behavior of the young.

President Hatcher provided strong leadership during this period of growth, although he did run into some student problems. During his first year, he ran into fraternity discrimination again, and like Ruthven, vetoed a requirement to ban such behavior. Students from South Quad and West Quad raided the women's dorms on the Hill–the first panty raids–and then gathered outside the President's House to display their trophies. However, President Hatcher, always the patrician, greeted them with the advice "Men, it is late and time to go to bed." At which point they returned to their dorms. The UM took great flak in the media, however, "Why was such horseplay permitted when other young men were dying in Korea?" It is ironic that the episode occurred at the very time that certain faculty members and student leaders were lamenting "student apathy". But change was beginning to occur in the student body as the 1960s approached.

1960s-1970s

The 1960s produced one of the most distinctive youth culture in collegiate history: anti-elitist, anti-establishment, and rejecting the materialism of its

The 1960s were a time of student protest.

John Sinclair and the Rainbow People's Party

parents. Old traditions such as the J-Hop, freshman hazing, class plays, and such disappeared. Fraternities and sororities faced hard times and had to take in boarders, dropping from 12% to 4.7% of the student body.

Of course Michigan had long attracted an activist student body, as evidenced by the well-known observation in the 1880s in Harper's Weekly that referred to one of Michigan's most interesting characteristics as "the liberal spirit through which it conducts education". But during the 1960s student activism was more strident. The University was pushed out of students' lives, the Code of Nonacademic Conduct disappeared (and was not reinstituted until 1992), and *in loco parentis* was forever banned from the Michigan campus.

By 1966 the students' insistence on control over their personal lives, including draft status and antiwar protest activity, collided with House Un-American Activities Commission request to the Hatcher administration for cooperation in investigating war protestors and the concerns of the Selective Service Bureau. The Students for a Democratic Society were particularly active. The Hatcher administration banned sit-ins in November, 1966 stirring enormous opposition from the Student Government Council. 1,500 students held a one-hour sit-in at the Administration (LSA) Building. This protest effort intensified when the Johnson administration ended student deferments. Draft card burnings at rallies began, and some students began to leave the country to escape the draft. The Diag became the center of activity for SDS and other groups.

Ann Arbor adopted its $5 pot law and established the annual Hash Bash celebration each May 1. John Sinclair and the Trans-Love Energies Tribe and Rainbow People's Party took over two large houses on Hill Street for communes. Drugs were an accepted part of campus life, at least by most students, with 90% using alcohol and 50% trying marijuana at least once. Co-ed dorms appeared, with only the Betsy Barbour, Newbury, Stockwell, and Martha Cook residences remaining restricted to women in 1970. Ironically, however, fraternity discrimination continued.

The Regents turned to Robben Fleming for leadership during these turbulent times, Fleming brought skills that seemed tailor made for the challenges of the 1960s. He was Chancellor of the University of Wisconsin, a peer institution, but he had also been a labor mediator, directing the Institute of Labor Relations at both Illinois and Wisconsin. With great patience, tact, and an understanding of the art of negotiations, Fleming would maintain the confidence of the University community through a difficult decade.

At an antiwar rally in Hill Auditorium in 1969, Fleming expressed the view that the war was a "colossal mistake". Following a UM football game the next day, 12,000 students marched from the Diag to Michigan Stadium to protest. On October 15, 1969, a rally was held in Michigan Stadium, encouraged by the Faculty Senate, and 20,000 showed up.

In March 1969, the Jesse James Gang, the militant wing of the SDS, attempted to provoke a confrontation by locking themselves in the room with a military

Calling for a commitment to diversity and inclusion.

Students disrupting a Regents meeting.

recruiter. Fleming just let them wear themselves out. Later, anti-ROTC militants took over North Hall, and again Fleming asked the police to just guard the building for safety and leave the back door unlocked. Eventually the students wore out once again and left.

Fleming did get caught in one incident: the battle over a student-operated bookstore. The Regents would not allow the students to control the store, and the Radical Caucus of SDS took over the LSA building. Concern about the security of faculty offices and student files, Fleming sought a restraining order. At 4:00 a.m., state and local policy forcibly evacuated the building, arresting 107 people. The arrests let students know there were some things that went too far.

Yet another volatile issue concerned minority issues. Low Black enrollment had been a growing concern. The snail's pace of progress led to the organization of the Black Action Movement, dedicated to assisting minority students and opening the University's traditionally white campus to wider minority participation. Unable to secure from the Regents the financial guarantees to meet its goal, BAM called for a campus-wide strike in March 1970. They sought a number of guarantees for financial aid, support services, support for the Center for African American Studies, and an increase in Black enrollment from 3% to 10%.

Fleming was under pressure to call in the National Guard. But he persuaded the Regents to bear with the unpleasantness, arguing that avoiding potential tragedy "calls for enduring a certain amount of damage, or intimidation, harassment and insult, in return for a more rational and sane means of dealing with the problem". Eight days after it began, the strike was settled, and the University gave approval to the essential BAM demands, including agreeing to work toward a goal of 10% Black enrollment by 1973.

While campus activism and protests during the 1960s irritated many, it should be acknowledged that these were frequently the mechanisms the campus used to address important social causes such as the international development (i.e., Kennedy's 1960 speech announcing the concept of the peace corps), the Vietnam war (i.e., the Teach-Ins of 1965), civil rights and racial diversity (i.e., the Black Action Movement of 1969), and environmental issues (i.e., Earth Day in 1972). To be sure, these were issues of great importance, and the voices of Michigan students and faculty were important both to the institution and to the nation. The nation's first Earth Day conference, sponsored by a campus group, was held on March 12-15, 1970. To attract media attention, a 1959 Ford sedan was "hacked to death" on the Diag.

Yet there is an ebb and flow to student activism, just as there is to broader political life, determined by social issues of the times–e.g., an unpopular war, the draft, an economic downturn, the lack of jobs for graduating students–and by the quality of student leadership, since pulling together such movements requires some talent. During the 1970s the energy crisis and a weakening economy put jobs on the front burner for most students. There were occasional flare-ups over important issues such as racial tolerance or gay rights, but there were

Smashing a car to celebrate Earth Day.

President Fleming was a calming influence.

also cosmic concerns such as establishing Ann Arbor as a nuclear-weapons-free zone that have long since been forgotten.

1980s

During the 1980s, the number of high school graduates in Michigan dropped by over 25%, as the post-war baby boom subsided. Although this led to a decline in the number of Michigan applicants to the University, increases in the number of out-of-state applicants more than offset this decline to the point where almost 20,000 students were applying for the 5,000 positions in the freshman class. While some of this increase in out-state application activity was no doubt due to the ease of filing multiple applications with personal computers, it was also due to the fact that Michigan had become a "hot school", a popular choice to students across the country because of its unusual combination of academic quality, attractive social life, excitement (athletics, politics, arts), and name recognition.

As the mood of the nation shifted away from confrontation and dissent in the 1980s, so, too, did the majority of Michigan's student body become more conservative and detached from the agendas of various special interest groups. As a result, those remaining activist elements of the student body became increasingly focused on narrow special interest agendas, even as the silent majority of students became more passive and focused instead on personal issues such as grades, social life, athletics...and job prospects!

This was reflected in student government, in which only the more activist–indeed, radical–students would care passionately enough about particular issues to expend the energy to run for elected office. It was also reflected, unfortunately, in the attitude of administrators and faculty toward such student activism, treating it with benign neglect until it burst into flames that required a fire drill. This tradition of activism, while a source of great energy and excitement, also had some drawbacks–particularly when the issues and agendas were not sufficiently compelling.

Student activism returned once again in the late 1980s, but the issues were common to those of most other campuses–e.g., military research on campus, gay rights, and racism–and could be viewed as resurgence of unsettled issues from the 1960s. Perhaps the most interesting event strategically was the Regents decision to divest only 90% of South African holdings in response to a law drafted by State Legislature Representative Perry Bullard prohibiting colleges from investing in South Africa because of its apartheid government. Although the University agreed in principle with challenging apartheid, it first sued the state to protect its constitutional autonomy, and after it eventually won in 1988, it divested the rest of its holdings. (This willingness to sue the state from time to time–or at least threaten suit–was a regular occurrence over the years, necessary to protect the constitutional autonomy of the University.)

64

1990s

Although the University had been worried about the impact of the demographic slide following the baby boom, in fact, student quality continued to improve throughout the 1980s and 1990s, with each class possessing academic credentials even stronger than the previous class. But student energy and activism remained, in part encouraged by the large number of staff in the student services area who had been members of the 60s generation and who harbored as much distrust and disrespect for "the establishment" as did the more activist students themselves. Indeed, it was not uncommon to find that many staff, themselves, were pot-stirring among the activist students, encouraging them to protest on various special interest agendas.

Key in changing a Michigan student culture, stagnating between those still trapped in the 1960s and those who had rejected student activism as irrelevant to their personal concerns, was the appointment of Maureen Hartford as Vice President for Student Affairs. Hartford came with extensive experience at other universities. But, more significant, she came with a deep respect, concern, and love for students that was immediately obvious to those on the search committee that recommended her appointment. During her first week on campus, she checked into the South Quad residence hall to spend several nights with students to learn more about their lives. She rapidly gained the respect of even the most activist students. Over time, she managed to stimulate a similar degree of respect for student concerns within the administration and the faculty. Within a few months it was clear that a true sea change had occurred in the student culture, and there was a rapid growth of interest in student government among our very academically strongest students.

But despite the mutual respect and affection between Hartford and the student body, she faced several particular challenges in which her reputation for toughness–with an earlier nickname of "Attila, the Hen"–would prove valuable. When she arrived on campus, Michigan had one additional issue that would have seemed almost absurd on other college campuses: the absence of any policy for student discipline and campus safety. One of the hangovers of the volatile days of the 1970s had been the elimination

Vice-President Maureen Hartford

of a code of student conduct. The elimination of this policy in 1974 had been intended only as a temporary lapse pending the development and adoption of a new code. But student government was given veto power over the process, and it had consistently exercised this veto to prevent the development or adoption of a new disciplinary policy. As a result, the University had gone for almost 15 years without any of the student disciplinary policies characterizing every other college or university in the nation. The only option available for student disciplinary action was to utilize an obscure Regents Bylaw that gave the president the authority to intervene personally to handle each incident. Although the University knew it was at some risk in the absence of such a student code–and, indeed, out of compliance with federal laws that required such policies to govern areas such as substance abuse–each time an effort was made to develop a code, activist students blocked it.

There was yet another issue of great concern to many students–but also providing opportunities for protest to others who resented any authority: campus safety. For most of the University's history, Ann Arbor was a rather simple and safe residential community. But as Southeastern Michigan evolved in the post-war era to "metroplex" with intricate freeway networks linking Detroit and its suburbs, Ann Arbor acquired more of an urban character, with all of the safety concerns plaguing any large city. While many aspects of campus safety could be addressed through straightforward and noncontroversial actions, such as improving lighting or security locks on residence hall entrances, there was one

Protesting the president

Cartooning the president

issue unique to the University that proved to be more volatile: the absence of a campus police force. Unlike every other large university in America, the University had never developed its own campus police and instead relied on community police and sheriff deputies. This had caused some difficulties in the activist days of the 1960s, when the Washtenaw Country sheriff had adopted a highly confrontational approach to student unrest. Throughout the 1980s it became more and more evident that local law enforcement authorities simply would never regard the University as their top priority. Their responsiveness to campus crime and other safety concerns was increasingly intermittent and unreliable. Furthermore, most other universities had found that the training and sensitivity required by police dealing with students was far more likely to be present in a campus-based police organization than in any community police force.

The issues of both the code of student conduct and a campus police came to a focus in 1992 when a University task force on campus safety strongly recommended that both be established. Although surveys indicated that most students supported both steps, a number of student groups–including student government–rapidly put together a coalition to protest "No cops, no codes, no guns". As the University took formal action to establish the campus police, a series of protests occurred, including one on a particularly warm day in December in which students camped out on the lawn of the President's House to "bury student rights"!

But, like most protests resisting efforts to bring the University in line with the rest of higher education, these rapidly faded as the campus police was established and not only demonstrated that they could reduce crime on campus, but further that they were far more sensitive to student needs and concerns than the local Ann Arbor police. Several years later students again protested–this time to urge more campus police in preference to the use of community police.

A series of actions were taken to improve campus safety, beyond the formation of a campus police organization. Major investments were made to improve campus lighting and landscaping. Special programs were launched such as the Sexual Assault Prevention and Awareness Center, the Night Owl transportation service, a Safewalk escort service in which students served as nighttime security escorts, and the Task Force on Violence Against Women. Broad programs were undertaken to address the concerns of substance abuse on campus, with particular attention focused on alcohol consumption. The University also addressed the hazards of smoking by making most of the campus a smoke-free zone, including all public spaces (even Michigan Stadium!) It developed programs to help members of the campus community stop smoking.

Greek life also changed significantly during the 1990s. Since the 1960s, the University had generally kept an arm's length distance from fraternities and sororities, even though over 6,000 undergraduates each year chose them as their residential community. This reluctance to become involved grew, in part,

Fraternity behavior became increasingly out of control.

from the University's concern about liability for the institution should it become too closely linked with Greek life. This attitude of benign neglect changed in the late 1980s, when the University–and the Ann Arbor community–became increasingly concerned about a series of fraternity incidents involving drinking and sexual harassment. The administration concluded that it had a major responsibility, to both its students and the Ann Arbor community, to become more involved with the Greeks.

To this end, it was decided that the president should call a special meeting with the leaders of all of the university's fraternities to address the growing concerns about their destructive behavior. The key message was to remind the students of Michigan's heritage of leadership and challenge them to strengthen their capacity to discipline renegade members through organizations such as the Interfraterrnity Council. Although beginning with a strong challenge for self-discipline, it was also stated quite clearly that the university would act with whatever force necessary to protect the student body and the surrounding community. More precisely, it was suggested that if their disruptive behavior continued, the president would come down on fraternities "like a ton of bricks." The ultimate threat was to deprive misbehaving fraternities of access to intramural sports, which was important for their visibility in recruiting new pledges.

Fraternity leaders picked up this challenge, and a new spirit of responsible behavior and discipline began to appear. Policies were adopted forbidding

drinking during rush along with strong sanctions for entertaining minors from the Ann Arbor community in the houses. The university took further steps by hiring a staff member to serve as liaison with the Greeks. This is not to suggest that misbehavior in Greek life vanished from the campus. Indeed, several fraternities suffered from such a pattern of poor behavior that their national organizations agreed to withdraw their charter, and they were removed from campus. But in general, the nature of Greek life became one of far greater responsibility and self-discipline.

2000s

The University of Michigan experienced major changes in the size, character, and culture of its student body as the century came to an end. In part because many of the concerns of students had been addressed and also because a challenging job market focused student attention on careers, student activism began to subside during the 1990s. But something else happened that changed the character of the student body more dramatically. In an effort to compensate for declining state support, in the late 1990s, the University began to rapidly increase enrollments, placing a premium on out-of-state students capable of paying private tuition levels. Enrollments were increased from 35,000 in the late 1990s to over 44,000 in 2015, an increase of 25%. Since many of these students came from affluent families capable of paying $60,000 per year or more for tuition, room and board, they frequently arrived on campus

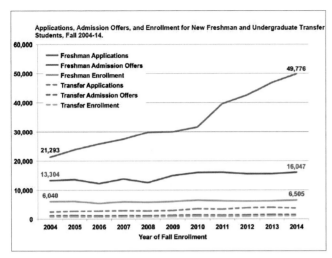

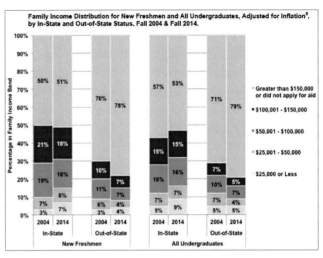

Soaring applications for admission

Soaring average incomes for out-of-state applicants

with more interest in the social aspects of university life than a rigorous academic experience. By the first decade of the new century, student protests had largely been replaced by student parties and athletics (at least if the increasing popularity of fraternities and sororities are any evidence of student priorities). The University became increasingly dependent on rich students who came here as much for fun as for learning.

Although entering student quality remained strong, at least as measured by high school grade point averages and scores on standardized entrance examinations such as the SAT and ACT, both the University's selectivity in admissions and yield rates lagged considerable behind those of many peer public and private universities. For example, in 2011 the University admitted 60% of instate applications, with a yield rate of 70%, while out-of-state selectivity was 40%, with a yield rate of 25%.

Although the growth in applications for admission from students continued to grow (largely because of the ease of application with the Common Application now used for most undergraduate programs), Michigan still competed very aggressively to attract high income students, since it was still regarded as a "safety" or backup school for most-out-of-state students. The University invested heavily ($650 million) to provide high quality residence experiences (complete with sushi bars and entertainment centers–"beer and circuses" in Roman terms), through infusing its athletic contests with "the wow factor", and turned lose its advertising power to push the Michigan brand to such students.

With these students have come numerous

challenges. Although the University had managed to tame fraternity excesses in the 1990s, the deluge of affluent students seeking fun rather than scholarship have ignited problems in Greek life once again, with excessive drinking, sexual assaults, and horrendous public behavior (e.g., the trashing of ski resorts during MLK weekend in 2015). Surveys find that today's students spend roughly half the time on their studies as earlier generations (e.g., typically 10-12 hours outside of class compared to 20-30 hours characterizing college students in the 1960s-1980s). While some of this can be blamed on student motivation, the faculty must also accept some of the blame for not assigning sufficient work!

In recent years there has been a growing concern, particularly on the part of the faculty, that as the University has become larger, more extended, and more complex, it has become less guided by academic priorities. Earlier the concern was raised about the erosion of the University of Michigan's long-standing public purpose of providing "an uncommon education for the common man". Clearly its leadership in providing exceptional educational opportunities to low income and underrepresented minority students has already declined as its state support has eroded.

But more seriously, the priority that the University has placed upon high-income students has been reflected in the drop of both students from impoverished backgrounds (e.g., Pell Grant recipients) and underrepresented minority students. In effect, it has shifted its public purpose to "providing an uncommon education for the uncommonly rich". But there are other signs of an increasing imbalance in the priority given to wealth, e.g., responding to the whims of generous donors, the private boxes and clubs characterizing Michigan athletics, wealthy students who attend Michigan "paying for the party," all activities, ironically, subsidized in part by the "common man" through the generous tax treatment of the payments for these premium services. (Armstrong, 2012)

A related concern is the current process universities with highly selective student admissions processes use to make admissions decisions. In 2010 most American colleges and universities with selective admissions process agreed to use a Common Application for admissions, in which students were required to complete a common application form and references to each of the institutions under consideration (augmented by a small number of specific elements for the most selective institutions). This enabled students to apply for admission to many institutions with essentially the same form, subject only to paying the small fee to each institution for admissions application processing. As a result, the number of applications received by selective institutions soared, with many students applying to 5 to 10 institutions in an effort to optimize their options for college attendance. With thousands of more applications, the selectivity of admissions at leading institutions such as the Ivy League dropped rapidly, below 10% in several cases.

Of course, since selectivity was used as an important indicator by college ratings schemes such as U.S. News & World Report, every effort was made to increase selectivity still further by marketing institutions to larger numbers of applicants, whether qualified or not. Yet enormous increase in applications triggered by the Common Application overloaded admissions offices and led unfortunately to the over dependence on quantitative measures such as grade point averages, SAT scores, and Advanced Placement courses as the first pass in the selection process in an effort to reduce the burdens on staff.

This was particularly serious for the University of Michigan, since it was regarded as a "safety" school, a backup application for students whose first choice was an Ivy League class institution with very low acceptance rates. The number of applications to UM soared to 52,000 and beyond, forcing the use of quantitative measures (GPA, SAT, AP) as initial criteria to reduce the remaining application inventory to manageable size for more subjective consideration.

Yet many of those with high quantitative scores came from affluent families that could afford special training programs for test taking and had access to strong secondary schools with ample AP offerings. Students from lower income families or secondary schools with limited resources were handicapped by the dependence on quantitative data forced by the Common Application, and hence eliminated early in the competition for admission. Unfortunately, the current admission process demanded by the Common Application process discriminates against the very type of student that Michigan really wants to enroll, i.e., "the common man with uncommon dreams"!

In 2015 the University joined a new group of 80 selective universities, the Coalition for Access, Affordability, and Success, which will adopt a new approach to admissions, working with students at an early ninth grade stage to build portfolios of achievements, and providing institutions with more flexibility in modifying applications to address their particular interests and characteristics. It is too early to assess the impact of the new approach, but it should be vastly preferable to the Common Application.

In summary, there is growing evidence that external factors including the dramatic decline in state support, the state's implementation of a ban on affirmative action, and the biases built into current admissions processes have put the University's public purpose at some risk. And to be fair, the University has spent heavily on providing financial aid packages that meet full cost of attendance to admitted students from Michigan. But this has been a formidable challenge in a state that provides the lowest level of need-based financial aid in the nation. Indeed, the degree to which the State of Michigan–and many other states–have turned their backs on the support of public education requires a more urgent warning, particularly to those of us in the "me" generation.

On a more positive note, the massive effort over the past several years to renovate all of the University's student housing while adding new facilities such as North Quad and the Munger Graduate Residence Hall

For most students, the ultimate goal today is commencement!

is highly comendable. These facilities are the living-learning environments for roughly one-third of the student body, and their quality is of major strategic importance to the university (even if the presence of food stations and sushi bars in the renovated dorms does suggest an effort to attract wealthy students as a part of this strategy...)

The Road Ahead

Over the past 15 years enrollments have grown 25% to almost 44,000 students. However essentially all of this growth has been at the undergraduate level, while graduate and professional enrollment has stayed relatively constant. This major shift in student composition deserves serious strategic effort, since it has strained the faculty and facilities resources that support our graduate and professional programs.

It has also been noted while the emphasis on attracting more out-of-state students capable of paying $60,000 for tuition, room and board has generated very substantial new resources, it has also shifted somewhat the student culture, away from the historic mission of "providing an uncommon education for the common man" and instead attracting more students from wealthy backgrounds, many of whom selected Michigan as a "safety school" backup to Ivy League applications or have chosen Michigan for its extracurricular life (i.e., have come "paying for the party"). While this shift in the student culture will be considered more specifically in Chapter 20 concerned with the public purpose of the University, it also is important to state here the concern about the low enrollments of students from low-income backgrounds. Much of Michigan's impact in the past came from students from working class families from the state's farms and factories who saw attending the University as a great opportunity to do something important with their lives, provided they worked hard enough. To serve more of these students, once the backbone of its student body, the University must restructure its admissions policies, financial aid, and outreach.

The University needs to throttle back Michigan's reputation as a party school (with big-time college sports) and instead rebrand itself as an institution determined to demand the student academic effort required for leadership roles later in life. More specifically, the University must insist that its faculty challenge its students through demanding academic programs. Here it might set a goal of demanding that through course assignments, students spend a minimum of two hours of effort for every one hour of class time, a metric used at leading universities through much of the last century. It also needs to provide more opportunities for student engagement with faculty in research, service, and professional activities. Here technology might help, since social networking has largely decoupled such engagement and interactions from space and time constraints.

It is also important for the University to provide its varsity athletes, roughly 1,000 in number, with similar academic experiences similar to other students. It must resist the tendency of coaches to dominate the lives of their athletes, demanding 40 hours or more a week of training and competition, and in some cases, even dictating their academic majors (e.g., the Bachelor of General Studies offered by LS&A). While the Athletics Department has built and staffed high quality learning facilities, these also tend to isolate athletes from other students (ironically, when these facilities were approved by the Regents, it was agreed that they would also be open to all students).

Although *in loco parentis* disappeared decades ago, the University has learned that it simply cannot ignore the behavior of students beyond the classroom. While most communities of young people experience the challenges of excessive alcohol consumption, drugs, and sexual misconduct and assault, large university communities are particularly vulnerable to these, as evidenced by Michigan's "leadership" in various national polls attempting to rate institutions as "party schools" or tragically, "sexual assault and misconduct". While the University has taken major steps toward addressing these concerns, the very scale and diversity of its many student communities will likely require new approaches.

Here particular attention must be given to "Greek life" on campus, since the unusually large number of students belonging to unregulated fraternities leads to a serious issue of adequate controls, as evidenced by the frequent instances of serious misbehavior and, indeed, even criminal conduct by fraternity members. While there is always a danger to the University in exposing itself to liability in becoming too engaged with these organizations, their damage to the University has been and remains today simply too great to ignore. While it is unrealistic to ban fraternities entirely as some institutions have done, the University should reinforce demands for appropriate behavior with strong penalties for misconduct, both for students as well as for the fraternities as organizations.

On a more positive note, Michigan's long history of student activism, while occasionally challenging to the University's leadership and governance, is something of great pride because of its social impact. Michigan must not only tolerate such student activities, including occasional disruption of University activities, but actually encourage it and remain attentive and responsive to student issues. Here, particular concern should be given to maintaining the University's long tradition of "truth and light", by throttling back efforts to manage information flow throughout the institution so that bad news is disguised and good news is marketed heavily. Students deserve the truth, the whole truth, and nothing but the truth from the institution responsible for their education.

Chapter 6

Faculty

The principal academic resource of a university is its faculty. The quality and commitment of the faculty determine the excellence of the academic programs of a university, the quality of its student body, the excellence of its teaching and scholarship, its capacity to serve broader society through public service, and the resources it is able to attract from public and private sources.

The inauguration address of 1988 of Michigan's 12th president began with the statement: "It is sometimes said that great universities are run by their faculties, for their faculties. Clearly the quality of our institutions is determined by the quality of our faculty–by their talents, their commitments, and their actions." (However this statement was quickly followed with the caveat: "I must hasten to add here that they are also run for their students and their society as well!")

Actually this faculty-centric statement reflected well our perspectives, shaped by decades of toiling in the faculty vineyards at Michigan, teaching, conducting research, advising students, hustling research grants, and serving on faculty committee after committee after committee. Both of us had served in numerous leadership roles with university faculty and community groups that played essential roles in the support of the University's faculty.

This empathy for faculty life evolved personal experience, understanding well the stresses of the promotion and tenure decisions, the relative poverty of junior faculty, and the frustrations of faculty politics. From this background, we understood clearly our obligation to serve the faculty of the university in various leadership roles–first as dean, then as provost, and as president. Yet even in these leadership roles, we continued to view ourselves as first and foremost members of the university's faculty community, on temporary assignment to administrative positions, a role we returned to after completing our leadership roles. We both have continued to work in many roles and on many agendas, both on the campus and in the community, as well as at the national and global level, to serve the University as best we could, always loyal and always dedicated to the faculty family.

1960s and 1970s

When we arrived in Ann Arbor, the Department of Nuclear Science and Engineering was the only academic program located entirely on the North Campus, spread out across several buildings, including the Phoenix Memorial Laboratory where most of our research laboratories and the Ford Nuclear Reactor were located. Furthermore, since this department offered only graduate degrees, all of its instruction, research, and students were also on that campus. In fact, its faculty and students probably had more interaction with other nuclear programs at MIT, Wisconsin, UC Berkeley, and Caltech than they did with other faculty members at Michigan. This isolation actually created a very close bond between faculty, graduate students, staff, and their families, working together, learning together, discovering together, and even playing together (all-night poker games, basketball, baseball, whatever).

Yet largely through involvement as both a member and a leader of the Faculty Women's Club, we began to develop relationships with faculty in other parts of the University. This would lead eventually to a role in faculty governance and teach us about some important characteristics of the Michigan faculty:

First, the unusual intellectual breadth of academic programs–schools and colleges, departments, research institutes and projects, etc.–provided evidence of

Our first "faculty home": the Department of Nuclear Science and Engineering: 1970 to 2012

just how low the barriers among disciplines were at Michigan and how easy it was to launch new interdisciplinary programs. For example, it was easy for engineering faculty to form relationships with mathematics and physics that would eventually lead to more formal programs such as applied mathematics and applied physics.

Second, although there was a University-wide faculty governance body, the Senate Assembly, in reality was rather weak. It served primarily as an advisory body on University-wide issues rather than faculty senates at many other univesities that were given executive authority (e.g., U Wisconsin and U California). Instead, at Michigan the true faculty power rested in the hands of elected executive committees at the level of schools, colleges, and departments. These influenced faculty appointments and promotions, budgets and instructional assignments, and even occasionally the selection of deans and chairs. And their elected participants were frequently some of the University's most distinguished faculty members.

Third, since the University was scattered about the small city of Ann Arbor, which was only of comparable size to the University itself (and actually smaller than the University on football weekends), one was likely to encounter other faculty members as neighbors, school parent-teacher organizations, restaurants, swim and tennis clubs, …just about everywhere. Hence one's social life with other faculty members naturally evolved far beyond one's academic department.

Fourth, although still in a relatively early stage, at the time, the decentralization of the University associated with the dispersion of power to the level of deans, directors, and chairs, was already well underway. Hence, the President, Executive Officers, and Regents of the University were far removed from the personal experience of most faculty members, except for the occasional article in the Michigan Daily or the Ann Arbor News, where one was more likely to read about Bo Schembechler than President Fleming or the Board of Regents. At the highest level, the administration and the governing board were largely out of sight and out of mind in faculty concerns. The most visible influence over faculty experiences and academic programs came from neither the central administration nor the governing board, but rather it was due to an invisible network of senior faculty members, distinguished in achievement, who had spent the majority of their careers at Michigan.

To be sure, those with influence and distinction were sometimes not the most visible and rarely the best compensated of Michigan faculty members. The latter were usually from the Medical School, as evidenced by the new cars that appeared each July in the parking lots of the city's tennis clubs shortly after the spring distribution of clinical income. Yet those with true influence over their colleagues and even at times the President and Regents, were" lifelong" members of the Michigan faculty who had committed their careers to the University, University leaders such as Bill McKeachie, Donald Katz, Angus Campbell, John Knott, Carl Cohen, and many, many others.

Of course many faculty members joined students during the 1960s to push for social justice, civil rights, and an end to the war in Vietnam. At times they were even sympathetic to student disruptive tactics such as classroom strikes or protests at Michigan Stadium. Fortunately the wise leadership of President Fleming recognized the importance of pervasive academic freedom, as long as academic values and the academic process were not put at risk. Tolerance was preferred to confrontation, and by the 1970s the flames of protest and activism had begun to smolder. The faculty largely returned to their classrooms, laboratories, and studios with their students, and Michigan turned instead to new challenges such as adjusting to the decline in state support and launching mammoth projects such as the new Adult General Hospital.

1980s

As state support began to decline more rapidly, with the loss of roughly one-third of state appropriations during the early years of the 1980s, there was increasing pressure on faculty to generate the research grants necessary to support their activities–and, indeed, part of their salaries and the support for their students.

At a university like Michigan, this can amount to an expectation that each faculty member will generate hundreds of thousands of research dollars per year, a heavy burden for those who also carry significant instructional, administrative, and service responsibilities. For example, imagine the plight of the young faculty member in Medicine: responsible for teaching medical students and residents; providing sufficient clinical revenue to support not only his or her salary but also the overhead of the medical center; securing sufficient research grants to support laboratories, graduate students, and postdoctoral fellows; exploiting opportunities for technology transfer and business start-ups; and building the scholarly momentum and reputation to achieve tenure. Imagine as well the conflict that inevitably arises among responsibilities to students, patients, scholarship, and professional colleagues. Not an easy life!

As a consequence, research universities such as Michigan began to develop a freewheeling entrepreneurial spirit, perhaps best captured by the words of one university president, "Faculty at our university can do anything they wish–provided they can attract the money to support what they want to do." In fact, one might view the contemporary university as a loose federation of faculty entrepreneurs, who drive the evolution of the university to fulfill their individual goals. In a sense, the research university has become a highly adaptable knowledge conglomerate because of the interests and efforts of our faculty. An increasing share of externally provided resources flow directly to faculty entrepreneurs as research grants and contracts from the federal government, corporations, and private foundations. These research programs act as quasi-independent revenue centers with very considerable influence, frequently at odds with more formal faculty governance structures such as faculty senates. The result is a transactional culture, in which everything is up for negotiation–let's make a deal, writ large!

The faculty members of research universities are well aware that their careers–their compensation, promotion, and tenure–are determined primarily by their research productivity as measured by publications and grantsmanship, since these contribute most directly to scholarly reputation and hence market value. This reward climate helps to tip the scales away from undergraduate teaching, public service, and institutional loyalty, especially when quantitative measures of research productivity or grantsmanship replace more balanced judgments on the quality of research and professional work.

Since the academic promotion ladder is relatively short, consisting essentially of the three levels of assistant professor, associate professor, and professor, the faculty reward culture can become one-dimensional, based primarily upon salary. Although faculty honors and awards are common in higher education, including endowed professorial chairs, many faculty members tend to measure their relative worth in terms of salary. Many public universities are required by freedom-of-information laws to publish faculty salaries. Even in private universities, one's salary can usually be compared with those of others either through the informal grapevine or by testing the marketplace by exploring offers from other institutions. Hence the faculty reward structure creates a highly competitive environment that extends beyond a single institution into a national or even global marketplace for the very best faculty talent.

These pressures began to drive noticeable shift in faculty priorities during the last decades of the 20th century. The strong commitment that had been made by earlier faculty to lifelong careers serving the University began to erode with an increasingly competitive marketplace for faculty, particularly those who could generate external funding for their research. Faculty members quickly learned that the best path to increased compensation and promotion–and for some, leadership positions–was to play the marketplace, moving from institution to institution in an effort to build a rewarding career. Those who chose to stay behind and commit a career to a single institution became a declining breed.

Deans quickly learned about the faculty marketplace, since in these roles, much of their time was spent attempting to counter offers that would lure Michigan best faculty elsewhere, while enticing top-notch faculty members into leaving their current institution and migrating to Michigan. In fact, deans and department chairs were increasingly evaluated by the scalps they raided from competing institutions. During the 1980s and 1990s it was customary to keep tabs on Michigan's success in this competition through what was called the annual "ebb and flow" charts of who the University attracted and who it lost in each program.

1990s

The growing pressures on faculty to generate the resources necessary to support their activities became even more intense during the 1990s. Since faculty compensation policies have major impact on recruiting, rewarding, and retaining top talent, this received increasing attention by the University leadership. A new faculty compensation policy was developed by the Executive Officer team and deans that aimed at achieving an optimum balance among criteria such as merit, market, and equity. Its key features, principles, and goals could be stated as:

The average compensation for full professors at Michigan should be set at the top of public universities.

However, the best faculty members at Michigan should be compensated at levels comparable to those of the best public and private universities.

The average compensation for assistant professors and associate professors should be set at the highest among public and private universities in the nation, since Michigan's tradition is to develop faculty from within rather than recruit at senior ranks through raids, and hence we needed to recruit the very best junior faculty.

Deans and directors should be compensated at levels comparable to the best public and private universities.

Annual salary increases should be based entirely upon merit (i.e., no cost-of-living increase), occasionally adjusted by market or equity considerations.

It was clear that it was the President's responsibility to attract the resources necessary to support such a policy and to make an effective case to the Regents, the State Legislature, and the public as to why such compensation was vital to the university's quality. The success of this aggressive strategy was demonstrated by the fact that by the early 1990s Michigan's faculty salaries had passed UC-Berkeley to become first among all public universities, and at the assistant and associate professor level, salary levels rose to first in the nation, ahead of all public and private peers.

Of course faculty members learn quickly that the best way to increase compensation and rise through the ranks is to periodically test their market value by exploring positions in other institutions. Although many professors would prefer to remain at a single institution throughout their career, the strong market-determined character of faculty compensation may force them to jump from institution to institution at various stages in their career. And here once again the influence of the president became important.

University presidents are usually not involved in routine faculty recruiting, since in the typical university, hundreds of searches are underway at any particular time. However, on occasion the president would be brought into the search process to lure a major faculty superstar to the campus. The president also occasionally played a similar role in attempting to persuade a distinguished faculty member to remain in the face of an attractive offer from another institution. Since so many of these efforts were in competition with West Coast universities, prior to a meeting with the faculty member, picture books on the San Francisco earthquake or other West Coast calamities (e.g., freeway traffic) were carefully placed on the coffee table in the President's office. There was also direct involvement as President in recruiting senior minority faculty, in part because of the hands-on involvement in the Michigan Mandate, the strategic effort to increase the university's commitment to diversity.

However, perhaps the president's most significant impact on faculty recruiting was through particular policy initiatives. Much of the momentum of academic institutions is driven by a few truly exceptional, visionary, and exciting appointments that set the pace for academic programs. Hence the University created a "target of opportunity" program intended to strongly encourage academic units to recruit such candidates. Usually faculty searches are heavily constrained by programmatic requirements, e.g., to search for an historian in Southeast Asian studies or a physicist in superstring theory. For this reason, the administrative team would set aside special funds intended to fund appointments for truly exceptional candidates, regardless of area of expertise. The academic units were challenged to identify such hiring opportunities and then bring us proposals for funding their positions. If these looked promising, the administration would commit from central resources the base and startup funding necessary to recruit these individuals. The target of opportunity was later extended to the recruiting of outstanding minority faculty with great success.

Of course such singular scholars are not always the easiest people to accommodate. Some are demanding prima donnas, requiring high maintenance by deans, provosts, and even presidents. It was the president's role to stroke these folks, sometimes assisting deans in meeting their needs and demands, at other times simply reassuring them that the university was honored to have them on our faculty and strongly supported their work. Yet it was their passion for their work, their unrelenting commitment to achievement, and their exceptionally high standards that accompanied their great talent, which set the pace for their students, their

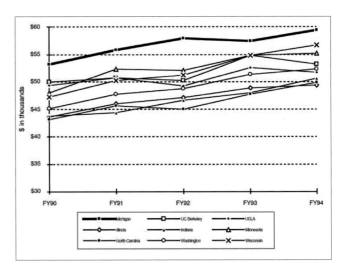

Average Assistant Professor Salary (1994)

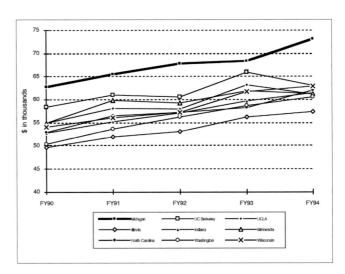

Average Associate Professor Salary (1994)

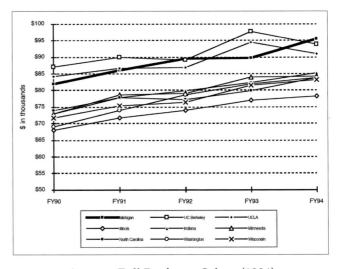

Average Full Professor Salary (1994)

In our roles in the positions of provost and president, we set a high priority
on community building events for faculty members and their guests.

colleagues, and the university.

There was one final element of faculty policy that was considered during the 1990s, although both sensitive and challenging: "the third rail" of tenure! Certainly the most controversial, complex, and misunderstood issue related to the faculty in higher education, at least in the minds of the public, is tenure. In theory, tenure is the key mechanism for protecting academic freedom and for defending faculty members against political attack both within and outside the university. In practice, it has become something quite different: job security, protecting both outstanding and incompetent faculty alike, not only from political intrusion but also from a host of other performance issues that could lead to dismissal in many other walks of life. And, of course, it is this presumed guarantee of job security that so infuriates many members of the public, some of whom have felt the sting of corporate downsizing or job competition.

Most university faculty members believe that tenure is a valuable and important practice in the core academic disciplines of the university, where independent teaching and scholarship require some protection from criticism and controversy. This privilege should also enable tenured faculty members to accept greater responsibility for the interests of the university rather than focusing solely on personal objectives. But even within the academy, many are beginning to question the appropriateness of current tenure practices. The abolition of mandatory retirement policies is leading to an aging faculty cohort, insulated from rigorous performance accountability by tenure, and this is depriving young scholars of faculty opportunities. Increasingly, the academy itself is acknowledging that both the concept and practice of tenure—particularly when interpreted as guaranteed lifetime employment— needs to be reevaluated.

Yet only the most foolhardy would attempt to do this within a single institution, since the marketplace for the best faculty is highly competitive. Hence any challenge to the status quo of tenure must be mounted by a coalition of institutions. To this end, during the 1990s the President's Council of the Big Ten Conference (which is actually as much an academic organization of 12 institutions–including the University of Chicago– as it is an athletic conference) invited the provosts

and chairs of the faculty senates of its universities to a daylong conference to discuss tenure and the faculty contract. Needless to say, one workshop does not a sustained movement make, but the discussion did suggest that the faculties of at least this set of research universities are more open to considering change than one might expect.

2000

As the University of Michigan entered a new century, faculty quality was increasingly challenged by the institution's struggle to retain top faculty in the face of increasing instructional loads, eroding compensation levels, and aggressive offers from competing institutions. There were growing concerns that the combination of heavier instructional loads driven by increasing enrollment in larger academic units (LS&A and Engineering) and faculty salaries, which were beginning to lag those of well-endowed private universities, wete making both the recruiting and retention of high quality faculty more difficult. More specifically over the period 2004 to 2011, the University lost 40% of faculty receiving offers from other institutions, including 55 to Harvard, 54 to UC Berkeley, 46 to Stanford, and 37 to Chicago, and 24 to Columbia. Of course, it had always been a challenge to compete with peer private institutions, particularly at a time when the gap between faculty salaries at public and private universities have grown to over 20%. But perhaps even more serious during this period were the growing losses to public universities, such as 33 to U Texas, 28 to U North Carolina, 25 to Maryland and 23 to Ohio State. Viewed from the perspective of many of our peers, Michigan was becoming a major supplier of many of their very best faculty members, and the loss to this University was immense.

Of particular concern was the evidence of a disturbing loss of many of our most talented junior faculty members. During the 15 years from 2000 to 2015, the University lost over 600 young faculty members to peer institutions. Of particular concern here is the loss of hundreds of recently tenured junior faculty, including many of the University's most outstanding women and minority faculty member, just as they are moving into the most productive part of their career.

Several of the University's schools and colleges (e.g., LS&A) had effective programs for successful mentoring of junior faculty members to the tenure stage. In fact, Michigan has long had a strong reputation for building an outstanding faculty through the recruiting and development of young talent, in contrast to many private institutions, which tend to recruit faculty at more senior levels after they have achieved tenure and established reputations elsewhere. For Michigan to have its young faculty members recruited away just as they have successfully achieved promotion and tenure not only raises the perception that the institution is serving as a "farm club" for other institutions, but furthermore raises a serious question about its continued capacity to build and retain its senior faculty through faculty development.

Unfortunately, the recent expansion in University enrollments, increasing by over 25% to 44,000 students, has had a significant impact both on the character of the University's academic programs and the nature of the Ann Arbor community. Since tenure-track faculty size has increased only modestly in those units undergoing major expansion (e.g., LS&A and Engineering), this has shifted lower division instruction toward an increasing dependence on part-time or nontenure-track faculty, who now provide over 50% of lower division undergraduate instruction. Teaching loads, as measured by students per full-time faculty member, are the highest in the University's history.

`On the other side of the ledger, the University launched an ambitious cost reduction effort during the past decade, aiming to trim roughly 1.5% to 2.0% each year off the base budget. Although some of these savings has come from more efficient management of energy and supply acquisition, and administration, much of the recent savings have come largely out of faculty-staff benefits for health care, retirement, and salary programs–and budget cuts imposed on academic and administrative units. Hence serious concerns have arisen that further cuts in benefits and support could cripple UM's efforts to attract and retain outstanding faculty and staff.

The University has compounded this top-down approach to cost containment by entering expensive contracts with external consultants (e.g., Accenture) that have attempted to impose corporate practices

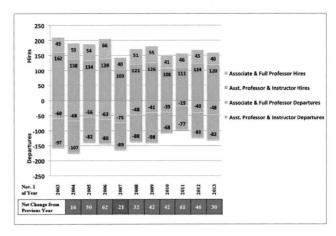

Faculty hires and departures

(e.g., centralizing all service activities) that have not only demoralized staff and enraged faculty, but have also been found to generate minimal savings of less than 0.1% of the University's budget (e.g., "penny wise but pound foolish"). To date administrative efforts have largely ignored the unprecedented expansions in administrative staffing and cost of growing peripheral activities such as public relations, marketing, and "institutional advancement" as well as the unusually high levels of compensation of senior administrators, now approaching extreme levels and questionable practices (e.g., hidden bonuses and deferred compensation) more appropriate for the corporate setting than higher education.

The Challenges Facing Today's UM Faculty

Market Concerns

Most of the faculty trends of the past decade have continued to intensify. The marketplace has become even more intense as faculty have become even more nomadic, now remaining less than a decade at each way station on their route to a professorial chair or administrative position. New elements have been added to the package of negotiations, including not only promotion, salary increases, startup funding, perhaps an endowed chair, but now dual-career family placement, more generous sabbatical leave options, etc. The competition among institutions has become every more intense.

It is important to note that faculty members of today

80

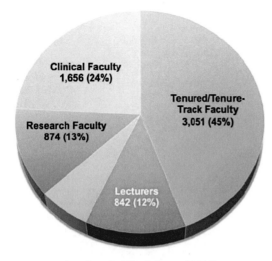

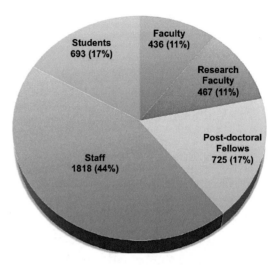

Academic Workforce (2014)

Research Workforce (2014)

actually work in several overlapping communities, e.g., their university, their discipline, their research communities, their teaching communities...all characterized by similar commitments, quality, rewards, reputation, etc. In contrast to years past when faculty members committed careers to a single institution (or disciplines), today faculty members are not only institutional nomads but also disciplinary nomads. They respond to a multiplicity of markets, pressures, and incentives, many of which are simply not under the control of the university.

The highly competitive nature of higher education in America, where universities compete aggressively for the best faculty members, the best students, resources from public and private sources, athletic supremacy, and reputation, has created an environment that demands achievement. However, while competition within the higher education marketplace can drive quality, if not always efficiency, it has an important downside. When serious imbalances arise in available funding, policy restrictions, and political constraints, such competition can deteriorate into a damaging relationship that not only erodes institutional quality and capacity, but also more seriously threatens the national interest. It can create an intensely Darwinian winner-take-all ecosystem in which the strongest and wealthiest institutions become predators, raiding the best faculty and students of the less generously supported and more constrained public universities and manipulating federal research and financial policies to sustain a system in which the rich get richer and the poor get

devoured.

This ruthless and frequently predatory competition poses a particularly serious challenge to the nation's public research universities. These institutions now find themselves caught with declining state support and the predatory wealthy private universities competing for the best students, faculty, and support. Of course, most private universities have also struggled through the recent recession, though for some elite campuses this is the first time in decades they have experienced any bumps in their financial roads. Yet their endowments and private giving will recover rapidly with a recovering economy, and their predatory behavior upon public higher education for top faculty and students will resume once again.

Faculty Incentives

The analysis of faculty attrition during the past 15 years finds that the loss of Michigan has been unusually high among junior faculty, and particularly among women and minorities. Although some of this is due to the long-standing process of tenure evaluation, the number of young faculty with distinguished records that leave the University for appointments at peer institutions (e.g., Harvard, MIT, Yale, Stanford, University of California) is cause for concern.

Of course, part of this may be due to the challenges of finding suitable opportunities for two-career families, since the small size of the Ann Arbor community and the weak economy of southeastern Michigan simply

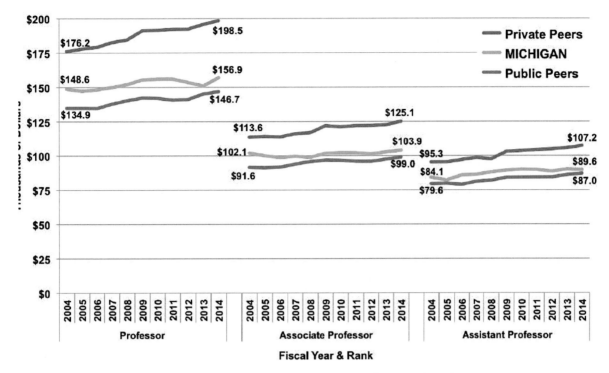

UMAA Faculty compensation over the past decade

cannot provide the job markets characterizing major metropolitan areas such as Boston or San Francisco. So, too, the large instructional loads driven by the University's dramatic increases in enrollments discourage many faculty members, particularly at the junior level.

But it also must be recognized that despite rhetoric to the contrary, faculty salaries simply have not been a priority of the University administration in recent years. Recent comparative analyses of faculty and administrator salaries with peer public institutions indicate that as of 2014, the average salary of full professors at Michigan has not only fallen 30% below those of private universities but also ranks only at the level of 16th among the 18th public and private institutions consided at its peers. In sharp contrast the compensation of senior administrators (Executive Officers, deans, and senior financial administrators) are 30% to 40% higher than all other peer public universities–and 40% to 50% higher when undisclosed bonuses are included (a topic to be discussed later in this report). The impact on faculty morale of excessive compensation of senior administrators and administrative staff has been considerable.

To be sure, the University has been under significant financial pressures during the past two decades with the decline of state support and the recession of 2008. Yet it has chosen to respond to these challenges by restraining faculty and staff salaries and reducing benefits rather than addressing the excessive compensation of the central administration. Indeed, during this period expenditures for administrative support have been increasing at an average annual rate that is 2 to 3 times the increases in expenditures for instruction, the primary measue of faculty salaries and benefits. (Ulsoy, 2012)

While much of this is driven both by the differing financial opportunities and challenges facing academic, auxiliary, and administrative activities, it is also due to an erosion of the academic voice in University leadership. For example, there has been a decided shift away from the long tradition of appointing senior administrators (including the Executive Officers of the University) with significant faculty experience. So, too, the long-standing practice of achieving a balance between the appointment of internal and external candidates for senior leadership positions such as deans in an effort to balance both the continuity provided by long-standing University employees with new viewpoints from outside seems to have been abandoned, with a decided

**Comparison of 2012 Faculty Salaries among
Provost's List of Peer Institutions**
(*Chronicle of Higher Education*, Feb. 12, 2015)

Rank	Institution	Average Salary		
		Prof.	Assoc. Prof.	Asst. Prof.
1	Stanford	195,400	131,200	109,800
2	Harvard	198,400	120,900	109,800
3	Penn	181,600	117,800	112,300
4	Duke	175,300	114,500	96,000
5	MIT	171,800	120,300	102,800
6	Northwestern	172,100	110,200	98,900
7	UCLA	162,600	107,400	87,400
8	Berkeley	154,000	104,600	92,300
9	Cornell endowed	161,800	113,000	97,000
10	Washington Univ. SL	172,400	100,200	96,800
11	Cornell	143,600	103,700	93,400
12	NYU	184,200	106,100	99,700
13	USC	155,900	105,300	93,300
14	Notre Dame	150,200	97,200	90,200
15	Virginia	151,600	95,000	80,300
16	UM	148,800	98,200	85,800
17	UNC	144,000	94,600	80,500
18	Texas	140,700	89,900	83,900

UM Rank: #16 out of 18

Faculty per *University Record*	35%
Staff per *University Record*	24%
Executive officers* per *University Record*	26%
Executive officers* actual (w/o bonuses)	52%
Executive officers* actual (with bonuses)	76%
Deans (w/o bonuses)	41%
Deans (with bonuses)	56%

Compounded UM salary increases over 2005-2014
(excluding President compensation)

university puts on the table to retain the individual, both can seriously distort the broader faculty compensation patterns. Furthermore, such offers usually go far beyond simply salary and can involve a considerable dowry including laboratory space, research support, graduate and research assistant support, and, yes, sometimes even a reduced teaching load.

Not only does such an effort tax the available resources of a university, but the recruitment package may seriously distort the existing faculty reward structure and lead to the loss of key faculty who may feel jilted by the offer to their new colleague. Even more serious are those instances in which an up-and-aspiring university recruits a big-name faculty member past his or her prime–an "extinct volcano." While the reputations of these individuals may add luster to the institution, their excessive compensation and declining productivity can discourage more junior faculty and actually harm program quality over the long term.

But beyond this, several of the wealthiest private universities play a particularly damaging role within higher education by preferring to build their faculties through raids on other institutions rather than developing them through the ranks from within. Their vast endowments allow them to make offers to faculty members that simply cannot be matched by public universities. When challenged about their predatory faculty raids on public universities, the elite private institutions generally respond by suggesting a trickle-down theory. Such free-market competition, they argue, enhances the quality of all faculties. "If you don't let these market forces work, institutions and people can stagnate." Yet in reality, this philosophy promotes the fundamental premise that the very best faculty members should be at the wealthiest institutions. Such predatory

preference toward external candidates in recent years.

The Faculty Marketplace

Academic leaders spend much of their time either attempting to recruit outstanding faculty members to their institution or fending off raids on their faculty by other institutions. Although there have been attempts in the past to impose certain rules of behavior on faculty recruiting–for example, through informal agreements that institutions will refrain from recruiting faculty just prior to the start of a new academic year or avoid using the promise of reduced teaching load to lure a research star—in reality, it is a no-holds-barred and quite ruthless competition. The wealthier and more prestigious the institution, the more aggressively it plays the game.

There is an insidious nature to this intensely competitive market for faculty talent. First, such recruiting efforts are a major factor in driving up the costs of a college education. The competition for faculty superstars can be intense and become VERY expensive. Whether it is the size of an offer put together to lure a star faculty member away, or the counteroffer the home

behavior can decimate the quality of programs in other universities by raiding their best faculty, who have been nurtured and developed at considerable expense. Even unsuccessful attempts to raid faculty can result in a serious distortion of resource allocation in the target institution as they desperately attempt to retain their best faculty stars.

The Erosion of Faculty Influence

Looking back over the past 50 years, it is clear that the career trajectories of the faculty have changed significantly. No longer do young faculty expect to pursue their career at a single institution but anticipate more of a nomadic path moving from institution to institution in order to rise up the promotion ladder. Yet even more seriously, the opportunities for establishing an academic career are dwindling, with non-tenure track appointments as post-doctoral scholars, lecturers, and adjunct faculty now providing the majority of lower division instruction, a feature driven by the efforts of universities to cut costs and improve productivity with a more flexible faculty workforce. As a consequence, today less than 25% of the instructional faculty is comprised of tenured professors.

Adopting corporate approaches to university management and leadership, coupled with the nomadic life it imposes upon today's faculty members, has also seriously damaged faculty loyalty to institutions. Here, Michigan provides a disturbing example of the impact of the increasingly "corporate" nature of large research university, with an increasing fraction of its central administration comprised of staff with little if any experience in higher education, and decision making largely detached from academic considerations (e.g., the efforts to recentralize resource control, weakening the power of deans and directors, launching new initiatives from the central administration rather than harvesting them from faculty and students, and imposing upon faculty and academic programs a corporate bureaucracy that is orthogonal to the spirit of academic freedom and creativity).

Noted scholar Cathy Davidson puts it well: "The distress in higher education today, our adjunct crisis, our overstuffed lecture halls, and our crushing faculty workloads, is a product of 50 years of neoliberalism, both the actual defunding of public higher education by state legislatures and the magical thinking that corporate administrators can run universities more cost-effectively than faculty members. They don't. The major push to "corporatize" higher education has coincided with a rise, not a decrease, in costs. The greedy, corporate brutality of far too many contemporary universities is reminiscent of medieval monasteries of old. Let's call it "turf and serf": real-estate land grabs, exploitation of faculty labor, and the burdening of students with crushing debt." (Davidson, 2013)

Little wonder than many of Michigan's most accomplished and distinguished faculty members have largely stepped back from efforts to influence the future of the University through service in a faculty governance role with little power or through initiatives that are usually ignored or overwhelmed by the public relations efforts of the central administration. In a very real sense, perhaps one of the greatest challenges to the University of Michigan today, as it is to other great public research universities, is to find a way to empower once again those faculty members whose contributions in teaching, scholarship, and service have been the key factor in establishing and sustaining the reputation of the University.

But perhaps most important has been the weakening of the voice and influence of the University's deans in recent years. The University of Michigan has long been known as a "deans' university", in which the authority and responsibility of deans as academic leaders is unusually strong. Deans are the key academic leaders most responsible for the priority, quality, and integrity of the University's academic programs. They select department chairs, recruit and evaluate faculty, seek resources for their school both within the university (arguing for their share of university resources) and beyond the campus (through private fundraising or research grantsmanship). As the key line officers for the faculty of the university, they have rather considerable authority that usually aligns well with their great responsibilities. Good things happen in the University's academic programs because of good deans, at least over the long term–and vice-versa, of course.

The Impacted Wisdom Group

During the mid-1990s, federal age discrimination laws eliminated the long-standing practice of mandatory retirement for university faculty. There was initial concern that this would lead to an "impacted wisdom group" of aging faculty retaining their appointments well past conventional retirement ages of 65 to 70, thereby preventing the opening of positions for new junior faculty. However the impact of the relative prosperity of the 1990s on faculty defined contribution retirement programs (e.g., TIAA-CREF) enabled many faculty members to continue to retire in the 60s with incomes comparable to their faculty salaries. Hence the elimination of mandatory retirement practices had little impact.

This situation changed with the 2008-2009 "Great Recession" that significantly dented retirement program accumulations, with losses in the 30% to 40% range. Although these accumulations have recovered in more recent years, the impact of the recession on confidence has not. Today a faculty member in reasonable health at age 65 has a 50%-50% probably of living until age 90, a period during which further major economic declines are likely to occur. Hence there is strong incentive for senior faculty members to continue to work as long as their health and their interests in their academic activities remain strong. In fact, recent surveys indicate that most faculty view the downside of retirement as the loss of the intellectual, cultural, and social benefits of being an active part of the academic community rather than financial concerns. Hence once again the concern that if retirements slow, positions for new faculty will similarly disappear.

Yet universities have also learned that the penalties for age discrimination can be very severe. Deans and department chairs are cautioned to be extremely careful in discussing retirement plans with faculty, since any attempt to push a faculty member into retirement is likely to result in expensive litigation. Today research universities are finding that each retirement has become a process of negotiation, with options such as phased retirement over several years, some continued engagement of emeritus faculty members, and other benefits such as access to libraries, retired faculty clubs, and possible partial appointments as "emeritus-in-service" for limited teaching and administration assignments. No longer is it sufficient to simply schedule a meeting for retiring faculty with a university financial consultant, who then takes away their parking pass and e-mail account and shows them the door.

Instead the approach should be to provide ways that faculty members can retain the intellectual, cultural, and social links that have been important parts of their lives and instead offer them an active role during their post-retirement. Put another way, senior faculty should be viewed as an important academic resource for the University rather than an aging challenge. For example, in Chapter 8 concerning the financial challenges facing the University of Michigan, we make a strong case for the wisdom of moving to a true year-round calendar that would be achieved through activating the May through August part of the calendar. This would be enabled not only by student demand (50,000 applications a year!), a modern physical plant (air-conditioned), and a calendar that is already divided into four-month long "trimesters" (although we call them "semesters"). Estimated additional tuition revenue would be $300 M to $400 M, while the financial impact on students choosing full-year enrollment allowing the completion of a baccalaureate degree in 2 to 2.5 years would not only be from reduced living costs but even more from getting into the work force with a college degree two years early!

But where would the instructional workforce come from, with current faculty members using the summer months for research projects or scholarly writing? From retired faculty members!!! Many of our senior faculty members are our most competent teachers, well known to students! While probably not interested in full time roles, they do love spending summers in Ann Arbor, and most would relish the opportunity to become re-engaged with students. Hence this untapped resource could actually be key to the University of Michigan's financial sustainability...

The Road Ahead

Ebbs and Flows Analysis

While department chairs and deans spend much of their time recruiting new faculty (and persuading their best faculty not to leave), this amount of faculty effort is difficult to assess at the University level. To be sure, a provost is usually sensitive to the "wins" and "losses" of a school or college when evaluating deans, but the broader University and its faculty are usually not aware of how the institution is doing in this competition for faculty. To this end, it might be useful to adopt a practice of the 1990s by creating each spring an "Ebb and Flows" chart identifying new faculty hires and losses at the department level, including where the gains came from and where the losses went. This would be analogous to a "business dashboard" exercise in the corporate world.

Essential Singularities

While the general faculty quality of a university across all departments, schools, and colleges is of great importance, determining the strength of its teaching and research, the visibility of the institution is frequently determined by truly exceptional individuals, so-called "essential singularities", whose intellectual impact is immense. At a large pubic university such as Michigan, these exceptional faculty members usually are first discovered as young hires, before their work has reached the attention of competing institutions. However once their work becomes visible, they are aggressively recruited by many other institutions, particularly leading private institutions such as the Ivy League, MIT, or Stanford, who can focus great resources to recruit them away from Michigan.

The University should think very strategically about how to provide a supportive environment for their unusual brilliance (not the easiest challenge in a community of outstanding scholars) and move them rapidly through the ranks in an effort to hold them to Michigan. Fortunately, we have been able to do this for many of our most outstanding junior faculty, but it remains a challenge of great difficulty and importance. However we might consider the approach taken by several other universities (e.g., UC Berkeley, the Canadian research universities) and create endowed chairs for exceptional junior faculty that would transition into senior endowed chairs subject to their continued achievements.

At the highest level, the University might consider the creation of professorial chairs with institution-wide appointments, such as the University Professors at the University of California or the Institute Professors at MIT. These provide exceptional faculty members with appointments in all academic units (and campuses in the case of Michigan), funded centrally by the institution, so that they have maximum flexibility for their research and teaching interests.

National Leadership

The national leadership of the University of Michigan is due almost entirely to the national leadership and influence achieved by members of its faculty in several areas:

Intellectual Leadership: e.g., stimulating, defining, and leading a particular field

Teaching Leadership: e.g., developing new pedagogy or reshaping a field through textbooks

Leadership in practice or application of knowledge: e.g., leading in a field of practice such as law or medicine or building a company through technology transfer

Academic leadership: e.g., achieving recognition as a department chair, dean, or university president

There are many paths to such leadership achievements, e.g., through research and scholarship, entrepreneurial activities, pedagogical development (e.g., award winning textbooks that dominate a field, intellectual leadership (e.g., election to a National Academy), and broader academic leadership (as chairs, deans, executive officers, and university presidents). However all of these paths to consequential leadership require not only talent, effort, and persistence, but they also require a supportive environment in the University and influence beyond its campus.

Hence the University not only needs to better encourage and recognize the national leadership of its faculty members, but it also needs to create an environment that supports such efforts, identifies and promotes opportunities, and remove barriers to such activities beyond the campus.

Emeritus Faculty

As we have noted, the disappearance of mandatory retirement age and the vulnerability of defined contribution retirement plans in a fluctuating economy have had a major impact on faculty retirement planning. But surveys have indicated that even more today, many senior faculty seek some level of continued engagement with their University following retirement, since their intellectual, cultural, and social lives have been shaped by these institutions.

We have suggested one possible contribution they might make should the University decide to move to year-round activity, since many emeritus faculty are not only among our best-known faculty through their earlier contributions (e.g., textbooks known to incoming students). Many universities have developed specific policies to encourage the engagement of senior faculty in productive roles, such as emeritus-in-service appointments providing them with the opportunity to continue teaching, research, and service at reduced appoint levels.

Yet beyond the desire to recapture faculty positions for new younger faculty from retiring faculty members within the current environment of limited funding, it is important to recognize that many emeritus remain among the University's most distinguished, dedicated, and capable teachers and scholars. Hence the senior retired faculty cadre should be viewed as an important asset of the University from a strategic viewpoint.

Appendix to Chapter 6
A Word about Faculty Compensation

The reputation of a university is determined primarily by the quality of its faculty. One cannot emphasize strongly enough just how competitive the current faculty recruiting (and retention) environment has become, and how intense the pressure has become on department chairs, deans, and executive officers to maintain faculty quality.

Some of the challenges faced by leading public research universitie includes:

The competition among the leading research universities has become what economists would characterize as a "winner-take-all" market. A great faculty enhances institutional reputation,…which enhances the ability to attract more great faculty and resources,…which enhances the institutional reputation relative to its competitors,… and so on, until only Harvard and Stanford remain standing. Put another way, the rich get richer, and the poor get devoured.

The impact of the booming equity market of the 1990s on the endowments of private universities, coupled with the meltdown of state economies during the early 1990s and then again during the past few years, has opened up a 20% gap in faculty salaries between the leading private and public universities–the largest gap in three decades.

This is aggravated by the predatory behavior of several of the private universities, which tend to build their faculty through lateral appointments of established faculty members (i.e., raiding other institutions) rather than developing them through the junior ranks from within. Here, at the top of the food chain is Tyrannosaurus Harvard; but several of the other Ivies (Princeton, Yale, Columbia) are almost as bad, tending to feed on the public research universities, weakened by state budget cuts and ponderously constrained by public regulations (e.g., sunshine laws).

The large public research universities face a particular challenge, since to fend off a raid by a rich private university, they may have to make a counter-offer that destabilizes other faculty members, stimulating them to look elsewhere to determine their own market value. Faculty retention during a period of limited resources can create a culture in which faculty come to believe that the only way to get a good raise or promotion is to demonstrate their worth on the open market, putting them in play for raids.

What might department chairs, deans, provosts, and others suggest to address these challenges?

1. While adequate compensation is important in faculty recruiting, the real keys are:

• The presence of world-class colleagues
• Outstanding students
• Great facilities
• Workload and service responsibilities that allow time for scholarship
• And a "dowry" to help them get their research up and going (which can run into the millions of dollars in the laboratory sciences)

An institution rarely attracts or loses an outstanding faculty member because of salary. Rather these other factors are where the key negotiations occur.

2. Furthermore, since many top faculty members make more from outside activities than from their faculty salary, policies governing academic leaves, consulting, intellectual property, and technology transfer can become important.

3. Global market comparisons of faculty compensation can be very deceptive. The marketplace tends to function at the microscopic level of individual faculty, specific academic areas, and faculty roles rather than at the macroscopic level of institutions. The recruitment of a world-class musician is totally different than that characterizing a laboratory-based nanotechnologist or first-amendment scholar. This market differentiation is rarely captured by faculty

compensation market studies at the institution level.

So much for the faculty. What about senior academic leadership, at the level of deans, executive officers, chancellors, and presidents? While executive search consultants love to stress the importance of competitive compensation (after all, that is how many of them set their fees), one should be very skeptical of just how important compensation is at this level. Instead,

• Believe it or not, most senior academic leaders are rarely lured by the dollars. To be sure, a competitive salary is viewed by some candidates as a measure of how much you want them. But it is rarely the deciding factor.

• Far more important is the challenge, opportunity, and prestige of building a top-ranked academic program.

• Many candidates are seeking new opportunities because they have been blocked by the narrowing pyramid of the academic hierarchy in their own institution.

• Some are after wealth and fame, but NOT from the university, but rather from outside their academic appointment through corporate boards, national commissions, or other opportunities.

• Some actually view academic leadership as a "higher calling", with emotional rewards and satisfaction that simply cannot be quantified in terms of compensation.

• In fact, some actually have acquired a sense of loyalty to a university and view such assignments as a duty of service.

If you think this sounds crazy, just look at the list of institutions with the highest executive salaries. Usually these are places you have to pay people to go, not at the very best institutions!

One more caution here. While it is the case that some public universities use their fund-raising foundations to supplement the salaries of senior leadership, this is usually provided as a payment for their development responsibilities. It is quite another matter entirely to solicit private support specifically to bring senior leadership salaries up to market levels. Not only does such a practice run into optics problems (remember, we are now in the post-Abramoff era), but it can start a public university down a very slippery slope where institutional integrity could be compromised by conflict of interest.

In summary, then, the incredible pressure on department chairs, deans, provosts, and chancellors to recruit and retain outstanding faculty in such a hypercompetitive marketplace, coupled with the challenge of recruiting top-notch senior leadership, demand adequate resources and flexibility, but within guidelines that are:

carefully crafted,
transparent,
well-understood,
broadly accepted, and
rigorously observed and implemented.

So what are the minimum essential requirements of modern faculty compensation programs? Of course, these are highly dependent on institution traditions, values, and character and hence are difficult to generalize.

Perhaps the best approach is to just tell you how we tried to set compensation at Michigan (since we have encountered and learned from most of the mistakes experienced by other public research universities).

The Faculty Compensation Strategy in the 1990s

The University of Michigan faculty and senior leadership compensation system was very simple, highly flexible, and entirely determined by the marketplace:

Market driven: Each department chair or dean was given the flexibility (within budget constraints) to adjust salaries to meet the marketplace characterizing each faculty member as an individual. All compensation was merit- and market-based, with no cost-of-living or other across-the-board adjustments.

Simplicity: Compensation is kept as simple and transparent as possible, avoiding deferred, incentive, and one-time compensation actions as much as possible, and utilizing a standard TIAA-CREF defined contribution retirement program (5% employee, 10% university).

Accountability: All academic administrators must be prepared to backup their compensation decisions with evidence of merit-, market-, and/or equity considerations (including outside offers).

Transparency and Optics: All compensation was fully disclosed, including the release of all employee compensation by name and appointment ("What you see is what they got..."). Furthermore, all compensation agreements and decisions were made with an assumption of eventual public scrutiny. (Chairs and deans were warned to imagine that any decision they make will eventually appear on the front page of the Detroit Free Press.)

Other Factors: Although chairs and deans have considerable flexibility in negotiating other elements of the package necessary to attract or retain faculty (e.g., moving, housing, laboratory space, research assistance, teaching and administrative loads), these packages were shaped by standard practice guidelines and monitored at the level of the provost. The same was true for early retirement or severance negotiations.

As an example of guiding compensation philosophy, during the 1990s the following goals were set and achieved:

1.   The average compensation for full professors at the University of Michigan was set at the top of all public universities.

2.   However, the best faculty members at Michigan were compensated at levels comparable to those faculty members of comparable quality in similar fields at the best public and private universities.

3.   The average compensation for assistant professors and associate professors was set to be the highest among public and private universities in the nation, since Michigan's tradition was to develop faculty from within rather than recruit at senior ranks through raids, and hence we needed to make certain we were recruiting the very best junior faculty.

4.   Deans and academic executive officers were compensated at levels comparable to the best public and private universities.

We used annual department-by-department surveys of faculty recruiting and retention experience (a so-called "ebb and flow" analysis) to monitor the success of the program.

Chapter 7

Staff

Students and faculty members tend to take the staff of a university pretty much for granted. While they understand these are the people who keep the trains running on time, who provide them with the environment they need for teaching and research, most view staff as only the supporting cast for the real stars, the faculty. When staff members come to mind at all, it is usually as a source of complaints, e.g., not fast enough to respond to request, too much regulation, too many coffee breaks, etc. To many faculty members, service units such as the Plant Department, Purchasing, and Internal Audit are sometimes viewed as the enemy.

Yet, with each step up the ladder of academic administration, we came to appreciate more just how critical the staff was to both the functioning and the continuity of the university. Throughout the university, whether at the level of secretaries, custodians, groundskeepers or the rarified heights of senior administrators for finance, hospital operations, or facilities construction and management, it became clear to us that the quality of the university's staff, coupled with their commitment and dedication, was actually just as important as the faculty in making Michigan the remarkable institution it has become. In some ways, even more so, since unlike many faculty members, who view their first responsibilities to their discipline or perhaps their careers, most staff members are true professionals, deeply committed to the welfare of the university as their highest priority, with many dedicating their entire careers to the institution.

The University of Michigan has been fortunate over its history in recruiting and retaining perhaps the most outstanding collection of staff members in higher education. In part this is due to the scale and complexity of the institution, which demand extraordinary competence. The knowledge, skill, and experience necessary to work with cutting edge technologies (e.g., the University's nanotechnology laboratories, performance venues such as Hill Auditorium, complex surgical procedures, and one of the most sophisticated IT environments in the world) attract outstanding talent. So too does the need for craftsmen of extraordinary skills (e.g., preservation of ancient documents and artifacts, design of performance venues, cutting-edge software development, and handling of hazardous materials). The supervision and management of the facilities, equipment, and financial operations characterizing the multiplicity of sophisticated environments necessary for cutting edge instruction, research, and service also require highly skilled staff. As The Michigan Daily once put it, "While the legend is that the President spins the Cube to start the day, it is the staff who truly make the University move."

One of the important reasons that the University is able to attract such outstanding staff is because our highly decentralized structure provides them with the freedom not only to perform their roles with minimal bureaucracy, but it also enables them to express their creativity in ways that frequently has impact far beyond the campus. For example, it was the great strength of the University's staff in networking, developed during the 1960s and 1970s for a statewide network connecting its universities, who developed the technology of the Internet. It has been staff who developed the modern surgical techniques and equipment that provide life-saving procedures to patients. The staff in finance managed the financial operations and integrity of a $7 billion/year institution, comparable in size to a Fortune 500 corporation, yet far more complex in the array of its many activities. And, in all such roles, these staff members play roles of great importance in teaching our students the skills and crafts critical both to their profession and achieving their educational objectives.

Finally, it is important to understand the importance of the role that staff members play in sustaining the momentum of the University and passing on from one generation to the next the corporate history critical to the institution's success. Students pass through for only the brief period of their studies. Faculty members are increasingly nomads, moving from university to university as the opportunity arises. But many of our staff members dedicate their entire careers to this University.

This was impressed upon us twice each year, when the president would host a banquet to honor staff with long-term service–20, 30, even 40 years. In a very real sense, it is frequently the staff who provide through their many years of service the continuity of both the culture of the university and its commitment to excellence. Put another way, it is the staff, as much as the students, faculty, or alumni, who perpetuate the institutional saga of the university.

1960s and 1970s

From the earliest days of the University, the quality of its staff stood out. In the 1950s and 1960s, Wilbur Pierpont was the Vice President and Chief Financial Officer (VPCFO) with a parallel appointment as Professor of Business Administration. In the late 1940s and early 1950s, it was Bill Pierpont who developed the concept and then negotiated the property acquisition that created the North Campus (and has been honored by the naming of the Pierpont Commons on that campus). When Alexander Ruthven developed health problems late in his tenure as Michigan President, it was Bill Pierpont who acted behind the scenes to keep the University on course. He recruited an outstanding team that served Harlan Hatcher, Robben Fleming, and later Harold Shapiro. His two successors as VPCFO, James Brinkerhoff and Farris Womack, also had wide responsibilities as well as faculty roles in the School of Business Administration and School of Education. Pierpont's predecessor, Robert Briggs, also later served as a Regent of the University, again providing evidence of the quality of the staff.

1980s

Our first experience working with staff members occurred while Dean of Engineering in the early 1980s. The College's Business Manager, Harold Harger, played a role very similar to that played by Bill Pierpont by providing both shrewd management of the assets of the College as well as helping to train a very young team of deans (including Chuck Vest, Dan Atkins, and Scott Fogler). Harger was a member of an important network of highly experienced business managers, scattered across the University who worked closely with deans and directors, who were, for the most part, faculty members with little experience with management issues. Although these business managers reported directly to their respect deans and had leadership responsibilities for the financial staff of their school, they also were part of a network of such senior staff that had a dotted line relationship with the VPCFO. Hence, if there were any problems within an academic unit, an alert would immediately be passed along to the VPCFO and hence the Executive Officers.

In fact, this network of experienced senior business managers was really the key to the decentralization of the University, since working arm-in-arm with the deans, they provided strong, experienced leadership with capability in both academic and financial matters. Their wisdom and integrity enabled the University to develop a remarkable capability to thrive even in the face of the most serious challenges, such as the loss of most of its state support.

It was also the case that the technology-intensive nature of engineering required a large number of highly skilled staff to build and operate critical equipment and facilities (e.g., think nuclear reactors). Because of their unique competence, such technical staff and faculty worked side-by-side in laboratories in a spirit of strong mutual respect. The same was true for secretarial and administrative staff who kept the ship moving ahead while chairs and deans worried about policy rather than operational matters. Indeed, the first advice we usually gave new faculty members was to quickly befriend the department secretaries, since they ran the University. (This was a lesson that we also learned in roles as provost and university president!)

92

Many of the staff who worked with us in the presidency

1990s

During the late 1980s the University recruited a new and highly experienced VPCFO, Farris Womack, who had served in that role both at the University of Arkansas and the University of North Carolina and was highly regarded as one of the most outstanding university financial officers in the nation. He was wise and experienced enough to immediately recognize the very considerable talent he had inherited in his organization and kept firmly in place, including not only one of the nations top financial teams (led by Chandler Matthews, Norman Herbert, Bill Krumm, Carl Smith, Bob Monart) and campus facility teams (Paul Spradlin, Fred Mayer, Russ Reister, Tom Schlauff, and many others), but as well outstanding technological capability (Doug Van Houweling, Dan Atkins, Randy Frank).

The achievements of this group were stunning. For example, Womack began by creating a central "bank" for the various units of the University, which allowed them to invest reserves as "funds functioning as endowment". Through wise leadership, augmented by a stellar group of financial advisors, Womack was able to increase the modest endowment of the University from $200 million to over $2.5 billion during his years at Michigan. Joining with Gil Whitaker as Provost, they were able to implement total quality management methods across the University that eventually raised the University's credit rating to the highest level of AAa, the first for a public university.

Yet there was another important role played by Womack and his predecessors in the role of VPCFO. Since most university presidents come to their role from backgrounds as faculty, they have relatively little experience in understanding and mastering the roles of university leadership. To be sure, most have been in other leadership positions, as deans or vice presidents. But the scale and complexity of a university such as Michigan, with a budget of $7 billion comparable to a Fortune 500 corporation, but with an array of activities far more diverse and complex, can be challenging indeed, particularly when presidential leadership requires so many skills, e.g., management, finance, politics, external relations, and fund-raiser extraordinaire. Hence at Michigan and most of its peers there is an unspoken additional role of the experienced chief financial officer: educating a new president on how to preside. This was the role that Bill Pierpont played with Harlan Hatcher, Jim Brinkerhoff with Robben Fleming and Harold Shapiro, and Farris Womack with our leadership team.

The word "team" is a very important word to use in describing the staff. Beyond their skill, competence, and dedication to the University, there was also a remarkable spirit of teamwork among staff members. The Executive Officer leadership team worked with staff not so much as supervisors but rather as colleagues, and in time we began to view our presidential roles as more akin to those of staff than faculty, in the sense that our first obligation was always to the welfare of the University rather than to our academic discipline or professional career.

While intensely loyal to the University, staff also require pastoral care from the president, particularly during difficult times such as budget cuts–sometimes involving layoffs–or campus unrest. It was important for the president and other senior officers to give the highest priority to events that demonstrated the importance of staff to the university and our strong support for their efforts. Whenever launching a major strategic effort, such as the Michigan Mandate or the Michigan Agenda for women, we would meet with numerous staff groups throughout the university to explain the effort and seek their advice and counsel. We made it a point to attend or host staff receptions, for example, to honor a retiring staff member or celebrate an important achievement. And, while we understood the central role of faculty in determining the quality of academic programs, we felt it was important that the president always be seen, in word and in deed, as committed to the welfare of the entire university community–students, faculty, and staff–in a balanced sense.

2000s

Unfortunately the University's leadership network of experienced staff, working together with deans and directors while maintaining the strong financial integrity, came to a screeching halt with the arrival of a new administration in the late 1990s. When Farris Womack decided to return to North Carolina,

94

the new president named a young staff member from New York's Metropolitan Museum of Art as Womack's successor. The resulting lack of financial and management experience triggered a stampede of departures of many of Michigan's most long-serving and valuable senior staff members, unfortunately to be replaced with successors not only unfamiliar with past University traditions and practices, but with limited understanding of their responsibilities in an institution of the University's scale and complexity. For example, in an effort to appease the faculty faced with an inadequate salary program, the new administration announced that since the faculty was more important than the staff, their salaries would be frozen so that any available funds could be used for a modest faculty salary program, both demoralizing and angering the staff. Although the new administration would last only four years, the damage that was done both through attrition and lack of respect for staff would last for well over a decade.

With the arrival of a new and more experienced administration, the disruption of staff activities began to subside, although morale remained low. With an agenda that was primarily focused on external activities, e.g., expanding the University medical center, fund-raising, and intercollegiate athletics, most attention was focused on recruiting new staff for the central administration. This resulted in a widening gap between the salaries of faculty and staff and the compensation (including bonuses and deferred compensation) of the central administration. The Regents were largely unaware of the damage that was being done to faculty and staff morale through this preferential compensation policy.

Although the overall staffing of the University increased only modestly during the past decade, there was a major shift of staffing away from core activities such as academic support and infrastructure maintenance and into externally focused activities such as development, marketing, and communications. Hundreds of new staff were added with little understanding or experience with academic institutions, a sharp contrast with earlier University practice. For example, the University launched a massive effort in "institutional advancement", in areas such as fund-raising, "branding" (read advertising), and social networking (e.g., webmasters, tweeters), and "global

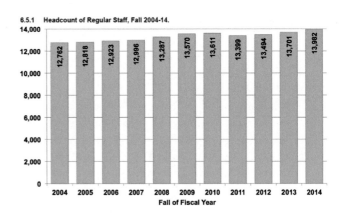

Total University Staff (2014)

communications" (which largely became a "Pravda-like" function hiding bad news and promoting the administration). By 2015 there were over 600 staff members in marketing and communications alone, in addition to another 500 in fund-raising.

This massive increase in staff members engaged i "institutional advancement" occurred not only in the central administration, but also at the level of schools and colleges. For example, the College of Engineering, listed 240 staff reporting to the Dean (compared to less than 30 people two decades earlier) in a host of new areas such as Entrepreneurship, Communication, Marketing, Web Development, and Industrial relations, although few in areas related to the core educational and research mission of the College. One of the consequences of this enormous staff was the burdens plance on the dean by staff issues at the expense of academic leadership, a situation faced by many other deans as their development and communications staff demanded more and more of their personal time for fund-raising and marketing rather than leadership. Again, the disappearance of the network of experienced business officers in academic units with dotted reporting lines to the chief financial officer removed the opportunity to identify and correct such excessive staffing.

Today's Concerns

Erosion of Appreciation for the Role of Staff

While great universities are known for their capacity to attract outstanding faculty and students, they

Highly skilled staff are essential to the complex laboratories of the University

Many staff have unique talents and skills that make them valuable teachers to students

require equally talented staff to support and sustain the environment necessary for high quality education, research, and service. At Michigan there is little doubt that many of our very best people are those among our staff, with extraordinary skills and deep commitment to the University.

Most faculty members realize the importance of staff, since they not only depend upon their talents, but they usually work side-by-side with staff in their teaching and research activities. Furthermore, many of our staff members are intimately involved with students, teaching them the subtle skills of the craft in the laboratory, the performance studio, or the medical procedure suites. This appreciation of the role of the staff is certainly present to those who both depend upon and work with them.

Yet in the same way that an increasingly corporate approach to University management and decision-making now threatens academic priorities, it also puts talented staff at great risk, as evidenced by the degree to which cost-saving ventures such as administrative shared services and reduction in benefits all too frequently have their most negative impact on the staff.

The Shared Services Fiasco

Perhaps the best example of the increasingly cavalier treatment of the staff is the recent effort by the central administration to implement a plan developed by Accenture consultants (and executed by two former Accenture employees who had become senior Michigan financial officers) to transfer several

hundred long-service administrative staff from academic units into an off-campus "shared services" facility. Another Accenture team of consultants proceeded with an attempt to "rationalize" IT services by requiring common desktop computing equipment ("MIWorkspace") and operating software, much to the chagrin of academic units dependent upon unique hardware and software demanded by their instructional and research programs.

The retention of such external consultants (at great expense) to apply corporate management methods to an academic institution, had a devastating impact on faculty and staff morale as resources and staff critical to research and teaching were withdrawn from academic units, and efforts were made to force the use of commodity equipment of inferior performance. Ironically, it was finally revealed that such heavy-handed projects would not achieve significant savings, both because of the costs of the Accenture consultants and the negative impact on University operations.

More generally it should have been apparent that the effort to centralize (or "rationalize") administrative responsibilities that may work quite well in some areas of corporate management could turn into a disaster if it pulls the University's best staff away from the academic units where the real innovation is driven by the interests of faculty and students working closely with outstanding staff with extraordinary skills. Similarly, to impose on the University's academic programs an enterprise-level of shared services unable to respond rapidly to the unique needs and technologies required for cutting-edge learning and discovery would cripple

Faculty per *University Record*	35%
Staff per *University Record*	24%
Executive officers* per *University Record*	26%
Executive officers* actual (w/o bonuses)	52%
Executive officers* actual (with bonuses)	76%
Deans (w/o bonuses)	41%
Deans (with bonuses)	56%

The increases in average salaries for various groups over the decade from 2004 to 2013.

Additional Pay	2004	2013	Variance	% increase
ADM: Admin Differential	3.982	12.487	8.505	214%
SAL: Salary Supplement	8.078	24.824	16.746	208%
UNS: Services Unrelated	0	6.971	6.971	N/A
ADD: Added Duties	0.732	1.814	1.082	149%
Total	12.792	46.096	33.304	260%
Increase in faculty salaries				28%
Increase in staff salaries				21%

The undisclosed salary supplements for admnistration over the decade from 2004 to 2013

the University's leadership as a research university. In 2014 a petition was circulated in which the majority of Michigan faculty opposed the efforts of the University administration to impose a shared services plan on academic units revealed the faculty concern about such corporate approaches, a reaction seen in other peer institutions. Over 1,100 signatures (representing over 50% of the faculty in the affected units) condemned the effort.

The impact on many leading faculty members of the shared services program has been serious, since it has taken away valuable and loyal staff who have long provided direct support not only for their oncampus teaching and research activities, but also for their ability to attract resources from outside (including the roughly $1 billion faculty members raise each year from external research sponsors). To impose an ill-conceived corporate strategy estimate to save less than $5 million per year (most of which will be used to pay off the Accenture consultants and necessary building renovations) that puts at risk a substantial share ($1.3 billion per year) of the University's budget is an extreme example of University leadership that has become "penny wise and pound foolish".

But of equal concern is the degree to which this undermined the treatment of valuable and loyal staff members. As one faculty member put it, "Instead of seeing employees as part of an organization, staff are now being perceived as interchangeable parts on an almost factory model."

Another long-standing faculty member put it even more bluntly, "This used to be a University I could be proud of in the way we handled our staff. Today, it isn't. The way shared services was handled revealed a side of a University I would not want to be proud of; I'm not even sure I'd want to be part of!" Or, as another faculty

member put it, "The pain stems not only from losing a colleague, whose office will no longer bustle with students and faculty wandering in and out, but also from the broken trust between staff and the University's leadership."

The shared services plan also damaged the trust in institutional leadership by the faculty, who were shocked not only by the withdrawal of some of their most important staff, but by the cavalier way that the University leadership launched this effort in secrecy and seemed determined to proceed with it. Fortunately, with the departure of the key administrative staff responsible for launching the effort and the appointment of a new president in 2014, there was an opportunity to reconsider such disruptive initiatives and their impact on the culture and character of the University.

Salary Inequities and Compensation Policies

There is ample documentation of the erosion in University staff compensation and benefits relative to peer institutions over the past two decades, similar to the erosion in faculty compensation. In sharp contrast has been the significant growth in compensation of senior adminstrators (executive officers and deans) and central administration staff who enjoy salaries far above those of the faculty. This inequity is compounded by the recent disclosure of a confidential system of bonuses and deferred compensation that has elevated administrative salaries to levels that now rank among the highest in higher education.

Beyond the lack of disclosure of such additional compensation, it has also become clear that such bonus compensation fails to meet the rigor demanded of similar practices in business and industry such as public disclosure of bonus compensation formulae that determine awards. Such an undisclosed and inadequately constrained compensation system for selected administrators has badly damaged both morale and confidence in university leadership by faculty and staff.

The Road Ahead

Thoughout the history of the University it has been apparent that whether at the level of secretaries, custodians, or groundskeepers or the rarified heights of senior administrators for finance, hospital operations, or facilities construction and management, the quality of the university's staff, coupled with their commitment and dedication, was comparable to that of the faculty in making Michigan the remarkable institution it has become. In some ways, it has been even more so, since unlike many faculty members, who view their first responsibilities as to their discipline or perhaps their careers, most staff members are true professionals, deeply committed to the welfare of the university as their highest priority, many dedicating their entire careers to the institution. Most staff members serve the university far longer than the faculty, who tend to be lured away by the marketplace.

It is from this strategetic perspective of the value of our staff that several suggestions seem appropriate:

It is important that the University develop and implement employee development programs comparable in scale and quality to most Fortune 500 corporations. While it is certainly true that many staff members develop unique skills of great value to the University, this should not be used as an excuse to lock them in place. Instead, they should be provided with the opportunity to develop new skills and explore new employment roles. The current University policy of allowing staff to take courses while employed is important to such career advancement.

Because of the scale, diverse, and unusually highly decentralized organization of the University, it is natural that considerable duplication can arise. For example, schools and colleges clearly duplicate many of the development and communications roles of the central administration. Clearly there is a need to achieve a better balance between central and unit staffing in many areas, since such redundancy represents considerable

cost escalation. However in this ongoing effort, it is very important to identify where staff can have the most impact, rather than simply gathering them together where they can be centrally managed. Here the damage done by the University's shared services program provides an excellence example of what should be avoided, since relocating valued staff from the units, where they were important for attracting and managing the $1.3 billion/year attracted for research projects by faculty in these units, to a central off-campus facility to save a relatively small amount (estimated at $5 million/year) is a classic example of mismanagement, robbing Peter to pay Paul, and penny-wise but pound-foolish!

The importance of the role of experienced financial managers in each of the many academic units, where most deans and chairs come from the ranks of faculty rather inexperienced in such management and financial roles. The EVPCFO should not only maintain a network of contacts with these managers at the unit level, capable of providing assistance or warnings when necessary, but should also be involved to some degree in both the appointment and evaluation of these staff. As noted earlier, it is this informal network of experienced management staff in the units linking to the EVPCFO that is the key to the financial integrity of such a massive and highly decentralized institution.

Finally, although the unique roles of staff throughout such a large, diverse, and highly decentralized organization should be respected, there needs to be a thorough review of salary practices to achieve equity across the institution. There are too many examples of inexperienced management providing inappropriate compensation through the undisclosed use of bonuses and other forms of one-time compensation, particularly at the central administration level. While making the total compensation of all employees of the University openly available for comparison, it is also appropriate to implement an ongoing compensation review to ascertain inequities that may arise across the university for similar staff roles. In particular, the University should adopt compensation policies consistent with best practices in the corporate sector for bonus and deferred compensation.

Resources

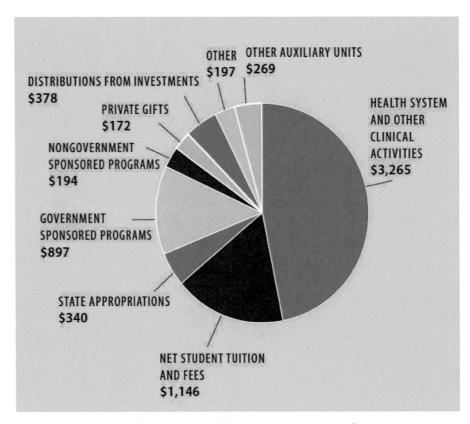

The 2015 Budget for the University of Michigan

Chapter 8

Financials

The story of the financial support of the University of Michigan over the past five decades is one of a continued decline in state support, which in turn has forced the University to become ever more dependent on student tuition, federal support of research, private giving, the building of significant endowment asets through wise investments, and the capacity of its auxiliary activities such as hospitals, student housing, and athletics to tap price-insensitive markets. When we first arrived at Michigan in the late 1960s, Michigan was clearly a state-supported institution with over 70% of the funding for our academic programs coming from state appropriations. However, over the next several decades, state support would be withdrawn year after year, so that Michigan was forced to make transitions from a "state-supported" to a "state-assisted" to a "state-related", and to a "state-located" institution, with less than 10% of our academic budget provided by the state. In fact, since today the activities of the University span not only the nation but have become worldwide, Michigan has become only a "state-titled" institution (e.g., the University of Michigan).

Despite this loss of state support, the University remains very much a public university, shaped as such throughout history and reflected in our characteristics (scale, breadth, and social engagement). But today 95% of the publics the University serves and the publics that support it are no longer located in our state. Our support comes almost entirely from students and their parents paying tuition, from the federal government providing grants for research and student financial aid, from alumni, friends, foundations, and industry providing private support, and from the wise investment of University assets such as its endowment.

The story of this forced evolution from a state-supported institution to one that became largely "privately supported, although still publicly committed" (in the words of former UM Provost and Cornell President, Frank Rhodes) is important not only for the University's historical record but also as a model for most of the other flagship public research universities in this nation, which are now experiencing the same erosion in state support.

First, however, it is useful to provide some background in university financing.

Financing the University: A Brief Tutorial

Like other enterprises in our society, the operation of a university requires the generation of adequate resources to cover the costs of activities. This is a complex task for academic institutions, both because of the wide array of their activities and the great diversity of the constituencies they serve. The not-for-profit culture of the university, whether public or private, requires a different approach to the development of a business plan than one would find in business or commerce.

Universities usually begin with the assumption that all of their current activities are both worthwhile and necessary. They first seek to identify the resources that can fund these activities. Beyond that, since there is always an array of worthwhile proposals for expanding ongoing activities or for launching new activities, the university always seeks additional resources. The possibility of reallocating resources away from ongoing activities to fund new endeavors has only recently been seriously considered. Strategies from the business world aimed at cutting costs and increasing productivity are relatively new to our institutions.

Most universities depend upon the following revenue sources:

- Tuition and fees paid by students
- State appropriations
- Federal grants and contracts
- Gifts and endowment income
- Auxiliary activities (such as hospitals, residence halls, and athletics)

Strategies for the expenditure side of the ledger include:

- Cost containment
- Strategic resource management
- Innovation through substitution
- Total quality management
- Re-engineering systems
- Selective growth strategies
- Restructuring the organization

The availability and attractiveness of each of these options varies greatly and depend upon the nature of the institution and the environment of which it is a part. Financial strategies also vary significantly with the particular circumstances faced by the institution. For many public institutions, more heavily dependent upon state appropriations, an appropriate strategy might be to build the political influence necessary to protect or enhance state support. Small private institutions with modest endowments depend heavily upon tuition and fees, and issues such as enrollments and tuition pricing and discounting play a key role in financial strategies. Small, highly focused research universities such as MIT and Caltech are heavily dependent upon federal research support and, needless to say, seek to influence federal research policies as part of their financial strategy.

The wise and efficient deployment of resources is as important as the effort to generate sufficient revenue when it comes to compensating for eroding public support. Understanding how to better use available resources to perform the many different missions of the contemporary university is key. Yet this can be a difficult task. Today's university is like a conglomerate, with many different business lines: education (undergraduate, graduate, professional), basic and applied research, health care, economic development, entertainment (intercollegiate athletics), international development, etc. Each of these activities is supported by an array of resources: tuition and fees, state appropriation, federal grants and contracts, federal financial aid, private giving, and auxiliary revenues. Part of the challenge is to understand the cross-flows, e.g., cross-subsidies, among these various activities.

Adapting to the Loss of State Support

Interestingly enough, both the university's early growth and its success in building an unusually broad array of world-class programs have had relatively little to do with the generosity of state support. For the first half-century following its founding in 1817, the University of Michigan was supported entirely from its federal land grant endowment and the fees derived from students. During these early years, state government both mismanaged and then misappropriated the funds from the Congressional land grants intended to support the University. The University did not receive direct state appropriations until 1867, and for most of its history, state support has actually been quite modest relative to many other states. Although there were periods during which state support matched those for other public universities, these were followed by long periods of deteriorating state support (e.g. the Depression years of the 1930s and then the recessions of the 1970s, 1980s, and 2000s.)

1950s-1960s

In the early decades following World War II, the substantial investments by the federal government in higher education as a public good essential for prosperity, public health, and national security were echoed at the state level for public universities. During this period, public institutions treated state and local governments as their primary revenue source, with tuition playing a relatively modest role. Even at private universities, the strong growth in federal research expenditures and student financial aid programs led to very significant increases in public support.

During the 1950s state appropriations to the

University of Michigan for both operations and facilities were generous, doubling from $15 M in 1951 to $30 M in 1957, with an additional $26 M for capital facilities. However there were occasional bumps in this road, including payless paydays on the campuses in 1959 and frozen state appropriations in the early 1960s, when UM fell to 17th place in salaries among universities while teaching loads increased rapidly. However this quickly turned around with significant growth resuming in the mid-1960s, although the efforts of state government to take over direct control of all campus construction in direct conflict with Regental authority led to a moratorium in state-funded campus construction during the late 1960s and much of the 1970s.

The UM Sesquicentennial fundraising campaign raised $55 M for new academic programs, fellowships, and buildings "to insure the vital margin" between state support for operations and the University's capacity to achieve excellence.

1970s

During the 1970s, the impact of the OPEC oil embargo and the emergence of strong competition from the Japanese auto industry weakened state tax revenues. The emergence of new universities such as Grand Valley State University and Saginaw Valley State University put more pressure on the state's higher education budget. In the short run, it probably did not help the University's financial position that the Regents twice sued the state for interfering with the powers of the Regents. In the long run, however, such challenges were vital for maintaining the autonomy of the University.

Unionization further complicated things. In 1968 there were two small unions: by 1974 the University was bargaining with numerous newly organized union locals, and strikes became a familiar routine in campus life. In 1971 the Intern-Resident Association unionized, followed in the same year by the Teaching Fellows Association who formed the Graduate Employees Organization (the Regents chose not to contest either, dominated as they were by newly elected Democrats).

The impetus for unionization was also caused by an unrelated and successful court challenge to the University's interpretation of instate residency. Anticipating a substantial loss of out of state tuition (although less than 1,000 were ultimately reclassified), the University eliminated the instate fee privilege or tuition waiver for graduate student teaching assistants.

Although the University of Michigan and the state shared in the support of the Replacement Hospital Project in the late 1970s and early 1980s, the drain of this mammoth project on the state funds once again severely limited state support for capital facilities for academic programs.

By the late 1970s, it was increasingly clear that the erosion of state support for higher education was a secular trend in Michigan that was likely to continue into the 2000s as the state's economy, based on low skill manufacturing, continued to decline. Indeed, over this three-decade period, state appropriations dropped from 70 percent of the University's operating budget in the 1960s to less than 10% in the mid-1990s. Further, as the state's tax revenue dropped below the national average, and other social needs such as K-12 education and prisons passed higher education as priorities, it was clear that further decline in state support was inevitable for the foreseeable future.

1980s

Although never a leader in state support of higher education, by 1975 the state slipped to 19th and by 1980 it would drop to 35th and was still falling. By the 1980s Michigan's state support was no longer strong enough to support even the instructional component of the University. Federal funding also continued to weaken in the 1980s as society turned its attention to mounting social and economic priorities.

With the accumulation of cutbacks, demands, and pressures leading to relentless financial contraction, it was clear that the academic quality of the institution would become seriously affected unless long-range planning was given a high priority. Hence it was fortunate in 1977 for the University to name as provost Harold Shapiro, an economist who had served as chair of the Budget Priorities Committee. It was even more fortunate when he accepted the position of President of the University in 1980.

If there was any hope that the state's financial

condition and support might improve, it was quickly dashed within a few months after Shapiro took office. By the early 1980s the state had entered a deep recession, with appropriations to the University of Michigan dropping by over 30%. Executive order cuts began to roll out of the Governor's office (since Governor Milliken was totally opposed to any new taxes). Coming as it did on the heels of the cuts and austerity measures adopted in the 1970s, the budget crisis of the early 1980s presented the UM with an intractable problem of increasing proportions. Michigan's growth rate for support of higher education dropped to 49th in the nation over the decade.

Although the erosion of state support slowed by the late 1980s, it never fully recovered, and it would continue a secular erosion for the next two decades, declining from 70% of the core support of the University's academic programs in the 1960s to less than 10% by 2010. In fact, by 2000, Michigan would drop to the bottom 10% of the states in its funding for higher education. The classic model of the public university no longer conformed to reality. When Shapiro took over, state support was 60% of the General Fund and 20% of the total budget. By the time he stepped down it had dropped to 50% of the General fund and 15% of the budget (and during the 1990s it dropped further to 30% of the General Fund and 10% of the budget).

Fortunately, the UM had a president in Harold Shapiro who understood that this burden of inadequate state support was likely permanent, and he assembled a team of experienced administrators capable of addressing it. He moved rapidly to put in place a series of major financial measures to sustain the quality and capacity of the University.

There were three key components to the Shapiro strategy: First, a major restructuring of both the culture and the financial management of the University by i) decentralizing authority for revenue generation and responsibility for expenditures, ii) stressing the importance of focusing resources to achieve excellence, iii) implementing conservative financial management of resources, and iv) during tough times, making tough decisions to set priorities.

Second, "right-sizing" tuition while maintaining the UM's long commitment of meeting the full financial need of all Michigan resident students. As the state subsidy of the costs of educational programs declined, it was necessary to compensate with major increases in tuition, highly differentiated between Michigan resident and out-of-state students. Between 1977-78 and 1987-88, tuition increased fourfold, raising annual tuition revenues from about $50 million to over $200 million. Students were also assessed for improvements in services that specifically benefited them, including the renovations of the Michigan Union and computer support. They were clearly being asked to pay for a greater percentage of their education since their state subsidy was disappearing. However, the increase in tuition was offset almost completely by inflation and declining state support. Students were being asked to pick up the portion of the bill the State was no longer willing to pay.

Third, an aggressive fund-raising effort was launched (including an $180 million campaign in the early 1980s). Shapiro hired Jon Cosovich, the major gifts officer at Stanford, to lead the new development efforts, who in turn began to work with the deans to develop more aggressive fund-raising strategies.

While these steps were important, even more so was Shapiro's belief that the key to Michigan's successful adaptation to a rapidly changing era, while sustaining its quality, would involve a profound decentralization of authority over resources and personnel to the lowest level where resources are generated and costs are incurred. As state support declined during the 1970s and 1980s, Harold Shapiro embraced this philosophy of decentralization to the level of deans and directors. An open market strategy evolved where deans were given the freedom as customers to decide for themselves where centralized services were more efficient and cost-effective than using outside vendors (e.g., facilities maintenance, communications services, etc.)

By the 1990s, more than 90% of the resources supporting the institution were attracted by individual units rather than the central administration. To be sure, the Executive Officers and Regents of the University had final authority, but this was generally exercised with considerable restraint to allow deans, directors, and department chairs significant authority. This realignment of both resource control and cost responsibility to the lowest levels of the organization where they occurred most naturally was key to the ability of the University to adapt to the very considerable financial pressures it would face by the late 20th Century. Michigan's long tradition of institutional autonomy positioned it well for such decentralization, a philosophy that was eventually adopted by many other public universities facing serious erosion of state support.

During the Shapiro administration, the provost and chief financial officer formed the team that worked together to refine the cost-containment activities, launching a major total quality management effort in the University Hospitals that, together with the completion of the new Adult General Hospital, was to position it as the most financially successful medical center in the nation during the 1990s. Major efforts to improve both the environment and incentives for sponsored research, coupled with an aggressive federal relations effort in Washington, stimulated rapid growth in the University's research grant activity. During the next several years Michigan moved to national leadership in its success in attracting research grants.

Although undergraduate education did not appear as prominently on the list of priorities as some felt it should, this was by design, not neglect. In times of financial crisis and dwindling public support, Shapiro turned first to the elements of higher education that society was willing to fund and stressed the one measure of higher education that Michigan had long championed and that most people seemed to understand—its academic reputation. A university that was recognized as a leader among its peers and that had financial strength and independence was one that could then afford and seek excellence in education.

The years of austerity, of reallocation, and of diversifying the University's support base, years that extended back into the Fleming presidency, began to pay off as Shapiro prepared to leave for the presidency of Princeton. The University not only met this challenge of declining state support, but it actually thrived during this transition period by intensifying the three-tiered strategy developed during the Shapiro years: effective cost containment, wise management of resources, and aggressive development of alternative revenue sources.

1990s

Although there was modest recovery in state support during the 1990s, it was essential to continue the strategy developed by Harold Shapiro stressing cost-containment and efficiency, adjusting tuition levels to reflect the loss of the subsidy through declining state appropriations, and to develop alternative sources of support through sponsored research and private fund raising.

Following the recommendations of a major task force on costs chaired by Business Administration Dean Gil Whitaker, the University implemented an institution-wide total quality management program in the early 1990s. This was patterned on the award-winning program in the University Hospitals. It empowered staff and faculty at all levels to seek ways to enhance the quality of their activities while constraining costs. In the mid-1990s, the University completed the decentralization of both resource and cost management to the unit level through a budgeting system known as responsibility center management, similar to that used in many private universities. In this system, units were allowed to retain all revenues. They were then assessed the costs associated with their activities, and taxed on all expenditures to support university-wide services such as safety. This system provided strong incentives for generating revenues and containing cost. It allowed local management controls at the unit level as key in more efficient operation.

As evidence of the effectiveness of these efforts, by the mid-1990s peer comparisons ranked the University's administrative costs (as a percentage of total expenditures) third lowest among major research universities. Yet another sign of the efficient use of resources was the fact that while essentially all of the University's programs were ranked among the top ten nationally in academic quality, the University ranked roughly 40th in terms of expenditures per student or faculty member. More specifically, it was able to provide an education of the quality of the most distinguished private institutions at typically one-third the cost!

The second element of the 1990s strategy involved far more aggressive management of the assets of the University—its financial assets, its capital facilities, and, of course, its most valuable assets, its people. VPCFO Farris Womack moved rapidly in the late 1980s to put into place a sophisticated program to manage the investments of the University. He built a strong internal investment management team augmented by knowledgeable external advisors, including several University alumni. Attention was focused on the management of the University's financial reserves such as operating capital and short-term funds. By establishing the concept of a centralized bank, Womack was able to bring more than $1 billion of additional funds associated with the various operating units of the University under sophisticated investment management.

Particular attention was focused on the University endowment, which amounted to only $200 million in 1988, small by peer standards and quite conservatively managed. Through Womack's aggressive investment management, coupled with a highly successful fund-raising effort, the University was to increase its endowment to over $2.5 billion by 2000–a truly remarkable growth of ten-fold with an average annual rate of return of 23%. During this period, Michigan consistently ranked among the national leaders in endowment earnings. This remarkable achievement established the nucleus of what today amounts to the 7th largest endowment in higher education, amounting to over $10 billion in 2015.

Womack's team put into place a plan for eliminating the backlog of deferred maintenance, which had grown during the difficult budget period of the 1980s. Since state support for maintenance had effectively disappeared, the University put into place a special student fee that generated roughly $10 million per year to maintain its physical infrastructure, with a priority given to classroom space.

The University also put into place a modern program to manage and develop its human resources. It established a senior position of Executive Director of Human Resources which pulled together all of the reporting lines in the personnel and affirmative action areas. It also took steps to address a number of key staff concerns, such as staff development, high performance workplace policies, flexible staff benefits, and dependent care.

The University also took steps to more realistically

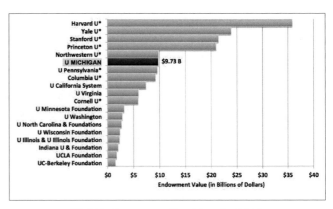

UM Endowment Ranking in 2015

price its services. One of the most difficult tasks from a political standpoint was to charge more realistic tuition levels for instate students. Although the University had long charged essentially private tuition levels to out-of-state students, acknowledging a state policy which dictated that state tax dollars could be used only for the support of Michigan residents, instate tuition had been kept at only token levels throughout the 1960s and 1970s. However, as state support declined, it became clear that the eroding "state subsidy" of the cost of education for Michigan residents no longer justified these low tuitions. Throughout the 1980s, the University began to raise instate tuitions to more realistic levels, although this frequently triggered political attacks from both state government and the media. By the mid-1990s, student tuition revenue had been increased to over $400 million, far exceeding the University's annual state appropriation of $290 million. Throughout this period of tuition restructuring, the University was able to increase the financial aid awarded students so that it could sustain its long-standing policy that no instate student should be denied a Michigan education for lack of economic means.

The financial strength of the University also benefited from the remarkable success of its faculty in attracting research grants and contracts from both the federal government and industry. As we noted earlier, the University rose to the position of national leadership by this measure of research activity, and by 1996 its sponsored research support was over $500 million per year–again substantially larger than state support.

The third resource stream of the University involved charges for auxiliary services it provided to the public, namely those activities such as clinical patient care and continuing education that generated revenues beyond those of the academic programs. Key in this effort was the remarkable success of the University Hospitals and related Medical Service Plans, which were generating almost $1 billion of revenue by the mid-1990s. Indeed, it was the revenue associated with these clinical activities that supported much of the remarkable growth of the Medical School. So, too, other auxiliary enterprises such as the Executive Management Education program of the Business School, the Housing Division, and the Department of Athletics also saw very considerable success during this period.

The University had been one of the first public universities to recognize the importance of private fund-raising, with the 55M campaign of the 1960s and the $180 million campaign of the 1980s. However, as the prospects for state support became dimmer, it became clear that private support would extend beyond providing simply the margin of excellence for the University's academic programs and increasingly provide their base operating funds as well. Early in the 1990s a very aggressive goal was set to build private support, as measured by the combination of gifts received and income distributed from endowment, to a level comparable to state support by the year 2000.

To this end, the University launched the largest fund-raising campaign in the history of public higher education by setting as a goal the raising of $1 billion by mid-1997. A sophisticated University-wide development effort was built and hundreds of volunteers were recruited across the nation. This fund-raising effort was extraordinarily successful. By 1996 the University had already gone well past its $1 billion goal, a year ahead of schedule, and would eventually exceed $1.4 billion. Annual gifts had grown from $60 million per year in 1988 to over $180 million per year in 1996. And, total annual private support, including endowment income exceeded $220 M per year, well ahead of schedule to surpass the state appropriation of $290 M per year by the end of the decade.

This combined strategy of effective cost containment, sophisticated asset management, and alternative resource development provided the University with extraordinary financial strength, despite the continuing deterioration of state support. As one measure of this financial integrity, in 1996 the University became the first public university in history to earn Wall Street's top credit rating of AAa, placing it on par with the wealthiest private universities. It would be this unusually high credit rating that would allow the University to borrow at minimum interest rates the resources to sustain further campus facility expansion and renovation despite the fact that the state support would continue to decline to one of the lowest levels in the nation (dropping to 47th among the states by 2010). Yet even as the University became predominantly supported by private resources (tuition and gifts) and federal grants (for research and student financial aid), it was able to sustain its strong commitment to serve the needs of the state.

2000s

As it usually happens, the transition to a new administration also resulted in a hard right turn (or perhaps "wrong turn" is more accurate) in financial strategy. The fund-raising campaign of the 1990s was brought to a conclusion in 1997 with a final total of $1.41 billion, which, while impressive, would have crossed the $2 billion mark had it been continued to 2000. The few capital construction projects launched by the new administration, such as the Life Sciences Institute, were funded by tapping existing assets such as those from University Hospital reserve funds rather than raising new funds. Efforts to contain costs or improve efficiency were largely terminated. And rather than fight the annual battle with Regents over increasing tuition to compensate for the loss of the subsidy provided by declining state support, the administration embarked on an alternative course by low-balling instate tuition and instead relying on major enrollment increases to generate new revenue by giving priority to the admission of out-of-state students capable of paying tuition at private levels.

Fortunately the tenure of this administration was brief, and during the brief interregnum before yet another administration, B. Joseph White, Dean of the School of Business Administration as Interim President, moved rapidly to appoint a new provost, Paul Courant, and VPCFO, Timothy Slottow. Working with this team, White resumed the major effort at cost reduction.

However the appetite for the new revenues

Education and General Spending By Standard Categories per FTE Student in CPI Adjusted 2010 Dollars

	2005	2006	2007	2008	2009	2010	Average Annual Percent Change (2005 - 2009)
Instruction	$18,139	$17,593	$18,176	$19,719	$20,142	$20,552	2.65%
Student Services	$1,606	$1,596	$1,649	$1,898	$1,969	$1,923	5.23%
Research	$15,603	$14,751	$14,875	$15,574	$16,654	$17,520	1.64%
Public Service	$2,922	$2,870	$2,746	$3,126	$3,151	$3,309	1.9%
Academic Support	$4,554	$4,749	$4,317	$5,756	$6,185	$6,072	7.96%
Institutional Support	$3,027	$3,107	$3,094	$3,877	$4,043	$3,867	7.51%
Operations and Maintenance	$5,896	$6,514	$6,530	$5,941	$6,544	$6,122	2.64%
Net Scholarships and Fellowships	$2,050	$2,141	$2,072	$2,280	$2,526	$2,569	5.37%
Education and General	$53,796	$53,320	$53,459	$58,172	$61,213	$61,936	3.28%

A careful tracking of expenditures over the past decade indicates that the largest growth was in administrative staffing rather than instruction (i.e., faculty salaries).

generated through the high tuition paid out-of-state students continued to be overwhelming, and when a new permanent administration was installed in 2002, enrollment growth was resumed as a key element of financial strategy. This would continue for the next decade, leading to a massive 25% enrollment growth of almost 10,000 students. Since this was accompanied by only modest growth in the number of tenure-track faculty (although major growth in the use of lecturers and part-time instructors), there was an associated productivity gain, at least as measured by students per faculty member (FYES/FTE). However instructional loads increased rapidly in the two units with large undergraduate enrollments, LS&A and Engineering, badly overloading both faculty instructional capacity and facilities.

The highest priority of the new administration was the launch of major private fund-raising efforts, the first during the mid-2000s, achieving $3.3 billion in funds and pledges, and the second launched in 2010 with the goal of $4 billion. While impressive in magnitude, once again these efforts also resulted in new costs associated with priorities of donors rather than the institution itself (e.g., the additional costs associated with an expansion of the Business School, the Athletic Campus,

and residence halls).

Under continued pressure to demonstrate cost savings, the new administration first turned to the most obvious source: reducing faculty and staff compensation expenses by increasing cost sharing requirements for medical plans, reducing retirement benefits, and, of course, limiting salary increases (for all job families with the exception of senior administrators, which continued to escalate rapidly). Ironically, in contrast to earlier efforts to increase productivity, the new priorities of the University–fundraising, marketing, and public relations–experienced massive staffing increases.

However the highly decentralized structure associated with responsibility center management still left control of 90% of University resources with the deans and directors, who were held responsible for both revenue generation and cost decisions. Hence the University administration moved rapidly to attempt to induce major cost-savings at the unit level through taxes on expenditures, although at the early stage deans and directors were given discretion in how this would occur.

The chart above reveals clearly the University financial strategy during these years as expenditures for institutional support, academic support, and student services (meaning the central administration) increased at 2 to 3 times the rate for instruction (which primarily reflects faculty salaries and benefits). Perhaps as evidence of the rapidly changing culture, several of the deans chose to respond by reducing faculty and staff support, while increasing the number of staff serving their needs for fund-raising, marketing, and public relations–just as the central administration.In fact, over the decade, thenumber of staff engaged in "institutional advancement" activities, increased to almost 1,100, with 500 involved in development (fund-raising) and over 600 in communications (marketing, public relations, and publications), with many of these staff added within the central administration.

As pressures for cost containment and efficiency increased, the central administration attempted to "recentralize" certain commodity services such as accounting, research grant management, and even computer services, much to the chagrin of the academic units that were heavily dependent on this support. With the arrival of a former partner from Accenture as a senior member of the University financial staff, it was not surprising that his former company would be given major contracts to implement new programs in "shared services" and "IT rationalization", with little effort to either seek input or even provide advance information about these efforts or to justify their cost-benefit advantages, which turned out were modest if not even negative in some cases. Not surprising, this ill-considered action caused an explosion of faculty and student activism to block its implementation, who voted overwhelming in a campus-wide petition to scrap the plan. This however was ignored by the executive officers, and the shared service program was put into place over the objections of academic units.

One other rather disturbing feature of the University's financial strategy over the past decade: the degree to which the auxiliary units of the University, the University Health System, Student Housing, and Intercollegiate Athletics, were largely absolved from the draconian cost-containment and staffing policies imposed on the academic units. In fact, the auxiliary units enjoyed very considerable growth in finances, facilities, and pricing even as the academic units were tightly constrained. Why did the auxiliaries so dominate University priorities when it was clear that it was the academic units that provided the reputation and fulfilled the fundamental missions of the University? That was a question that was frequently asked by the faculty of the University, without a response from its leadership.

Today's Financial Challenges

Today much of American higher education is still recovering from the impact of the Great Recession of 2008 and 2009. State support on a per student basis has continued to drop by over 30% over the past decade to the lowest levels in three decades. Faculty and staff layoffs and furloughs are still common.

Yet in the 2000s and beyond the University of Michigan appeared to be enjoying a period of relative peace, prosperity, and growth. In contrast to much of the rest of higher education, Michigan appears to be financially secure, having completed a $3.3 billion fundraising campaign several years ago and launching a new effort with a goal of $4 billion by 2018. It touts a series of efforts to reduce costs and improve productivity in its business activities to keep its top Aa1 credit rating intact. Student applications and enrollments continue to grow, as do research expenditures, exceeding $1.3 billion per year. The spirit of the campus seems upbeat, confident, and secure. Or at least so we are told.

Yet, below the surface there are growing concerns about whether the University has a realistic and sustainable financial model as the University prepares to enter its third century. As state support declined over the past five decades, the University of Michigan has found itself a predominantly "privately-supported" public university, in the sense that roughly 95% of its revenues came from non-state sources such as student tuition, clinical fees, research grants, private gifts and endowment earnings that are determined by competitive markets (as shown in charts detailing the 2014 financials of the University).

While the University's state appropriation today at $300 million (UMAA) is still very important, state support has fallen behind all of the University's other patrons including students (tuition), the federal government (research grants and student financial aid), and private contributors (gifts and endowment income). This erosion in state support is demonstrated

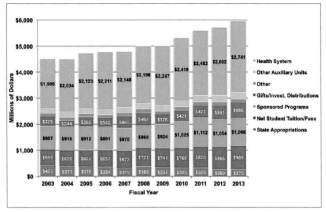

Operating Revenues (inc Hospitals)

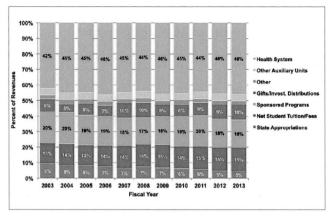

Operating Revenues (w/o Hospitals)

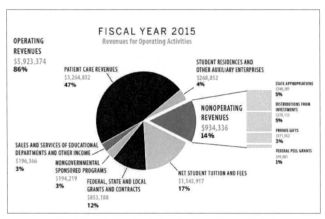

UM Total Budget (including hospitals)

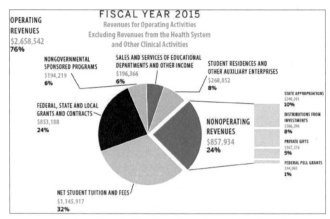

UM Academic Budget (without hospitals)

Revenue Budgets	2005	2006	2007	2008	2009	2010	2011	2012	2013	2014	2015
State Appropriation	320,562	314,733	325,796	320,156	329,908	316,572	315,148	268,803	273,057	279,109	295,174
Tuition and Fees	675,392	725,108	777,367	840,566	894,487	948,461	1,015,952	1,090,540	1,156,647	1,217,808	1,277,842
Indirect Cost Recovery	156,458	165,384	170,560	164,710	171,569	180,191	212,467	218,291	211,616	219,303	213,874
Other Revenue	10,870	15,260	21,325	22,230	12,830	9,785	9,678	9,603	7,820	7,920	8,020
Total Revenues	1,163,382	1,220,485	1,295,048	1,347,661	1,408,794	1,455,010	1,553,245	1,587,037	1,649,140	1,724,140	1,794,910

Expenditure Budgets by Unit											
Schools and Colleges	674,235	705,376	744,999	779,497	812,445	821,383	890,861	910,684	959,038	994,068	1,018,185
University Academic Units	45,233	46,213	47,715	49,475	57,640	59,294	59,543	60,468	62,000	63,995	66,003
Research Units	4,251	4,191	3,608	4,305	4,116	3,158	4,314	4,969	4,943	4,779	3,326
Academic Program Support	35,050	35,455	41,987	49,233	58,328	70,592	81,860	62,991	63,548	69,073	79,912
Capital Renewal Fund	-	-	-	-	-	-	2,507	16,566	30,300	41,894	44,905
Executive Officer and Service Units	218,942	218,134	230,229	233,298	234,949	238,196	240,365	245,712	248,989	256,646	259,499
North Campus Research Complex						11,341	15,324	20,342	6,888	12,298	14,403
Financial Aid	78,099	84,759	90,920	99,058	106,594	117,790	126,056	134,255	144,768	161,170	183,444
University Items	107,572	126,357	135,590	132,795	134,723	133,254	132,416	131,050	128,065	119,318	125,232
Total Expenditures	1,163,382	1,220,485	1,295,048	1,347,661	1,408,794	1,455,010	1,553,245	1,587,037	1,649,140	1,724,140	1,794,910

UM Budget Revenue (2014)

Revenue Budgets	2005	2006	2007	2008	2009	2010	2011	2012	2013	2014	2015
General	1,163,382	1,220,485	1,295,048	1,347,661	1,408,794	1,455,010	1,553,245	1,587,037	1,649,140	1,724,140	1,794,910
Designated	101,475	112,625	119,750	140,075	143,420	134,770	136,270	137,400	137,540	143,190	172,489
Expendable Restricted	759,741	845,416	881,390	879,590	898,481	969,709	1,053,733	1,110,109	1,094,334	1,097,197	1,054,926
Auxiliary Activities	2,041,115	2,260,687	2,392,303	2,415,498	2,617,270	1,646,668	2,838,824	2,932,963	3,198,411	3,406,856	3,593,864
Total Revenues	4,065,713	4,439,214	4,688,491	4,782,824	5,067,965	5,206,156	5,582,073	5,767,599	6,079,425	6,371,383	6,616,189

Expenditure Budgets											
General	1,163,382	1,220,485	1,295,048	1,347,661	1,408,794	1,455,010	1,553,245	1,587,037	1,649,140	1,724,140	1,794,910
Designated	101,475	112,625	119,750	140,075	143,420	134,770	136,270	137,400	137,540	143,190	172,489
Expendable Restricted	759,741	845,416	881,390	879,590	898,481	969,709	1,053,733	1,110,109	1,094,334	1,097,197	1,054,926
Auxiliary Activities	2,022,677	2,217,388	2,335,475	2,359,287	2,581,993	1,641,130	2,773,513	3,015,247	3,239,005	3,495,268	3,638,271
Total Expenditures	4,047,275	4,395,914	4,631,663	4,726,614	5,032,687	5,200,618	5,516,761	5,849,883	6,120,019	6,459,795	6,660,596

Table entries are dollars in thousands.

UM Budget Planned Expenditures (2014)

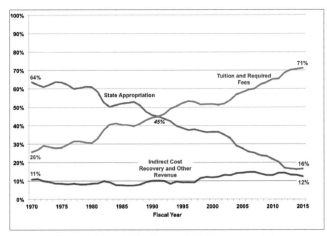

General contribution of state support to
the UMAA General Fund budget

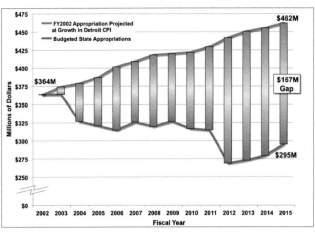

The "Jaws" diagram showing the erosion in
state support compared to the CPI

convincingly by charts showing the elements of the General Fund (academic) budget as well as an estimate of the loss in state support over the past decade (the so-called "jaws" diagram).

A more detailed discussion of the current strategy for compensating for the loss of state support and financing the University is provided below:

1) Enrollment Increases: These charts make it apparent that the University has been able to adjust revenues to compensate for the loss of state support largely by increasing enrollments (by 25% or 10,000 students), increasing student tuition (particularly for non-resident students, now in excess of $45,000/year), and shifting the student mix of instate to out-of-state students. Yet here there are worries about the future. While once the state appropriation was viewed as providing the tuition discount provided instate students, this is clearly no longer the case. A very rough estimate of the annual cost of education at Michigan (across all undergraduate and graduate/professional programs) would range between $25,000 to $30,000 per student, a cost similar to other leading public universities such as UC Berkeley, U Wisconsin, and U Virginia. State support of the roughly 27,000 instate students enrolling in the University averages out roughly to $7,000, which when combined with instate tuition still falls roughly $10,000 short of the actual cost. Hence it seems clear that the higher tuition charged out-of-state students ($45,000 and up) generates a sufficient surplus over actual costs to partially subside instate students and financial aid.

Put another way, the high tuitions charged to out-of-state students are covering the cost (subsidizing the education) of Michigan resident students. While this may strike some as robbing Peter to pay Paul, it is perhaps better to frame it as a Robin Hood approach to university financing since weathy out-of-state students are being asked to subsidize the education of low-income instate students.

However there are several serious concerns about this strategy. First, while the loss of state support has largely been compensated for with nonresident tuition, this has approached a ceiling. Today the current out-of-state undergraduate tuition of $45,000 has caught up with leading private universities such as Harvard and Stanford. Furthermore although there are strong financial pressures to continue to grow enrollment, while holding permanent faculty lines relatively constant, the increasing instructional load in UM's large undergraduate colleges, LS&A and Engineering, are already becoming unbearable for many faculty members, particular those with research grants.

Finally, as we have noted earlier, this strategy of increasing the enrollment of students capable of paying essentially private tuitions has distorted both the economic distribution of the student body as well as the culture of the University. This has also placed the public purpose of the University in jeopardy, since it is in part responsible for the major decline in the number of low income and underrepresented minority students. However here one should properly also place the blame on state higher education policies that place

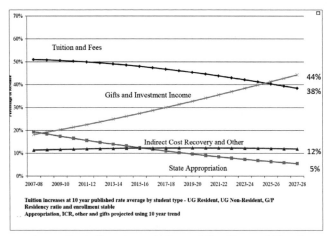

An optimistic extrapolation of the General Fund
over the next decade (Hanlon)

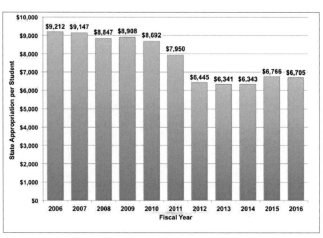

State Appropriations per student

Michigan at the bottom of the states in the level of need-based financial aid it provides to resident students.

2) Sponsored Research: If the University is successful in sustaining the quality of its faculty, it should remain among the national leaders in the level of sponsored research expenditures. However, as we noted early, since roughly 30% ($380 million in 2014) of research expenditures are provided by the University itself both to cover inadequate indirect cost recovery and cost sharing, this high level of research activity also imposes additional costs on the University that must be addressed by revenue from other activities such as student tuition and patient fees (unless, of course, research sponsors such as the federal government can be persuaded to cover more of the indirect costs of the research they procure).

3) Fund Raising: Clearly private support has been essential to the welfare of the University. As state support for major capital facilities disappeared in the 1990s, this provided a critical source of funding for new buildings. It has also been critical for ongoing operations, bringing in roughly $100 M/y to $150 M/y for this purpose. Private gifts also provide much of the funding for the University's essential student financial aid programs. But its most critical impact is building an endowment whose growth can then be managed to provide significant ongoing support for academic programs for the long term. The ability of the University to build its endowment through fund-raising campaigns and effective asset management has been impressive, resulting in endowment growth to $10 billion in 2015 after recovering from the 2008 recession.

However several caveats are important here: Although the UM completed a successful $3.3 billion fund-raising campaign in the 2000s and has recently launched a $4 billion fund-raising campaign associated with the Bicentennial, these largely provide only marginal resources within a $7 billion per year budget–and could well result in launching new initiatives demanded by donors that dilute academic programs even further. Furthermore, in recent years Michigan has been able to achieve only an average annual fund-raising activity (currently ranked 20th), lagging not only leading privates but several publics as well (Wisconsin, Indiana, Texas, U California, etc.) While it is understandable that a very large university like Michigan would not attract the deep loyalty and commitment of Ivy League institutions, it also does not seem to be attracting the support characterizing several other large public institutions. The most successful fund-raising is by clinical units, understandable because of the personal impact they have on donors. Perhaps the problem is that there are just not enough exciting things happening on campus to attract the interest of donors.

It is also important to recognize that most large gifts for capital facilities fail to cover either the full construction or operating costs of the building, requiring substantial additional University expenditures. This is a particularly serious issue for those naming gifts (i.e.,

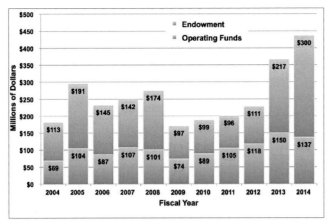

Gifts to the University

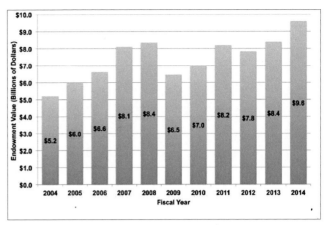

Endowment Growth

"the edifice complex") for facilities that are not among the University's highest priorities. Furthermore, most of the University's endowment is for specified purposes (including those funds associated with hospital reserves) and not available for general support.

As we noted, while the University's current development and marketing staffing is several times that of the 1990s, it has failed to achieve any real growth in annual giving, ranking below many other public and private universities. In a similar sense, although the total goals of the major campaigns appear large ($3.3 B and 4.0 B), when adjusted for inflation, these are comparable in scale to the $1.4 B campaign of the 1990s and furthermore are dependent upon major gifts that require substantial additional University investment in low priority activities (e.g., the Munger graduate resident hall and the expansion of the Athletics campus).

4) Endowment: Although Michigan's endowment appears impressive, its impact is limited by the size of the University. As a rule of thumb, the wealthiest private institutions achieve endowments capable of sustaining their institutions only when their endowments reach a level of $1 million per student (since this generates sufficient payout at 4.5% to 5% to cover tuition levels). With the rapid growth in Michigan's enrollment, its endowment support for academic purposes (paying out 4.5% of the total endowment each year) amounts to only $230,000 per student. Hence while impressive, the University's endowment falls far short of that required to provide independence from state support with our current enrollment.

Two comparisons illustrate the relative importance of endowments vs. student tuition:

Percent of academic budget from endowments
Harvard: 35%
Stanford: 20%
Michigan: 10%

Percent of academic budget from tuition
Harvard: 10%
Stanford: 17%
Michigan: 36%

It is also important to observe that most of the growth of Michigan's endowment is coming from investment income rather than additional gift contributions.

5) Cost Containment: On the other side of the ledger, the University has launched an ambitious cost reduction effort during the past decade, with the goal of trimming roughly 1.5% to 2.0% each year of annual expenditures. While this has resulted in part from more efficient management of energy and supply acquisition and administration, many of these savings have been achieved by taxing the expenditures of academic units to leverage reductions in their budgets and by increasing employee and retiree contributions to staff benefits. Both approaches put academic quality at risk. It is clear that efforts to enhance efficiency, productivity, and cost containment must be broadened to include both academic units and revenue-generating activities such as development and marketing.

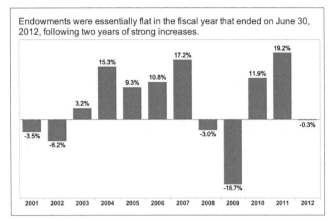

Endowment returns over past decade

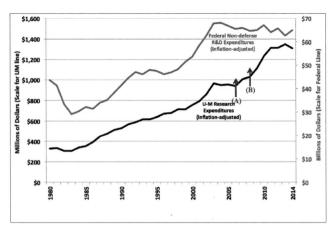

Growth in research expenditures (inflation adjusted)

Furthermore, the massive expansion of the staffing in areas such as communications (600) and development (500), coupled with the dramatic increase in compensation of senior administrators and staff in the central administration, raise serious concerns about the viability of the current cost containment strategy.

There are several longer-term concerns that should be kept in mind about future options for strengthening the University's financial situation

6) State Support: Since much of the State of Michigan's tax revenue base has been eliminated by the tax policies of recent conservative Republican administrations, it is unlikely that there will be significant restoration of state appropriations for higher education for many years. Michigan is likely to continue to rank in the lowest quartile of the states in its support of its public universities. Since the population of college age students in Michigan is projected to drop by 20% over the next decade, it is likely that state support will at best track inflation and will not increase sufficiently to cover the funding cuts of the past two decades.

7) Enrollment Growth: Although there will likely be strong pressures to continue to grow enrollment while holding tenure-track faculty size constant, the concerns about the negative impact on academic quality of further enrollment growth, the pressure on faculty retention driven by increasing instructional load, and the fact that out-of-state tuition rates are approaching

the ceilings experienced by private universities, suggests that this option may be limited.

8) Cost Containment: Much of the highly touted recent "savings" of the University have come largely out of faculty-staff benefits, cutting health care, retirement benefits, and salary programs. Furthermore faculty and staff compensation have been modest, dropping 20% below several of its private university peers and lagging behind even other leading public universities. Hence there is a serious concern that further cuts in benefits would cripple UM's efforts to attract outstanding faculty and staff. Instead, it is becoming clear that the University must simply assess more carefully those areas where most staff growth has occurred (e.g., communications and development). Furthermore the Regents must demand more rigorous and defensible compensation policies for senior administrators comparable to peer institutions.

9) Securing the University's "Public Purpose": As we will discuss later in Chapter 20, the loss of state support coupled with the enrollment of large numbers of out-of-state students paying high tuition has seriously eroded Michigan's public purpose. The fraction of low-income and first-generation college students has dropped below that of most public universities and even several leading private universities, leading to UM's characterization as "an engine of inequality". Furthermore, the fraction of underrepresented students enrolling in the University has also dropped significantly from its peak in 1996.

In fact, the percentage enrollment of African American students has dropped from 9.5% in 1996 to 4.3%, the lowest level since the 1960s.

There seems to have been a shift in University priorities from a fundamental public purpose of "providing an uncommon education for the common man" to selling our services to the highest bidder–in fact, to the "top 1%. Clearly this would characterize those out-of-state students whose parents could afford $60,000 per year to attend Michigan. But it also applies to those who can afford access to many other University activities, e.g., an average price of $230 per game for football tickets (except for students, who still pay $50 per game for standing in long lines for open seating… the highest student pricing in the nation).

11) Competition among Academic vs Auxiliary Units: There is increasing concern about the very significant growth in the auxiliary units of the University, which operate in relatively price-insensitive markets with few Regent constraints such as those imposed on tuition. Yet this unbridled growth has serious implications for academic units. For example, the University's debt capacity is determined by tuition revenue rather than auxiliary revenues, thereby raising the concern that to some degree auxiliary facilities growth could well constrain academic opportunities. More serious is the aggressive growth in the fund-raising activities of auxiliary units that are now going after prospects and fund-raising opportunities in competition with academic units. An early example of this was the degree to which the University Musical Society has managed to capture most of the private gifts that in earlier times would have funded the Music School. Most recently, the Athletics Department has been rapidly expanding development staff and set a campaign goal of $350 million, comparable to and likely competitive with LS&A. Again this clearly raises the relative priority given to academic and auxiliary units by the leadership of the University.

In summary, the University's current financial model looks increasingly unsustainable: Its academic programs are largely sustained by high tuition from out-of-state students, which is approaching both enrollment and tuition ceilings. Fund-raising seems increasingly suspect, achieving modest results even with excessive staffing, poorly aligned with university priorities, and insufficient to have the major impact characterizing private universities. Although the University faculty remains highly successful in attracting sponsored research support, roughly 30% of the $1.3 billion of annual research expenditures is currently provided by the University itself. While the University had taken advantage of low interest rates to enable massive investments in auxiliary enterprises ($650 million of resident hall renovations, $2 billion of medical center expansions, and $750 million in new or renovated athletic facilities), the capability of longer term revenues to support both the debt and operating costs of these facilities is questionable.

The Bottom Line

So how might we assess the financial state of the University over the past 50 years. To be sure, the University has survived in the face of losing over 50% of its state support, with its reputation largely intact. On the positive side, Michigan has managed to preserve most of its quality and its reputation even while losing over 80% of its state support. In fact, in the 1990s the National Academy ratings of academic quality ranked the University of Michigan 3rd in the nation (and world) behind only Stanford and the University of California Berkeley in the quality across the full spectrum of its graduate programs.

But it could be argued that this was primarily because of decisions and actions taken during the three-decade period from the 1970s to through the 1990s. Tuition was increased to more realistic levels reflecting the decline in state subsidy. Strong support and incentives were provided to encourage the faculty in obtaining external research support (with Michigan moving to 1st in the nation in research activity as a result). Authority and accountability for resources was decentralized to the level of deans and directors, where assets are acquired and costs are incurred. The effort was launched to more aggressively manage the University's endowment increasing it by 10 fold to over $2.5 B. And a central "bank" was created by the VPCFO to manage University assets in a highly creative and effective manner. Largely as a result of these actions, the University was able to achieve in 1997 the top AAa credit rating and maintain this rating through the past decade and a half.

In contrast, during from the late 1990s to the 2010s, a series of short term actions have been taken that may have walked the University out on a financial limb. The dramatic increase of 25% in student enrollments, designed to generate additional tuition particularly from out-of-state students, has both overloaded instructional capacity and seriously damaged the socioeconomic diversity of the student body. Furthermore, launching massive debt-financed capital facilities projects in auxiliary enterprises to take advantage of market-insensitive pricing and low interest rates has not only incurred significant debt but encumbered much of the University's borrowing capacity (determined primarily by student tuition and fee revenue rather than auxiliary revenues).

Hence today there remain serious concerns about the University's financial sustainability, since enrollments have now reached (or in some cases exceeded) instructional and facilities capacity. Nonresident tuition is approaching the ceiling experienced by the top private institutions, while instate tuition continues to be highly constrained by political factors. While endowment has continued to grow, endowment-per-student is at only one-tenth the level of leading private institutions.

During the past half-century, the auxiliary units (i.e., health system, student housing, and intercollegiate athletics) have thrived. UM's AAa rating coupled with inelastic consumer markets experienced by auxiliary activities has allowed a massive investment in new facilities (e.g., the adult general hospital, the Mott Children's hospital, and many other new clinical care and research facilities for the medical center; an investment of over $650 million in renovating and building new student residence halls; and comparable investments in Michigan Stadium and other athletic facilities). Yet this massive growth in auxiliaries has also raised a concern about the balance between auxiliary and academic priorities.

Perhaps most serious is the fact that the University has failed to sustain its public purpose. While it achieved significant progress in racial diversity during the 1990s, minority enrollments have since fallen back to the low levels of the 1960s. Largely because of the growth in the enrollment of high-income nonresident students coupled with the low level of state support (particularly in the absence of state-based financial aid programs), the University has lost much of its economic diversity. Indeed, some even question whether the University's long-standing commitment to providing "an uncommon education for the common man" has now been replaced by efforts to attract and educate uncommonly rich students.

The Road Ahead

Clearly, in the face of the impact of aging populations and the global financial crisis on state and federal budgets and hence on support for higher education, the nation's public research universities must intensify their efforts to increase efficiency and productivity in all of their activities. In particular, they should set bold goals for reducing the costs of their ongoing activities. Many companies have found that cost reductions and productivity enhancement of 25% or greater are possible with modern business practices such as lean production and total quality management. While universities have many differences from business corporations–for example, cost reductions do not drop to the bottom line of profits–there is likely a very considerable opportunity for process restructuring in both administrative and academic activities.

Of course, in the face of deep cuts in state appropriations, most public research universities have already been engaged in intense cost-cutting efforts, particularly in non-academic areas such as financial management, procurement, energy conservation, competitive bidding of services, and eliminating unnecessary regulation and duplication. They have cut hundreds of millions of dollars of recurring costs from their budgets. But it is now time to consider bolder actions that require restructuring of academic activities as well.

First, let us provide a realistic assessment of financial opportunities for each source of support:

Restore state support? Not for years, if ever...
Raise tuition? Perhaps for instate, but outstate
tuition is already at Harvard levels
Private fund raising? Questionable as a major

source relative to needs

Endowment: Absolutely, but it will grow henceforth primarily through wise financial management

Federal support: Absolutely, both for financial aid and research support (subject to ICR)

Rather than distracting ourselves with penny-wise and pound-foolish actions such as "shared services" (that will undercut the staff support of our teaching and research) or IT "rationalization" (that will stifle the innovation and creativity in our academic units), while achieving only marginal savings (less than 1% on the average), we should consider "pound-wise and penny-foolish" approaches that would have very major impact on the University.

1. Re-establish the control of the Provost over budgets, expenditures, and financial discipline by recreating the Committee on Budget Administration and the Budget Priorities Committee, each chaired by or reporting to the Provost.

The massive increases in administrative staffing and expenditures both in administrative units such as Development and Communications and in Schools and Colleges (particularly Engineering and Business Administration) suggest both a lack of discipline and control of expenditures. From 1970 to 2000, the authority as chief budget officer of the Provost was sustained by the Executive Officers convened as the Committee on Budget Administration and chaired by the Provost and by the Budget Priorities Committee, a blue-ribbon body comprised of faculty, staff, deans, and executive officers reporting to the Provost. Note the Provost maintained control over all operating and capital expenditures through these mechanisms, a control and discipline authority that is clearly missing today.

However as we suggested in Chapter 7, the role of experienced financial managers in each of the many academic units is critical since most deans and chairs come from the ranks of faculty rather inexperienced in such management and financial roles. The EVPCFO should not only maintain a network of contacts with these managers at the unit level, capable of providing assistance or warnings when necessary, but should also be involved to some degree in both the appointment

and evaluation of these staff. As noted later, it is this informal network of experienced management staff in the units linking to the EVPCFO that is the key to the financial integrity of such a massive and highly decentralized institution.

2. The Provost should implement a series of actions to establish greater discipline and cost containment.

For example, all capital projects that are either not fully funded (for BOTH capital expenditures and operating costs) or central to the academic programs of the University should be put on hold. Similarly, private gifts that either do not address significant University priorities (e.g., Munger Hall) or entail significant additional expenditures (expansion of Ross School of Business Administration) should be declined. It is absolutely essential that the Executive Officers contain those activities that convey a false impression of the University's prosperity or compete with the academic core for resources. Here, the biggest threats are the unconstrained growth of the Athletics Department and the plush designs of renovated student housing (complete with sushi bars and exercise rooms). Any auxiliary or University-related activities that compete directly with academic units for private giving or University subsidy should be constrained. Finally, the salaries of senior administrators, including the President, should be clearly linked to faculty and staff salaries rather than simply market-driven (which is largely a fictitious rationale for compensating what are "public callings" similar to many government positions).

3. Moving to year-round operation

In the early 1960s the University switched to a trimester calendar of three 4-month terms to allow operating year-round at full capacity (with the spring-summer term divided into two 2-month half terms). The students and faculty liked it, but the state never stepped up to add in the additional appropriation necessary to subsidize state resident students during the spring summer term. Hence year-round operation was abandoned. Yet, interestingly enough, the University kept the trimester calendar, except we now call each

116

trimester a "semester" and give faculty the month of May as "academic non instructional time".

Since state support today provides only 8% of the support for the University's activities, it is no longer a major factor in determining the University calendar. Hence it is logical for the University to consider the possibility of bringing the third spring-summer "semester" to full capacity. Furthermore today both our instructional facilities and residence halls are completely renovated to handle year-round operation (even in a future of global warming). At the current net tuition level of $1 billion for two terms, this would have the potential of generating an additional $400 million a year. Moveover, it would provide students flexibility in how they schedule their calendar. In fact, students entering with advanced placement credits could conceivably earn a bachelor's degree in two years, thereby providing as well very considerable savings in the cost of their education (particularly through both living costs and additional employment opportunities).

Since our buildings and utilities are fixed costs, whether they get used or not, the primary concern would be instructional costs. Although most faculty use the spring-summer term for research, the University could rely on senior and/or emeritus faculty as the major teaching staff for the summer (perhaps negotiating a reduced salary).

There are questions, of course. In our current calendar, the state appropriation provides (in theory) the discount between instate and nonresident tuition, amounting to roughly $150 million per term. Would we need to generate a similar subsidy to operate in the spring-summer term? Or would we attract a different student mix? How would we handle the balance between full-time Michigan students and students from other colleges taking a summer term at Michigan?

4. Tax auxiliary units to support the academic core

The auxiliary units of the University, i.e., hospitals, student housing, intercollegiate athletics, depend heavily on the reputation and capacity of the academic core of the institution. Furthermore the auxiliaries currently operate in a less price sensitive market and are less constrained by political issues than tuition (e.g., Regents).

Hence it seems perfectly appropriate to "tax" the expenditures of the auxiliary units to help support the academic core. A tax of 5% of expenditures = $150 M/y. Indeed, such a tax on expenditures might provide an additional brake on unnecessary spending, such as capital facilities expansion.

5. Lobby to restore state support to adequate levels

During the 1980s and 1990s the University successfully led a statewide coalition of public universities and their most influential alumni to make the case for state support (the so-called "treetops" strategy). During the past decade there has been little effort to build such a unified approach. It is clearly time to repeat the "treetops" strategy of the 1990s to restore state appropriations either to inflation-adjusted levels that would amount to an increase from 2015 level of $300 M to $468 M to match the inflation-adjusted level of 2002.

6. Join in the National Academy Agenda

Recently the National Academies of Science, Engineering, and Medicine have engaged in a major effort to restore the priority of research universities in America. If higher education is able to get traction on the ten actions requested of Congress, funding for the nation's research universities would increase by roughly 25% ($70 billion/year) over the next decade.

Michigan's share of this would be $1.5 B/y, or equivalent to a $30 B endowment.

Yet, while many of the nation's research universities are actively engaged in this effort, Michigan has been conspicuously absent from the table. Perhaps it should get up off the bench and join in the effort

Other ideas

Spin off companies in which the University owns equity interests. (After all, isn't that what Michigan Athletics has become?)

Apply peer comparisons to determine staffing levels appropriate for activities such as fund-raising and marketing (meaning Harvard, Stanford, U. Wisconsin, and U California).

Conduct a thorough analysis of executive salaries (using compensation practices for corporate boards)

Learn to say "no" to the offer of gifts that run counter to University interests or require excessive UM cost-sharing (e.g., Munger Hall?)

And the list goes on and on and on…

A final observation…

Clearly, current financial models for most American research universities are unsustainable and must be restructured. Yet, while efficiency, streamlining, cost reductions, and productivity enhancement are all necessary, eventually stakeholders of American higher education must address the dramatic decline in research university support through investments from all sources–federal government (particularly for graduate education), states, private sector, and students (tuition). As any business executive knows all too well, relying entirely on cost-cutting and productivity enhancement without attention to top line revenue growth eventually leads to Chapter 11!

We will return to this issue in Chapter 19.

Chapter 9

Buildings

While outstanding faculty, students, and staff are the key assets of a great university, the quality of facilities clearly influences the ability both to recruit outstanding people and to support their efforts to achieve excellence. As Winston Churchill once stated: "We shape our buildings. Thereafter, they shape us." Maintaining and enhancing the quality of the campus, buildings, grounds, and other infrastructure is a major priority of the university, and it must be a responsibility of the president. In most cases, the need for facilities and other campus improvements bubble up from the various programs of the university, and then the deans and the president work together to acquire the resources necessary to support these projects.

One of the more visible challenges faced by the University over the past half century arose from the burden of its aging physical plant. Our academic buildings, many fifty to one hundred years old, had served us well. Thousands of students had skipped up stairs, rushed down halls, and scooted out doors, on to other commitments, leaving behind scuffed walls, drafty windows, and heating and cooling systems of a by-gone era. These buildings desperately needed renovation to meet the educational needs of today and tomorrow. For example, modern research methods required more space than was allotted decades ago. Changing teaching styles demanded flexible classroom spaces that could accommodate small seminars and group projects as easily as large lectures.

Outside these buildings, many more lumens of light were needed to bathe campus landmarks and illuminate sidewalks and footpaths to create a safer environment for all members of the community. Behind the flora, miles of fiber optics were necessary to link libraries, research laboratories, and residence hall rooms to the information super highway.

With the disappearance of federal support for higher education facilities during the 1980s, universities had been forced to depend primarily upon private support, student fees, or limited state support—for public universities—to rebuild their physical plants. The growth in the equity markets enabled some well-endowed private universities to take important steps toward addressing these needs during the 1990s. But many other less affluent institutions, including Michigan, continued to struggle with inadequate facilities for their educational programs.

Although the needs of academic units should take precedence in capital improvements, any visit to a university campus will soon reveal that much of the activity exists in auxiliary units, such as the medical center, student housing, and intercollegiate athletics because of their independent capacity to generate funding (e.g., patient fees, rents, ticket income, television revenue, or gifts).

The majority of capital expansion at most research universities these days occurs in their medical centers, driven by the need for renovation or growth in clinical facilities, the desire for additional research space in the biomedical sciences, and the availability of substantial income from clinical activities. This is not surprising, considering that medical center budgets have typically increased at twice the rate of academic budgets throughout the past two decades (e.g., 10 percent per year for the medical center versus 5 percent per year for the rest of the university). The desire to increase clinical income drives the continual expansion of facilities, particularly in such lucrative areas as surgery and internal medicine, but also in satellite clinics designed to expand primary care activities that feed patients into university hospitals. Similarly, the extraordinary growth in federal support of biomedical research, now

The University of Michigan campus (1970)

The University of Michigan campus (2000)

The University of Michigan campus (2010)

representing over 60 percent of all federal research and development on university campuses, has stimulated staggering investments in expensive new research facilities in the life sciences, such as molecular biology, genomics, proteomics, and biotechnology. There is a certain irony here: in contrast to pharmaceutical companies that tend to invest in "throwaway" research buildings because of the rapid obsolescence of research technology, universities prefer to hire expensive architects to design monumental facilities to last generations, even though these facilities will require several times their original capital costs for the renovations necessary to track technological changes.

In recent years, there also has been a comparable level of capital expansion in athletic facilities. The wacko culture characterizing intercollegiate athletics presumes that the team that spends the most—or builds the most—wins the most. Hence, there has been a costly arms race to invest hundreds of millions of dollars in expanding football stadiums and basketball pavilions, specialized training facilities, academic counseling centers, plush offices for the ever-expanding athletic staff, and even museums designed to impress recruits and fans alike with past athletic accomplishments. While much of this investment (e.g., in bigger and better training facilities or the most expensive artificial turf fields) is driven by competitive forces, some of the largest investments (e.g., skyboxes for wealthy fans and corporate clients, sophisticated television systems, or on-campus stores for marketing sports paraphernalia) have been made as a marketing device. Most athletic departments tend to borrow the funds to build such facilities, depending on future revenue from ticket sales, television contracts, or licensing to cover the debt, although most of these loans are actually secured with a university pledge of income from student fees. The debt load on several of the major athletic programs is considerable, ranging into the hundreds of millions of dollars for many institutions and requiring that new revenue be generated through clever and occasionally even coercive mechanisms, such as seat taxes and skyboxes for premium seating (ironically given a highly favorable, if somewhat perverse, tax treatment by the Internal Revenue Service as "charitable donations for educational purposes").

Although the core activities of the university involve teaching and scholarship, capital investments in facilities for academic programs tends to lag far behind investments in auxiliary activities, such as medical care and intercollegiate athletics. In part, this has to do with constraints on the funding sources available for academic facilities (e.g., state appropriations, private gifts, or debt financing based on student fees). But it is also due to the relative autonomy of most auxiliary units, portraying (at least in myth, if not in reality) their financial independence from the rest of the university. Most universities tend to be far more parsimonious when spending funds on new classroom or library space than when investing in major expansion of the football stadium or university hospital. Such was true for Michigan, both during the 1970s and 1980s as state support collapsed and then again in the early 2000s as University priorities shifted from academic facilities to large investments in auxiliary activities (e.g., a large expansion in the medical center, student residence halls, and Michigan Stadium).

1960s - 1970s

During the late 1950s and early 1960s, growth of the University's campus was dependent not only on student demand but on the availability of state appropriations to fund the necessary capital facilities. There was strong state support of both operations (amounting to roughly 80% of instructional costs) and new facilities, including the School of Music, Engineering laboratories, a cyclotron laboratory, and the Institute of Science and Technology on the North Campus, the Undergraduate Library, the Physics and Astronomy Building, and the giant Mary Markley residence hall on the Central Campus, and the new School of Dentistry, at $17 million, the largest state-funded building in the University's history at that time ($140 million in today's dollars).

Yet rapid growth of the campus began to slow in the late 1960s, both because of the weakening of state appropriations, but even more so because of action by the State Legislature to allocate all monies for planning and constructing university buildings through the state controller, including planning and letting contracts. The conflict of state control with the independent authority demanded by the University's constitutional autonomy blocked state funded construction for almost a decade.

By the mid-1970s the impact of the energy crisis on the state's economy, coupled with the impact of the growing competitiveness of the Japanese automobile industry on Detroit, and later the shifting priorities of an aging population, signaled the beginning of a more permanent erosion of state support that would continue for several decades. Student fee revenue, federal research grants, and private gifts allowed limited construction of student residences such as Bursley Hall on the North Campus, research facilities such as the School of Public Health, and the Schools of Art and Architecture on the North Campus.

Although state appropriations for campus projects resumed during the 1970s, the increasing competition from other public colleges and universities competing for state fund and the impact of the Arab oil embargo and Japanese auto imports on state revenues kept state capital for UMAA academic facilities at marginal levels. By the early 1980s the state had entered a deep recession, with appropriations to the University of Michigan dropping by over 30%, requiring a major restructuring of the University's financial strategy with deep budget cuts, program discontinuance, increasing tuition, and a major effort to build private support of the University.

1980s

But there was yet another factor competing with the funding of academic buildings due to the University's own priorities. By the 1970s it had become apparent that "Old Main", the University Hospital built during the 1920s, was in desperate need of replacement. Yet the projected expense was formidable. President Fleming launched the planning effort for the Replacement Hospital Project, which he chaired to make certain it was a reasonable plan. Success was finally achieved in 1979-1980 during the transition year when Allan Smith served as interim president and then followed with the leadership of Harold Shapiro, based upon a unique partnership in which both the State of Michigan and the University would each sell $180 million of bonds to finance the $360 million project. This was the largest state-funded project since the Mackinac Bridge. Indeed, the size of state funding required for the Replacement Hospital Project ($180 million) took a significant bite

The new Adult General Hospital

out of the state capital outlay dollars available for all of higher education in Michigan during the 1980s.

The massive project began in the early 1980s at a time when the State of Michigan was coping with a major national recession, which followed the usual pattern of state's fortunes: "When the nation economy catches a cold, the state of Michigan catches pneumonia!" While the Replacement Hospital Project benefited from low construction costs during the recession, the construction on the rest of the campus was largely dormant with the exception of privately funded health care facilities such as the W. K. Kellogg Eye Center and the Taubman Health Care Center along with biomedical laboratory facilities funded through research grants, e.g., Medical Science Research Buildings I, II, and III, which together with the Replacement Hospital Project amounted to a $500 million investment in the University Medical Center during the Shapiro years.

At a much smaller, but nevertheless critical, level was the completion of the move of the College of Engineering to its North Campus site. Actually this provides an interesting example of how, even in the worst of economic times, a bit of pragmatic planning and good luck can lead to progress. In 1980, Engineering found itself split with most instructional activities in the old Central Campus buildings of West Engineering and East Engineering, and most research activities in laboratories on the North Campus. The enrollment of the College had grown by over 35% during the 1970s, so there was a desperate need for more space. An overly optimistic fund-raising campaign conducted

122

1950s Early Saarinen plan for the North Campus

1970s Early construction on the North Campus

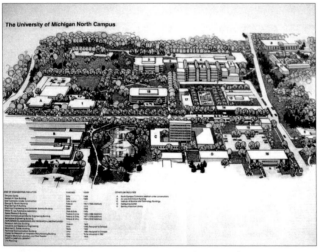

1980s Engineering moves to the North Campus

1990s Major expansion with the Media Union

2000s The Engineering Campus is complete.

2020??? The North Woods Master Plan

Transforming the University of Michigan's North Campus

The Economics Building destroyed by fire in 1982

in the 1970s raised sufficient funds for only the first phase of a grand plan for a three-building complex to accommodate the move of the College. When a new team of deans was appointed in the College in 1981, it quickly became apparent that they would have to cobble together a much more realistic plan based as much on trading space as new construction.

Key to success was the tragic loss of the University's oldest academic building, the Economics Building, when on Christmas Eve of 1982 a disgruntled graduate student set fire to it and burned it to the ground. The College immediately turned to Provost Billy Frye and offered him temporary space in its East Engineering building for the displaced Economics Department until it could be moved to Lorch Hall, if he could provide the funds to allow us to move part of the College into under-utilized space on the North Campus. Next the College persuaded Harold Shapiro to let the deans go to Lansing to lobby for a state-funded building that would complete our move. Although Shapiro was skeptical that in the state's current economic condition we would be successful, he nevertheless agreed to let us go, albeit accompanied by one of the University's most skillful state relations staff, Keith Molin. Sometimes miracles happen, as they did in this case when we managed to land the state-funded Electrical Engineering and Computer Science (EECS) Building and complete the move!

Hence by sacrificing a grand plan based on overly optimistic fund-raising goals of the 1970s and settling for reallocated facilities, the College was finally able to launch its move to the North Campus in 1983.

This EECS Building would be the last state-funded building for many years to come, as state funding for higher education buildings would largely collapse. Throughout the 1970s and 1980s, the state had provided little support for campus facilities, aside from the commitment to rebuild the University Hospitals, which had diverted state dollars that would have otherwise been available for academic facilities to the support of patient care. Hence future academic facility needs of the University would have to be met through private gifts or debt-financing pledged against student tuition revenue.

1990s

Despite the lack of state support, the University of Michigan's Ann Arbor campus continued to grow into one of the largest university campus in the nation, with almost 26 million square feet of space by 2000. Yet many of the most distinguished academic programs of the University were housed in ancient buildings, in bad need of repair, and totally inadequate for modern teaching and research. Heating systems were antiquated, windows drafty, and teaching and laboratory facilities were outdated. During the previous several decades, the campus environment had declined significantly. A two-decade long freeze on state funding for capital construction, coupled with the age and obsolescence of many of Michigan's facilities, was having a serious impact on the quality of the University's academic programs and the morale of faculty, students, and staff. Classrooms were dilapidated, laboratories were no longer adequate for state-of-the-art research, and major book and art collections faced serious risk. Even the appearance of the campus looked dismal, with trash littered everywhere, posters taped to any bare space, and chalked messages scribbled across the sidewalks and building walls. It was clear that many of the students and faculty had lost any sense of pride in the appearance of the campus, and they treated it like the slum it had become.

Yet, during the 1990s, several factors converged simultaneously to provide the University with a remarkable window of opportunity for rebuilding its campuses. First, falling interest rates, coupled with the University's high credit rating, made it quite inexpensive to borrow money. Second, because of a weak economy,

The key to rebuilding the campus: Farris Womack, VPCFO, who put together the financial plan, Paul Spradlin, who managed the vast complexity of the many projects, and University Architect Doug Hanna.

there were few competing construction projects underway in the private sector, and hence construction costs were quite low. Third, the University's success in auxiliary activities, including private support, clinical revenue, and continuing education fees, was beginning to generate substantial revenue. And, fourth, the University was able to convince Governor Engler to launch a major state capital facilities programs, with the understanding that the University would match the state effort through the use of its own funds.

But there was one final ingredient. The Executive Officers managed to convince the Regents that the University should debt-finance critically needed academic facilities using student fees. While this was a common device in private universities, Michigan had generally used student fees to finance only non-instructional facilities such as Crisler Arena, depending instead on state funding for academic facilities. To make this step more politically palatable in the face of concerns about rapidly rising tuition, the administration developed a plan of shared sacrifice in which faculty and staff salaries were held level during the first year of the new fee. (This latter step earned some harsh criticism from faculty members, even though the lapse in salary increases was only temporary and more than made up through strong salary programs in later years.)

The Medical Center led the way with a series of new teaching, research, and clinical facilities that augmented the new Adult General Hospital. A new Child and Maternal Health Care Hospital replaced Mott and Women's Hospitals. A high-rise Cancer and Geriatrics

Center was constructed. A trio of sophisticated research laboratories, Medical Science Research Buildings I, II, and III came on line to keep the Medical School at the forefront of biomedical research, while also housing the Howard Hughes Medical Research Institute. As the Medical Center growth began to strain against the limits of its downtown Ann Arbor site, the University Hospitals acquired a large site northeast of Ann Arbor and began to develop its East Medical Campus to respond to the need for additional primary care facilities. It also developed new primary care facilities throughout southeastern Michigan, including a major concentration in the Briarwood area in south Ann Arbor.

The last remaining facilities needed to complete the North Campus were completed, including the FXB Building for aerospace engineering, the Lurie Engineering Center, and the Media Union, a remarkable digital library and multimedia center. Further, the eminent American architect–and University alumnus– Charles Moore was commissioned to design a striking carillon, the Lurie Bell Tower, that rapidly became the symbol for the North Campus.

There was also extensive construction activity on the South Campus of the University, including the renovation or construction of most athletic facilities. Michigan Stadium was renovated, and a natural grass field was installed. In the process, the stadium floor was lowered so that an additional 3,000 seats could be added, thereby increasing the capacity of the stadium to 106,000. Other new or substantially renovated

Central Campus New Buildings and Renovations during the 1990s

Angell Hall Renovation

Angell Hall-Haven Connector

Angell Computer Cluster

Shapiro Undergraduate Library

Randall Laboratory Addition

Chemistry Building (Dow)

Kraus Building

C. C. Little

Chemistry Building (Old)

West Engineering Building

Lorch Hall

East Engineering Building

Business Administration Education

Health Service

Business Executive Education

School of Social Work

Margaret Bell Pool Addition

Student Activities Heutwell Center

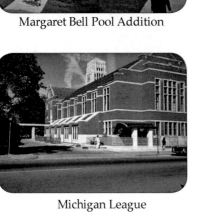

Michigan League

Ingalls Mall/Diag Re-construction

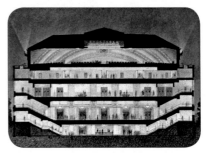

Hill Auditorium Plan

North Campus New Buildings and Renovations during the 1990s

Media Union

Lurie Bell Tower

Lurie Engineering Center

Francois-Xavier Bagnoud Building

Maya Lin's Wave Field

Francois-Xavier Bagnoud Building

Herbert H. Dow Building

North Campus Reflecting Pool

Electrical Eng & Computer Science

Medical Campus new Bildings and Renovations during the 1990s

University Hospital

Medical Science Research I, II, III

Taubman Health Care Center

Cancer Center

C. S. Mott Children's Hospital
Women's Hospital,
Maternal & Child Health Care Center

Medical Center Drive
Parking Structure

East Medical Complex
Plymourh Road

Detroit Observatory

South Campus New Buildings and Renovations during the 1990s

Golf Course Improvements

Michigan Stadium

Tennis Center

Donald B. Canham Natatorium

Michigan Stadium (and turf)

Donald B. Canham Natatorium

Glenn E. Schembechler Hall

Weidenbach Administration Building

William D. Revelli Band Rehearsal Hall

Continuing Legal Education

facilities included Canham Natatorium, Schembechler Hall, Keen Arena, Weidenbech Hall, Yost Arena, the Michigan Golf Course, the varsity track, and the new Michigan Tennis Complex. New facilities were provided to support business operations, including the Wolverine Tower and the Campus Safety Office.

Most encouraging of all was the great progress in addressing the critical needs of the Central Campus. The Undergraduate Library, appropriately referred to as the "ULGI", was surrounded by an attractive shell, totally renovated, and dedicated as the Harold and Vivian Shapiro Library. The Physics Department benefited from a major new research laboratory promoted by it chair, Homer Neal. A major building was constructed between Angell and Haven Halls to serve the LS&A faculty. Total building renovations were accomplished for East Engineering, West Engineering, C. C. Little, Angell Hall, the LS&A Building, Frieze, Mason, and Haven Halls. And a marvelous new building was built for the School of Social Work.

This massive campus renaissance, eventually amounting to almost $2 billion of facilities construction and renovation, was made possible by a combination of state support for capital improvements; federal support of research facilities; private gifts and grants; the reallocation of internal UM funds including contributions from the University's auxiliary units; and student fees. Its tremendous success was due to the vision, commitment, and hard work of a great many individuals at the University. Of particular note here was the incredible effort of VP Farris Womack in leading the effort to finance the projects, Paul Spradlin in directing the projects, and Jack Janveja, Tom Schlauff, and Fred Mayer in the design, management, and execution of the complex effort.

By the conclusion of this massive effort, essentially every building on Michigan's three campuses had either been substantially renovated or replaced with modern, state-of-the-art facilities. The infrastructure necessary for modern research and teaching was installed, including extensive investments in networking the campuses and installing modern information technology systems. Furthermore, this massive construction effort provided an opportunity to significantly enhance the appearance of the University's campuses with exciting new architecture and new landscaping. Finally, by taking advantage of modern technology, the University was able to design facilities to lower lifetime operational costs.

The University of Michigan had moved rapidly from an aging campus to a leader in the quality of environment it was able to provide for its academic program. It would enter the new century, confident of working from a firm foundation of cutting-edge teaching, research, and support facilities. By 1996, essentially all of the projects to rebuild the University of Michigan were either completed, underway, or funded. Over the next two years several dozen of these facilities projects would be completed and dedicated. During spring of 1996 the University had managed to obtain a commitment to provide an additional $137 million of state appropriation, including $79 million for the Ann Arbor campus. This amount was sufficient to complete the renovation of the Central Campus, including the last key LS&A facilities: the LS&A Building, Haven Hall, Mason Hall, Frieze Hall, West Hall, and the Perry Building. Since this required a 20% University match, the University had developed a funding plan that would use University funds to renovate Hill Auditorium and the Rackham Building as the University's contribution (in fact, $20 million was set aside for the Hill Auditorium project). Since Farris Womack had realized that construction costs were likely to increase rapidly with a prosperous economy, we arranged to have these projects fast-tracked with the intent to have them completed by late 1998.

The funding was in place, the plans had been completed, and the University was ready to proceed through the state capital construction process. Unfortunately, these important projects came to a halt in 1997 with the arrival of a new administration.

2000s

With a new administration in the late 1990 came a new campus master planning architect, Venturi-Scott-Brown, led by noted architect Robert Venturi. Previously funded University projects were put on hold for several years to allow the development of a new master plan. Although the University eventually moved ahead with the Venturi-designed Life Sciences Institute (ironically a copy of an earlier Venturi design of a larger biomedical sciences laboratory at Yale), there was little effort to resume the projects to renovate important Central Campus academic buildings. During this delay, the original construction estimates of $80 million later soared to over $300 million because of the delay. The master plan for completing the North Campus met a similar fate. Although the University benefited greatly from the successful effort to rebuild the various campuses of the University during the 1990s, this effort was halted even when most of its plans were close to completion.

Although there was an attempt to signal a strong interest in architecture by directing Venturi to decorate Michigan Stadium with a surrounding "halo", proclaiming the Michigan fight song in 10 foot high letters (and angering fans so much that the Regents directed that it be quietly removed a year later), Venturi's major effort was to design the key research facility in a new Life Science Institute, aimed at attracting Nobel-quality biomedical researchers to the campus. Rather than seek new funding for this multi-building center, the administration instead simply funded it from UM Hospital reserves ($80 million). The biomedical research complex on Huron and Observatory (later named the Taubman Biomedical Laboratory) was important for the continued expansion of research activity in the life sciences, as was the acquisition of the former Pfizer Global Research campus for the site of North Campus Research Center.

A more strategic campus development effort was launched in the mid-2000s by the next administration, beginning with two major complexes designed by architect Robert Stern, Weill Hall (for the Ford School) and North Quad, which provided elegant entrances to the Central Campus. However when the late decision was made to add a 450 student residence hall tower to the North Quad complex, it not only delayed the project by a year but resulted in a construction cost per student comparable to a small house in Ann Arbor. Similarly a major expansion of the Business School (labeled "the flower pot" by its faculty) ended up costing five times ($150 M) the present worth value of a "naming" gift $30) and almost bankrupted the School–a painful lesson about the costs associated with gifts consisting of pledges rather than cash.

Of course, much of this growth was highly opportunistic. Low interest rates and the University's high credit rating enabled the auxiliary units to launch a series of major projects. The University Medical Center continued its rapid expansion with a new Cardiovascular Center ($300 million), a major expansion of the East Medical Campus, and the massive new Mott Pediatrics Hospital ($750 million), along with planned expansion of the Medical School. A major series of renovations was launched for student residence halls ($650 million), felt to be necessary not only to house growing enrollments but also attracting high quality (and high tuition paying) students. The Athletics Department launched a $260 million project to add skyboxes and dining clubs to Michigan Stadium, funded from additional fees for season tickets ("seat licenses") and increasing ticket prices for both fans and students alike to the highest in the nation. Similar premium seating (funded by major increases in ticket prices) was added to Crisler Arena (basketball) and Yost Arena (ice hockey). In addition there was further capital facilities growth fueled by philanthropy including a $150 million expansion of the Ross Business School, a $100 million gift for expansion of the Athletic Campus, and a $110 million gift toward a $180 million project to build a graduate residence hall, with a $261 million biological sciences building approved by the Regents in 2014 (although funding was specified only as "internal sources"...meaning debt-financed).

Of course, with such growth came both risk and controversy. The financing of the construction of new research facilities heavily dependent upon sponsored research support such as the Public Health addition faced the risk of declining federal research budgets. The massive scale of the new Mott Pediatrics Hospital ($750 million) quickly drove the budget of the University Hospitals into the red, with operating losses in excess of $200 million per year. The aggressive ticket pricing program of the Athletics Department, with ticket prices (including "seat licenses") averaging $230 per game in Michigan Stadium, drove many long-time faculty, staff, and townspeople season ticket-holders away, while student ticket prices (at $305 per season, the highest in the nation) and policies (open seating requiring queuing hours before game-time) quickly eroded student attendance. And while private giving stimulated further campus construction, donors

Venturi's early design for a "circus look" halo for Michigan Stadium

The Venturi Halo goes up...

The Venturi Halo comes down!

Venturi's UM Life Sciences Institute

Venturi's Yale Biomedical Research Laboratory

North Quad

Weill Hall

Life Sciences Institute

Biomedical Sciences Building

Ross School of Business Administration

Law School South Hall

Mott Children's Hospital

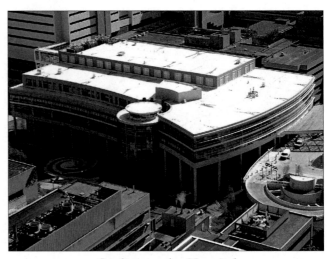

Cardiovascular Hospital

Hill Dining Hall

East Quad Renovation

Michigan Stadium

Chrisler Center

School of Nursing

Beyster Laboratory

Ross Addition to Business Administration

Munger Graduate Resident Hall

tended to give to their own priorities rather than the University's needs (e.g., the $140 M Munger graduate residence hall that was roundly panned by graduate students for its "dormitory-like character").

Many of the gift-funded facilities required substantial additional University contributions because of the nature of the gift (e.g., through pledges and bequests that led to present worth values that fell far short of the proclaimed size of the gift) and the requirement of further cost sharing by the University for the both the construction of the facility and its eventual operation. Here the lesson frequently overlooked was that large donors usually give money for what they want rather than what universities need, hence all too frequently incurring sizeable additional university expenses for resources only peripheral to academic priorities. It quickly became clear that the University had failed

to adequately assess the true cost of these building, resulting in considerable additional expenses.

There were also more general concerns. Most of the campus growth (75%), at least in terms of investment ($2.5 B), occurred in auxiliary units (i.e., clinical activities, housing, athletics) and were funded by auxiliary revenue streams, albeit with debt secured by student fee revenues. Those buildings responding to academic needs have generally depended upon anticipated federal research support (e.g., Public Health Annex) or private funding (Ross Business School, Weill Hall). This raised a serious question as to just how, in the absence of state support, the University could meet the future capital facilities needs of those academic units that had no donors or other external revenue sources (e.g., federal R&D).

Furthermore, the debt of the University rose to

$1.835 billion with an additional estimate of interest charges over the borrowing period as $577 million.

The Road Ahead

While capital facilities (or bricks and mortar) are necessary and important assets for the teaching, research, and service activities of a university, they also have other characteristics that can pose risks. For example, they sometimes have a monumental character, symbolizing the history and tradition of an institution. Hence they provide an important objective for university leaders, from deans to presidents to trustees, to build something designed by a "big name architect" to symbolize the impact of their leadership. In a similar way, many donors have an edifice complex, with the intent to mark the campus with a major facility bearing their name. It is perhaps not surprising that these other objectives sometimes conflict with the actual need for the building or the serious consideration of its construction and long-term operating costs.

A brief walk across the campuses of most prominent American research universities will quickly spot these architectural gems (or just as frequently, white elephants), although the assessment of whether they are really needed by the institution or adequately financed requires further analysis. This is particularly the case with buildings financed in part through gifts from donors in return for naming rights. As a rule of thumb, most universities set the gift requirement for naming a building after a donor as at least 50% of its construction costs. But there are two caveats here. Since donors frequently pay off their pledge over time, the actual value of their gift is usually much less. The long-term operating costs of a building today are estimated to be two to three times its construction costs. Hence, naming gifts for new construction typically walk the university out on a long limb of continued expenses many times the value of the gift itself.

Here the lesson is that universities should think very carefully about the financial burden they are assuming by building an edifice for a donor. They should at least demand a gift in excess of 50% of the actual construction costs in constant dollars. They might even consider seeking an additional endowment to provide further support for the operations of the facility.

Chapter 10

Technology

The University of Michigan has long provided national leadership for higher education in the application of technology to teaching and research. Perhaps no area illustrates this more vividly than its leadership in the development and application of computers and, more broadly, information and communications technologies. Michigan has not only easily adapted to each transformation in these technologies, but it has led in the transitions of early mainframe computers to timesharing to networked computer workstations to the Internet and today's global networks of data centers, search engines, big data, and open knowledge resources.

1950s and 1960s

During the post WWII era, Michigan was among the earliest universities to explore the use of the digital computers. Michigan faculty member Arthur Burkes participated in the development of the first electronic computer, ENIAC, and obtained a portion of this machine for display in the University's Computer Science and Engineering Building. The University's Willow Run Laboratories installed an early computer, MIDAC (Michigan Digital Automatic Computer) in 1952, but the use of computers in teaching and research really began with a series of IBM mainframe computers, the IBM 650, 704, and 7040, installed on campus during the 1950s and 1960s. University faculty members including Bernard Galler, Donald Katz, James Wilkes, and Brice Carnahan led the efforts to apply these computers to both teaching and research, developing the first courses in computer programing and later new academic degree programs such as Computer and Communications Sciences (in LS&A) and Computer Science and Engineering (in Engineering).

But more significantly, the University led in the development of the software for these computers, first developing the MAD (Michigan Algorithm Decoder) programming language in 1960 and then one of the first time-sharing operating systems, MTS (Michigan Terminal System), for building a University-wide network using the IBM 360/67 mainframe computer in 1966. The MTS system, operated by the University Computer Center directed by Robert Bartels, not only became the workhorse of the University's teaching and research activities, but soon was adopted by many other universities. (Wilkes, 2014)

The University's leadership in networking technology soon led to a statewide computer network, MERIT, (Michigan Education Research Information Triad), linking together the major universities in Michigan (initially UM, MSU, and WSU), which was to play a major role in creating the Internet in the 1980s.

1970s and 1980s

The University's time-sharing system continued to evolve through the 1970s and 1980s, moving from IBM mainframes to more powerful Amdahl computers, and gaining a reputation as one of the nation's leading computer environments for teaching and research. But the very success of the MTS system, its centralized structure, and its home-grown character, rapidly lost ground to the new generation of minicomputers such as Data Equipment Corporation's VAX minicomputer systems for science and engineering applications. By the end of the 1970s, most engineering and science departments at top research universities had acquired their own VAX systems. Yet, Michigan remained not only moored to the increasingly aging mainframe-based MTS system, but also to centrally administrated

138

From sliderules and calculators to Eniac to early IBM mainframes and finally to the Michigan Terminal System

computer policies that prevented academic programs from breaking away and acquiring more advanced computing environments. In fact, every purchase of a computer had to be approved by a central committee at the University.

This was a topic of personal interest, since Jim's own career had largely paralleled that of the digital computer. His particular area of research, nuclear energy systems (nuclear reactors, nuclear rockets, thermonuclear fusion), was not only heavily dependent upon state-of-the-art computing, but it had actually driven much of computer development. During the 1960s and 1970s much of this research was accomplished using Atomic Energy Commission supercomputers at AEC laboratories such as Los Alamos and Livermore. Although the research made use of the very fastest computers in the world, several of our faculty members (including Dick Phillips and Bill Powers of Aerospace

Engineering) stimulated interest in the use of the first microcomputers such as the TRS-80 and Apple II for instructional purposes. In fact, this led to one of the very first introductory computer courses on these systems in the late 1970s. From these experiences, it was clear that the College of Engineering simply had to break away from the University's MTS system and build its own computing environment, more suited to its needs. We were convinced that the digital computer would rapidly evolve from simply a tool for scientific computation and information processing into an information technology infrastructure absolutely essential to all of our activities, from research to instruction to administration. Hence, to build a leading engineering college, it would have to become a leader in information technology. This view was shared by many members of the College.

Dan Atkins assumed the leadership for this effort, assisted by Dick Phillips, Lynn Conway and other members of the faculty. They set a rather ambitious goal: To build the most sophisticated information technology environment of any engineering college in the nation, an environment that would continually push the limits of what could be delivered in terms of power, ease of use, and reliability to our students, faculty, and staff. The system was called CAEN, the Computer Aided Engineering Network, a name reflecting its functional architecture as a sophisticated information technology network integrating the College's instruction, research, and administrative activities together with both oncampus users (students, faculty, staff) and offcampus participants (industry, government, alumni). More technically, CAEN was envisioned as a distributed intelligence, hierarchical computing system linking personal computer workstations, superminicomputers, mainframe computers, function-specific machines (CAD/CAM, simulation) and gateway machines to national networks and facilities such as supercomputer centers. The network was designed to support not only general scientific computing, but computer-aided instruction, administrative services, and access to technical and bibliographic databases.

The College first had to fight a battle with the University administration to allow us to break away from the MTS system. Fortunately it was easy to convince Harold Shapiro and Bill Frye that they needed to encourage more diversity in computing, and in particular, allow some units to move far out on the curve of advanced computing as pathfinders for the rest of the University. Engineering and Business Administration were given the go-ahead to build their own environments (which would eventually lead to the disappearance of MTS, although it would take almost a decade).

The College of Engineering moved ahead with the transition from a mainframe time-sharing system to microcomputer/workstation networks by first providing every member of the faculty with a personal computer (a choice of either an IBM PC or an Apple II computer). Actually, there was an interesting wrinkle to this offer, since the College asked each faculty member also to take a second computer home, the rationale being the likelihood that their families would serve as an additional stimulus to become "computer literate". Interestingly enough, this program had unexpected

impact when the teenage sons of one faculty member became so adept at programming the Apple II computer brought home by their father, that they managed to develop commercially successful software for editing photographic images. You may have heard of the software…Adobe's Photoshop! (Tom Knoll and John Knoll together developed this software that revolutionized the field of digital photography. John Knoll later became a leader in the field of computer animation at George Lucas's Industrial Light and Magic and today is leader of CGI at the Walt Disney Company.)

The College next began to acquire several networked clusters of state-of-the-art computer workstations for research (Apollo, Sun, HP, Apple Lisas, Silicon Graphics). We faced a very major challenge in providing adequate computing resources for our students, since our large enrollments (6,000) would require a massive investment. To address this, we took two very important steps: We persuaded the University to allow us to charge students a special $100 per term computer user fee to help support their computing environment. This generated $1.5 million each year that we then could use to buy (or even debt-finance) computer equipment. We made absolutely certain that every penny of these fees (along with significant contributions from the College) went entirely to equip numerous student computing clusters that would be restricted solely for the use of students. To provide a vivid demonstration of just what the students were getting for their fees, we converted two large lecture rooms on the first floor of the Chrysler Center into a gigantic computer cluster, equipped with over 100 of the new Apple Lisa workstations. This was quite a sight—probably the largest collection of Apple Lisas that ever existed—and it really impressed the students. The College adopted the philosophy that these were the students' computers, without any constraints on how they could use them. Similar computer clusters were later distributed across the University.

The second element of the plan for students involved developing a mechanism to help them purchase their own personal computers, since we realized that the University would never have sufficient assets to equip all enrolled students. The College explored the possibility of negotiating very deep discounts (60% or more off list price) with key vendors such as Apple

From Apple II to IBM PCs to Apple Lisas to the Computer Aided Engineering Network (led by Dick Phillips, and Dan Atkins with the help of Steve Jobs) and finally the MacIntosh and beyond.

and IBM. They were quite willing to do this, but the principal hangup was with the University, nervous that the local computer stores might complain to the state legislature that we were undercutting their business. After considerable effort, we finally managed to convince Shapiro and Brinkerhoff that the leading universities would be achieving massive deployment of personal computers to students through such bulk discounts, and that Michigan would rapidly fall behind if we did not do the same. Since I suspected that the impact on local retailers would be very positive from the secondary hardware and software sales stimulated by the student program, the University negotiated a separate agreement with them to sell their wares when the students picked up their computers through the University. Since the first major deliveries occurred early in the fall, we began to call these events the Fall Computer Kickoff Sale. It was quite a hit with the students, particularly when new systems such as the Macintosh appeared. The number of University students acquiring their own computers began to increase rapidly, stimulating both the College and the University to install appropriate networking capability in the residence halls and University buildings.

The final step in bringing CAEN to the level of sophistication we had envisioned was made possible by a $2 million gift from General Motors that allowed us to acquire over 350 high-end computer workstations, connected with high speed networks, to serve the advanced needs of students and faculty. Our philosophy was simple: The College was determined to stay always at the cutting edge, but with a very strong service focus. It sought to remove all constraints on computing, with no limit whatsoever on student and faculty use. The College went with a multivendor environment, moving with whatever technology was most powerful.

Needless to say, these were highly controversial issues in the early 1980s, particularly at the University of Michigan. But as a result, by the mid-1980s the University could boast one of the most sophisticated computing environments in the world, a fact of major importance to recruiting outstanding faculty and students.

But more important, the leadership and experience of the University, both in the development of distributed workstation networks and in the statewide MERIT network led directed by Eric Aupperle, coupled with the recruiting of Douglas van Houweling as chief information officer, led to an effort to join with IBM and MCI (a 1980s telecom company) to compete successfully for a grant to build a national network (NSFnet) that would link the nation's scientists with the supercomputer centers of the National Science Foundation. The MERIT-IBM-MCI team was able to address the explosive use of this new network, growing at rates of 10% a month, both because of the Michigan experience and the decision to use the TCP-IP protocols developed by the Department of Defense Arpanet. Because of this success, the federal government supported the extension of the NSFnet scientific network to include other national networks, creating an "Internetwork", which would be managed by Michigan and its partners until the early 1990s. Of course, this was the Internet, which the Michigan team led through a new organization, Advanced Network Technologies, until it was finally spun off to the commercial sector in 1993.

1990s

The opening of the Media Union in 1996 was yet another significant and tangible commitment by the University of Michigan, in partnership with the State of Michigan, to provide all members of the University community access to some of the most sophisticated and transformational tools of the emerging digital revolution. Conceived as a model for "the university of the future", the North Campus deans viewed the Media Union project as an effort to create a physical environment to meet the rapidly changing character of teaching and research for many years to come, in a sense of "…designing a building full of unknowns."

The University retained the architectural firm descended from the famous architect, Albert Kahn, who had designed much of the University campus in the early 20th century, as well as many of the leading buildings in Detroit. The design team of deans, faculty, and staff responsible for the program of the new facility envisioned it as more akin to the MIT Media Lab for students and faculty of the North Campus academic programs. It was designed as a high-tech collection of studios, laboratories, workshops, performance venues and gathering and study space for students. Its original program statement in 1993 portrayed it as an Internet portal to the world (since the Internet was still rather new at that time). Although it was designed to provide space for the library collections of the College of Engineering and Schools of Art and Architecture, its function as a "traditional" book-based library was never a major part of the vision. Instead it was a place intended for collaboration and innovation in teaching and learning, a place where students, faculty, and staff could access a technology-rich environment, a place open to all "who dared to invent the future".

More specifically, the resulting 250,000 square foot facility, looking like a modern version of the Temple of Karnak, contained over 500 advanced computer workstations for student use. It had thousands of network jacks and wireless hubs for students to connect their laptops to work throughout the building or in its surrounding plazas and gardens during the summer. The facility contained a 500,000 volume library for art, architecture, science, and engineering, but perhaps more significantly, it was the site of several of the nation's major digital library projects (including the JSTOR project, the first of the national digital libraries). There was a sophisticated teleconferencing facility, design studios, visualization laboratories, and a major virtual reality complex. Since art, architecture, music, and theater students worked side-by-side with engineering students, the Media Union contained sophisticated recording studios and electronic music studios. It also had a state-of-the-art sound stage for digitizing performances, as well as numerous galleries for displaying the results of student creative efforts. To serve the unique needs of students and faculty in these areas, the Media Union was designed to open 24 hours a day, seven days a week, so that students have round-the-clock access to its facilities.

Over the past two decades since it opened, this facility "full of unknowns" has become the home for a large and evolving collection of new information and communications technologies far beyond the resources that any one school or college could acquire and maintain. The Media Union's collection of digital assets and resources requires constant renewal with the latest versions of software and hardware, and an expert team of professionals who enable U-M users to get up-to-speed and use them productively for innovative research and teaching. The Media Union rapidly became one of the most active learning spaces in the University, providing thousands of students with 7x24 hour access to rich resources including libraries, advanced technology, workshops, performance venues, and high quality study and community gathering spaces. The center has evolved into an innovative center for discovery, learning, invention, innovation, demonstration, and deployment utilizing state-of-the-art technologies and facilities and assisted by expert staff. In a sense, it serves as a new form of public good, an innovation commons, where students and faculty would come to work together with expert staff mentors to develop the skills and tacit learning acquired through studios, workshops, performance venues, and advanced facilities such as simulation and immersive environments. The Media Union encourages experimentation, tinkering, invention, and even play as critical elements of innovation and creative design.

Rationalizing significant investments in cutting-edge resources by enabling free access to a shared, expertly supported collection of assets has enabled a widespread culture of innovation in digital technologies at the U-M. Students and faculty are free both to envision and to lead, hands-on, change in disciplines being transformed by the digital revolution – from engineering, the performing and design arts, and medicine, to economics and government.

In 2004, in keeping with a long-standing tradition of naming an appropriate building after each former president, the Media Union was renamed the James and Anne Duderstadt Center, or more commonly known to students simply as "the Dude". Perhaps one student best captured the role of the center when asked to explain its purpose as: "The Dude is the place you go to make your dreams come true!"

The University also continued its leadership in advanced network technology. After spinning off University management of the Internet in 1993, Doug van Houweling launched a new initiative, Internet2, which created a consortium of research universities and companies to build and operate an advanced network for research purposes. The State of Michigan recognized the importance of this effort and invested $10 million to help it get up and running. For several years this effort

The Media Union (later named the Duderstadt Center) provided
state of the art cyberinfrastructure environments for students

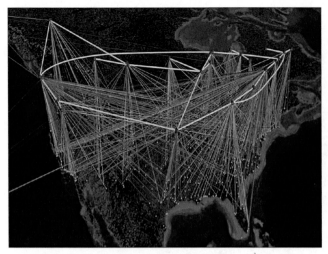

Internet 2 and the Abilene Computer Network

The Michigan Virtual University

was managed by the University of Michigan, until after a change in UM leadership, the leadership role was passed along to Indiana University.

During the 1990s the University seriously considered launching a "skunkworks" operation to explore and develop various paradigms for what a 21st Century university might become. Eventually, rather than building an independent research center, the University instead decided to take its smallest academic unit, the former School of Library Science, and put at its helm one of our most creative scientists, Dan Atkins, with the challenge of developing new academic programs in "knowledge management." The result was the rapid evolution—indeed, revolution—of this unit into a new School of Information, the first such academic program in the nation.

This new school was committed to developing leaders for the information professions who would define, create, and operate facilities and services enabling users to create, access, and use information they need. It intended to lead the way in transforming education for the information professions through an innovative curriculum, drawing upon the strengths of librarianship, information and computer science, business, organizational development, communication, and systems engineering. Its activities ranged from digital libraries to knowledge networks to virtual educational structures. Although initially launched as graduate programs at the M.S. and Ph.D. level, the School of Information broaden in later years to also offer undergraduate degrees.

In 1996 the University created a new institution, the Michigan Virtual Auto College, designed to explore the implications of digital technology for higher education. This was a collaborative effort among the University of Michigan, Michigan State University, the State of Michigan, the state's other colleges and universities, and the automobile industry. It was formed as a private, not-for-profit, 501(c)3 corporation to broker technology-enhanced courses and training programs for the automobile industry, including the Big 3 and Tier 1, 2, and 3 providers.

MVAC served as an interface between higher education institutions, training providers, and the automotive industry. It worked to facilitate the transfer of credits between and among institutions to facilitate certificate and degree attainment for those participating in courses and training programs offered under its auspices. MVAC offered courses and training programs, ranging from the advanced post-graduate education in engineering, computer technology, and business administration to entry level instruction in communications, mathematics, and computers. Capitalization for MVAC was provided by members of the partnership: the State of Michigan ($5 million), the universities ($2 million), and the automobile industry ($5 million). However it was expected that the effort would rapidly become self-supporting, based on student fees. The schedule for the MVAC was an aggressive one, with formal incorporation in fall of 1996, delivery of the first array of pilot courses by February, 1997 and a full curriculum in place by

Google Books

Hathi Trust

Fall of 1997. The MVAC paradigm was sufficiently successful that it broadened its curriculum into a full range of undergraduate curricula and was renamed the Michigan Virtual University in 1998, with participation by both public universities and community colleges throughout the state.

2000

University activities in the development of digital information and communications technology continued throughout the 2000s, although there were some minor setbacks. For example, the Internet2 project, founded by Douglas van Houweling to develop a consortium of institutions to build the next generation of the Internet, received little support with the arrival of a new University of Michigan administration in the late 1990s. The University's leadership role in this effort was assumed by Indiana University, and after further difficulties in receiving adequate support from Michigan, the headquarters of Internet2 was moved from Ann Arbor to Washington, DC.

On a more positive note, Daniel Atkins was asked to chair a major National Science Foundation blue ribbon commission on the future of cyberinfrastucture, the new term for the technology infrastructure provided by computer hardware, software, personnel, and policies. In a response to the recommendations of this study, the NSF invited Atkins to create a new Office of Cyberinfrastructure that managed the nation's efforts in areas such as advanced scientific computer and

software development. Atkins returned after several years to lead a similar effort to bring the University of Michigan to a leadership role in cyberinfrastructure development. Jim's own role included chairing a major National Academies study of the impact of computing on research universities and then assuming the chairmanship of the NSF Advisory Committee on Cyberinfrastructure.

Yet another major contribution of the University during the 2000s traces its antecedents to the 1990s when Michigan joined several other universities to examine the possibility of digital libraries for the National Science Foundation. Led by Randy Frank and Dan Atkins, the University already had the experience of building the JSTOR library of the Mellon Foundation for digital archiving and providing access to scholarly work in history and economics. Among the students working on NSF project was a young Michigan computer science student, Larry Page, who continued on to graduate school at Stanford (also part of the NSF digital library project), where he and Serge Brin developed the Page-Rank algorithm that was the key to the Google search engine.

In 2004 Page returned to Michigan and offered to have Google digitize our entire library (all 8 million volumes), which would become the nucleus of a major book search service by Google, now up to over 22 million volumes. Led by Paul Courant and John Price Wilkins, Michigan went beyond this to lead a group of universities and libraries (80 thus far) in pooling their digital collections to create the Hathi Trust ("Hathi"

Angell Haven Computer Clusters

Visualization stations

means "elephant" in Hindu), adding over 400,000 books a month to form the nucleus (already at 14 million books, with 5 million of these already open for full online access) of what could become a 21st century analog to the ancient Library of Alexandria. While many copyright issues still need to be addressed, it is likely that these massive digitization efforts will be able to provide full text access to a significant fraction of the world's written materials to scholars and students throughout the world within a decade. Michigan has also played an important role in opening up access to both scholarly publications and digital archives critical to the advancement of knowledge in an increasingly digital world.

Michigan has provided leadership in developing sophisticated course managements systems with its Sakai software, now serving as the learning system for several major universities and supporting the CTools system at the University. With this experience, the University was well positioned to participate in the emerging use of cyberinfrastructure on instruction through MOOCs (massively open online courses), first participation in the Coursera organization and later creating a new consortium, Unizen, for creating such online curriculum resources.

In the 2010s, Michigan joined with several other universities, national laboratories, and industry to create CASL, the first of the Department of Energy innovation hubs, a new research paradigm aimed at building government-university-industry partnerships to translate basic research into commercially valuable products. The $125 M CASL project (Consortium for Advanced Simulation of Light Water Reactors) goal was to use the world's fastest supercomputers (so-called exaflop technology, capable of 10^{18} arithmetic operations per second) to use fundamental physics to design the next generation of nuclear reactors. University faculty members William Martin and Tom Downer led the successful effort to development key elements of the key CASL product, the VERA virtual environment for reactor analysis.

Most recently, in 2015 the University announced a major $100 million effort to build an interdisciplinary research effort in "big data", involving the College of Engineering, the Medical School, the Institute for Social Research, and many other faculty across the University. A related project to couple data-intensive computing with supercomputing modeling and simulation was also launched with the assistance of the National Science Foundation.

Today's Concerns

The primary missions of the University, its teaching, research, and service activities (or alternatively, its activities of learning, discovery, and engagement with society) are increasingly dependent on cyberinfrastructure, i.e., information and communications technology. The rapid advances in these technologies are not only reshaping but creating entirely new paradigms for research, education, and application not only in science and engineering but

UM hosted NSF meeting on cyberinfrastructure

Daniel Atkins hosting NSF Session

in all of the academic and professional disciplines. It has been clear for sometime that to maintain world-class academic programs, the University must also achieve leadership in the quality and relevance of the cyberinfrastructure it provides at the level of each of its highly diverse teaching and research programs.

This is particularly challenging since the features of information technology such as processing speed, memory, and bandwidth, have been increasing in power at rates of 100 to 1,000 fold per decade since WWII. This is one of the major reasons for the continued surprises we get from the emergence of new applications–the Internet, social networks, big data, machine learning–appearing in unexpected ways at a hyper exponential pace. We have learned time and time again that it makes little sense to simply extrapolate the present into the future to predict or even understand the next "tech turn". These are not only highly disruptive technologies, but they are highly unpredictable. Ten years ago nobody would have imagined Google, Facebook, Twitter, etc., and today, nobody really can predict what will be a dominant technology even five years ahead, much less ten!

In 2013 the University of Michigan hosted a major conference concerning the impact of rapidly evolving cyberinftrastructure on the activities of discovery, innovation, and learning. The workshop convened an unusually broad spectrum of thought leaders from multiple disciplines and venues of research, technology development, and education to consider the changing nature of cyber-enabled learning and discovery in broad terms, spanning learning at all levels and institutions and discovery including research, development, innovation, invention, design, and creativity.

The topics considered by the Michigan workshop considered the impact of powerful technologies such as always-on, ubiquitous connectivity (anywhere, anytime, everyone); social networking, crowd sourcing, collaborative learning and discovery, functionally complete cyberinfrastructures, emerging learning paradigms such as massively open online courses (MOOCs), cognitive tutors, gaming, immersive experiences; big data, data-intensive discovery, learning analytics, intelligent software agents: and possible surprises such as cognitive implants. Of particular concern were the impact of emerging technologies capable of transforming learning institutions (schools, colleges, workplace training, lifelong learning, open learning) and paradigms (from learning about, to learning to do, to learning to become). Similarly consideration was given to the way in research paradigms were likely to change (Pasteur's Quadrant, citizen scientists, crowd sourcing, open knowledge). In particular, the workshop roundtable was challenged to suggest a framework for the conduct of research concerning the impact of possible emerging technologies on the conduct of scientific research, technological innovation, and STEM education. Of particular interest was the identification of possible advances in technology that could radically transform the existing paradigms for these activities.

Many participants stressed the importance of

"craft", of the contributions of truly talented staff who drive innovation in units where they are most competent. These people are attracted to universities such as Michigan to work in academic units with faculty and students where they are highly valued and have the freedom to do exciting work. In fact, its great strength and contribution to society arises from this very unusual diversity in ideas, experiences, and people. Again, this argues for an organic plan, essentially a diverse ecosystem that will continue to mutate and evolve in ways that we cannot anticipate.

Just what purposes should drive IT strategy. To support the university mission? What mission? Of the University writ large? Of the academic units? Of generic language like teaching, research, and service… or discovery, learning, and engagement…or "Change the world!"…or what?

What should be the focus on solutions that are easily created and replaced? Agility to be sure. But what about resilience? And maturity? What about "optimum redundancy", so important to academic processes. For example, while Michigan formed a partnership with Google in 2012 at the enterprise level to Google, it soon learned that relations with companies with "startup" encountered difficulties in the support of "mission critical" applications such as university instruction. The University learned to be careful about becoming overly dependent on companies still embracing a "startup", e.g., high-risk, culture.

Who should the University regard as priorities for IT services? Students? Faculty? Staff? Administrators? New learning paradigms such as blended education; experiential, personalized learning. Actually, all of these activities have been part of the university's portfolio since the 19th century! Even the massive markets enabled by MOOCs is not really new. UM TV was teaching courses for credit with over 100,000 students through live TV in the early 1950s.

What is the appropriate strategy for enterprise-wide IT development? Most of the University's IT Strategic Plan is aimed at providing a cyberinfrastructure environment on campus. But the anyplace-anytime character of today's world leaves hanging the majority of the time spent working by our students, faculty, and staff, which is off campus in their homes, dorms, cars, wherever. Without a major plan for high-speed connectivity throughout the community, this is a very incomplete strategy. Most of the strategic investments associated with the NextGen infrastructure seem to be focused on-campus…WiFi networks, high capacity networks in data centers, labs, etc., use of clouds. But most of the time our people (faculty, students, staff) will be tethered to our resources through 4 MB/s cable or telcom carriers. Hence, without robust connectivity beyond the campus, these major investments will fall far short of our needs.

Where is the subject of institutional collaboration? Today our faculty work more with colleagues on the other side of the globe than across the hall; our students bring multi-institution study groups with them from their high school days…and Facebook, of course…most of our faculty are nomadic, moving from institution to institution every few years, just as our students will move on to other endeavors and institutions when they finish their studies. Again, more consideration needs to be given of life beyond the campus…and with institutions beyond our own.

Too much of the current focus is shaped by today's technologies, not tomorrow's. Cloud services, big data, analytics. Again, overdependence on commodity products, particularly to the degree we constrain the cyber environments of academic units through policies such as purchasing and shared services, will harm the loosely coupled adaptive culture of the university that is one of our greatest strengths. This is particularly dangerous if we become overly dependent on particular vendors because of top-down rather than bottom-up forces. The reality is (and always has been) that it has been our faculty, staff, and students who spot the next big trends in technology and then drive change upward through the institution.

It is becoming increasingly clear that we are approaching an inflection point in the potential of rapidly evolving information and communications technology to transform how the scientific and engineering enterprise does knowledge work, the nature of the problems it undertakes, and the broadening of those able to participate in research activities.

Arden Bement, Director of the National Science Foundation stressed that , "We are entering a second revolution in information technology, one that may well usher in a new technological age that will dwarf, in sheer transformational scope and power, anything we have yet experienced in the current information age". (Bement, 2007) The implications of such rapidly evolving technology for the future of the discovery, innovation, and learning are of great importance to the prosperity, health, and security of our nation as it faces the challenge of an increasingly knowledge-and innovation-driven world. Such cyberinfrastructure will not only be increasingly important to higher education, but it will drive the evolution of the university as a knowledge institution.

The Road Ahead

Fortunately, the University of Michigan has been able to respond to such rapid technological change in the past–and, indeed, achieved leadership–because it has functioned as a loosely coupled adaptive system with many of our academic units given not only the freedom, but also the encouragement, to experiment and to try new things. We have intentionally avoided the dangers of centralizing these activities, although every once in awhile someone tries to recentralize, e.g., riding the MTS mainframe model while the rest of the world was switching to minicomputers (PDPs and VAXs) and microcomputers, or overly constraining university-wide IT with models appropriate for the business world but highly constraining, indeed disastrous, for research and teaching. We must be very careful to learn from these past mistakes and not go down these roads again.

To be sure, the tension between centralization (whether MTS or "rationalization") and decentralization (where cacophony leads to innovation) can be very threatening, particularly to those parts of the University that need to make the trains run on time (e.g., financial services, hospitals, etc.) Fortunately, in the past, the wisdom of maintaining a loosely coupled adaptive system at the academic level finally bubbles up to the leadership of the institution, and academic units are set free once again. An example here was when Harold Shapiro set Engineering and Business Administration free to develop networks of powerful workstations as the alternative to the MTS-Amdahl time-sharing system. One of the results was CAEN, which rapidly evolved beyond MIT's Athena and CMU's Andrew systems to achieve leadership.

Some particular warnings here are appropriate. It is important not to attempt to standardize the campus cyberinfrastructure environment. The university in general–and Michigan in particular–is one of the most intellectual diverse organizations in the world. In fact, its great strength and contribution to society arises from this very unusual diversity in ideas, experiences, and people. Again, this argues for a much more organic plan, essentially a diverse ecosystem that will continue to mutate and evolve in ways that we cannot anticipate.

While dependence on commodity services, particularly those provided through the cloud, can be cost-effective, it can also become highly constraining for the creative enterprise that characterizes research universities. Overdependence on commodity products can become debilitating to the academic process, particularly to the degree we constrain the cyber environments of academic units through policies such as purchasing and shared services, that can harm the loosely coupled adaptive culture of the university that is one of our greatest strengths. This is particularly dangerous if we become overly dependent on particular vendors because of top-down rather than bottom-up forces. The reality is (and always has been) that it has been our faculty, staff, and students who spot the next big trends in technology and then drive change upward through the institution.

To be sure, the University has important responsibilities that require mission critical computing. But it is at the level of academic units rather than the enterprise level where innovation and leadership must occur. Why? Because they are driven by learning and discovery, by experimentation, by tolerance for failure, and by extraordinarily talented faculty, students, and particularly, staff. While sometimes duplicative and inefficient, it has made MIT, Carnegie Mellon, and Stanford leaders, as well as Michigan with CAEN and MERIT (i.e., NSFnet and then the Internet).

In a sense, it is amazing that the university has been able to readily adapt to these extraordinary transformations of its most fundamental activities, learning and scholarship, with its organization and structure largely intact. Here one might be inclined to observe that technological change tends to evolve much more rapidly than social change, suggesting that a social institution such as the university that has lasted a millennium is unlikely to change on the timescales of tech turns, although social institutions such as corporations have learned the hard way that failure to keep pace can lead to extinction. Yet, while social institutions may respond more slowly to technological change, when they do so, it is frequently with quite abrupt and unpredictable consequences, e.g., "punctuated evolution".

Admittedly, futurists have a habit of overestimating the impact of new technologies in the near term and underestimating them over the longer term. There is a natural tendency to implicitly assume that the present will continue, just at an accelerated pace, and fail to anticipate the disruptive technologies and killer apps that turn predictions topsy-turvy. Yet, we also know that far enough into the future, the exponential character of the evolution of Moore's Law technologies such as info-, bio-, and nano- technology makes almost any scenario possible.

Organization, Leadership, and Governance

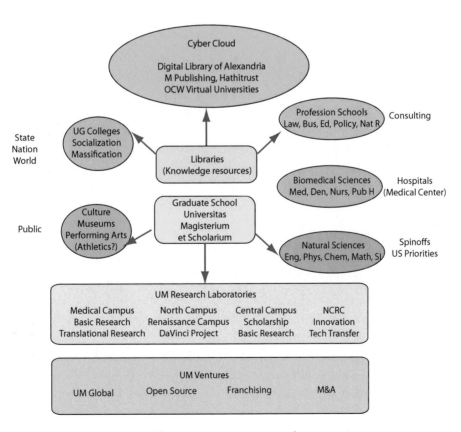

A diagram of the 21st Century research university

Chapter 11

Organization

The nature of the contemporary university and the forces that drive its evolution are complex and frequently misunderstood. The public still thinks of us in very traditional ways, with images of students sitting in large classrooms listening to faculty members lecture on subjects such as literature or history. The faculty thinks of Oxbridge—themselves as dons, and their students as serious scholars. The federal government sees another R&D contractor or health provider—a supplicant for the public purse. And armchair America sees the university on Saturday afternoon as yet another quasi-professional athletic franchise. The reality is far different—and far more complex.

The classic and highly simplified triad of higher education, of teaching, research, and service, branches extensively. Once during a planning exercise at Michigan during the 1980s, we attempted to list the various activities of the university in the hopes that we might be able to red-pencil all but the most important of these activities—our "core competencies"—in our efforts to reallocate limited resources. Our brainstorming sessions led to a network of activities that went on for pages and pages. After identifying these multiple missions, we asked the planning group to cross off all but the most critical activities. Not surprisingly, we managed to cross out only a few of the items on the list. All of the other activities were felt to be essential by someone in the group. (And those we had marked out were later reinstated by several members, after further reflection.)

This branching network of multiple missions creates a very different image of the modern research university than that commonly perceived by students, faculty, or society: that of a very complex, international conglomerate of highly diverse businesses. To illustrate, consider a simple organizational diagram of "business lines" of the University of Michigan, Inc.

The University of Michigan, with an annual budget of roughly $7 billion per year, and an additional $15 billion of assets under active investment management, would rank roughly 350th on the Fortune 500 list. The University educates over 70,000 students on its several campuses at any given time. This would correspond to an educational business line with a budget of roughly $3.5 billion per year. The University is also a major federal R&D laboratory conducting over $1.3 billion a year of research, supported primarily from federal contracts and grants. Its health care system averages two million patent visits per year in its various hospitals, providing care to a population of two million, and characterized by a $3.0 billion budget. The university's activities are truly international in scope, providing educational, research, and service activities throughout the world through both an array of partnerships with institutions abroad as well as through Internet services. Even its sports entertainment business line, the Michigan Wolverines, has scale more comparable to professional franchises with a budget of $150 million–even larger since Michigan Stadium's capacity of 115,000 is the largest in the nation. Other characteristics of note include 36,000 employees, an endowment of $10 billion, and over 36 million square feet of facilities.

The University of Michigan has become actively involved in providing a wide array of knowledge services, from degree programs offered in Shanghai, Hong Kong, Seoul, and Paris, to cyberspace-based products such as online continuing education and massively open online courses (MOOCs). In fact, Michigan played a leading role in building and managing the Internet in the 1980s and 1990s, and

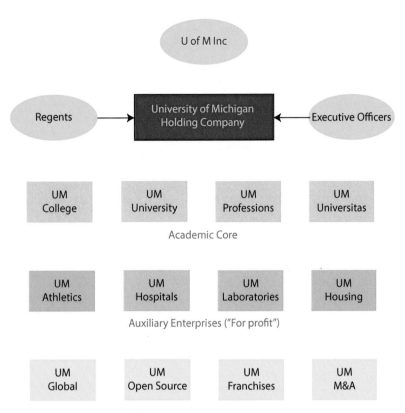

Michigan's "corporate" structure

today it is the world's leader in capturing, curating, and archiving digital materials, as evidenced by its creation and management of the HathiTrust, the largest digital library in the world with over 14 million volumes.

The corporate organization chart shown above would compare in both scale and complexity with many major global corporations. And it is not unique to Michigan. Most of the major research universities in America are characterized by very similar organizational structures, indicative of their multiple missions and diverse array of constituencies. The contemporary university has become one of the most complex institutions in modern society. It is comprised of many activities, some non-profit, some publicly regulated, and some operating in intensely competitive marketplaces. It teaches students; conducts research for various clients; provides health care; engages in economic development; stimulates social change; and provides mass entertainment (athletics). It is far more complicated than any corporate structure, not only in missions but frequently also in extent, spanning the world in both activities and influence in both the public and private sectors.

1950s-1970s

As we have noted, the early years following WWII were a time of rapid growth for American colleges and universities, sustained by strong public support from both states and the federal government for expanding academic programs, building campuses, funding research, and supporting students. Fortunately, during the 1930s and 1940s, Michigan's Alexander Ruthven had transformed the earlier "headmaster" character of University leadership into more of a corporate model, expanding the number of executive officers to handle the growing activities of the institution and utilizing Regents as a true board of directors. Of particular note here was the emergence of Wilbur Pierpont, a former faculty member in the Business School, as a wise and effective chief financial officer capable of guiding and financing the growth of the University throughout the 1950s and 1960s.

Hence when Harlan Hatcher arrived from Ohio State in 1952, there were relatively few changes that he needed to make in the organization, where most resource decisions were made at the executive office

154

The University of Michigan's Ann Arbor Campus (2014)

and Regent level. Put in simplest terms, each year the University would drive its budget "truck" up to Lansing, fill it with generous state support, and then drive it back and distribute it among the deans and directors of the various academic program and auxiliary activities. To be sure, many of these units were led by powerful and visionary deans capable of building both the quality and size of their programs. But since most support came from state appropriations and research grants, they had relatively little control of their overall funding.

Robben Fleming inherited this organization when he arrived in the late 1960s, but already changes were appearing on the horizon. The growth of other public colleges and universities in the state–particularly Michigan State University–provided strong competition for state funding. State support of campus construction stalled with new government policies that threatened the University's constitutional autonomy. And campus activism and occasional disruption weakened state priorities for the support of higher education. Hence Fleming acted early to reorganize his executive officer team, distributing more broadly both the responsibilities and accountability for controlling the resources of the University. Key in this was the creation of two

powerful executive officer committees, the Committee on Budget Administration, chaired by the Provost and Vice President for Academic Affairs of the University, who assumed the role as both chief academic officer and chief budget officer of the University, and the Plant Extension Committee, chaired by the chief financial officer, who presided over the buildings, grounds, and construction projects of the campus. Again expressed in simplified terms, in this system the role of the president became that of generating the money to support the University, the provost had the power to determine how these dollars would be spent, and the chief financial officer had the responsibility to make certain the dollars would be spent the way the provost wanted them to be.

This new system clearly made the provost at Michigan not only second-in-command to the president, but as both chief budget officer and chief academic officer, one of the most powerful such positions in the country. As Fleming once put it, "If you start out as a president with a VPAA and VPCFO who are superb people, you are about three-quarters of the way down the path of success, because these are your critical areas." Fortunately during the Fleming years the role of provost was assumed by three individuals of truly extraordinary ability: Allen Smith, former Dean of the

Harlan Hatcher

Robben Fleming

Harold Shapiro

Allan Smith

Frank Rhodes

Billy Frye

Wilbur Pierpont

James Brinkerhoff

Farris Womack

Law School; Frank Rhodes, former Dean of LS&A; and Harold Shapiro, former chair of Economics. Note that all would later assume critical university leadership roles, Smith as interim Michigan president, Rhodes as president of Cornell University, and Shapiro as president of both Michigan and Princeton. Similarly, Fleming's two VPCFOs, first Wilbur Pierpoint and then James Brinkerhoff, were highly regarded as among the very best financial officers in the nation.

Interestingly enough, despite their power, the Michigan provosts of the 1970s not only appointed deans and directors of unusual ability, but they also began a gradual process of transferring more and more control over resources, appointments, and policy to them in their leadership roles of academic and administrative units. They realized that as the University continued to grow while becoming ever more complex, and the erosion of state support would require more diverse sources of revenues, most of which would be generated by the deans and their units (e.g., tuition revenue, research grants, and private gifts), the capacity of the executive to manage the institution through centralized authority was no longer advisable or even practical.

1980s-1990s

To set the framework for the further evolution of the organization of the University during the 1980s and 1990s, it is important to remember one of its most unusual and important characteristics: constitutional autonomy. Because the University had already been in existence for two decades before the State of Michigan entered the Union in 1837, and because of the frontier society's deep distrust of politics and politicians, the new state's early constitution in 1850 granted the university an unusual degree of autonomy as a "coordinate branch of state government". Michigan's constitution delegated full powers over all university matters granted to the University's governing board of regents, although surprisingly enough it did not state the purpose of the university.

This constitutional autonomy, together with the fact that the university traces its origins to an act of Congress rather than a state legislature, has shaped an important feature of the university's character. Throughout its history the university has regarded itself as much as a

national university as a state university. Furthermore, Michigan's constitutional autonomy, periodically reaffirmed through court tests and constitutional conventions, has enabled the university to have much more control over its own destiny than most other public universities.

Hence, it should not be surprising that the various academic units of the University also evolved with a strong sense of autonomy over their academic objectives and decisions. To be sure, the Executive Officers and Regents of the University had final authority, but this was generally exercised with considerable restraint to allow deans, directors, and chairs significant authority.

This decentralization of authority and autonomy throughout the University became even more important as state support began to erode in the late 1970s. By the 1990s, more than 90% of the resources supporting the institution were generated by the actions of individual units rather than by the central administration. Hence it was natural to cede even more authority over expenditures along with responsibility and accountability for costs incurred to the deans and directors of the University's various units. An open market strategy evolved where deans and directors were given the freedom as customers to decide for themselves where centralized services were more efficient and cost-effective than using outside vendors (e.g., facilities maintenance, communications services, etc.)

This realignment of both resource control and cost responsibility to the lowest levels of the organization where they occurred most naturally was key to the ability of the University to adapt to the very considerable financial pressures it would face by the late 20th Century. Michigan's long tradition of institutional autonomy positioned it well for such decentralization, a philosophy that was eventually adopted by many other public universities facing serious erosion of state support.

Yet such decentralization has occasionally had a negative impact, particularly when it has allowed the auxiliary units of the University (e.g., those without public support) to effectively decouple from the institution. At Michigan there is some truth to the old saying that the academic core of the contemporary university is a quite fragile institution striving to survive between the pressures exerted by the football stadium on one end of the campus and the university hospital on the other. But more serious is the issue of how one sustains the highest priority for the academic core of the university in an increasingly resource-driven (and for many academic units, resource-starved) environment constrained by "fund accounting", in which it is increasingly difficult to provide cross-subsidies from one unit to another (and particularly from auxiliary units to academic units).

During the 1980s and 1990s, the University had evolved into a highly adaptable knowledge conglomerate. Put another way, Michigan's organization culture had become a loosely coupled, adaptive ecosystem that evolved and excelled based on the extraordinary talents, dreams, and commitment of faculty, staff, and students. In particular, faculty members were provided with the freedom, the encouragement, and the incentives to move toward personal goals in highly flexible ways. One might even suggest that the University had become, in an organizational sense, an intellectual holding company of faculty entrepreneurs, who drove the evolution of the University to fulfill their individual goals. A transactional culture had emerged in which everything was up for negotiation–except for fundamental academic values. The university administration saw its role as managing the university as a highly decentralized federation. It had set some general ground rules and regulations, acted as an arbiter, raised money for the enterprise, and tried—with limited success—to keep activities roughly coordinated. In fact, university leaders viewed their role as less similar to that of a corporate manager and more akin to that of a conductor of an orchestra comprised of highly skilled and highly valuable knowledge professionals.

2000s

Although Michigan's high degree of decentralization of authority and responsibility had been key to its quality and capacity, allowing the University to enhance academic quality even while losing state support, this culture proved difficult for new university leaders and administrators to accept, coming as most did from other universities and experiences (including several from the business world). It was not surprising

that beginning the late 1990s and continuing into the 2010s, numerous efforts were launched to attempt to impose practices from the corporate sector to recentralize authority within the institution. For example, following the recommendation of business consultants, the University attempted to adopt a "shared services" organization, where key staff were pulled out of academic units and placed in central organizations to provide "commodity" services such as personnel, financial, and procuring activities. A similar approach was launched in the information technology area through a "rationalization" process that attempted to force the adoption of commodity technologies and extract key staff from the academic units to support University-wide services.

Yet another approach to centralize power in the University involved imposing heavy taxes on the expenditures of the academic units to support central services, particularly burdensome at a time when both staffing and compensation in the central administration were increasing rapidly.

Finally, and perhaps most damaging, the central administration launched a major effort to recruit an increasing number of external candidates for deans and executive officers (roughly 70% of administrative appointments during the decade of the 2000s came from outside the University) in an effort to dilute the long-standing Michigan culture of powerful deans that had been handed down through generations of internal appointments.

To be sure, the tension between centralization (e.g., to achieve efficiency) and decentralization (where cacophony leads to innovation) can be very threatening, particularly to those parts of the University that need to make sure that the trains run on time (e.g., financial services, hospitals, etc.) They prefer a coordinated approach at the enterprise level, a so-called "rationalization" of services that seeks to reduce redundancy with strong central control. Yet while this approach might work well in corporate settings, it began to damage the University by pulling some of the best staff away from the academic units where the real innovation is driven by the interests of faculty and students working closely with outstanding staff with extraordinary skills. Similarly, to impose on the University's academic programs a central administration unable to respond rapidly to the unique needs and technologies required for cutting-edge learning and discovery would threaten the University's leadership as a pathfinder and trailblazer. In sharp contrast to business enterprises, technological diversity and redundancy is frequently a requirement for the conduct of world-class academic programs.

But there was one other important organizational characteristic that disappeared during the 2000s and 2010s: the availability of open, accurate, pervasive, and accessible information throughout the entire University. After all, a university is the ultimate knowledge organization, and any attempt to hide, distort, or manipulate information can seriously damage its most fundamental activities of discovery, learning, and engagement.

To be sure, such an open form of communications can be alien to those from activities such as advertising, marketing, public relations, fund raising, and politics. Yet without complete access to accurate information– both good news and bad news–universities are seriously hindered. Any attempt to sequester information, replacing truth with fiction, or attempting to propagate myths or distortions to further a particular agenda should be challenged and revealed as damaging to the academic process. This is particularly important in these times when the role of the traditional media supporting investigative journalism and openness has been challenged by the pervasive character of electronic media and social networking.

The effort of the 2000s and beyond to launch a massive communications, public relations, marketing, and branding effort that emerged at Michigan with the goal of "institutional advancement" in reality represented an attempt to manipulate both internal and external opinions. It rapidly became not only an extraordinarily expensive endeavor, growing to over 600 staff by 2015, but it also engaged in highly inappropriate and damaging activities to the long-standing traditions and quality of the University. While such media manipulation is common in the world of commerce or politics, it has no place on any university campus, since it corrupts the university's fundamental goals of *veritas et lux*, e.g., "truth and light".

However, from a more positive viewpoint, the inability of recent administrations to tame the decentralization of the University provides strong evidence that today the institution is so large and complex that as a loosely coupled adaptive ecosystem, it can no longer be managed through top-down directives. Like other complex biological systems, it has developed the capacity to reject "invasive species" that try to change its culture (or in other terms, its "institutional saga"). It is quite capable of defending itself against attacks both from the inside and outside.

For example, when a former corporate CEO attempted to transform the Michigan athletics program into a commercial entertainment business, he quickly encountered the long tradition of a highly decentralized but dedicated Michigan community that insisted upon traditional values, including not only longstanding and loyal fans, but also students and faculty. In a sense, the University responded by repelling this "invasive species" and terminating its leadership. There are numerous other examples when externally-recruited leadership of academic programs, deans and department chairs, have attempted to acquire the power to radically challenge the Michigan grass-roots culture and have found themselves quickly repelled and rejected.

The Road Ahead

The trail-blazer character of the Michigan saga demands a risk-tolerant environment in which initiatives are encouraged at all levels among students, faculty, and staff. For example, the university intentionally distributes resources among a number of pots, so that entrepreneurial faculty with good ideas rarely have to accept "no" as an answer but instead can simply turn to another potential source of support.

The most important play in the Michigan playbook for entrepreneurs is the end-run, since the University culture not only tolerates but encourages faculty, students, and staff to bypass bureaucratic barriers. For example, it is quite common for faculty to bypass deans and appeal directly to the provost or president, just as many, including the deans–and occasionally even a coach or athletic director–will occasionally find opportunities to execute an end-run to the Regents, a relatively easy thing to do since half of them live in Ann Arbor. Once faculty, chairs, and deans learn the

Michigan culture, they quickly learn that the university also tolerates end-runs to state or federal government, e.g., the governor, legislature, congress, or federal agencies. To be sure, sometimes a senior administrator might growl at them–particularly the vice-president for government relations worried about coordinating university relations with the state, or a president worried about inappropriate influence on a Regent. Most Michigan presidents soon learn that since these end-runs are so ingrained in the culture of the university, they will happen quite naturally, and attempts to stifle them are likely to be not only ineffective but could discourage many of the most creative, loyal, and well-intentioned people in the university. Hence it is far better to accept the end-run as a University tradition. It has been suggested that some Michigan presidents even quietly encouraged this practice, since they had used it quite effectively themselves during their earlier roles as faculty members and deans!

Perhaps because of this long tradition of decentralization–even anarchy–university-wide faculty governance through a faculty senate has been relatively ineffective at Michigan. Just as with the administration, the real power among the faculty and the ability to have great impact on the institution resides at the school, college, or department level, where powerful senior faculty, executive committees, chairs, and deans have the authority to address the key challenges and opportunities facing their academic programs. Should this power structure become distorted with poor appointments or weak faculty, the end-run culture acts as a check and balance by rapidly communicating such problems up or around the chain of command to the provost, president, or even the Regents.

From this discussion, it should be apparent that a top-down leadership style is quite incompatible with the Michigan culture. Those presidents who have chosen to ignore this reality or attempted to reign in this distributed power, to tame the Michigan anarchy, have inevitably failed, suffering a short tenure with inconsequential impact.

Not to suggest that Michigan will tolerate a weak president. Presidents unable to adapt to the Michigan trailblazing saga, who are hesitant to push all the chips into the center of the table on a major initiative or incapable of keeping pace with the high energy level of the campus, will soon be rejected–or at least ignored–by the faculty. Michigan embraces bold visions, and without these, effective leadership is simply impossible. But, as we have stressed, the University's history strongly suggests that such visions arise most naturally from the grassroots efforts of the faculty, students, and staff involved in academic activities that, in turn, are embraced and supported by the leadership rather than imposed from on high.

Of course, Michigan probably represents one of the extremes of a highly decentralized academic anarchy, although many other institutions with exceptionally strong faculty lie in a similar regime of the governance spectrum. There are other institutions that not only tolerate strong, centralized leadership but actually require it. Some are at an early stage of evolution and require strong, top-down leadership to set the priorities and make the tough lifeboat decisions to move the institution to the next rung in quality.

While the extreme decentralization of authority and accountability throughout the University was radical when introduced in the 1980s and 1990s in response to the decline in centrally obtained resources such as state support, it aligned well with the increasing complexity and scale of the University that evolved beyond centralized control. Hence, the message that today should be provided to all new leadership recruited from outside is that "Michigan exists today and must remain highly decentralized in authority, and its evolution must be driven by the talent, achievements, and goals of faculty, students, and staff at the grass-roots level. Don't attempt to challenge this. Learn how to live with it!"

Yet, as the influence of powerful forces such as the changing needs of society, globalization, and technology reshape the activities of the university, one can expect its organization and structure to continue to evolve, albeit while preserving its decentralized character. Many research universities are already evolving into so-called "core in cloud" organizations in which academic departments or schools conducting elite education and basic research, are surrounded by a constellation of quasi-academic organizations— research institutes, think tanks, corporate R&D centers—that draw intellectual strength from the core university and provide important financial, human, and

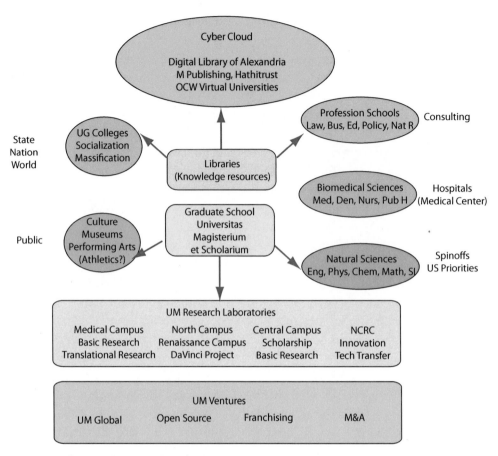

The University of Michigan as a "Core-in-Cloud" Organization

physical resources in return. Such a structure reflects the blurring of basic and applied research, education and training, the university and broader society.

More specifically, while the academic units at the core retain the traditional university culture of faculty appointments, tenure, and intellectual traditions, for example, disciplinary focus, those organizations evolving in the cloud can be far more flexible and adaptive. They can be multidisciplinary and project focused. They can be driven by entrepreneurial cultures and values. Unlike academic programs, they can come and go as the need and opportunity arise. And, although it is common to think of the cloud being situated quite close to the university core, in today's world of emerging electronic and virtual communities, there is no reason why the cloud might not be widely distributed, involving organizations located far from the campus. In fact, as virtual universities become more common, there is no reason that the core itself has to have a geographical focus. It could exist in cyberspace, independent of space and time.

To some degree, the core-in-cloud model revitalizes core academic programs by stimulating new ideas and interactions. It provides a bridge that allows the university to better serve society without compromising its core academic values. But, like the entrepreneurial university, it can also scatter and diffuse the activities of the university, creating a shopping mall character with little coherence. And it can create a fog that distorts the true nature of the university by the public.

If these institutions are to respond to future challenges and opportunities, the modern university must engage in a more strategic process of change. While the natural evolution of a learning organization may still be the best model of change, it must be guided by a commitment to preserve its fundamental values and mission. Universities must find ways to allow its most creative people at the grassroots level to drive their future. The challenge is to tap the great source of creativity and energy associated with this natural entrepreneurial activity in a way that preserves the university's core missions, characteristics, and values.

Appendix for Chapter 11
A Handy-Dandy List of UM Operating Principles

How is the University of Michigan organized and managed?

1. The University of Michigan is a "loosely coupled, adaptive system," with a growing complexity, as its various components respond to changes in its environment. This entrepreneurial character of the university has made it remarkably adaptive and resilient.

2. The University provides faculty with the freedom, the encouragement, and the incentives to move toward their personal goals in highly flexible ways. One might even view the organization of a university–particular research universities–as a holding company of faculty entrepreneurs, who drive the evolution of the university to fulfill their individual goals.

3. The university administration manages the modern university as a federation. It sets some general ground rules and regulations, acts as an arbiter, raises money for the enterprise, and tries—with limited success—to keep activities roughly coordinated. In fact leading a university is less similar to that of a corporate manager and more akin to that of a conductor of an orchestra comprised of highly skilled and highly valuable knowledge professionals.

4. Budget authority is delegated to the lowest level where assets are acquired and costs are incurred. (Typically this is at the level of deans and directors.)

5. The most important voice for academic priorities usually comes from the deans, particularly when acting as a group. For this reason, every effort should be made to encourage the deans and provost to function as a true team.

6. Faculty governance works most effectively at the level of department, school, and college executive committees. In contrast to the Senate Assembly or SACUA, the executive committees are generally comprised of UM's strongest faculty.

7. The free flow of information is absolutely critical to the success of the loosely-coupled character of the University. Attempts to keep bad news in confidence and promote only good news (or exaggerated information) may benefit a few individuals but will seriously harm the University over the long term.

How do faculty get things done around here.?

Rule 1: NEVER accept "no" for the answer to a request. In a highly decentralized organization, there are lots of folks who may have the capacity to say "yes".

Rule 2: The most important play in the Michigan playbook is the "end run"…around chairs to deans, around deans to provosts, around presidents to Regents, and around the University to Lansing, Washington, or donors. Administrators should never try to block this, since the University would soon cease to function as an entrepreneurial organization.

Rule 3: it is usually better to seek forgiveness than ask permission.

Rule 4: Under no circumstances should faculty (or academic leaders) allow themselves to be constrained by staff in areas unrelated to core activities (e.g., development, communications, public relations, government relations). These individuals work to support the academic units, not to constrain them.

Some operating rules for UM academic leaders.

1. In simplest terms, the president's job is to raise the money, the provost's job is to determine how to spend it, and the VPCFO's job is to make certain folks spend it the way the provost wants them to. In hierarchy, the president trumps the provost, and the provost trumps everybody else.

2. It is critical that any administrators with major authority have strong backgrounds in higher education… or at least supervisors with such backgrounds.

3. To reaffirm the role of the provost, both the Committee on Budget Administration and the Budget Pri-

orities Committee should be reinstituted and chaired by the provost.

4. Because of the decentralization of the University, every effort must be made to benchmark all operations against best practices at other institutions (e.g., funding, staffing, achievements). In a similar sense, a rigorous audit operation (both external and internal) is critical.

5. Finally, since universities are based on truth and learning, every effort must be made to assure the flow of accurate information throughout the organizaton. Pravda-like organizations should never be tolerated!

Chapter 12

Leadership

As we have stressed in the preceding chapter, the modern research university has many of the characteristics of an international conglomerate of highly diverse businesses. It is not surprising that such a global enterprise requires capable management and visionary leadership. Many of the University's activities, such as its hospitals and high-technology research, require the rigor and accountability of mission-critical corporations. Yet the unique culture of the academic core of the University has a character almost orthogonal to the modern corporation since its most valuable employees are faculty members characterized by deep and highly valued knowledge and skills. They furthermore are protected from traditional top-down management methods by two unique characteristics: academic freedom and tenure. In fact, some describe academic leadership as more akin to pushing wheelbarrow full of frogs, since if you jostle them too much, they will jump out (into an intensely competitive higher education marketplace).

Hence the demand for leadership of such a large complex organization goes beyond competence and experience in academic administration. It requires a complex system of management talent covering a range of disciplines expertise that would be unusual even for a large multinational corporation. For example, beyond the expertise necessary for a large educational institution, it requires leadership capable of managing large medical centers, research facilities that are characterized by unusual characteristics (such as extremely hazardous radioactive or biological materials), computer facilities and networks at the cutting edge of technology, commercial activities in tech transfer, educational services, and college sports, and on and on. And most of all, it requires the sensitivity more akin to a political leader than a corporate CEO.

Hence while such discussions tend to focus primarily on the senior leadership of the University as an academic institution, it must be kept in mind that many of their responsibilities require a network of leaders with capabilities and experience in decidedly nonacademic areas.

The Zoology of University Leadership

University Presidents

Early college presidents were expected to provide primarily academic leadership. In some 19th century institutions, the president was not only the most distinguished scholar, but the only scholar. The intellectual influence of presidents on the faculty, the governing board, and the students was profound, as suggested by a Michigan student's admiration of President Tappan: "He was an immense personality. It was a liberal education even for the stupid to be slightly acquainted with him." (Peckham, 1994)

Today the president's role in academic affairs remains important but it must be exercised in a more delicate fashion. Technically, the shared governance policies of most universities delegate academic decisions to the faculty (e.g., criteria for student admissions, faculty hiring and promotion, curriculum development, awarding degrees). Hence the faculty usually expects the university president to focus on political relations, fund-raising, protecting their academic programs from threats such as intercollegiate athletics and the medical center, and keep hands off academic matters.

Yet in reality the most successful university presidents are capable not only of understanding academic issues but also of shaping the evolution of academic programs and enhancing the academic reputation of their university. After all, if the success or failure of a presidency will be based on the goal of leaving the university better than one inherited it, it is hard to imagine how one could achieve this without some involvement in the core activities of the institution, teaching and scholarship. Yet this requires both skill and diplomacy, since faculty reaction to a president's heavy-handed intrusion into academic affairs can be fierce. Presidential influence is more generally exercised through the appointment of key academic leaders such as deans or department chairs, by obtaining the funds to stimulate the faculty to launch new academic programs, or by influencing the balance among academic priorities.

There are some presidents–unfortunately a rarity these days–who have had both the scholarly credentials and interests to play a significant role in shaping the intellectual direction of the university. Michigan has benefited from several such leaders: for example, James Angell, who attracted extraordinary scholars such as John Dewey; Harlan Hatcher, himself a distinguished scholar and professor of English literature who raised the quality of the university even as it doubled in size; and Harold Shapiro, who brought his own deep understanding of the history of the university and the changing nature of a liberal education in his efforts as provost and then as president to enhance the quality of the university's students, faculty, and programs.

This leadership role is complicated by the scale and diversity of the contemporary university, comparable to that of major global corporations or government agencies. Today's university conducts many activities, some nonprofit, some publicly regulated, and some operating in intensely competitive marketplaces. Universities teach students, conduct research for various clients, provide health care, engage in economic development, stimulate social change, and provide mass entertainment (e.g., college sports). Of course the university also has higher purposes such as preserving our cultural heritage, challenging the norms and beliefs of our society, and preparing the educated citizens necessary to sustain our democracy.

The executive responsibilities of university presidents demand at least some degree of management skills. Fortunately most presidents have developed these through a sequence of earlier leadership experiences (e.g., department chair, dean, and provost). But this can also be taken to the extreme where the president becomes more of a technocrat or corporate CEO than an academic leader. Still others adopt more of a military approach, commanding their executive staff much as a general would command the troops. Of course, while the administrative staff of a university can adapt to such authoritarian styles, the creative anarchy characterizing the faculty will rebel or simply ignore general-presidents and continue with their own agendas.

Regardless of personal proclivities, successful presidential leadership styles must be responsive both to the nature of the institution and the demands of the times. The character of each institution, its size, mission, culture, and most important, its institutional saga, will tolerate certain styles and reject others. Authoritarian leadership might be effective or even demanded at some institutions, but the culture of creative anarchies such as Michigan, Berkeley, or Harvard will demand a more subtle approach to building grass-roots support for any initiative. Similarly, the turbulent 1960s and financially stressed 1980s required different leadership styles than the market-driven challenges and opportunities of the early 21st century. It is important that university presidents be capable of adapting their own leadership styles to fit the needs of their institution. Rigidity is not a particularly valuable trait for either the effectiveness or even the survival of university leaders!

Yet, despite the fact that university presidents have executive responsibilities for all of these activities and purposes, the position has surprisingly little authority. The president reports to a governing board of lay citizens with limited understanding of academic matters and must lead, persuade, or consult with numerous constituencies such as faculty and students that tend to resist authority. Hence the university presidency requires an extremely delicate and subtle form of leadership, sometimes based more on style than substance, and usually more inclined to build consensus rather than take decisive action. The very phrases used to characterize academic leadership such as "herding cats" or "moving cemeteries" suggest the complexity of the university presidency. Universities are led, not managed.

Each Michigan president seems to have filled a

Harlan Henthorne Hatcher (1951-1967)

Robben Wright Fleming (1968-1979)

Harold Tafler Shapiro (1980-1987)

James Johnson Duderstadt (1988-1996)

Lee Bollinger (1997-2001)

Mary Sue Coleman (2002-2014)

particular leadership role for the University, perhaps less because of how they were selected than the degree to which the institution and its needs shaped their presidency. For example, the post-war years of the 1940s and 1950s were a time of prosperous economy, growing populations, and an expanding demand for higher education, first as a consequence of returning veterans under the G. I. Bill and later through the efforts of the Truman Commission to extend the opportunity for a college education to all Americans. Hence it was a time for university presidents who could grasp the opportunity to grow their institutions, for example, Harlan Hatcher at Michigan and John Hannah at Michigan State.

In contrast, the 1960s and early 1970s were a time of protest, triggered first by the Free Speech Movement and Civil Rights, and then later by the Vietnam War (and the draft). University leaders were sought with the skills to handle dissent and confrontation, many coming from backgrounds in labor mediation such as Robben Fleming at Michigan and Clark Kerr at the University of California. There were also many casualties among those presidents from an earlier time who simply could not adapt to the confrontational climate of the 1960s.

The late 1970s and 1980s required still different leadership styles as the economy weakened, driven first by rising energy prices (the OPEC oil embargo) and later industrial competition from Japan. While the nation fell into recession, many industrial states such as Michigan faced depression-level hardships, with serious tax revenue shortfalls and consequently deep cuts in appropriations to higher education. This was a time of retrenchment, of focusing resources on highest priority, and generating new revenue streams through private fundraising and student fees. Leaders with strong financial skill (and intuition) such as Harold Shapiro at Michigan, Jack Peltason at the University of California, and Arnie Weber at Northwestern were key to the abilities of their institutions to restructure themselves financially to thrive in an era of constrained resources.

Although financial pressures relaxed–at least temporarily–in the late 1980s and 1990s, universities required strong entrepreneurial leadership capable of grasping the opportunities presented by the end of the Cold War, the increasing diversity of the American population, the forces of globalization, and the extraordinary transformation of our economy from making things (manufacturing) to creating and applying new knowledge, driven in part by rapidly evolving technologies such as the computer, telecommunications, and transportation. Perhaps indicative of the needs of higher education during this period was the appearance of university presidents with science and engineering backgrounds. While these university leaders were comfortable with the technology reshaping our society, even more important was a leadership style stressing teamwork, risk-taking, and entrepreneurial energy and capable of providing new visions for the university of the 21st century.

Executive Officers

One of the great myths concerning higher education in America–and one that is particularly appealing to faculty members, trustees, and legislators alike–is that university administrations are bloated and excessive. In reality, most universities have quite lean management structures, inherited from earlier times when academic life was much simpler and institutions were far smaller. Typically the number of administrative positions (and executive officers) in a university is only a small fraction of the number of senior administrators found in corporations or government agencies of comparable size. Furthermore, in contrast to corporations or government agencies, universities have quite shallow organizational structures. For example, there are typically only five organizational levels in the academic ranks (president, provost, dean, department chair, faculty member), leading to an exceptionally broad, horizontal organization structure at the senior level.

The direct line reports of the university president are the executive officers of the university, with titles such as vice-president or vice-chancellor in various functional areas–e.g., academic affairs, research, student affairs, business and finance, fund-raising, and government relations. Since the success or failure of the university president depends upon the quality of these appointments, one of the most important responsibilities of the president is recruiting, building, and leading a quality team of executive officers.

Surprisingly for one of the nation's largest

and most complex universities in the world, the University of Michigan always had a very small central administration–at least until the 2000s. It was characterized by a very lean executive officer team, with only six vice-presidents plus two chancellors for the Dearborn and Flint campuses, only one-half to one-third the number of executive officers as most other universities. Such a lean administration could only succeed with outstanding people, and hence a premium was placed on developing or recruiting the very best people into these key positions. Their success required, in turn, recruiting outstanding senior staff in each of their organizations, a stress on quality that tended to propagate throughout the institution.

At Michigan the two key executive officer positions are the provost (and vice president for academic affairs) and the chief financial officer (and vice president for business and finance). Much as in corporate organization, the president-provost-VP-business represented the executive leadership core of chief executive officer (CEO), chief operating officer (COO), and chief financial officer (CFO). In 1992 the modifier "executive" was added to the titles of the provost and VPCFO to distinguish their line-reporting responsibilities for all academic and administrative units of the university, including the regional campuses in Dearborn and Flint. Other vice presidents such as those for research, student affairs, development, and government relations generally had staff roles, although in some cases they had large administrative units reporting to them (e.g., student housing and research administration).

Next to the president, the provost (or vice president for academic affairs or "chief academic officer") is the most important leader in the university. In effect, the provost is the chief operating officer of the university, with the line-reporting responsibility for all of the academic units of the university, i.e., schools and colleges through their deans, centers and institutes through their directors, and a host of academic service units such as admissions and financial aid. The provost also serves as second-in-command and backup to the president and is usually tapped as acting president when the president is on leave or absent for an extended period.

Clearly the position of the provost at a major university is daunting, as suggested by the formal role definition we use at Michigan: " The provost is the intellectual and scholarly leader of the university, with ultimate responsibility for all academic programs, operations, initiatives, and budgets". Note here that to clearly establish the priority of the academic mission of the institution, the Michigan provost also functions as the chief budget officer, preparing the budget that determines the detailed allocation of resources throughout the university and thereby integrating the academic and budget functions and priorities.

Perhaps because of its vast size and complexity, Michigan has usually selected insiders as provosts until quite recently. Hence it was logical that the provost-president relationship would frequently be an inside-outside division of roles, in which the provost served as chief operating officer, managing the internal affairs of the institution, while the president served as CEO and "chairman of the board," managing the external relationships (state and federal government, fund-raising, public relations, intercollegiate athletics) and the sensitive relationships with the governing board (which could be extraordinarily time-consuming with a politically elected body).

The unusual responsibility and authority of Michigan's provost position and the quality of the academic leaders who have served in this role give it high visibility and influence on the national scene. However, it also identifies the position as an important source of university leadership, as evidenced by the number of Michigan provosts who have gone on to university presidencies. Yet the turnover in the position can be a considerable challenge to the president. There was an informal and quite unspoken rule that each Michigan president was allowed only three provost appointments. After that, they had to step down. Ironically this trend has continued to today!

Deans

The University of Michigan is known throughout higher education as a "deans' university". Because of our size and our highly decentralized organization, deans of our many schools and colleges have unusual freedom and authority, albeit with considerable responsibility and accountability. Most of the progress

The Deans Team during the 1980s

made by schools and colleges can be traced to the leadership of their deans–although, of course, the same can usually be said for the consequences of any shortcomings.

Clearly, being a faculty member is the best job in a university–the most prestige, the most freedom, the most opportunity. However, if one has to be an academic administrator, the best role is as a dean–at least at Michigan. Although some academic units such as the College of Literature, Science, and the Arts or the School of Medicine rival major universities in their size, financial resources, or organizational complexity, for most University of Michigan schools and colleges, both the size and intellectual span is just about right to allow true leadership. To be sure, a dean has to answer in both directions, to the provost from above and their faculty from below. But their capacity to control both their own destiny and that of their school is far beyond that of most administrators.

The cadre of deans is usually quite remarkable at a leading university. To be sure, there is always a pecking order among deans, with the "big dogs"– LS&A, Medicine, Engineering, Law, and Business– sometimes standing apart from the "little dogs"–

Music, Art, Architecture, Social Work, Education, Pharmacy, Dentistry, Nursing, Natural Resources, and Public Health. The Rackham Graduate School is usually an anomaly and, in fact, can sometimes serve as an intermediary between the superpowers and the nonnuclear states.

Although the deans generally meet regularly in a large council with the provost–once called the Academic Affairs Advisory Council but more recently called the Academic Policy Group–the size of this body mitigates against substantive discussion. In the late 1970s, when Al Sussman, former dean of the Graduate school, was serving as interim provost, he formed a clandestine group of deans known as the "SOUP" Group (for "Seminar on University Priorities") for the purpose of breaking the deans into smaller discussion units. While this group, consisting of LS&A, Engineering, Law, Business, Social Work, Pharmacy, and Rackham was sometimes useful, it later evolved into an exclusive fraternity with members selected more for personality than priority of school (e.g., how could one possibly leave out Medicine while including Pharmacy). Nevertheless, for the most part, the family of deans was remarkable for the quality of its members and their commitment to the University.

Since the University of Michigan is so heavily dependent on the quality of its deans, most presidents and provosts make a great effort to attract the very best people into these important positions. It is important for the president and provost to work closely together not only in the appointment and support of these key academic leaders but also to build a sense of community among them, establishing friendships and bonds, since these, in turn, glue together the university. Perhaps because of our own experience as members of the "deans' family," we were always on the lookout for new ways to involve the deans more intimately in the leadership of the university.

To be sure, there are many drawbacks to academic leadership roles, such as department chairs or deans. These positions rarely open up at a convenient point in one's career, since most productive faculty members usually have ongoing obligations for teaching or research that are difficult to suspend for administrative assignments. Although an energetic faculty member can sometimes take on the additional burdens of chairing a major academic committee or even leading a small department or research institute, the time requirements of a major administrative assignment such as department chair or dean will inevitably come at the expense of scholarly activity and the ability to attract research grants. The higher one climbs on the academic leadership ladder, from project director to department chair to dean to executive officer, the more likely it is that the rungs of the ladder will burn out below them as they lose the scholarly momentum (at least in the opinion of their colleagues) necessary to return to active roles in teaching and research.

University of Michigan Professor Dan Moerman, an anthropologist by training and longstanding member of faculty governance, suggests a very interesting perspective of the role of a dean as a broker between the two cultures of the university: the faculty (collegial, center-periphery, colleagues, peer respect) and the administration (hierarchical, top-down, bosses, performance evaluations). Moerman observes that, "When a president discusses things with deans, he calls a meeting; with the faculty, the president invites them to dinner. The dean is the mediator, the connecting link, between the two cultures. To be credible to the faculty, the dean must have scholarly credentials. But to relate to the administration, the dean needs to be competitive rather than collegial. This leads to a certain intentional ambiguity to the role. The dean is a broker, a middleman, betwixt and between–a trickster like Coyote or Janus." Since deans must represent the views of the faculty and never be seen as losing, they must become quite conservative, seeking to minimize risk and maximize flexibility. A president who interacts directly with the faculty becomes very threatening to a dean. ("If man can talk to God, what need is there for a priest?") What to do? As Moerman suggests, "Kick ass" says the administrator; "consult" says the faculty; "confuse" thinks the dean...

UM Academic Leadership, Decade by Decade

1960s-1970s

During the early years after WWII, the University faced the opportunity for rapid growth, sustained by strong and increasing state appropriations. Harlan Hatcher provided thoughtful and distinguished leadership in a patrician style, while the Board of Regents consisted primarily of wealthy Republicans who viewed their role much as members of a corporate board of directors, responsible primarily for the integrity and financial sustainability of the University, but staying far removed from its detailed management. Both the president and the Regents allowed the deans to provide strong leadership for the academic programs of the University.

However this rapidly changed during the 1960s and student and faculty activism began to appear around issues such as student rights, the Vietnam War, and minority enrollments. The strength of this effort challenged the more passive leadership of earlier years and stimulated the Regents to lure Robben Fleming, Chancellor of the University of Wisconsin Madison and experienced labor negotiator to address the growing activism on the campus. Fleming's skills of engagement and negotiation served the University well, calming the more radical disruptions and protecting the quality and integrity of the University during a difficult period. Fleming always maintained that university presidents were not all that important

Presidential teams of the 1960s, 1970s, 1980s, and 1990s

for massive universities such as Michigan. The role of the president was to keep things moving smoothing and make outstanding appointments to key leadership positions, such as the provost (which he demonstrated through appointments of outstanding leaders such as Allen Smith, Frank Rhodes, and Harold Shapiro. But those who lived through the decade knew better since while many presidents floundered and failed, Michigan successfully weathered a painful period of transition.

Some presidents are particularly skillful at grasping opportunities, or rescuing victory from the jaws of defeat. Robben Fleming exhibited this skill at a particularly important moment, when campus disruptions could have seriously and permanently damaged the institution. His long experience as a labor mediator had taught him that sometimes conflict is necessary to create the most effective path to compromise.

1980s

By the late 1970s there were already signs of weakening state support, along with the disappearance of state funding for facilities because of political issues. The acceptance of the Cornell presidency by Provost Frank Rhodes provided Fleming with the opportunity to appoint Harold Shapiro, a distinguished economist, to lead the efforts to restructure the financing of the University as state support declined, while he worked to secure funding for the Replacement Hospital Project, a massive $300 million effort that would later involve both Allen Smith as interim president and Harold

Shapiro when he became president in 1980.

Shapiro's style was well-suited to addressing these issues, since he was highly strategic and data-driven in these decisions. He launched a three-phase set of initiatives involving increasing tuition (particularly for out-of-state students), launching a major fund-raising campaign, and pushing hard for cost reductions. To carry out this agenda, he appointed the LS&A Dean, Billy Frye, as provost, who worked closely both with a University-wide task force, the Budget Priorities Committee, and the faculty Senate Assembly on a Five-Year financial plan that included discontinuance of several academic and administrative units. Both Shapiro and Frye appointed a distinguished group of leading faculty members as deans, and began to transfer to them both the authority over their resources and the accountability for their expenditures, the first of what would be a sequence of steps during the 1980s and 1990s to decentralize power in the University to the level of deans and directors where resource decisions were best made.

Perhaps the most important theme of the 1980s was Shapiro's insistence on the goal of excellence–in teaching, research, and service; students and faculty; and the quality of academic and administrative units, despite the decline in state funding. This commitment set Michigan on a course to become a leader in many areas during the 1990s. From his early days as provost and then through his presidency, he was absolutely insistent on the highest academic standards for the university. Although his determination to raise the bar on faculty hiring, promotion, and tenure sometimes rankled complacent faculty and occasionally undermined deans, it clearly elevated the quality of the university to a degree that few others were able to achieve. It also demonstrated quite convincingly that academic leaders can have a major impact on institutional quality–if they are determined enough, have the academic background to recognize quality, and the courage to point out where it is weak.

1990s

By the late 1980s, state support finally began to stabilize (although it never increased to its earlier levels, while state funding for facilities remained modest). Since Harold Shapiro had given Jim, his successor as provost, the initial assignment to launch an ambitious planning effort essential to restoring both the momentum and leadership of the University, the transition to president two years later was straightforward. Furthermore Shapiro left behind an unusually strong team of deans and executive officers recruited largely by Shapiro.

This last point is very important, since the University has a long history of looking inside for its academic leadership. To be sure, the Regents have frequently gone outside for University presidents–with only five of its 14 presidents selected from within. But both the deans and executive officers have generally come from internal appoints. In fact, during Shapiro and Jim's tenure, 15 of Michigan's 18 deans came from within, bringing with them considerable experience in University activities. Similarly of the 15 appointments made to executive officers during the 1990s administration, only 3 came from outside: Farris Womack, as chief financial officer, Maureen Hartford as vice president for student affairs, and Walter Harrison for external relations. For provost, it was particularly important to continue the long-standing tradition of internal appointments drawn from the Michigan deans (e.g., Charles Vest, Gilbert Whitaker, and Bernard Machen).

With this leadership experience, the University embarked on implementing the earlier planning effort, with strong engagement from the faculty, that led to exciting visions and initiatives to shape the future of the University such as the Internet and Internet2, the School of Information to provide leadership in technology,

the Michigan Mandate and Michigan Agenda for Women, which led the University to leadership roles in serving underrepresented minorities and women, new programs in areas such as genetic medicine and international studies, a major stress on improving the quality of undergraduate education, and providing faculty with the incentives and support necessary to propel Michigan to national leadership in the amount of research conducted on its campus.

Although state support remained stagnant, the University launched the largest fund-raising effort in the history of public higher education, led by Joe Roberson and Tom Kinnear, to raise over $1.4 billion. Vice President Womack provided skilled management of the University's endowment, increasing it by over a factor of 10 from $200 M in the 1980s to $2.5 B by the end of the 1990s, laying the foundation for what would become the largest endowment in public higher education.

2000s

By some measures, with the arrival of Lee Bollinger as the new president, Michigan's leaderhip in higher education began to erode. Many of the major efforts of the 1980s and 1990s such as the diversity agenda (the Michigan Mandate), technology (the Internet), and completing the rebuilding of the University's academic campuses were set aside by the new administration in favor of new ventures such as the arts (the annual visits of the Royal Shakespeare Theatre and planning for a new theater for a professional repertory group), big name architects (Robert Venturi and the Life Sciences Institute), and legal activities (preparing to successfully defend affirmative action before the Supreme Court in 2003). Such shifts in priorities were both expected and traditional with a change in administration.

However the new administration went further and rapidly replaced several of the University's key executive officers with inexperienced outsiders. They, in turn, replaced several layers of experienced business and physical plant staff, actions that would set back the management of the University for years to come. Furthermore, the decision to throttle back fund-raising and instead depend on increasing enrollment to compensate for the loss in state support with increased

Position	Name	Where	Why	Search	Successor
Senior Officers					
President	Jim Duderstadt	UM Faculty	Escape	Flawed search	Lee Bollinger
EVP-Provost	Bernie Machen	Pres, Utah	LB Push	Wired search	Nancy Cantor
EVP-CFO	Farris Womack	Retired	Escape	Failed search	Robert Kasdan
VP-Research	Homer Neal	UM Faculty	Escape	Failed search	Fawwaz Ulaby
VP-Health Aff	Rhetaugh Dumas	Retired	GW Push	Flawed search	Gil Omann
VP-Student Affairs	Maureen Hartford	Pres, Meredith	Escape	???	
VP-University Rel	Walt Harrison	Pres, Hartford	Escape	Failed search	
VP-Government Rel	new position			No search	Cynthia Wilbanks
VP-Development	Tom Kinnear	UM Faculty	Escape	No search	Susan Fagan
Secretary	Roberta Palmer	Undecided	LB Push	No search	Lisa Tedesco
General Counsel	Elsa Cole	NCAA	LB Push	???	Marvin Krislof
Chancellor-UM Flint	Charlie Nelms	U Indiana	Escape	Failed search	Interim
Chancellor-UM Dearborn	Jim Renick	Chan, NCA&T	Escape	???	
Chief of Staff	Ejner Jensen	Back to faculty	Push	No search	Chacona Johnson
Deans					
Medicine	Giles Bole	Retired	Retired	Failed search	Alan Lichter
Rackham	Nancy Cantor	UM Provost	Pull	Wired search	Earl Lewis
Architecture	Bob Beckley	UM Faculty	Retired	Failed search	Filled
Pharmacy	Ara Paul	UM Faculty	Retired	Normal search	Filled
Education	Cecil Miskel	UM Faculty	Retired	Normal search	Interim
Public Policy	Ned Gramlich	Fed Reserve	Pull	Normal search	John Chamberlain
Music	Paul Boylan	Retiring	Retiring	???	
LS&A	Edie Goldenberg	Retired	Escape	Virtual search	Pat Gurin

Position	Name	Where	Why	Status	Successor
Bus Admin	Joe White	Looking	Escape		
Law	Jeff Lehman	Looking	Escape		
Engineering	**Steve Director**				
Social Work	**Paula Allen-Meares**				
Information	Dan Atkins	Stepped down	Escape	Search	Interim
Public Health	Noreen Clark	Stepping down?			
Dentistry	**Bill Kotowicz**			Interim	
Art	Allen Samuels	UM Faculty	Pushed	Interim	
Natural Resources	Gary Brewer	Faculty	Escape	Normal	Dan Mazmanian
Other Senior Academic Administrators					
VPr-Acad Out	Doug Van Houweling	Internet II	LB Push	Eliminated position	
University Librarian	Don Riggs	Looking	Push	Failed search	Interim
Director, Mus Art	Bill Hennessey	NC	Pull	Normal search	
Athletics Director	Joe Roberson	Retired	LB Push	No search	Tom Goss
AVP	Randy Harris	VP, Houston	Escape	Wired	
AVP	Paul Spradlin	Retiring	Escape	Held up	Hank Beier
AVP	Bob Holbrook	Retiring	Retired	Wired	Paul Courant
AVP	Susan Lipschutz	Deceased	Deceased	Wired	Pam Raymond
AVP	Jackie McClain	CSU	Escape	Open	
AVP	Roy Muir	Retiring	Retiring	Open	
AVP	Lisa Baker	Resigned	Escape	Open	
AVP	Norm Herbert	Looking	Escape		
V Pr	**Lester Monts**				

The "Big Broom" chart, tracking the
turnover of senior staff in the late 1990s,

tuition revenue from more out-of-state students would launch the University down a road of growth that would later prove to be unsustainable.

The administration of the late 1990s was short-lived, lasting for only four years. The Regents selected experienced academic leaders from within for the interregnum between administrations, including B. Joseph White, Dean of the Business School, as interim president, and Paul Courant, Chair of the Department of Economics, as provost. Both were long-standing members of the University faculty, experienced leaders, and highly skilled in both financial management and strategic planning.

However Regents once again looked outside for the next president, although this time they sought experienced leadership for the next administration. They selected Mary Sue Coleman, the President of the University of Iowa, as Michigan's next president. Since interim president White had strengthen the executive officer team inherited by Coleman, this allowed the new president to focus early attention on important strategic issues such as the challenges faced by the University Hospitals, the financial operation of the University, and perhaps most important, private fund raising. The provost and vice-president for research assumed primary responsibility for the leadership of the academic units of the University.

Unfortunately, state support continued to decline throughout the 2000s, dropping even faster in the aftermath of the recession of 2008 and amounting to a decade-low drop of over 50% on a per student basis. To compensate for this loss, the administration continued the pattern of enrollment increases (with a bias toward out-of-state students) while launching two major fund-raising campaigns, the first successfully raising $3.3 B and the second, a $4 B campaign launched just as the University began a search for a new president. Fortunately because of the major success of VP Womack in increasing the University endowment to $2.5 B by the end of the 1990s, the University was able to benefit from continued growth of this resource through equity investments to the level of $10 B by 2015.

However during this period of eroding state support, there was a major shift in University priorities and attention to the auxiliary activities of the University–the medical center, student housing, and intercollegiate athletics–because of the dependence of these activities on the support from markets that were largely price insensitive (health care, student rents, and athletic ticket and media revenue). Massive investments were made in new facilities for these units, e.g. a $300 M cardiovascular center and a $750 M pediatrics hospital, $650 M for student housing renovation and construction, and $300 M for adding skyboxes and premium club facilities to Michigan Stadium and Crisler Arena. Since this was occurring during a period when there was very limited funding for academic facilities, the faculty became increasingly concerned that auxiliaries were dominating academics for the attention of the Regents and the executive officers.

Because of the priority given both the auxiliaries and activities such as fund-raising and public relations (e.g., "branding" the University), and the relative benign neglect of the academic programs, there was a major increase in both the number of administrative staff and their compensation (much of it coming from confidential bonuses and deferred salary agreements). Indeed, the compensation of senior administrators rose to levels exceeding that of even the leading private universities, while faculty salaries remained stagnant,

Vice Presidents' Salaries (2012-2013)

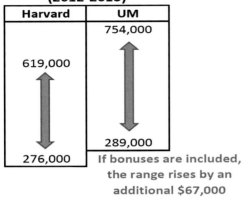

Harvard	UM
619,000	754,000
276,000	289,000

If bonuses are included, the range rises by an additional $67,000

UM Executive Officer compensation have risen to levels characteristing leading private universities.

Additional Pay to Executive Officers and Deans:
From $17K in 2000 to $1.4 Million in 2014

Position	2000-01	2005-06	2010-11	2013-14
Provost	0	0	3,250	0
U. Secretary	0	10,600	37,894	38,052
U. Librarian	0	0	250	19,000
VP Development	0	30,000	100,000	145,000
VP Finance, CFO	0	0	0	50,000
VP Comm.	0	0	49,812	25,000
VP Research	0	0	0	0
VP Legal	0	38,315	0	0
VP Student Affairs	0	0	0	0
VP Health Affairs	0	177,590	439,390	412,350
Dean CA & UP	0	2,205	30,900	72,684
Dean Art & Design	0	1,128	1,128	50,000
Dean Business	0	13,268	38,287	100,000
Dean Dentistry	1,250	93,750	35,000	77,614
Dean Education	0	3,750	3,000	500
Dean Engineering	0	0	0	0
Dean Information	0	2,705	30,000	118,000
Dean Kinesiology	0	0	0	58,717
Dean Law	0	4,861	4,861	25,000
Dean LSA	0	0	10,000	8,333
Dean Medical	16,057	124,835	243,237	98,500
Dean Music	0	0	0	0
Dean SNRE	0	0	0	123,895
Dean Nursing	0	1,898	0	0
Dean Pharmacy	0	0	0	0
Dean Public Health	0	0	60,000	0
Dean Public Policy	0	1,500	0	0
Dean Rackham	0	0	0	0
Dean Social Work	0	0	0	0
Totals:	17,307	506,405	1,087,009	1,422,645

falling behind most peer institutions. New forms of hidden compensation such as "signing bonuses" and deferred compensation were used to buy the loyalty of key administration staff with little oversight and a level of secrecy that was a clear departure from the University's long-standing practice of open reporting of staff salaries.

A massive public relations effort largely disguised these efforts and prevented most of the campus, including the faculty, from realizing what was occurring. Slowly but surely, not only the deans but the faculty were losing their influence though limited engagement with the University and through the weakening of existing faculty governance.

Concerns Raised and Lessons Learned

The most serious recent trend in University leadership over the past two decades has been the erosion of the power of the deans and directors. As we have noted, the strength of the University's academic programs has been due in large measure to the quality of the leadership of the deans and directors. The deans are the key line officers of the University. They are also the ones most responsible for maintaining its academic priorities and quality. Great deans create and lead great schools and colleges, not to mention generating over 90% of the resources of the University. During the last half of the 20th century, high priority was given to dean appointments consistent with their considerable authority and responsibility. Since deans, directors,

and department chairs are the key players in leading Michigan's path finding ventures, great care must be taken both in their selection and their understanding both of the Michigan heritage and culture and the quality of their faculty and staff.

Yet in recent years there is some evidence that the traditional roles and power of the deans have been weakened. The rigid application of 10 year limits on the appointments of deans, with little attention given to easing their transitions to "life after leadership", has been very discouraging and led to the departure of several of the University's most talented leaders. So too, there has been a clear trend to fill most open dean positions with outsiders with little experience with decentralized management. From the 1960s through the 1990s, over 80% of the University's dean positions had been filled from internal candidates. Yet by 2015, 13 of 19 dean positions had been filled with external candidates, in sharp contrast to the University's long-standing traditions of looking inside for dean candidates.

Traditionally, it was the provost's role to form the deans into a cohesive team working together to address the challenges and opportunities facing the University. Formed into a group, not only were they an important source of wisdom and strength, with unusual capacity to promote academic values in the face of occasional threats. Yet in recent years little attention has been given by the provost and president to building and sustaining a cohesive team among the deans or giving their voice adequate influence.

There has been similar erosion in both the academic credentials and experience of the executive officers. In the past, most of the University's senior leadership team had sufficient academic experience to merit faculty appointments in addition to their administrative assignments. Today, however, only four executive officers (president, provost, VP Research, and EVP Health System) have faculty credentials. The recent trend to appoint senior officers without academic background or experience has decoupled the central administration from the academic core of the University to an alarming degree. It is challenging enough to have a governing board with little experience in the core "business" of the university, but to then hire an executive team of administrators with little academic experience raises many concerns, particularly during a time of great challenge and change.

The Road Ahead

The role of leaders in a major public research university such as Michigan is complicated by its scale and diversity, comparable to that of global corporations or government agencies. Today's university conducts many activities, some nonprofit, some publicly regulated, and some operating in intensely competitive marketplaces. Universities teach students, conduct research for various clients, provide health care, engage in economic development, stimulate social change, and provide mass entertainment (e.g., college sports). Of course the university also has higher purposes such as preserving our cultural heritage, challenging the norms and beliefs of our society, and preparing the educated citizens necessary to sustain our democracy.

Inside Out

To be sure, it is important to seek a balance in leadership, bringing in leaders from outside for new ideas and energy while relying on internal appointments to sustain important traditions and values. When this balance is distorted, perhaps due to complacency with the status quo, or more serious, an effort by newcomers, frustrated with the University's resistance to change, to bring in too many outsiders in key roles as deans or executive officers in an effort to change the culture of the institutions. Fortunately, the decentralized organization of the University is not only capable of responding to a changing environment but also repelling invasive species that attempt dramatic change.

So what balance should be sought? Certainly the majority of deans should be chosen from inside, perhaps in a ratio of two to one over outsiders. To be sure this is difficult in an era in which universities are increasingly dependent upon executive search consultants, tempted to push their existing stable of external candidates and motivated by compensation indexed to the compensation negotiated by selected candidates. At the executive officer level, perhaps a balance closer to 50%-50% seems best, balancing internal and external experiences.

While a similar balance is probably appropriate at the presidential level, Michigan's history reveals that most of its presidents have come from outside (Tappan, Angell, Burton, Little, Hatcher, Fleming, Coleman, and Schlissel) with only four from inside (Hutchins, Ruthven, Shapiro, Duderstadt, and Bollinger), which reverses the 2 to 1 inside to outside pattern of deans. To some degree this is probably because the Board of Regents led the search and made the choice, reflecting perhaps a "devil you don't know always looks better than one you do".

Interestingly enough, one finds a correlation between the distinction of the university and its tendency to appoint insiders as presidents, with Harvard, Yale, Princeton, Stanford, and the University of California as prominent examples of leadership from inside. However any speculation about this arising from confidence that one's own people make the best leaders of outstanding universities is obliterated by the case of Cornell, which has chosen five of its presidents from Michigan!

Anyway, this balance between the selection of leadership from within or without should be tracked very carefully, since it could lead to difficulties over time.

Leadership Development

It is very important to view leadership development as a strategic issue for the University. While most faculty prefer to remain in academic roles, some are willing to accept additional responsibilities in leadership roles. Every effort should be made to encourage and support such activities, providing opportunities for further leadership development, albeit with strong evaluation of leadership ability. Interestingly enough, since academic leadership usually requires not only time and effort, but also sacrificing one's scholarly activity, such willingness to participate in faculty service or even governance should be recognized as a sign of possible leadership interest.

Some Suggestions for Presidential Leadership

A recent study on academic leadership by the Association of Governing Boards provided some important recommendations concerning the university presidency that should be kept in mind. (AGB, 2007)

1. To reconnect the president with the core academic mission of the university, i.e., learning and scholarship. It is important to resist the tendency to view the presidency as simply just another CEO role, dominated by fund-raising or lobbying, and instead re-establish academic leadership as a president's highest priority.

2. To urge boards, faculties, and presidents themselves to view the university presidency not as a career or a profession in and of itself, but rather as a calling of immense importance, similar to those of other forms of public service, rather than seeking personal

compensation and benefits far removed from the academy.

3. To seek to establish what the AGB study termed *integral leadership*, a new style of collaborative but decisive leadership: A president should exert a presence that is purposeful and consultative, deliberative yet decisive, and capable of midcourse corrections as new challenges emerge. Integral leadership succeeds in fulfilling the multiple, disparate strands of presidential responsibility and conceives of these responsibilities as parts of a coherent whole. Leadership of this sort links the president, the faculty, and the board together in a well-functioning partnership purposefully devoted to a well-defined, broadly affirmed institutional vision."

Presidential Compensation

One of the most controversial issues in American higher education today is the alarming increase in the compensation of university presidents, now rising to the million-dollar levels more characteristic of corporate CEOs that academic leaders. This not only has undermined public confidence in the leadership and governance of the nation's universities, but it has also decoupled the university president from the faculty.

To some degree this is due to governing boards who fail to understand that academic leadership is a public calling more akin to public leadership roles such as governor or national leadership than corporate management. It has also been driven by the increasing use of professional search consultants whose fees tend to be indexed to compensation. But there is also an alarming tendency of university leaders to set aside the concept of academic service in favor of greed.

It is worth observing here that UM's president of the late 1990s, Lee Bollinger, sought to become the first $1 million public university president. He failed in this quest at Michigan, but he won the war in 2015 when he became the nation's highest paid president at Columbia with a salary of $4.6 M. A refreshing counterpoint was provided by President Gregory Fenves of the University of Texas at Austin who refused a $1 million salary in favor of the $750,000 salary of his predecessor.

Perhaps such excessive compensation is not

surprising in institutions willing to pay football and basketball coaches truly astronomical salaries. But it nevertheless is damaging, both to the public perception of financial behavior of academic institutions as well as to the reputation of their governing boards. While ambition and greed are frequently present in the negotiation of presidential compensation, hopefully some degree of public commitment and responsibility should also be encouraged.

Appendix

Some Comments on Executive Compensation

What about the compensation of senior academic leadership, at the level of deans, executive officers, chancellors, and presidents? While executive search consultants love to stress the importance of competitive compensation (after all, that is how many of them set their fees), one should be very skeptical of just how important compensation is at this level.

Believe it or not, most senior academic leaders are rarely lured by the dollars. To be sure, a competitive salary is viewed by some candidates as a measure of how much you want them. But it is rarely the deciding factor. Far more important is the challenge, opportunity, and prestige of building a top-ranked academic program.

Many candidates for senior leadership roles are seeking new opportunities because they have been blocked by the narrowing pyramid of the academic hierarchy in their own institution. Some are after wealth and fame, but NOT from the university, but rather from outside their academic appointment through corporate boards, national commissions, or other opportunities.

Some actually view academic leadership as a "higher calling", with emotional rewards and satisfaction that simply cannot be quantified in terms of compensation. In fact, some actually have acquired a sense of loyalty to a university and view such assignments as a duty of service. If you doubt this, just look at the list of institutions with the highest executive salaries. Usually these are places you have to pay people to go, not at the very best institutions!

One more caution here. While it is the case that some public universities use their fund-raising foundations to supplement the salaries of senior leadership, this is usually provided as a payment for their development responsibilities. It is quite another matter entirely to solicit private support specifically to bring senior leadership salaries up to market levels. Not only does such a practice run into optics problems (remember, we are now in the post-Abramoff era), but it can start a public university down a very slippery slope where institutional integrity could be compromised by conflict of interest.

Higher education should be viewed as both a "public good" to society as well as an individual benefit to graduates. As such, academic leadership roles have a "calling" character that should be understood and accepted as a public service, much like other public leadership roles. Leading an academic organization should be viewed as both a privilege and a responsibility, not as merely a route to fame and fortune.

Indeed, many in higher education today view the frequent institution hopping and excessive compensation of senior academic and administrative leaders in higher education as one of the unfortunate trends that has seriously undermined our society's understanding of the contemporary American university and its public good character.

We believe it is particularly important that governing boards view university leaders as *public servants* rather than corporate executives, both in their unique responsibilities, their accountability, and their compensation. To impose such a corporate culture, values, and compensation practices on an academic institution is both disruptive and dangerous to its fundamental purpose and mission.

Unfortunately, these policies while both accepted and effective during the 1980s and 1990s, were largely abandoned during the 2010-2015 period, More specifically, Michigan faculty salaries not only dropped more than 20% below private university peers, but also dropped below several public universities including the University of California (both UCLA and Berkeley), Rutgers, Virginia, and Texas, even as adminstrative salaries and undisclosed compensation through bonuses and hiring incentives exploded to extreme levels. (Ulsoy, 2012)

Chapter 13

Governance

American universities have long embraced the concept of shared governance, involving public oversight and trusteeship, collegial faculty governance, and experienced but generally short-term administrative leadership. While shared governance engages a variety of stakeholders in the direction of the university, it does so with an awkwardness that tends to inhibit change and responsiveness.

The politics swirling about governing boards, particularly in public universities, both distracts them from their important responsibilities and stewardship, while discouraging many of our most experienced, talented, and dedicated citizens from serving on these bodies. The increasing intrusion of state and federal government in the affairs of the university, in the name of performance and public accountability, can trample on academic values and micromanage many institutions into mediocrity. Furthermore, while the public expects its institutions to be managed effectively and efficiently, it weaves a web of constraints through public laws that make this difficult indeed. Sunshine laws prevent substantive discussions between governing boards and administrators. Even the most sensitive business of the university must be conducted in the public arena, such as its search for a president. And even the selection of the president is subject to intense public scrutiny and influence.

Efforts to include the faculty in shared governance also encounter obstacles. To be sure, faculty governance continues to be both effective and essential for academic matters such as faculty hiring and tenure evaluation. But it is increasingly difficult to achieve effective faculty participation in broader university matters such as finance, capital facilities, or external relations. The faculty traditions of debate and consensus building, along with the highly compartmentalized organization of academic departments and disciplines, seem increasingly out of sync with the breadth and rapid pace required of the university-wide decision process.

The Nature of Governance at the University of Michigan

Much of the University of Michigan's strength and leadership has arisen and been sustained because of a very unusual decision about its governance made during the earliest days of its history. Because the University had already been in existence for two decades before the State of Michigan entered the Union in 1837, and because of the frontier society's deep distrust of politics and politicians, the new state's early constitution in 1850 granted the university an unusual degree of autonomy as a "coordinate branch of state government". Actually this also reflected the importance of freedom as a key Enlightenment theme embraced by Jefferson and his colleagues in defining the early structure of the republic. It was later an important founding principle of the Northwest Ordinance that led to the creation of the University. Michigan's constitution delegated full powers over all university matters to the University's governing board of regents, although surprisingly enough it did not state the purpose of the university. This constitutional autonomy, together with the fact that the university traces its origins to an act of Congress rather than a state legislature, has shaped an important feature of the university's character.

Throughout its history the university has regarded itself as much as a national university as a state university, as exemplified by the declaration of its early Regents, "The doors of all its Departments are open to students from Every State in the Union, upon the same terms as to those of our own State; so that it may, in some sense, with propriety, be styled a National Institution, and every State in the Union has an interest in its prosperity." Furthermore, Michigan's constitutional autonomy, periodically reaffirmed through court tests and constitutional conventions, has enabled the university to have much more control over its own destiny than most other public universities. (Peckham, 1963)

Hence it is apparent that the real key to the University's quality and impact over its two centuries of history has been the very unusual autonomy granted the institution by the state constitution of 1850. The University has always been able to set its own goals for the quality of its programs rather than allowing these to be dictated by the vicissitudes of state policy, support, or public opinion. Put another way, although the University is legally "owned" by the people of the state, it has never been obligated to adhere to the priorities or whims of a particular generation of Michigan citizens. Rather, it has been viewed as an enduring social institution with a duty of stewardship to commitments made by generations past and a compelling obligation to take whatever actions were necessary to build and protect its capacity to serve future generations. Even though these actions might conflict from time to time with public opinion or the prevailing political winds of state government, the university's constitutional autonomy clearly gave it the ability to set its own course. When it came to objectives such as program quality or access to educational opportunity, the University of Michigan has always viewed this as an institutional decision rather than succumbing to public or political pressures.

The University of Michigan is certainly no exception in facing the multiple challenges of university governance. But our institution is anomalous in another respect. We are one of the very few American research universities whose governing board is determined through statewide popular election, involving partisan candidates nominated by political parties. With two of our eight regents up for election every two years, the frequently changing political stripes of our governing board present a particular challenge both to the University and to its president.

To some degree this anomaly in the selection of the university's governing board is balanced by another unusual feature of the university's governance. As we noted earlier the Michigan constitution grants the university an extraordinary degree of autonomy as a "coordinate branch of state government," by giving its regents full powers over all university matters. More specifically, the constitution authorizes the board to "have the general supervision of the university and the direction and control of all expenditures from university funds." But the constitution also directs the board to elect a president who should preside, without vote, at all their meetings. This latter detail is very important, since it clearly identifies the president as both "chief executive officer" and "chairman of the board" (at least their meetings), a stature held by few other university presidents who generally attend governing board meetings only as observers. It allows the president both to determine the agenda and orchestrate the activities of the governing board. Through this mechanism, the state constitution deftly relieves the regents of the ability to administer the university. In theory, at least, they need only to determine policy–and, of course, hire and fire the president.

Faculty governance is also unusual at Michigan. To be sure, the university has a long tradition of strong faculty governance at the level of individual academic units such as departments or schools through faculty executive committees. Here the clearly identified responsibilities (hiring, promotion, tenure, budget priorities) attract the participation of our best faculty members and provides effective faculty governance. But at the university-wide level, the limited authority of the faculty senate all too frequently transforms it into a debating society more concerned with "p-issues" (e.g., pay, parking, and the plant department) than strategic academic issues facing the university.

To be sure, most of those citizens and faculty members serving on various governing bodies do so with the best of intentions, loyal to the institution and committed to its welfare and capacity to serve. Yet all too frequently they do so within an awkward structure of shared governance that allows political forces to inhibit access to both adequate information and communication. It is also a structure that can easily be hijacked by those with strong personal or political agendas that could harm the university.

1950s-1960s

Throughout much of the 1950s and 1960s the University's elected board was unusually stable. Moderate Republican politics dominated the state and wealthy Republican men were nominated to run and elected as Michigan Regents. Stalwarts such as Paul Goebel, Robert Briggs, William Cudlip, and even a former Michigan football coach, Harry Kipke, were elected, and the Regents operated much like a corporate board of directors.

But there were occasional challenges at the state level to the power of the University's Board of Regents. A new state constitution was drawn up at the convention of 1963, reaffirming the autonomy of the University of Michigan, which had been established in the constitution of 1850 and reaffirmed in the revision of 1908 and extending autonomy to the other public universities in the state. The new constitution created a new State Board of Education, which was to have general supervision over all public education "except as to institutions of higher education granting baccalaureate degrees". "The power of the boards of institutions of higher education in this constitution to supervise their respective institutions and control and direct the expenditure of the institution's funds shall not be limited by this section."

However, a controversy developed over the powers of the State Board of Education. It objected to enlargement of the Flint Senior College into a four-year college branch of the University, as requested by the Flint Board of Education. The attorney general went on to say that the State Board of Education had the power to determine the location of colleges and the addition of departments to existing colleges. Such power to authorize departments was a distinct invasion of the autonomy of the Board of Regents and of the governing boards of any of the state universities. Thus, the scene was set for a continuing and ongoing battle over the autonomy of the Regents. Such challenges by state government to the constitutional power of the Regents would continue throughout the next several years, requiring occasional litigation (or at least the University's threat of litigation to protect its autonomy).

During the 1950s and 1960s, the faculty had grown so large that it accomplished little in the semiannual meetings of the Faculty Senate, and its committee structure was cumbersome. In an effort to reflect faculty views more efficiently and more quickly, the Senate reorganized itself in 1966 by electing a legislative Assembly of sixty-five members, representing all schools and colleges, to meet monthly. In turn, the Assembly selected a nine-person Senate Advisory Committee for University Affairs (SACUA) as its active executive committee.

Throughout the 1960s and 1970s both University wide through SACUA and the Senate Assembly, and at the school, college, and department level through executive committees, tended to be led by distinguished senior faculty members with broad University interests, such as Shaw Livermore, Brymer Williams, and Arch Naylor. This experienced faculty leadership proved invaluable as the University faced financial difficulties during the late 1970s and into the 1980s.

1970s

In the early 1970s, organized labor became more active in nominating and electing Democratic candidates to the Board of Regents since the University was an attractive target for further unionization. In 1968 there were two small unions: by 1974 the University was bargaining with numerous newly organized union locals and strikes became a familiar routine in campus life. In 1971 the Intern-Resident Association unionized, followed in the same year by the Teaching Fellows Association who formed the Graduate Employees Organization (the Regents chose not to contest either, dominated as they were by newly elected Democrats sponsored by organized labor).

Although of a different party, the Regents of the 1960s and 1970s continued to be prominent men such as Eugene Power, Robert Nederlander, and Paul Brown, with corporate leadership experience. Furthermore, both Harlan Hatcher and Robben Fleming could look to experienced VPCFOs such as Wilbur Pierpont and James Brinkerhoff to work closely with the Regents, particularly on key financial issues. From time to time a conservative candidate from Western Michigan would run and be elected to the Board, such as Deane Baker, but throughout the 1970s and 1980s the Regents could be characterized as a moderate Democratic body.

My 1988 public interview with
the Regents for the UM presidency

A meeting of the University of Michigan Regents

1980s

During the early 1980s the transition from Republican governors (George Romney and William Millikan) to Democrat James Blanchard was evidence of more balanced politics in the state, which led to greater political balance among the candidates elected to the university governing boards. There was also more opportunity to diversify boards with both women and minority candidates. However with Regent nominations occurring during mid-August party conventions prior to statewide fall elections, there was less attention paid to party nominations, and over time these began to reflect either special interests or party fund-raising. Furthermore, as the statewide visibility of nominations for Regent dropped (surveys indicated that fewer than 10% of the electorate had any knowledge of most candidates), incumbents had a significant advantage in being nominated and elected to multiple terms. Finally, since the statewide ballots placed the election of university governing board members far down on the ballots, election of Regents became increasingly dependent on the coattail effects from the top of the ticket. In general, whichever party carried the governor or senate post would also capture the Regent elections (although in a close election, usually women candidates had an advantage).

The consequence to the University was an increasingly divided Board of Regents in terms of both political party and political philosophy. Put

more bluntly, the board became more divided among liberal Democrats nominated by organized labor and Republicans nominated by its conservative wing. Such divided boards posed more of a challenge to University leadership, since Regents began to vote more along party lines, e.g., Republicans always opposing tuition increases and Democrats always supporting the unionization of various job families in the University. Such was even more the case on social issues such as affirmative action and gay rights, since it was important that Regents maintain a highly visible stance on political issues in an effort to better position themselves for the next election. And since for some members, their position as a Regent was their most visible role, there was an increasing tendency to stand for multiple terms. If they conformed to their party's political agenda, they could be relatively certain to be renominated as an incumbent and could only lose their seat through a strong sweep of the ticket by the opposing party.

1990s

Throughout the 1990s the Board of Regents became increasingly divided to the point that in the 1994 elections, with a strong Republican governor at the top of the tickets, two Republicans were elected, sweeping out not only the Democratic chair and vice-chair of the Board, but creating the horror of a 4-4 political division. Although the president chaired the meetings of the Board, the University administration was increasingly

182

preoccupied with the challenge of making certain that it obtained at least a 5-3 majority on any critical issues (such as tuition) and avoided a majority vote on anything that would damage the institution (such as firing the president).

In a confidential survey taken of deans and executive officers during this period, there was a unanimous consensus that the most serious challenge facing the university was the deterioration in the quality of its Board of Regents. They went further to suggest that the primary responsibility of the President and the Executive Officers must become that of protecting the university from its own governing board. This challenge also plagued the other two public universities with elected boards, Michigan State University and Wayne State University. In a meeting with the senior editor of one of the state's leading newspapers, he warned that the University administration's most difficult challenge would be that of preventing the Board from harming the University. Ironically, some of our Board members agreed with this assessment.

This situation was complicated by a similar division on the part of faculty governance, as a small group of faculty from the Medical School managed to take control of SACUA and began to rattle sabres against both their school and the University administration more generally.

As concerns grew, the University administration set out on a dangerous course of attempting to improve the quality of its governance. It attempted to restructure the meetings of the governing board to allow more discussion of key strategic issues facing the university rather than allowing the agenda to be dominated by the usual flow of routine business decisions. It assisted the Regents in developing internal leadership and discipline so that the occasional antics of maverick board members would not hold it hostage.

A similar effort was directed at improving faculty governance.The deans were encouraged to urge their faculties to nominate strong candidates for the university's Senate Assembly. The executive officers met regularly and frequently with the leadership of the faculty senate and most faculty advisory committees. Efforts were made to engage the executive committees of the university's schools and colleges in university-wide strategic issues. To facilitate interactions with faculty, the administration brought into the President's Office former leaders of faculty governance to serve both as liaison and Secretary of the University.

Yet it seemed that each painful step forward would quickly be followed by two steps backward. An incumbent Regent would become irritated and attempt to retaliate against our UM Alumni Association's efforts to encourage interested alumni to stand as candidates for Regent. The local newspapers would become attracted to our strategic discussions and attempt to use the state's sunshine laws to pry into more sensitive areas such as business strategies or property acquisitions. A cabal of discontented faculty members in a particular school (usually Medicine) would engineer a coup to take over the faculty senate in an effort to push their personal agendas.

2000s

The governance of the University stabilized somewhat during the late 1990s and early 2000s. New members of the Board of Regents, who adopted a somewhat more constructive role in supporting institutional leadership, replaced those few who had assumed a more confrontational role. The board became more diverse in gender and age, although still dominated by lawyers as the most common occupational background.

However faculty governance became weaker, as faculty members from the Flint and Dearborn campus began to be elected to SACUA, and new administrations increasingly comprised of senior officers with little faculty experience tended to ignore faculty concerns. A glaring example occurred during the late 1990s when the Athletic Director convinced the President that the Board in Control of Intercollegiate Athletics that enabled faculty influence over important issues such as student eligibility and athletic budgets, should be replaced by an Advisory Board on Intercollegiate Athletics chaired by the Athletic Director. Furthermore, over the next several years additional language was inserted in the Regents Bylaw to make it clear the new ABIA has only weak advisory authority. In fact, a final explanation point on this weakening of faculty influence over athletics was made when one of the former Regents, was appointed as Athletic Director, with little interest in even convening the Advisory Board.

The weakening of faculty governance at Michigan stands in sharp contrast to the role that faculty governance was playing at other peer institutions. A particularly striking example was the role that the Faculty Senate played in blocking the efforts of several members of the University of Virginia Board of Visitors to support a vicious attack on the institution's administration and force the resignation of its new president, Teresa Sullivan, a former provost at Michigan. The faculty senate stepped up, taking a vote of no confidence in the board and strongly supporting the president, which forced the governing board to back off. Yet many of the governance problems still remain.

Yet, even with this recent expression of faculty concerns, Michigan's faculty governance has been remarkably stable in comparison to much of the rest of higher education. In fact, when the majority of the Michigan faculty voted overwhelmingly against the imposition of the "shared services" program, which would transfer many of their most valuable staff into a central administrative unit, the outgoing President simply announced that the University would move ahead despite their concerns. Needless to say, this created a wound unlikely to heal in the near term that might even re-ignite faculty activism once again.

Lessons Learned

The challenges facing the current model of university governance can be illustrated by several contrasting quotes:

"In the 1850s, when the current forms of lay board governance were established, the average American college had fewer than one hundred students and less than 1% of while males attended college. Over the past century, universities have evolved from a trustees-plus-president "imperium" to a more faculty-based hegemony to a somewhat more broadly based sovereignty that includes government (state and federal) and students."
Harold T. Shapiro

"Our antiquated systems require seemingly interminable consultations with every interested group, provide virtual vetoes for those affected by any significant change, and fail to lodge authoritative power in any office."
Nan Keohane

"For years now the trustees of many colleges and universities have rolled over as academics and administrators within the institutions they're supposed to govern have run amok. While trustees turn a blind eye, faculty and administrators have politicized and dumbed down the curriculum, instituted draconian speech and sexual-conduct codes that they have then enforced with all the liberalism of the Court of the Star Chamber, and instituted an immoral and often unconstitutional system of admissions apartheid."
Wall Street Journal

"In reality, the practice of shared governance—however promising its original intent—often threatens gridlock. Whether the problem is with presidents who lack the courage to lead an agenda for change, trustees who ignore the institutional goals in favor of the football team, or faculty members who are loath to surrender the status quo, the fact is that each is an obstacle to progress. If higher education is to respond effectively to the demands being placed upon it, the culture of shared governance must be reshaped."
National Commission on the Academic Presidency

"In an attempt to improve institutional effectiveness and accountability, a call goes out for stronger leadership, quicker decisions, and a more business-like approach to decision-making. Battles over who has decision-making authority over academic policy, technology, diversity, tenure, and administrative issues are growing in higher education."
William Tierney

To understand these varied perspectives, it is important to recognize that shared governance is, in reality, an ever-changing balance of forces involving faculty, trustees, and administration. It represents the effort to achieve a balance among academic priorities, public purpose, and operating imperatives such as financial solvency, institutional reputation, and public accountability. Different universities achieve this balance in quite different ways. For example, at the University of California a strong tradition of campus and system-wide faculty governance is occasionally called upon to counter the political forces characterizing the governing board, examples being the loyalty oath controversy of the 1950s, the Reagan takeover of the UC Board of Regents in the 1960s, and the debates over the use of affirmative action in student admission during the 1990s.

In contrast, at the University of Michigan, campus-wide, elected faculty governance has historically been rather weak, at least compared to faculty influence through executive committee structures at the department, school, and college level. Hence the tradition has been to develop a strong cadre of deans, both through aggressive recruiting and the decentralization of considerable authority to the university's schools and colleges, and then depend upon these academic leaders to counter the inevitable political tendencies of the university's regents from time to time. When the deans are strong, this checks-and-balance system works well. When they are weak or myopically focused on their own academic units, the university becomes vulnerable to more sinister political forces.

Where is the influence of the university administration–and particularly the president–in this balancing act? Usually out of sight or perhaps out of mind. After all, senior administrators, including the president, serve at the pleasure of the governing board. They are also mindful of faculty support, since they may be only one vote of no confidence away from receiving their walking papers–a long-standing academic tradition recently re-established by Harvard and several other universities. While it has always been necessary for the American university president to champion the needs of the academic community to the governing board and the broader society while playing a role in ensuring that the academic community is in touch with society's interests and needs, it is also not surprising that the administration is usually quite reluctant to get caught publicly in skirmishes between the governing board and the faculty.

The danger of such a bilateral balance of power arises when one party or the other is weakened. When the faculty senate loses the capacity to attract the participation of distinguished faculty members, or when a series of poor appointments at the level of deans, executive officers, or president weaken the administration, a governing board with a strong political agenda can move into the power vacuum. Of course there have also been numerous examples of the other extreme, in which a weakened governing board caved into unrealistic faculty demands, e.g. by replacing merit salary programs with cost-of-living adjustments or extending faculty voting privileges to part-time teaching staff in such a way as to threaten faculty quality.

Part of the difficulty with shared governance is its ambiguity. The lines of authority and responsibility are blurred, sometimes intentionally. Although most members of the university community understand that the fundamental principals of shared governance rest upon the delegation of authority from the governing board to the faculty in academic matters and to the administration in operational management, the devil in the details can lead to confusion and misunderstanding. Turf problems abound. One of the key challenges to effective university governance is to make certain that all of the constituencies of shared governance–governing boards, administrations, and faculty–understand clearly their roles and responsibilities.

Nothing is more critical to the future of higher education than improving the quality and performance of boards of trustees and attracting distinguished faculty members into leadership positions in faculty governance. Today during an era of rapid change, colleges and universities deserve governing boards comprised of members selected for their expertise and experience, members who are capable of governing the university in ways that serve both the long-term welfare of the institution and the more immediate interests of the various constituencies it serves. Trustees should be challenged to focus on policy development rather than intruding into management issues. Their role is to provide the strategic, supportive, and critical stewardship for their institution and to be held clearly publicly, legally, and financially accountable for their performance and the welfare of their institutions.

It is not hard these days to find examples of university governing boards under fire for what critics regard as bad behavior. In recent years boards of trustees have been accused of ignoring problems (Penn State), meddling in campus leadership (University of Virginia), pursuing an ideological agenda (University of Texas), and forcing clearly unqualified presidents on a university with political objectives (University of Iowa). A National Commission formed by the Association of Governing Boards to recommend changes in higher education governance says actions like these jeopardize not only the institutions but also the public trust in higher education. "Far too much time and talent and too many resources are preoccupied with institutional advantage, the preservation of the status quo, internal disputes over governance roles and authority, and the advancement of political and individual agenda.". (AGB)

For public boards, the need is particularly urgent. As long as the members of the governing boards of public universities continue to be determined through primarily political mechanisms, without careful consideration or independent review of qualifications or institutional commitment, and are allowed to pursue political or personal agendas without concern for the welfare of their institution or its service to broader society, the public university will find itself increasingly unable to adapt to the needs of a rapidly changing society. Every effort should be made to convince leaders of state government that politics and patronage have no place in the selection of university governing boards or efforts to determine their administrative leadership. Quality universities require quality leadership and governance. Even as public university governing boards have become increasingly political and hence sensitive to special interests, they have also become increasingly isolated from accountability with respect to their quality and effectiveness. Not only should all university governance be subject to regular and public review, but the quality and effectiveness of governing boards should also be an important aspect of institutional accreditation.

The Road Ahead

Despite dramatic changes in the nature of scholarship, pedagogy, and service to society, American universities today are organized, managed, and governed in a manner little different from the far simpler colleges of a century ago. We continue to embrace, indeed, enshrine the concept of shared governance involving public oversight and trusteeship by governing boards of lay citizens, elected faculty governance, and experienced but generally shorter and usually amateur administrative leadership. Today, however, the pace of change in our society is exposing the flaws in this traditional approach to university governance.

Hence it is appropriate to question whether the key participants in shared governance–the lay governing board, elected faculty governance, and academic administrators–have the expertise, the discipline, and the authority, not to mention the accountability, necessary to cope with the powerful social, economic, and technological forces driving change in our society and its institutions. More specifically, is it realistic to expect that the shared governance mechanisms developed decades (or, in some cases, centuries) ago can serve well the contemporary university or the society dependent upon its activities? Can boards comprised of lay citizens, with little knowledge either of academic matters or the complex financial, management, and legal affairs of the university be expected to provide competent oversight for the large, complex institutions characterizing American higher education? What is the appropriate role for the faculty in university governance, and is this adequately addressed by the current determination and conduct of faculty governing bodies? Can academics with limited experience in management serve as competent administrators (deans, provosts, presidents)? And, finally (and most speculatively), what works, what does not, and what to do about it?

As the contemporary university becomes more complex and accountable, it may even be time to set aside the quaint American practice of governing universities with boards comprised of lay citizens, with their limited expertise and all too frequently political character, and instead shift to true boards of directors similar to those used in the private sector.

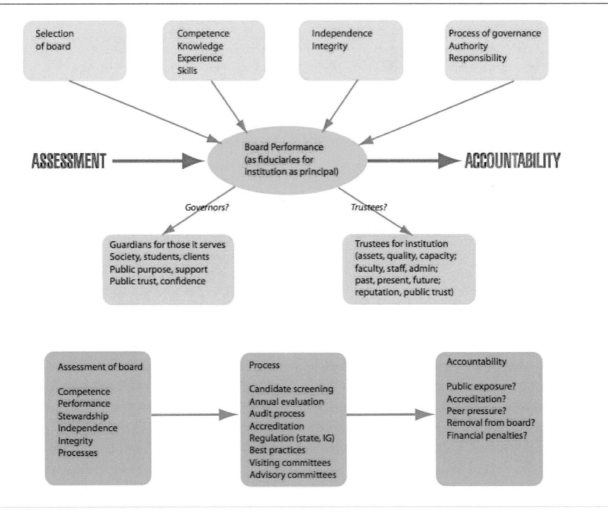

A prescription for assessing and improving govering board performance

Although it may sound strange in these times of scandal and corruption in corporate management, there is increasing evidence today that university governing boards should function with a structure and a process that reflects the best practices of corporate boards. Corporate board members are selected for their particular expertise in areas such as business practices, finance, or legal matters. They are held accountable to the shareholders for the performance of the corporation. Their performance is reviewed at regular intervals, both within the board itself and through more external measures such as company financial performance. Clearly, directors can be removed either through action of the board or shareholder vote. Furthermore, they can be held legally and financially liable for the quality of their decisions–a far cry from the limited accountability of the members of most governing boards for public universities.

While it is important to provide board members with sufficient tenure to develop an understanding of the university, it is also important to avoid excessively long tenures. It is probably wise to limit university board service to a single term, since this would prevent members from "campaigning" during their tenure for future appointment or election to additional terms.

Again drawing on the experience of corporate boards, let us make the more radical suggestion that university presidents should have some influence over the selection of board members, just as their colleagues in private universities and CEOs in the corporate sector. Here it is not suggested that university presidents actually should nominate or select board members. But consideration should be given to their right to evaluate and possibly veto a proposed board member if the individual is perceived as unduly political, hostile, or just simply inexperienced or incompetent.

All university governing boards, both public and private alike, would benefit greatly from the presence of either active or retired university presidents, senior administrators, and distinguished faculty members from other institutions among their membership. Since the experience of most lay board members is so far removed from the academy, it seems logical to suggest that boards would benefit from the experience such seasoned academicians might bring. After all, most corporate boards find it important to have experienced business leaders, either active or retired, among their membership. University boards should do the same.

An equally controversial variation on this theme would be to provide faculty with a stronger voice in true university governance by appointing faculty representatives as members of the governing board. This would be similar, in a sense, to the practice of some corporate boards in providing a seat for a representative from organized labor. However, there would need to be a clear sense of accountability and liability in such an appointment, so that the faculty board members would not simply become advocates for the faculty position and instead be responsible to the entire institution.

Every effort should be made to convince leaders of state government that politics and patronage have no place in the selection of university governing boards or efforts to determine their administrative leadership. Quality universities require quality leadership. Even as public university governing boards have become increasingly political and hence sensitive to special interests, they have also become increasingly isolated from accountability with respect to their quality and effectiveness. Not only should all boards be subject to regular and public review, but also the quality and effectiveness of governing boards should be an important aspect of institutional accreditation.

Perhaps the simplest approach to identifying possible reforms in faculty governance is to examine where it seems to work well and why. From the experience as a faculty member, a former member of faculty governance at both the academic unit and university level, and a university president–faculty governance seems to work best when focused upon academic matters such as faculty searches, promotion and tenure

decisions, and curriculum decisions. Why? Because the rank and file faculty members understand clearly that not only do they have the authority and integrity to make these decisions, but that these decisions are important to their academic departments and likely to affect their own teaching and research activities. As a result, the very best faculty members, namely those with the strongest reputations and influence, are drawn into the academic governance process, either through formal election or appointment to key committees (hiring, promotion, tenure, curriculum, executive) or at least consulted for influential opinions in their role as department mandarins.

In sharp contrast, most active faculty members view university-wide faculty governance bodies such as faculty senates primarily as debating societies, whose opinions are invariably taken as advisory– and frequently ignored–by the administration and the governing board. Hence, rare is the case when a distinguished faculty member spares the time from productive scholarship, teaching, or department matters for such university service. Of course there are exceptions, but more common is the squeaky wheel syndrome, where those outspoken faculty members with an axe to grind are drawn to faculty politics, frequently distracting faculty governance from substantive issues to focus instead on their pet agendas.

Hence a key to effective faculty governance is to provide faculty bodies with executive rather than merely advisory authority, thereby earning the active participation of the university's leading faculty members. Advisory bodies, paid only lip service by the administration or the board of trustees, rarely attract the attention or the participation of those faculty most actively engaged in scholarship and teaching. The faculty should become a true participant in the academic decision process rather than simply a watchdog on the administration or defenders of the status quo. Faculty governance should focus on those issues of most direct concern to academic programs, and faculty members should be held accountable for their decisions. Faculties also need to accept and acknowledge that strong leadership, whether from chairs, deans, or presidents, is important if their institution is to flourish, particularly during a time of rapid social change.

Because of the unusual nature of faculty governance

at Michigan, vested in both university-wide structures such as the Senate Assembly and school and department level executive committees, some specific suggestions are appropriate for our University. First it is essential that the voice of the faculty on both academic and institutional matters be strengthened by restoring the executive powers of school and college executive committees. It is essential that newly appointed deans understand both the bylaws and past practices that have granted and recognized the executive powers characterizing these bodies.

Consideration should also be given to strengthening the Senate Assembly and the Senate Advisory Committee on University Affairs, both by providing some degree of executive authority and perhaps a new structure capable of attracting the engagement of the University's most distinguished faculty members into service on these bodies. One possibly would be moving to a bicameral organization comprised of both elected faculty members from general ranks ("the house") and a "senate" of appointed senior faculty with endowed or honorific chairs.

In conclusion, we should recognize that the current form of university governance, evolving over many decades is more adept at protecting the past than preparing for the future. All too often shared governance tends to protect the status quo–or perhaps even a nostalgic view of some idyllic past–thereby preventing a serious consideration of the future. During an era characterized by dramatic change, we simply must find ways to cut through the Gordian knot of shared governance, of indecision and inaction, to allow our colleges and universities to better serve our society. Our institutions must not only develop a tolerance for strong leadership; they should demand it.

The complexity of the contemporary university and the forces acting upon it have outstripped the ability of the current shared governance system of lay boards, elected faculty bodies, and inexperienced academic administrators to govern, lead, and manage. It is simply unrealistic to expect that the governance mechanisms developed decades or even centuries ago can serve well either the contemporary university or the society it serves. To blind ourselves to these realities is to perpetuate a disservice to those whom we serve, both present and future generations.

Missions

Education

Research

Service

The core missions of the research university

Chapter 14

Education

Mention higher education and most people think about "going to college," that is, undergraduate education, as the core mission of the university. It is certainly true that undergraduate students outnumber graduate and professional students on most of our campuses. Furthermore, an undergraduate education frequently is a formative experience in one's life, since this generally coincides with both emotional and intellectual maturation.

Yet much of the evolution of the American university–and the University of Michigan, in particular–during the decades following World War II was focused on activities such as research and graduate education, professional education and service, extension and continuing education, and auxiliary enterprises such as medical centers and intercollegiate athletics. Indeed, a quick glance at the balance sheet for any major university reveals that the majority of its resources, whether financial or personnel, are certainly not directed at undergraduate education. At Michigan, only about 15% of our budget is directed toward this activity; only one-third of our faculty teaches undergraduates.

Actually, this is also the image that much of the American public has about large research universities. They tend first to think of the commitments that public universities have made to the professions, to law and medicine, engineering and agriculture. We also might acknowledge the responsibilities of these institutions to serve the public or their important research programs. But few would think first about their commitment to undergraduate education. Rather, the image of undergraduate education in large public universities is one of thousands of students wandering in and out of large lecture courses in a largely random fashion, taught by foreign teaching assistants, possibly on their way from their fraternity or sorority house to the football stadium. We think of undergraduate students in these institutions as identified only by their I.D. number until the time of their graduation, where they are asked to stand and be recognized along with thousands of their fellow graduates.

Yet well over half of the students on the campuses of major public universities are undergraduates. Indeed, at Michigan we enroll over 29,000 undergraduates, including 20,000 in our liberal arts college, which makes it the largest commitment to liberal arts education of any university in the nation. Studies confirm that the undergraduates from flagship public universities comprise the largest source of professionals, scholars, and leaders of our society. At Michigan we have led the nation for many years in the number of our undergraduates who go on to professional careers such as teaching, law, engineering, and medicine.

Hence, for Michigan, the challenge of its educational mission is multifaceted. On the one hand, the strength of its professional schools and the strong research and scholarly orientation of our faculties should not be compromised. On the other hand, the University needs to generate a fresh commitment to cultivating a spirit of liberal learning among its undergraduates and its faculties, to encourage major efforts to improve the quality of teaching and learning. The University attempts to provide resources to ensure that these efforts can go forward in an atmosphere of continuous experimentation–of intelligent trial and error. Broad faculty participation is essential, and the unprejudiced testing of alternative ideas can be expected to generate vigorous debate. This is as it should be, since the stakes are high. The University aims to prepare its students not merely to function in our complex society, but to serve as leaders shaping society's future directions.

Undergraduate education is a core activity even in research universities such as the University of Michigan.

For several decades following World War II, most large public universities focused their attention on building strong programs in the professions—building high-quality schools of law, medicine, business, engineering, agriculture, and so forth. Perhaps this was due to a sense of public responsibility. Or perhaps it was due to the demand for these programs from both students and employers. Whatever the reason, it is probably true that most institutions have invested the lion's share of new resources in recent years in the graduate and professional schools rather than the quality of our undergraduate programs.

One might explain this by saying that curriculum reform is cyclic, and the pendulum is now swinging back after the deconstruction of undergraduate education accompanying student unrest in the 1960s. Clearly market forces are also at work. In many parts of the nation we experienced a major decline in the number of college-age students during the 1990s as we coasted down the backside of the post-war baby boom. Nothing like a demographic crunch to stimulate educational institutions to improve their product!

No more compelling challenge has faced our universities—particularly, our research universities—than reaffirming our commitment to education, especially for undergraduates. If our undergraduate students are to love the process of learning, they must work closely with those who are deeply involved in the excitement of discovery. Students, we have learned, must be involved in the struggles for new knowledge.

At the University of Michigan, instead of apologizing for our size, we began to take advantage of our unique strengths. We worked to connect undergraduates more directly with the vibrant intellectual activity going on around them—whether through hundreds of small seminars, student participation in faculty research projects, or broader community projects. Increasingly, even our youngest students are learning to question the authority of intellectual sources, instead of simply imbibing accepted truths. We assume they are creative actors, not just listeners. Our curriculum aims to involve students in the deep complexity of real-life problems, problems that have no "right" answers. Instead of giving students the facts of science or history, we strive to introduce them to the critical world views of scientists and historians.

Today's complex social and intellectual problems overwhelm the limited resources of isolated individuals. In universities, in government, and in the business world, those who succeed are now those who collaborate with others. At the University of Michigan, from our science laboratories, to our engineering classes, to our art studios and concert halls, and beyond, we realized the need to organize student inquiry increasingly around teams.

Our professional schools also faced dramatic transformations. Our medical and business curricula needed to be restructured to reflect modern changes in practice. Our graduate programs required reform in order to reduce time to degree and to create more

192

opportunities for interdisciplinary majors. And technology such as MOOCs and connected learning drove new educational paradigms.

1960s

Although we have referred to the 1960s as a time of student protest and rejection of the established paradigm for the university, it was also a time of rare opportunity for experimentation in higher education. The "greatest generation" was determined to provide educational opportunities for their children, the baby boomers, and committed the necessary tax resources to build and expand the campuses of public universities. The University of California and the California Master plan are the most vivid examples of this, launching several new university campuses to explore different approaches to higher education, e.g., UC San Diego to explore an Oxbridge college approach to graduate education, UC Santa Cruz to focus on new approaches to undergraduate education, and UC Irvine, UC Santa Barbara, and UC Riverside to provide expanded education opportunities for a rapidly growing population.

In the early 1960s Michigan also benefited from relatively generous appropriations for both operations and facilities that allowed significant experimentation. New learning paradigms were explored with the Pilot Program of Alice Lloyd residence hall, a new program based on writing and the arts; the Residential College, a major living-learning effort located in East Quad and patterned after the colleges at Yale and Oxbridge, and the Honors Program, an interdisciplinary major for outstanding students. The University also developed a novel dual degree, Inteflex, which enabled strong students to enroll jointly in LS&A and Medicine, thereby not only gaining assurance of admission to Medicine when they first entered the University, but coordinating programs to cut a year off of the time required for the M.D. Engineering launched the world's first curricula in new technologies such as nuclear engineering and computer engineering.

Unfortunately, by the late 1960s, state funding was already beginning to show signs of instability, and state funding for academic facilities began a slow decline.

Furthermore, as the baby boomers moved through college ages, a baby bust was projected that provided little incentive for further expansion of higher education in the state.

1970s and 1980s

With the emergence of disruptive student activism and then later the erosion of state support, the University had other priorities during the latter years of the 1960s and the 1970s, and the innovation in academic programs languished. Facing a 30% drop in state support over a three-year period in the early 1980s, the University launched a major "lifeboat" exercise in an effort to better focus limited resources. Initially three academic units were selected for review: the Schools of Education, Art, and Natural Resources, using the classical trilogy of quality, centrality, and cost. In the end, only the School of Education took a major cut, 50%, along with several other units such as the University Extension Service and Michigan Media.

Ironically, over the course of the decade there were not only cuts but growth in some units. The path to a better university focused efforts on research, graduate education, professional training, and professional service, since these (and not undergraduate education) were the key to the University's reputation. The leadership believed that only if the University was recognized as a leader among its peers and had financial strength and independence could it then afford and seek excellence in education. The economic needs of the state stimulated major growth in engineering and business programs. And the appearance of pervasive computer networks through the learning environment gave rise to efforts to explore new technology-intensive learning paradigms.

Yet, as our colleagues in elite private institutions have known for so long, the cornerstone of any distinguished academic institution is its undergraduate college. This college and those intellectual disciplines that derive from these programs form the academic heart, the intellectual core of our institutions, and over a period of time will determine both the distinction of the institution as well as the strength of its other endeavors in the professions, in research, and in service.

New facilities were created for undergraduates and new international programs were launched.

1990s

The University of Michigan has long been firmly committed to the principle that research universities can and should play an important but unique role in undergraduate education. To reflect this, during the 1990s the University leadership was determined to provide our undergraduates with an experience which draws on the vast intellectual resources of the modern research university: its scholars, its libraries and museums, its laboratories, its professional schools, its remarkable diversity of people, ideas, and endeavors.

The intent was to expose our students to the excitement of great minds struggling to extend the bounds of knowledge. Of course we recognized that the scholars we placed in the classroom were not always the best teachers of knowledge in the traditional sense. But we were convinced that only by drawing into the classrooms faculty with strong commitments to scholarship could we stimulate our students to develop the skill at inquiry across the broad range of scholarly disciplines that is so essential to life in an age of rapidly expanding knowledge.

Michigan aimed to develop in our students both the ability and will to strive for knowledge. We believed that a critical component of an undergraduate education in a research university is the development of the will to seek and the skill to find knowledge. We should expose our students to the diversity, the complexity, and the pluralism of peoples, cultures, races, and ideas

that can only be found in the intellectual melting pot of the modern research university. And we must also accept our mission to educate the leaders of American society. Indeed, if past experience is any guide, most of the leaders of this nation will continue to be produced by our great research universities.

The University set firm priorities on restoring core support for both LS&A and improving the quality of undergraduate education. This was done both through the provision of additional operating funds as well as special initiatives which benefited LS&A, e.g., the priority given to rebuilding the natural sciences, additional funding designed to improve the quality of first year undergraduate education, and special salary programs for outstanding faculty. However, in later years, the University went beyond this to launch an ambitious program to renovate or rebuild all of the buildings housing LS&A programs, which had deteriorated during the 1970s and 1980s as the University had addressed other capital priorities such as the new University Hospital. In the decade from 1985 to 1996, the University invested more than $350 million in capital facilities for LS&A, essentially rebuilding the entire Central Campus area.

Improving the quality of the undergraduate experience became a clear priority of the University with the creation of the Undergraduate Initiative Fund to provide over $1 million per year of grants to faculty projects aimed at improving undergraduate education. The common thread throughout these

The University has also provided state-of-the-art facilities for cyberenabled
learning, such as the Duderstadt Center and the Angell-Haven cluster.

initiatives was grassroots involvement. The University
sought proposals, ideas, and participation in defining
programs from our faculty, students, and staff. It aimed
to invest resources in a way that would motivate our
most creative people to become involved and to become
committed.

The first awards in this program created an
interesting portfolio of new initiatives. It supported
the development of a new series of core curriculum
courses in the liberal arts. Instruction in science and
mathematics for the first two undergraduate years
underwent major revisions. New initiatives were
aimed at better integrating the arts such as theater,
dance, and music into the undergraduate curriculum.
Major pedagogical needs were addressed in areas as
teaching assistant training. Substantial action was taken
to improve counseling and sensitivity to pluralism in
the University. The Undergraduate Initiative Fund also
approved a number of student proposals, ranging from
undergraduate colloquia to faculty fellow programs
in the residence halls, to on-line counseling and
information services on our campus computer network,
to an alternative career center.

LS&A launched a major effort to improve the quality
of its introductory courses, and it received national
acclaim for its efforts in areas such as chemistry,
biology, and mathematics. It introduced a broad array
of seminar courses taught by senior faculty for first
year students. And efforts were made to create more
learning experiences outside of the classroom through

student research projects, community service, and
special learning environments in the resident halls.
So, too, other schools such as Engineering, Business
Administration, Art, and Nursing launched major
efforts to improve undergraduate education.

Similar efforts were launched to improve the quality
of graduate and professional education. The School
of Medicine completely restructured the medical
curriculum to provide students early in their studies
with clinical experience. Business Administration
redesigned its MBA program to stress teamwork and
community service. Engineering introduced new
professional degrees at the masters and doctorate level
to respond to the needs of industry for practice-oriented
professionals. The School of Dentistry underwent a
particularly profound restructuring of its educational,
research, and service programs. The Institute for Public
Policy Studies was restructured into a new School of
Public Policy. The School of Library Science evolved into
a new School of Information, developing entirely new
academic programs in the management of knowledge
resources.

The University's professional schools continued to
develop and offer high quality continuing education
programs. Of particular note was the Executive
Management Education of the Business School–ranked
by some as the nation's leading program–and an array
of postgraduate professional education programs
conducted by Medicine, Law, and Engineering.

International education was also given high priority

during the 1990s. Following planning efforts led by the provost in the 1980s, a series of steps were taken to broaden and coordinate the University's international activities. Michigan joined its Big Ten colleagues as a member of the Midwestern University Consortium for International Activities (MUCIA), the leading university organization for international development. The University created a new International Institute to coordinate international programs. It continued to expand its relationship with academic institutions abroad, with particular emphasis on Asia and Europe. Of particular note were the distance learning efforts of the Business School, which used computer and telecommunications technology, along with corporate partnerships, to establish overseas campuses in Hong Kong, Seoul, Paris, and London.

2000s

Perhaps the largest change in the nature of education at Michigan during the first decade of the 21st century was due to the impact of the massive enrollment growth of over 10,000 students (25%) designed to increase tuition revenue from out-of-state students. This has had a major impact on the nature of instruction in those academic units with large enrollments, i.e., LS&A and Engineering, and within these colleges, large departments such as economics, psychology, electrical engineering, and mechanical engineering. Since tenure-track faculty size has grown only modestly during this period, most of the additional instructional load has been handled using non-tenure track instructors, e.g., lecturers, adjunct faculty, and graduate teaching assistants.

These schools have attempted to moderate the impact of increasing dependence on lecturers, part-time faculty, and teaching assistants by providing additional seminars and explored the possibility of technology-based learning such as blended classrooms. Yet the reality is that the lower division of undergraduate instruction has become quite similar to that provided by community colleges, with very little opportunity for first and second year students to become engaged with senior faculty members of the University.

Another change in the educational environment of a more national character has been the dramatic decline over the past decade in the time students spend on academic pursuits. The rule of thumb during the 1960s-1980s was that for every hour spent in class, students were expected to dedicate two hours of study and class preparation (e.g., for a 15 credit hour course loads, students were expected to spent 30 hours in additional study). Yet recent surveys indicate that today's student spends less that 10 hours a week studying. Of course, part of the burden of this reduction in learning effort must rest with the faculty whose assignment loads apparently no longer require such effort. And it is also the case that there are many extracurricular activities available with significant learning opportunities. Yet it is also the case that an increasing number of students, particularly those from affluent backgrounds, come to the university to "pay for the party", with a priority given to social activities such as fraternities and sororities or entertainment venues such as big-time college sports.

A third change in the educational experience in recent years has been driven by rapidly evolving technology. To be sure, many students spend inordinate time in social networking, e.g., Facebook and Twitter. However technology infrastructure plays a critical role in course management systems (e.g., CTools and Canvas) that enable not only the management of lectures and assignments but also access to instructors and other students. As we will note later, new learning paradigms such as Massively Open Online Courses (MOOCs) and cognitive tutors could drive massive change in the learning paradigms. But thus far, on most major campuses such as Michigan, these more advanced learning technologies are still used only by a few faculty members in a highly experimental phase, such as "flipped" classes in which students are expected to come to class prepared to enter discussions rather than listen to lectures.

However there is one area where technology has already penetrated deeply into the curriculum by providing students with unusual tools and environments for creativity. For example, the creation of objects using 3-D printers, virtual reality environments, hacker fairs for software development, or the design and creation of new electronic devices has now become commonplace in the advanced workspaces and studios of the University. Key in these "maker" efforts are not only the tools but even more important expert staff with both skills in the crafts of such technology but also the ability to teach students these skills. In fact, many of our most outstanding teachers are those craftsmen who can train students in the use of advanced technology to help them transform their ideas into reality.

The Road Ahead

To most students and parents, the purpose of a college education is to earn the college degree necessary for a good job, for personal economic security and well-being. Many of today's students approach their college education with very definite career goals in mind. They enroll with plans to become doctors or engineers or lawyers or teachers. While many will change their minds during their undergraduate years, most will emerge with specific career goals still uppermost in mind.

Employers reinforce this utilitarian approach. The recruiters they send to campus are looking for very definite skills. Perhaps they seek something highly specific such as a particular undergraduate major or Internet navigation skills. Or perhaps they seek some evidence that the student can communicate well and work comfortably in a diverse environment. Students are extremely sensitive to these signals from the employment marketplace, and the experience other students have with job interviews and placements can have a very significant impact on their own educational plans.

In a sense, the university is caught between the contradictory forces of responding to more pragmatic goals of students and employers while providing the liberal education that provides a student with the broader skills important for good citizenship and a meaningful life. Furthermore, in a world of ever-changing needs, one objective of an undergraduate education certainly must be to prepare a student for a lifetime of learning. The old saying that the purpose of a college education is not to prepare a student for their first job but rather their last job still has a ring of truth.

Two data points provided by recent surveys are of interest in this regard. In longitudinal studies of their graduates, several universities asked alumni to rank the value of their various experiences while undergraduates. Inevitably the alumni tended to rank as most valuable their interactions with faculty and other students (the community theme again). Lowest in value was the actual content learned through formal courses.

A more recent survey actually suggests that the earnings potential of those students with liberal arts majors may in fact be greater than those in more technical majors such as business. Of course one reason might be that students from the liberal arts generally plan on further education at the graduate level in various professional programs such as law or medicine. But this advantage could also be due to the broader learning experiences characterizing the liberal arts, which better prepare students for adapting to multiple careers later in life.

This view is reinforced by surveys of CEOs of major American corporations who when asked what they most sought in today's college graduates, tended to respond: the ability to communicate, the willingness to continue to learn, the capacity to value and manage diversity, and the desire to drive change. Again, particular curricular content was not high on the list.

There is a certain irony here. The contemporary university provides one of the most remarkable learning environments in our society—an extraordinary array of diverse people with diverse ideas supported by an exceptionally rich array of intellectual and cultural resources. Yet we tend to focus most of our efforts to improve undergraduate education on traditional academic programs, on the classroom and the curriculum. In the process, we may have overlooked the most important learning experiences in the university.

Think about it from another perspective. When asked to identify the missions of the university, we generally respond with the time-tested triad: teaching, research, and service. Yet undergraduate education is usually thought of only from the perspective of the first of these missions, teaching. Clearly, we should broaden our concept of the undergraduate experience to include student involvement in other aspects of university life.

For example, at a research university, every undergraduate should have the opportunity—or perhaps even be required—to participate in original research or creative work under the direct supervision of an experienced faculty member. While the few students who have been fortunate enough to benefit from such a research experience usually point to it as one of the most important aspects of their undergraduate education, most see their education only through the more standard curriculum. Interestingly enough, many faculty members who have supervised undergraduate research projects also find it to be an exhilarating role, since undergraduate students are frequently more questioning and enthusiastic than graduate students!

So too there is ample evidence to suggest that students' learning benefits significantly from community or professional service experiences. Such activities provide students with experience in working with others and applying knowledge learned in formal academic programs to community needs. Since many students arrive on campus with little experience in relating to broader community values, the experience of doing something for others can be invaluable.

In fact, major studies suggest that knowledge is created, sustained, and transformed in "communities of practice." Learning is seen as a form of membership that evolves as the individual engages in the practices and activities of the community, which becomes the living repository of knowledge. While there are numerous opportunities for volunteer community service in all universities, a more structured approach would be valuable in better aligning these experiences with the goals of an undergraduate education. Indeed, such community or professional service might even be considered as a requirement for an undergraduate degree.

There seems little doubt that the undergraduate experience needs to be reconsidered from a far broader perspective. Better alignment with the multiple missions of the university—providing undergraduates with education through teaching, research, and service—would seem an appropriate goal for most universities. All too frequently each of the missions of the university is associated with a different component—a liberal education and teaching with the undergraduate program, research with the graduate school, and practical service with professional schools. However, in reality, all components of the university should be involved in all of its missions—particularly undergraduate education.

Today's college graduate will face a future in which

perpetual education will become a lifetime necessity since they are likely to change jobs, even careers, many times during their lives. To prepare for such a future, students need to acquire the ability and the desire to continue to learn, to become comfortable with change and diversity, and to appreciate both the values and wisdom of the past while creating and adapting to the new ideas and forms of the future. These objectives are, of course, those that one generally associates with a liberal education.

What is unique about education at universities such as Michigan? What is the "market niche" of the comprehensive research university? We all share a serious commitment to scholarship as well as a commitment to unusual breadth across a rich diversity of academic disciplines, professional schools, and social and cultural activities. We have all achieved an unusual degree of diversity in our students, faculty, and staff. Our campuses demonstrate an unusual degree of participation of faculty and students in the university decision process. And we all share in an unusually strong commitment to the quality of our students, our faculty, and our programs.

In a sense, the strength of our institutions depends upon our efforts to achieve an optimum blend of quality, breadth, and scale. We attempt to do a great many things, to involve and benefit a great many people, and we attempt to do everything very well. Furthermore, we attempt to achieve a balance among teaching, research, and service, as well as undergraduate education, graduate education, professional education, and faculty scholarship and development. It is important to note that we do not view achieving this balance as a conflict among competing goals. Rather we view it as an opportunity to exploit an important creative tension.

It is this blend of missions that provides the research university with such a unique environment for undergraduate education. We are not, nor should we try to imitate, a small liberal arts college, with a faculty chosen primarily for their teaching skills and with a curriculum limited both by design and resources. Rather, we are large, comprehensive universities, spanning almost every intellectual discipline and profession. We have the capacity to attract and sustain many of the world's leading scholars. We provide intellectual resources unmatched elsewhere in our society, whether in the extent of our library and museum collections, or in the laboratory facilities we provide, or in the exotic new tools of our intellectual trades ranging from supercomputers, to the sophisticated equipment required for solid-state electronics and recombinant DNA research, to the expensive instrumentation used for positron emission tomography in our medical centers.

Yet it is important to stress that Michigan's approach to undergraduate education is built upon the liberal arts–the humanities and arts, the social and natural sciences–as conveyed by its College of Literature, Science, and Arts. As President, Harold Shapiro once framed the objectives of a liberal education at Michigan as:

> "The need to better understand ourselves and our times, to discover and understand the great traditions and deeds of those who came before us; the need to free our minds and our hearts from unexamined commitments in order to consider new possibilities that might enhance both our own lives and build our sympathetic understanding of others quite different from us; the need to prepare all thoughtful citizens for an independent and responsible life of choice that appreciates the connectedness of things and peoples." (Shapiro, 1988)

So, where do the liberal arts fit into the contemporary university? Of course, for the medieval university, they comprised the curriculum for free men (from the Latin *liberalis*) rather than those skills characterizing the servile arts (like masonry and engineering). Although, originally identified by the disciplines of the *trivium* (grammar, logic, and rhetoric) and later the *quadrivium* (geometry, arithmetic, astronomy, and music) that comprised the curriculum of the medieval university.

Each age has added further to the liberal arts, e.g., the humanities, the physical and biological sciences, and the social sciences in the 19th and 20th century. Still excluded from the liberal arts are topics that are specific to the professions such as medicine, pedagogy (i.e., education), business, and of course, engineering!

As Shapiro notes, additional objectives have also been added to the concept of a liberal education, such as freeing of the individual from previous ideas, the disinterested search for truth, the pursuit of alternative ideas, the development and integrity of the individual, and the power of reason. Here, it is important to acknowledge that the content of a liberal education for the 21st Century continues to evolve.

As difficult as it is to define and as challenging as it is to achieve, perhaps the elusive goal of liberal learning remains the best approach to prepare students for a lifetime of learning and the capacity to both adapt to and occasionally drive change.

Chapter 15

Research

During past eras of challenge and change, Congress has acted decisively to create innovative partnerships to enable its universities to enhance American security and prosperity. While engaged in the Civil War, Congress passed the Morrill Land-Grant Act of 1862 to forge a partnership between the federal government, the states, higher education, and industry aimed at creating universities capable of extending educational opportunities to the working class while conducting the applied research to enable American agriculture and industry to become world leaders. The results were the green revolution in agriculture that fed the world, an American manufacturing industry that became the economic engine of the 20th century and the arsenal of democracy in two World Wars, and an educated middle class that would transform the United States into the strongest nation on earth.

A hundred years later, emerging from the Great Depression and World War II, guided by a critical report, *Science, the Endless Frontier,* drafted by Vannevar Bush, head of the wartime research, Congress acted once again to strengthen this partnership by investing heavily in basic research and graduate education on the campuses. The national research policies adopted at that time created a partnership between the federal government and the nation's leading universities. These policies were based on the premise that the nation's health, economy, and military security required continual deployment of new scientific knowledge, and that the federal government was obligated to ensure basic scientific progress and the production of trained personnel in the national interest. They declared that federal patronage was essential for the advancement of knowledge. These policies also accepted a corollary principle: that the government had to preserve "freedom of inquiry," to recognize that scientific progress results from the "free play of free intellects, working on subjects of their own choice, in the manner dictated by their curiosity for explanation of the unknown."

This effort succeeded in building the world's finest research universities, capable of providing the steady stream of well-educated graduates and scientific and technological innovations central to our robust economy, our vibrant culture, our vital health enterprise, and our national security in a complex, competitive and challenging world. This expanded research partnership enabled America to win the Cold War, put a man on the moon, and develop new technologies such as computers, the Internet, GPS, and new medical procedures and drugs that have contributed immensely to national prosperity, security and public health.

As important as research universities are today in our everyday lives, it seems clear that in the future, they will play an even more critical role. They will become the key players in providing the knowledge resources—knowledge itself and the educated citizens capable of applying it wisely—necessary for our prosperity, security, and social well-being. As Erich Bloch, former Director of the National Science Foundation, stated in Congressional testimony: "The solution of virtually all the problems with which government is concerned, health, education, environment, energy, urban development, international relationships, space, economic competitiveness, and defense and national security, all depend on creating new knowledge—and, hence, upon the health of America's research universities."

The University of Michigan can lay claim to being one of the earliest research universities in America, adopting *Wissenschaft,* a culture of scholarship, from the German universities, hiring faculty who were scholars as well as instructors, and building one of the largest telescopes in the world in the 1850s under the leadership of its first president Henry Tappan. He expected his faculty to teach, to push back the frontiers of knowledge, and to initiate their students into a world of intellectual exploration.

1950s-1960s

From its creation, Michigan has provided leadership in research that continued well into the 20th century, intensifying following WWII with federal policies that established university campuses as the source of the majority of the nation's basic research. Michigan participated aggressively in this new environment. The University's involvement in wartime research was quickly transformed into major research activities through Project Michigan at the Willow Run Laboratories in areas such as electronics, remote sensing, and computing. The presence of one of the nation's leading programs in aerospace engineering established Michigan as a leading research center in rocket science and spaceflight, including astronaut training. The relocation to the University of leading social science research programs from WWII established the Institute for Social Research, which in turn stimulated the rapid evolution of the social science disciplines on the campus into world leaders. Similar advances were made in biomedical research, with the clinical trials demonstrating the effectiveness of the Salk vaccine in the 1950s, heart transplant surgery in the 1960s, and the early development of human gene therapy with the discovery of the gene responsible for cystic fibrosis and the subsequent effort in molecular medicine of the 1980s.

It was also during the post-World War II era that Michigan became known as a world leader in interdisciplinary programs. Much older programs, such as our many international area studies programs and the Horace H. Rackham School of Graduate Studies, were joined by new ones, including the Michigan Memorial Phoenix Project, the Institute for Social Research, the Howard Hughes Medical Research Institute, the Institute for Science and Technology, and literally hundreds of other institutes, centers, programs, seminars, and other informal groups.

1970s

In the late 1960s and 1970s, under President Robben Fleming, the University reviewed its research priorities. At that time, over half of the research funding at Michigan came from military projects, and a number of investigators were engaged in classified research. After much debate and campus protests, the faculty voted to restrict classified studies. At the same time, the University divested itself of the Willow Run laboratories, which were supported almost entirely by the military, dropping the level of military funding on campus to below 10 percent of the total. Finally, in another important decision, the faculty established the "end-use" rule, prohibiting "any classified research contract with the specific purpose of which is to destroy human life or to incapacitate human beings." This again represented a new post-war realization of the importance of university research to the rest of the world, and of the University's responsibility to consider the ultimate impact of its discoveries.

Although few new departments were created during this period, the tendency toward specialization within departments increased. Departments became more splintered of loose confederations of faculty in rarefied subfields who had more in common with peers in their disciplines at other universities than with campus colleagues. Generous funding for the sciences also widened the already immense gulf between the social sciences, the natural sciences, and the humanities.

Since the effort of faculty to attract external grants for funding research and graduate education was so critical, the University explored special efforts to provide incentives for grantsmanship, as well as to make the case for faculty support of indirect cost recovery as critical to adequate funding research grants. While chair of the Academic Affairs Advisory Committee to both Provost Frank Rhodes and Harold Shapiro, Jim was able to make the case for strong incentives for such efforts, including grants based on the percentage of indirect cost recovery and PhD student participation. Although this was not implemented in the 1970s, it was later funded in the 1980s by Provost Billy Frye and remains in place today.

1980s

Simultaneously with the effort to encourage faculty to seek grants, the University also moved to adopt a far more aggressive stance toward technology transfer. In the late 1980s it modified its intellectual property policies to provide more faculty incentives for transferring knowledge developed on the campus through patents, startup companies, and industrial partnerships. Advisory groups were formed to assist in technology transfer and small business development. The University also worked to build strong partnerships with private sector companies, for example, the partnership to develop the Internet with IBM and MCI, the Fraunhofer Institute with the German government and local industry, and the Tauber Manufacturing Institute with a consortium of business partners.

The University was successful in convincing the State of Michigan to create an annual Research Investment Fund that would invest $25 million each year in technology ventures aimed at economic development in the State. The College of Engineering was able to capture $10 million of these funds for three initiatives: the Solid State Electronics Laboratory, Advanced Manufacturing program, and Robotics effort. In addition, it also received $1 million per year to create an Applied Physics program between Engineering and Physics. Over the next several years these funds became a part of the base budget of the College.

1990s

The chairmanship of the National Science Board, both the nation's leading science policy body as well as the board of directors for the National Science Foundation, provided Jim an excellent opportunity as the University's president to strengthen the University's research activities.

Four key themes were converging during the 1990s: i) the importance of the university in an age in which knowledge had become a key factor in determining security, prosperity, and quality of life; ii) the global nature of our society; iii) the ease with which information technology and telecommunications enabled the rapid exchange of information; and iv) networking, the degree to which informal cooperation and collaboration among individuals and institutions was replacing more formal social structures such as governments and societal structures.

Michigan was determined to play a significant role in all of these arenas. During the 1980s, the University had recruited some of the nation's leaders in these areas, including Doug Van Houweling from Carnegie-Mellon, Lynn Conway from Xerox, Doug Hofstadter from Indiana, and Randy Frank from Utah, who joined campus leaders such as Dan Atkins, Bernie Galler, John Holland, Richard Phillips, and Eric Aupperle. Drawing from the experience of major projects such as the statewide MERIT computer network, Van Houweling headed up a major effort that led the University to join corporate partners IBM and MCI to build and manage the NSFnet, the backbone of the rapidly developing Internet. This positioned the University to play a key leadership role in the evolution of the "information superhighway", as it evolved into a worldwide network linking hundreds of millions of people. Even as the University provided this national leadership, it was continuing to make substantial investments in its oncampus information technology environment that kept it at the cutting edge for students, faculty, and staff.

Rather than focusing its efforts to develop sophisticated computing capability for a handful of scholars, as did many other universities who invested in supercomputers, Michigan instead followed a philosophy of "power to the people"–namely, to provide as much computer and networking capability as possible to as many members of the University community as it could. It was determined to provide students and faculty with maximum flexibility and few constraints, so they could let their creativity and curiosity drive their use of these resources.

Through close cooperation with industrial leaders such as IBM, Apple, Sun, MCI, Xerox, and Hewlett-Packard, the University established itself as a clear leader in the quality of its information technology environment for teaching and research. It played a key role in developing much of the technology used today in the Internet, and it managed the transition from time-sharing mainframe systems to client-server networks. Through innovative programs such as the Fall Kickoff Computer Sales by which sophisticated computer systems were sold to students at deep discount, the

Chair, National Science Board

Chair, Advsory Committee on Cyberinfrastructure

Member, NRC Committee on Science, Engineering
and Public Policy (COSEPUP

Chair, NRC Committee on Information Technology
and the Reseach University

Rescomp program that placed numerous clusters of advanced computers directly into the residence halls, and the unusual array of oncampus computing resources and centers–including massive facilities such as the Angell-Haven Computer Center and the Media Union–it provided students with extraordinary access to this technology.

By the mid-1990s, Michigan was recognized throughout the world as one of the most important leaders in the development, application, and use of digital technology. It was exceptionally well positioned for leadership as this rapidly evolving technology revolutionized the nature of an increasingly knowledge-driven civilization.

The University also began to play a leadership role in the digital age, through its leadership of the national digital library project, the evolution of its School of Library Science into a new School of Information focused on the management of digital information, and the Media Union which established Michigan as a leader in the development and use of multimedia technologies. Major investments were made in the research capability of the University through new research facilities (e.g., three major medical science research buildings, new physics and chemistry laboratories, and a major expansion of the laboratories of the College of Engineering).

Furthermore, the University's government relations efforts in both Lansing and Washington were increased with the establishment of permanent offices and

Duderstadt Center

Angell-Haven Computer Center

additional staff, as well as a strategic focus on key research initiatives. Similarly, the University was far better positioned to compete effectively for major federal research grants, including the establishment of major national centers such as the NSF Center for Ultrafast Optics, the National Cancer Research Center, the Human Genome Project, and the many programs of the Institute for Social Research.

As a result, the University of Michigan's ranking with respect to the amount of sponsored research activity rose from its traditional rank of 7th or 8th nationally to overtake MIT and Stanford to be ranked 1st in the nation. Put another way, by this measure, by the 1990s, the University could rightly claim the title of America's leading research university. Beyond the impact that such research had on society in areas such as genetic medicine, public policy reform, information technology, and humanistic studies, this dimension of University activity greatly added to the intellectual excitement on campus and brought instructional programs to the cutting edge of the knowledge base.

2000s

Throughout the first decade of the 21st century, the University of Michigan has remained one of the world's leading research universities. The level of its research activities continued to increase. However there were new challenges.

Although there was initially optimism that the federal government was prepared to make the strong investment in its research universities with the doubling of the budget of the National Institutes of Health, other federal priorities such as two wars (Iraq and Afghanistan), health care for an aging population, tax cuts, and a weakening economy soon undermined this research support. While the NIH budget was initially doubled, stimulating universities to build new biomedical research facilities and hire more faculty and postdoctoral researchers, this support has fallen off by over 40%. The hope generated by the passage of the American Competes Act in 2007 that would have doubled the funding of NSF, DOE Science, and NIST has rapidly faded with new pressures on Congress to limit expenditures (although there was a brief burst of support associated with one-time funding aimed at stimulating the economy following the recession of 2008-2009). A conservative Congress has shifted its attention away from investments in the future through research and education, putting large research universities at risk.

The University of Michigan maintained its status as the nation's leader in research expenditures (rising to $1.32 billion in 2013). However the erosion of NIH funding by Congress coupled with stagnant funding in the physical sciences and engineering forced the University to commit more internal resources ($384 million in 2013) to sustain research groups and service the debt on new research facilities.

Despite the erosion in federal research support, the University continued its efforts to increase its research activity with the acquisition of the Pfizer

Michigan Energy Institute

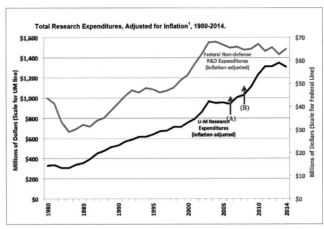

Growth in UM Research Volume (inflation adjusted)

Global Research Center to build a North Campus Research Center, funded by $108 million by the Medical Center and providing facilities for joint University-industry research. There was also heightened activity in identifying promising intellectual property and assisting faculty in entrepreneurial efforts to bring it to market.

There were also many new research programs. The University had long been a leader in research in energy sciences, technology, and policy. However a presidential committee recognized that more was needed to position Michigan for the unusual challenges and opportunities presented by the need to increasingly shift the nation to carbon-free energy sources. To this end the faculty recommended and the Regents approved a new Michigan Energy Institute that would support multidisciplinary energy research across the University. The Institute was designed as an enabling rather than an operational or managing organization, serving to focus the broad spectrum of University energy expertise and programs. Its functions are to coordinate (research projects, partners, or clients), to serve as a clearinghouse linking expertise both on and off campus, to assist in identifying and developing research opportunities (perhaps enabled with seed funding), to market the University's capabilities in energy research (to government, industry, and the public), to stimulate the development of educational programs, and to manage those facilities designed to support University-wide, multidisciplinary research activities. New facilities for the Michigan Energy Institute were built adjacent to the Phoenix Memorial

Laboratory, which also broadened its research activities beyond nuclear research.

A second major program, also created by a University-wide committee, was the program in Science, Technology, and Public Policy (STPP) located in the Ford School of Public Policy. In response to increasing demand for experts in the politics and processes of science and technology policymaking as well as a need for sustained intellectual engagement on these issues, the STPP aims to develop both educational and research initiatives in this area. This program addresses two primary questions. First, it explores "science and technology for policy": how science and technology are used to develop public policy in a broad array of domains such as national security, public health, economic competitiveness, and environmental sustainability. Second, it examines "policy for science and technology": how policies are developed to promote beneficial scientific and technological development at the international, national, state, and local levels, such as the allocation of research funding and regulation of new research and technologies. As one of the world's leading research universities, typically ranked among the top three in the nation in research activity across an unusually broad range of disciplines, the STPP program provides the University of Michigan with both an important opportunity and significant obligation to influence policy development in science and technology.

Of particular importance were the various leadership roles Jim was able to play in organizations such as the National Academies of Science, Engineering, and

University R&D Expenditures, U-M and Other Leading Institutions, FY2004-13.										
Institution	2004	2005	2006	2007	2008	2009	2010⁶	2011	2012	2013
Johns Hopkins U⁷	$1,375M	$1,444M	$1,500M	$1,554M	$1,681M	$1,856M	$2,004M	$2,145M	$2,106M	$2,169M
U MICHIGAN	$769M	$809M	$800M	$809M	$876M	$1,007M	$1,184M	$1,279M	$1,323M	$1,375M
U Washington	$714M	$708M	$778M	$757M	$765M	$778M	$1,023M	$1,149M	$1,109M	$1,193M
U Wisconsin	$764M	$798M	$834M	$841M	$882M	$952M	$1,029M	$1,112M	$1,170M	$1,124M
UC San Diego	$709M	$721M	$755M	$799M	$842M	$879M	$943M	$1,009M	$1,074	$1,076M
UC San Francisco	$728M	$754M	$796M	$843M	$885M	$948M	$936M	$995M	$1,033M	$1,043M
Harvard U	$354M	$388M	$423M	$432M	$460M	$449M	$583M	$650M	$799M	$1,013M
Duke U	$521M	$631M	$657M	$782M	$767M	$805M	$983M	$1,022M	$1,010M	$993M
U North Carolina	$417M	$441M	$444M	$477M	$526M	$646M	$755M	$869M	$885M	$973M
UCLA	$773M	$786M	$811M	$823M	$871M	$890M	$937M	$982M	$1,003M	$967M

SOURCE: National Science Foundation, Higher Education Research and Development Survey.

UM Ranking in research expenditures

The 2015 Vannevar Bush Award

Medicine, federal agencies such as the Department of Energy, the National Science Foundation, and various White House initiatives, which greatly enhanced the visibility and influence of the University. In recognition of this leadership role in serving the nation through public service, in 2015 he received the Vannevar Bush Award, the nation's leading recognition for leadership in science and technology policy.

The Road Ahead

Today, our nation faces new challenges, a time of rapid and profound economic, social, and political transformation driven by the growth in knowledge and innovation. A decade into the 21st century, a resurgent America must stimulate its economy, address new threats, and position itself in a competitive world transformed by technology, global competitiveness, and geopolitical change. Educated people, the knowledge they produce, and the innovation and entrepreneurial skills they possess, particularly in the fields of science and engineering, have become key to America's future.

Restoring the nation's research capacity will require a balanced set of commitments by each of the partners—federal government, state governments, research universities, and business and industry-to provide leadership for the nation in a knowledge-intensive world and to develop and implement enlightened policies, efficient operating practices, and necessary investments. It is important to create linkages and interdependencies among these commitments that provide strong incentives for participation at comparable

levels by each partner. Success will require a decade-long effort when both challenges and opportunities are likely to change, evolving from an early emphasis on more efficient policies and practices to later increases in investment as the economy improves.

Yet today, many research universities are forced to subsidize underfunded sponsored research grants from resources designated for other important university missions, such as undergraduate tuition and patient fees for clinical care. This is no longer acceptable and must cease. If the federal government and other research sponsors would cover the full costs of the research they procure from the nation's research universities, they, in turn, could hold steady or reduce the amount of funding from other sources they have had to provide to subsidize this federal research. Universities should be able to allocate their various resources more strategically for their intended purpose. Both sponsored research policies and cost recovery negotiations should be applied in a consistent fashion across all academic institutions.

In a similar spirit, both the federal government and the states should reduce or eliminate regulations that increase administrative costs, impede research productivity, and deflect creative energy without substantially improving the research environment.

Over the past two decades, in the face of shifting public priorities and weak economies, states have decimated the support of their public research universities, cutting appropriations per enrolled student by an average of 35 percent, totaling more than $15 billion each year nationally. (McPherson, 2009) Yet,

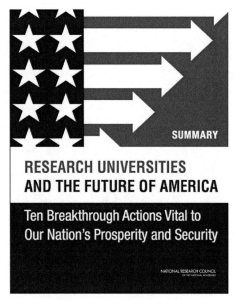

National Academies Study of Research Universities

American Academies Study of U.S. Research

even as the states have been withdrawing the support necessary to keep these institutions at world-class levels, they have also been imposing upon them increasingly intrusive regulations. As the leader of one prominent private university put it, "The states are methodically dismantling their public universities where the majority of the nation's campus research is conducted and two-thirds of its scientists, engineers, physicians, teachers, and other knowledge professionals are produced." (Holliday, 2012)

Hence, the nation must challenge the states to recognize that the devastating cuts and meddlesome regulations imposed on their public research universities is not only harming their own future, but also putting at great risk the nation's prosperity, health, and security. While strongly encouraging the states to begin to restore adequate support of these institutions as the economy improves, we also urged them to move rapidly to provide their public research universities with sufficient autonomy and agility to navigate an extended period with limited state support. One way to stimulate this would be new federal programs to support critical university needs such as new faculty positions and infrastructure needs (e.g., cyberinfrastructure) though funds that would require match from state or private contributions.

It is important that the relationship between business and higher education should shift from that of a customer-supplier—of graduates and intellectual property—to a peer-to-peer nature, stressing collaboration in areas of joint interest and requiring joint commitment of resources. Strong support of a permanent federal tax for research and development and more efficient management of intellectual property by businesses and universities to improve technology transfer are also needed. Such a tax credit would stimulate new research partnerships, new knowledge and ideas, new products and industries in America, and new jobs. Better management of intellectual property would result in more effective dissemination of research results, thus also generating economic growth and jobs.

Although universities seek high efficiency in their teaching and research–particularly public universities in the face of eroding state support, it is essential that the nation's research universities strive even harder to address the concerns of the American public that their costs are out of control. To this end, universities should set and achieve bold goals in cost-containment, efficiency, and productivity. They should strive to constrain the cost escalation of all continuing activities—academic and auxiliary—to the national inflation rate or less through improved efficiency and productivity. This will require the development of more powerful, strategic tools for financial management and cost accounting, tools that better enable universities to determine the most effective methods for containing costs and increasing productivity and efficiency. It is essential that universities, working together with key constituencies, intensify efforts to educate people about the distinct character of American research universities and cease promoting activities that create a public sense of unbridled excess on campuses.

Research universities should restructure doctoral education to enhance pathways for talented undergraduates, improve completion rates, shorten time-to-degree, and strengthen the preparation of graduates for careers both in and beyond the academy. (Wendler, 2010) To this end, the federal government should achieve a better balance of fellowships, traineeships, and research assistantships. Both universities and research sponsors should address the many concerns characterizing postdoctoral research appointments including the excessive length and low compensation of such service and the misalignment of these experiences with career opportunities. Such efforts would increase cost-effectiveness and ensure that we can draw from the "best and brightest" for our nation's future doctorates.

Research universities should intensify their efforts to improve science education throughout the education ecosystem, including K-12 and undergraduate education. Furthermore, all research partners should take action to increase the participation and success of women and underrepresented minorities across all academic and professional disciplines and especially in science, mathematics, and engineering. As careers in STEM fields continue to expand, recruiting more underrepresented minorities and women into those fields is essential in order to meet the workforce needs of our nation and to secure economic prosperity and social well-being.

Federal agencies should make visa processing for international students and scholars who wish to study or conduct research in America as efficient and effective as possible, consistent also with homeland-security considerations. This should include the possibility of granting residency to each foreign citizen who earns a doctorate in an area of national need from an accredited research university ("attaching a green card to each diploma").

While achieving these goals will be challenging, particularly in a rapidly changing economic environment, it is important to state what is needed and then to develop implementation strategies in collaboration with the various constituencies that are key to achieving these goals.

Clearly such actions would require significant policy changes, productivity enhancement, and investments on the part of each member of the research partnership: the federal government, the states, stakeholders such as business and philanthropy, and most of all, the nation's research universities. However, these recommendations do comprise a fair and balanced program that will generate significant returns to the nation. Such commitments are necessary for the future prosperity, health, and security of America.

Chapter 16

Service

The comprehensive university is a distinctively American institution. These unique institutions are a primary societal mechanism for the creation, preservation, and dissemination of knowledge through their educational and research activities. They are also expected to apply this knowledge to serve society as a whole. In many ways, the university has become the very embodiment of the American dream. It provides opportunity through education. Its research fuels the progress of industry, the quality of health care, and the security of our nation. Its cultural activities enrich our lives. It helps to protect our natural environment. It accepts a profound responsibility to serve our society at a multitude of levels.

Public service represents the "real-world" extension of the research, teaching, and professional expertise of the faculty. The support of public universities through general taxation implies particular service responsibilities, and the commitments that such institutions are willing to assume for society cannot remain implicit. The public has the right to ask how public universities are responding to its needs, and these institutions have an obligation to provide a clear answer.

Our universities are also at the forefront of efforts to create new jobs from new knowledge. Our technology-transfer activities encourage researchers to bring their discoveries to the marketplace. As the world economy enters a time of unpredictable change, the university is working hard to ensure that our nation sustains momentum as an economic powerhouse. We work directly with business and industry, helping to produce and compete more efficiently.

Research universities are particularly responsive to national needs, working closely with government and industry to strengthen national security in both wartime

and peace. They have embraced a mission to stimulate economic prosperity through the transfer of technology from the campuses into industry and the marketplace.

As a haven for those in critical need, our medical centers have served society with the most advanced care for decades. Each year, our emergency helicopters transport thousands of critically-ill patients, our hospitals serve millions, and our doctors develop the medical breakthroughs of the future. From cuts and bruises to the most traumatic injuries and life-threatening illnesses, our academic health centers provide a sense of security and hope.

Most large universities have launched a diverse range of efforts to strengthen local communities. Many programs draw on the expertise of all the university's schools and colleges, supporting local communities with healthcare, economic development, environmental assessment, and other services. Some programs are based on student volunteers and internship. As critical catalysts for change, community service projects draw students, faculty, and staff into neighborhoods to serve and to learn that our true community encompasses the world, not just the campus.

Many public universities have extended their reach and impact beyond their communities, states, and the nation to address global needs. Since modernizing agriculture was one of the primary goals of the land-grant acts, it is not surprising that the nation's land-grant universities have been long involved in international activities, first extending the green revolution of modern agricultural science and today embracing broader agendas such as feeding the world–not an insignificant challenge with the population explosions in underdeveloped regions such as Africa (anticipating feeding a population of 2.3 billion in 2050.) The land-grant universities have been joined by those with the

The scale of the University of Michigan is shown in the colored areas on an aerial of Ann Arbor.

health sciences providing global outreach in public health and medical care.

Today's university is more heavily involved than ever in public service activities, ranging from economic development to health care delivery to strengthening inner-city schools. Yet, in this world of intense economic competition, technological change, and social complexity, public universities are continually besieged by requests, demands, and exhortations to do even more to serve the public.

In the late 20th Century, the public's willingness to support higher education tends to be determined not by the value placed on its traditional missions of teaching and scholarship, but instead, by the perception of direct and immediate benefit stemming from its public service activities. Populism and parochialism are again affecting public attitudes toward higher education. The themes of today are no longer "excellence in teaching and research," but, rather, "excellence for whom and for what purpose"—or, more to the point, "What have you done for me lately?"

Michigan's Service Mission

Clearly the University of Michigan has great impact on the state. Consider for example, some of its state-specific statistics

200,000 alumni, 42,000 employees who live and work in Michigan
24,000 students enrolled from the state of Michigan
2 million visits by state residents to UM hospitals and clinics
$1.5 billion in UM purchases from 45,500 Michigan companies
$7 billion of revenue attracted into the state

Yet the more directed activity of public service has always been an important component of the mission of the University of Michigan. Perhaps President James Angell articulated this best:

"Perhaps in no other particular is the contrast between the old college and the new university more marked than in the close relation of the university, and especially the university in the West, to the public and to the schools. It is not easy for us to realize how great an extent the college of 50 years ago was isolated from the public. By the great mass of common people it was regarded as the home of useless and harmless recluses, of the mysteries of whose life they knew nothing and for whose pursuits they cared nothing. But we all know how conspicuous most of the universities have been in recent years. They have abandoned their monastic seclusion. They have sought to make their aims and their life known to the public and to interest all classes of men in their welfare. Public and private generosity thus rival each other in the hearty support of the universities which have had the wisdom to dedicate themselves with all their resources to public service."

The University evolved with the State of Michigan, responding to its needs as its economy and society expanded and diversified. From the earliest days the

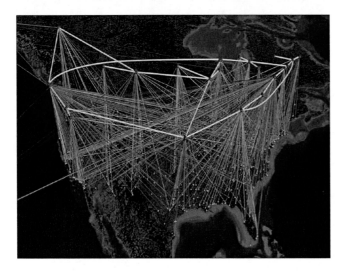
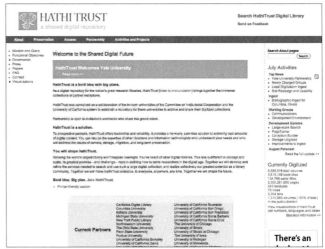

The impact of the service activities of the University have been immense, from nuclear science to industrial technology to pharmaceutical research to robotics to the Internet to the Hathitrust.

University was animated by social purpose through the social responsibility expected of its graduates to justify public investment, the faculty commitment to educating undergraduates to civil and practical life, and the improvement of public institutions throughout the state. Later, as research, professional training, and graduate education took firm hold, these too were infused with public purpose. Indeed, from its founding, the University of Michigan has been identified as one of the most progressive forces in American higher education, establishing a strong tradition of service to the society that supported it.

Michigan engineers and scientists were instrumental in developing the technologies necessary to defend the nation during world wars, including remote sensing and satellite reconnaissance. Michigan was heavily involved in both aeronautical engineering and space science and spaceflight. The University developed the first research and educational programs concerning the peaceful uses of atomic energy. Their School of Public Health performed the clinical trials for the Salk polio vaccine, and their medical school developed not only an array of clinical treatments but also launched early programs in human gene therapy. And its work in computer networks and digitization led to the Internet and digital libraries.

To illustrate this in more detail, it is useful to consider two of the most significant areas of the University's public service: clinical care and economic development.

An Example of Public Service:
The Academic Medical Center

Perhaps the best example of the manner in which the missions of education, research, and service interweave is the academic medical center, certainly the most complex component of the university. Furthermore, its missions of education, research, and clinical care are conducted all on a scale that dwarfs most other university programs. There is also no part of the university that has experienced such powerful forces of change in recent years because of the profound changes in the ways in which health care is delivered and financed. There is also no part of the university that has required so much time and attention of university leaders.

American universities have long been an important source not only of physicians, nurses, dentists, pharmacists, and other health care professionals but also for health care through their hospitals and clinics. Medical education and practice has been an important priority for the University since its earliest days in Ann Arbor, and during the late 19th century Michigan, together with Penn and Columbia, defined the character of medical education within a graduate paradigm based upon laboratories and teaching hospitals. With one of the largest hospitals in the nation, built during the 1920s, the University became one of the leading providers of health care to the state and of medical research for the world.

Both the Medical School and the University Hospital experienced rapid growth throughout the post-war decades. This growth continued throughout the 1970s and 1980s, even as there were pressures to reduce the enrollments in the Medical School, arising from the growing awareness that there was an over supply of physicians—specialists in particular. Even though the Medical School reduced its enrollment of medical students by 30 percent during the 1980s (to 180 students per class), the number of faculty in the School continued to grow to its present level of over 1,200, driven by the increasing clinical needs of the hospitals. Similarly, both the physical size and the level of patient activities of the University Hospital—more correctly "hospitals," since the medical center spawned separate facilities for activities, such as pediatrics, maternal care, geriatrics, cancer treatment, ophthalmology, and so on—continued to grow through the 1980s and 1990s. Today, the university health system receives almost two million patient visits per year, with total revenues of $3.0 billion/year, ranking it as one of the largest academic medical centers in the nation.

The primary reason for this extraordinary growth was both the increasing health care needs of an aging population, and, of course, the need to generate revenue from patient care. Since the University Hospitals operates as an auxiliary unit of the University, without state or University subsidy, it needs to generate sufficient revenues to cover its expenses. Since scale determined market competitiveness, there were strong incentives for growth.

Yet the Medical Center faced major challenges in

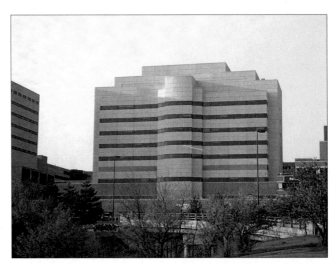

The clinical services of the University of Michigan Hospitals
provide an extraordinary resource to the citizens of the State of Michigan.

the later half of the 20th century as medical practice changed and the University's clinical facilities needed to be upgraded. The University presidents of those years, notably Presidents Fleming, Smith, and Shapiro, "bet the ranch" on the Replacement Hospital Project, at $350 million, the largest project in the history of the University. Although this was an extraordinary gamble, particularly during the early 1980s when the state's economy was in a deep recession, the new facility provided the University Medical Center with a highly competitive advantage as it came on line in the late 1980s. This, coupled with a series of restructuring and cost-reduction efforts led by UMH Director John Forsyth, rapidly positioned the University Hospitals as among the most profitable in the nation. Indeed, during the early 1990s, the Hospitals were routinely generating surpluses of $50 million or more each year. Hospital reserves grew to over half-a-billion dollars, and a combination of Hospital reserves and clinical income generated by Medical School faculty funded an extraordinary period of new research and clinical facilities, including sophisticated research laboratories, a new pediatric and women's hospital, a cancer center, a geriatrics center, and extensive outpatient facilities.

Yet the changes in health care delivery and financing continued to accelerate as increasing resistance to health care costs led to strong market forces driving intense competition and new health care organizations to provide managed care. Again, the leadership of the Medical Center was visionary and launched major new efforts such as the M-Care HMO, a network of primary care facilities scattered throughout southeastern Michigan, including a new medical campus in northeast Ann Arbor and important strategic alliances with hospitals and health care insurance providers.

As each wave of changes in health care swept across the nation, the University Medical Center, both because of commitments made in the past and an aggressive vision for the future, seemed to thrive and become even stronger. Today the renamed University Health System has grown to over $3.2 billion in clinical activity, and together with the teaching and research activities of the Medical School, represents almost 50% of the budget of the entire University. Yet today there are increasing concerns that the University Hospitals may have moved too far out on a limb in the expansion

of clinical facilities. The massive investments in new facilities during the past decade (the $200 million Cardiovascular Center and the $760 million Mott Pediatrics Hospital) have driven operating revenues into the red, running deficits in the range of $100 million to $200 million a year over the past several years. While the $2.2 billion of UMH reserves generate sufficient investment income to compensate for these operating losses, the University soon will face the need to replace the massive Adult General Hospital, which is already showing obsolescence after only 30 years of operation (in part because of the new restrictions to private rooms because of the risk of infection and infrastructure such as elevator towers no longer able to handle the changing characteristics of the population served by the Hospital such as patient weight).

Today all academic medical centers are under great stress, because of both federal policy and the changing nature of the marketplace for health care. The rapid growth of managed care organizations (where payment is not structured around clinical services but on a fixed basis for maintaining the health of each individual) has changed dramatically the nature and financing of health care. The marketplace has become intensively competitive because of an excess of hospital capacity, and the entry of for-profit organizations. Because of the high costs associated both with the tertiary clinical mission and teaching function, many academic medical centers face serious financial challenges today that threaten their very survival.

Compounding these challenges is the Affordable Health Care Act, passed in 2010, which attempts to rapidly expand the availability of health care to the millions of Americans currently without health care plans, while controlling costs. Although under continual attack by conservative political forces, the role of government in creating and supporting national health care policy has been adopted by almost all nations, and the further evolution toward more government influence on the marketplace seems inevitable.

In simple terms, what is really occurring is a shift in the risk associated with providing health care. In the past, the "fee-for-services" payment system placed most of the risk on third-party payers, such as the federal government or insurers. Physicians and patients were focused on the quality, rather than the costs, of health care, since others picked up the tab. Managed care shifts the risk from third party payers to health care providers. Managed care organizations negotiate a fixed cost per person, regardless of the costs of their medical treatments. The burden is placed on health care providers to manage the costs of maintaining the health of the "managed lives" in the contract. In most academic medical centers, this risk has been borne initially by the hospitals.

It is increasingly clear that for teaching hospitals to survive, they must have increasing freedom to control their costs—to operate like a business—with attention given to the bottom line, even if this conflicts on occasion with their teaching and research mission. In particular, most teaching hospitals are taking a far more aggressive stance toward negotiating physician services from their associated medical schools. In practical terms, this means that they are seeking to shift the risk associated with health care costs once again, this time to the clinical faculty and the medical school. The implications, both for medical schools and their host universities, are serious indeed.

Economic Development

Research universities have become important players in regional economic development. The key ingredients in technology-based economic development are technological innovation, technical manpower, and entrepreneurs. Research universities produce all three. Through their on-campus research, they generate the creativity and ideas necessary for innovation. Through their faculty efforts, they attract the necessary "risk capital" for economic development through massive federal R&D support. Through their education programs they produce the scientists, engineers, and entrepreneurs to implement new knowledge. They are also the key to knowledge transfer, both through traditional mechanisms, such as graduates and publications, as well as through more direct contributions such as faculty/staff entrepreneurs, the formation of start-up companies, and strategic partnerships with business and industry.

The Bayh-Dole Act of 1980 reflected the federal interest in the transfer of technology from the campuses into the marketplace and permitted universities and small businesses to retain title to inventions developed with federal R&D funds. Furthermore, there is ample evidence to support the impact of research universities on technology-driven economic development. We need only look at MIT's impact on the Boston area, Stanford's and UC-Berkeley's impact on Northern California, Caltech's impact on Southern California, and the Research Triangle activity stimulated by the University of North Carolina, North Carolina State University, and Duke University.

In examining such experiences, one can identify several key stages to technology transfer:

To attract the key people;
To create the knowledge;
To facilitate the transfer of knowledge;
To create a sufficiently entrepreneurial culture both on and off campus;
To form or attract new companies; and
To help these companies grow and flourish.

The new knowledge necessary to stimulate economic activity flows directly from the research performed by universities. Estimates suggest that over 50 percent of the new job growth in America can be traced to new knowledge coming out of our research laboratories. Through research grants and contracts, the federal government, augmented by industry, foundations, and internal university support, supplies the resources for the development of new knowledge. But here it is important to keep in mind that such support continues to be provided primarily through a competitive process based upon merit review. The quality of the faculty and students determines the quality of the proposals and hence the success in attracting external support for research. There is strong evidence that the most highly ranked universities attract the most research support, generate the most new knowledge, and thus stimulate the most regional economic development. Excellence determines impact.

Research universities—particularly public research universities—have a major obligation to make every effort to transfer intellectual properties resulting from their academic activities into the private sector where they will benefit society more broadly, in a manner consistent with their academic missions, of course. Such

The Industrial Technology Institute

The North Campus Research Center

technology transfer will occur most rapidly when those who create the new knowledge—faculty and staff—have maximum incentive, opportunity, and support to transfer it to the private sector. A research university's ability to recruit and retain outstanding faculty and staff will be increasingly influenced by the environment it provides to allow, encourage, and facilitate such knowledge-transfer activities. There is strong evidence suggesting that in many cases the best "academics" and "entrepreneurs" are one and the same!

Furthermore there is considerable evidence that interaction with the broader society is a critical factor in stimulating creative research in some areas. Knowledge transfer activities can have a positive impact on the quality of basic research since they create pressures to work in exciting, high risk, interdisciplinary areas to achieve the quantum leaps in knowledge not normally available in the industrial setting. In this sense, it is wrong to equate commercial value with applied research. Frequently the real barriers to application are due to a shortage of basic knowledge, only gained through fundamental research.

The University of Michigan has long accepted the role of transferring technology from its research programs to local and regional economic development. During the 1960s and 1970s, numerous companies were created in the Ann Arbor area, assisted by the University's efforts to create sources of venture capital. In the 1990s, intellectual property policies of the University were modified to give inventors not only streamlined legal and technology transfer activities, but to provide

inventors with the right of refusal and ownership if they believed they could be more efficient in creating companies and products. New organizations such as the Industrial Technology Institute and the North Campus Research Center were launched to encourage and incubate spinoff activity.

However it should also be acknowledged that while technology transfer has been long regarded as an important mission of the University, it has been difficult to ignite the same level of economic activity that characterizes other high-tech hot spots such as Silicon Valley, Route 128, or the Research Triangle. In part, this has to do with the State of Michigan's culture of "the big", i.e., big companies, big unions, big government, and big universities. Hence the infrastructure of financial institutions and management expertise does not provide the nurturing environment for startups that characterize many other parts of the nation. In fact, several Michigan students and faculty members have been quite successful in starting technology-based companies elsewhere.

Yet there are several cautions that should be noted. Although many research universities look to reap financial benefits from equity interest in spinoff activities, the reality is that less than ten universities today generate more revenue from technology transfer activities than they spend on the lawyers and staff in their technology transfer offices. In almost every case where an actual "profit" has been made on the spinoff activity, this has resulted from a single big hit, usually in the pharmaceutical area (e.g., Wisconsin and Columbia).

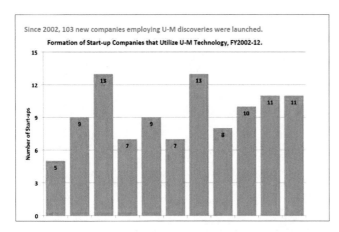

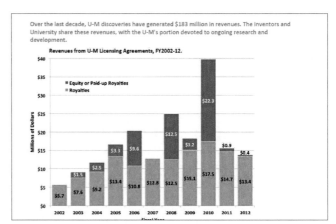

The intellectual property resulting from the University's research
is used to generate new companies and prosperity.

Hence it seems unlikely that most universities will reap substantial income through direct control of intellectual property through mechanisms such as patent licenses and equity interest in spin-off companies, at least in the near term. Institutions could gain substantial indirect benefits from aggressive technology transfer efforts through increased public support and private gifts. The strong support of Stanford by William Hewlett and David Packard is but one example. But the real motivation for technology transfer from the campus to the marketplace should be viewed as a form of public service, not as a profitable business.

Universities must take care to avoid a paternalistic attitude toward their faculty and staff. In perhaps well-intentioned efforts to protect them from the harsh, cruel world of private enterprise, the university may constrain and frustrate those already experienced in such activities. It would also prevent the development of a learning process among others (albeit sometimes by the school of hard knocks), while removing the incentive for widespread faculty involvement in technology transfer activities. It is best to begin with the premise that faculty and staff in universities are mature, responsible individuals who will behave properly in balancing the university's interests and their own responsibilities for teaching and research against their interests in intellectual property development and technology transfer. The key to avoiding conflict of interest is public disclosure.

In summary, knowledge transfer from the campus to the market will only succeed if we recognize that it is highly people-dependent. It is essential to stimulate and encourage the individual researcher-inventor to participate in these activities and to remove the constraints to provide maximum incentive and opportunity for this process to occur, but also to view this as a public service, indeed obligation, rather than as a source of riches.

Perhaps more important is the formation of strategic alliances between university researchers and industry and government. Such university-industry alliances should be viewed as symbiotic associations between two unlike organisms for the benefit of each. Of course, both industry and university have a "service to society" component. But their fundamental goals are quite different: industry seeks to make a profit, while universities seek to create and maintain knowledge and impart it to students. In a university-industry partnership, it is important that each partner focuses on what it does best.

While industry partnerships have existed for many years, they have tended to rely on traditional relationships, such as the hiring of graduates, the use of faculty consultants, or the sponsorship of research. Today, we face new challenges. The time required for technology transfer from university to industry must be reduced dramatically to meet the needs of existing companies and to spawn new industries. Yet academic institutions are ill equipped to respond to the highly focused immediate needs of industry without considerable disruption of on-campus responsibilities. We need to improve mechanisms for achieving direct industrial support of academe through financial assistance, equipment donations, and visiting staff. It is clear that both industry and academia need stronger, more sophisticated, and sustained relationships with each other in order to respond to the needs and capabilities of each type of organization.

While technology transfer is important and the launch of new companies is an appropriate subject for instructional activities, the University should avoid jumping on the bandwagon of hype about creating "centers for entrepreneurship" or entrepreneurship courses for undergraduates in the hopes that the next Bill Gates, Larry Page, of Mark Zuckerberg will spring from their campuses. Only a tiny fraction of students have the character to become a true entrepreneur, and most of these will fail many times before achieving the rare success.

A final caution is appropriate here. Today many universities view technology transfer as a new source of wealth. They see dollar signs in the vision of the next Apple or Microsoft or Facebook (although these were all started by college dropouts...) But as we have noted earlier,, there are few riches available to most universities in technology transfer. Rather, their primary motivation for such activities should be serving society. Indeed, some universities are even considering viewing the intellectual property produce on their campuses as a "public good", available to anybody subject to licensing restrictions that prevent it from being patented by others and restricted in use.

Other Service Activities

Services provided by the academic medical center and technology transfer represent highly organized and quite substantial organizations to provide University services. But for a major research university such as Michigan, there are countless service activities provided by faculty, staff, and students. For example, many faculty members contribute their time to important public service activities such as serving on scientific advisory bodies such as the National Academies of Science, Engineering, and Medicine or serving as technical consultants to federal agencies such as the National Science Foundation, the Department of Energy, or the Department of Defense. Many provide consulting services to industry or state agencies.

Major universities with a world-class presence also contribute important international services such as public health, economic development, or conflict resolution. Although such missions as international development were once a key mission of land-grant universities with their strong expertise in agricultural sciences, today all public universities have major international outreach activities. For example Michigan has extensive programs to assist sub-Saharan Africa in the development of public health and education. It has long had strong engagement with Asian nations, dating from over a century ago when President Angell, then serving as envoy to China, arranged for the reparation payments for the Boxer Rebellion to be kept in China to found a major technical university, Tsinghua, that today has become comparable to MIT in its quality and impact. Yet it is also very important today to avoid "colonial" approaches to globalization, e.g., establishing campuses in other parts of the world, but instead developing these as true peer-to-peer partnerships with other institutions seeking international activities. A good example here is the joint school of engineering operated by the University of Michigan and Shanghai Jiao Tong University.

Although the University does not have a school of agriculture, during the 1990s it joined with the land-grant universities as a member of the Midwest University Consortium of International Activities, participation in addressing global public health and economic development activities. With the emergence of the Internet, such global service activities became even more of a priority.

Lessons Learned

As we have noted, the relationship between the university and American society has evolved over the years and continues to do so today. In this sense, the mission of the University naturally acquires a trinity character of teaching, research, and service, or in more contemporary terminology, learning, discovery, and engagement.

The Land Grant acts established a model through which universities distributed and applied existing knowledge to serve an emerging industrial nation. The federal government-university research partnership shifted the emphasis to the generation of new knowledge through campus-based research. Today, as the role of the federal government as a major agent in addressing social concerns has shifted to the states and the communities, the university will be expected to assume new roles. For example, the increasing pace in the development and application of knowledge requires forming new relationships with both private industry and government agencies. So, too, does the direct support of university activities by institutions in both the public and private sector. Our colleges are drawn into new and more extensive relationships with each passing day.

This is understandable because research universities have vast resources capable of contributing to public needs. They are civic institutions with a long history of building the nation through their educational, research, and service activities. Yet, despite this past history and contemporary need, few universities are strategically situated for public service. Few university leaders and even fewer faculty members would place public service toward the top of the university's priorities. As Derek Bok put it, "Most universities continue to do their least impressive work on the very subjects where society's need for greater knowledge and better education is most acute."

To be sure, the public service role can, if not carefully managed, undermine the stability of our educational institutions. Part of the challenge here is not only knowing what are appropriate public service activities to conduct, but also knowing when it is time to cease or spin off a particular service activity, and then to accomplish this task without alienating important constituencies of the university. There are times when a particular service activity has simply outlived its usefulness. At other times, a service activity might be more effectively and appropriately performed by other social institutions, perhaps in the private sector. And there are some occasions when the service activity becomes so large and complex that it begins to distort the fundamental academic character of the university.

Many faculty members are concerned that much of university public service is simply not linked closely enough to its academic mission. But this may be in part a matter of definition, for it is clear that a very wide range of university activities do benefit both the campus and the public alike. For example, universities

benefit the public directly through their libraries and museums (preservation of knowledge), their theaters and concerts (provision of aesthetic experiences), intercollegiate athletics (entertainment for the masses), their custodianship of the young, and a host of direct services including hospitals, testing laboratories, publishing companies, hotels and restaurants, and so on. While not an "extension service" in the traditional sense, these activities certainly provide important services to the public.

The basic functions of the university continue to be core academic activities. Other major activities of the university gain legitimacy only to the degree that they are linked with education and scholarship. In this sense, public service that is based on teaching and research is not a function but one of a number of principles that animate and guide the basic work of a university.

For example, the early growth of the Internet was managed by a consortium of universities through federally sponsored projects such as NSFnet. But in the 1990s it became apparent that the rapid evolution of the Internet and its increasingly commercial character required that it be spun off to private contractors. Today there are many signs that the changing nature of health-care delivery and financing may require the spin-off of major academic medical centers and health care systems. And some would contend that intercollegiate athletics—at least the commercially dominated sports of football and basketball that serve as a source of public entertainment—so threaten the academic integrity of the university that it is time that they be spun off before they damage our institutions.

This growing demand for our services may be one of our greatest contemporary challenges. Increasingly, the public's willingness to support higher education tends to be determined not by the value placed on its traditional missions of teaching and scholarship, but rather by the perception of direct and immediate benefit through its public service activities.

One of the greatest challenges is balancing the various complex roles of the modern research university, even as these roles are rapidly changing. How does one achieve an optimum balance between teaching and research? Public service versus our role as an independent critic of society? The liberal arts and the professions? The tensions among these various roles occur in part because of the incompatibility in the needs, values, and expectations of the various constituencies served by higher education.

This challenge is particularly difficult for the public research university since so many different constituencies must be served. In a sense, each of its constituencies responds to a different aspect or role of the university. The tax-paying public and its elected state representatives expect these institutions to serve state and national interests while providing access to education for peoples of diverse racial, cultural, and economic backgrounds. These groups tend to emphasize the teaching function of the university, which is both demanding and essential for the dissemination of knowledge.

Other constituents such as industry and the federal government believe these institutions also have important obligations as research centers to achieve and maintain the highest possible level of excellence in the discovery of ideas and knowledge. Governments and public-interest groups seek expertise applicable to current social problems, foreign policy issues, or health care needs. At the same time, various publics expect the university to create an environment that sustains the research and inquiry that sometimes requires years of labor before coming to fruition. The interaction of these various functions can be creative and enriching, but the contrasting expectations of diverse constituents can also lead to a conflict in missions.

Public service, in a restricted sense, is comprised of those activities that are aimed at serving the needs of society, as dictated by an agenda set by the public and its representatives, rather than the institution itself. Public service is in this context primarily a responsive activity, designed to respond to societal needs, rather than a proactive effort that is in alignment with the primary academic objectives of the university. Another common restricted definition construes public service as work that draws upon one's professional expertise—an outgrowth of one's academic discipline. This includes applied research for an external client, consultation and technical services, clinical work or performance, or instruction within continuing education programs. In this sense, public or "professional" service is an applied version of teaching or scholarship.

Unfortunately, it has been precisely these restrictive definitions of public service that have led to the diminishment of public support for higher education. While there continue to be complaints that higher education is unresponsive to the needs of society, quite the opposite is true since the competitiveness of American universities causes them to pay close attention to their constituencies. This intense desire to respond has, in fact, led many institutions to reallocate limited resources away from their primary responsibilities in teaching and research in an effort to generate more direct public awareness and support.

By attempting to respond to unrealistic public aspirations and expectations, by attempting to be all things to all people, higher education has whetted an insatiable public appetite for a host of service activities of marginal relevance to its academic mission. A quick glance around any community with a local university provides numerous examples of this, from extension offices for continuing education to medical clinics to incubation centers for high-tech business formation to athletic camps for K-12 students.

Yet such responsiveness to the needs—indeed, even the whims—of society by higher education may, in the long run, be counterproductive. Not only has it fueled an inaccurate public perception of the primary mission of a university and an unrealistic expectation of its role in public service, but it has also stimulated an increasingly narrow public attitude toward the support of higher education. A "What-have-you-done-for-me-lately?"attitude now permeates federal, state, and local government. This fuels powerful forces of parochialism that force institutions to spread themselves ever more thinly as they scramble to justify themselves to their elected public officials.

The Road Ahead

There is little doubt that the need for and the pressure upon universities to serve the public interest more directly will intensify. The possibilities are endless: economic development and job creation; health-care; environmental quality; the special needs of the elderly, youth, and the family; peace and international security; rural and urban decay; and the cultural arts. There is also little doubt that if higher education is to sustain both public confidence and support, it must demonstrate its capacity to be ever more socially useful and relevant to a society under stress.

As we enter the age of knowledge, the traditional articulation of the mission of the university as a triad of teaching, research, and service may be too narrow. We need to consider more contemporary forms of our fundamental mission of creating, preserving, integrating, transferring, and applying knowledge.

Yet, as the University responds to both the need and opportunity to intensify service activities, several caveats and suggestions seem appropriate:

While there continue to be complaints that higher education is unresponsive to the needs of society, quite the opposite is true, since the competitiveness of American universities causes them to pay close attention to their constituencies. This intense desire to respond has led many institutions to reallocate limited resources away from their primary responsibilities of teaching and research in an effort to generate more direct public awareness and support. By attempting to respond to unrealistic public aspirations and expectations, to be all things to all people, higher education has whetted an insatiable public appetite for a host of service activities of only marginal relevance to its academic mission.

Yet such responsiveness to the needs—indeed, even the whims—of society by higher education may in the long run be counterproductive. Not only has it fueled an inaccurate public perception of the primary mission of a university and an unrealistic expectation of its role in public service, but it has also stimulated an increasingly narrow public attitude toward the support of higher education. Powerful forces of parochialism compel institutions to spread themselves ever more thinly as they scramble to "justify" themselves to their elected public officials. Faculty and administrators alike feel under intense pressure to demonstrate their commitment to public service, even when they recognize that this will frequently come at the expense of their primary academic missions.

It is important to always remember that education and scholarship are the primary functions of a university, its primary contributions to society, and hence the most significant roles of the faculty. When universities become overly distracted by other activities, they not only compromise this core mission but they

also erode their priorities within our society. Yet, public service must be a major institutional obligation of the American university. The public supports the university, contributes to its finance and grants it an unusual degree of institutional autonomy and freedom, in part because of the expectation that the university will contribute not just graduates and scholarship, but the broader efforts of its faculty, staff, and students in addressing social needs and concerns. It is some concern that the role of public service in higher education has not received greater attention in recent years, since this was an original mandate for many of our institutions.

Our institutions need a continually refreshed vision of their role that responds to the ever-changing needs of the society we serve. As we evolve along with broader society, the linkages between us become more varied, complex, and interrelated. Within this context of change, it is clear that public service must continue to be an important responsibility of the American university.

Chapter 17

Athletics

Mention Ann Arbor, and the first image that probably comes to mind is a crisp, brilliant weekend in the fall: walking across campus through the falling leaves to Michigan Stadium; gathering at tailgate parties before the big game; the excitement of walking into that magnificent stadium–"the Big House"–with 110,000 fans thrilling to the Michigan Marching Band as they step onto the field playing "Hail to the Victors."

Intercollegiate athletics provide some of the very special moments: The excitement of a traditional football rivalry such as Michigan vs. Ohio State. Or, perhaps, special events such as a Rose Bowl or a NCAA Final Four. Intercollegiate athletics programs at Michigan are not only an important tradition at the University, but they also attract as much public visibility as any other University activity.

They are also a critical part of a university president's portfolio of responsibilities. As any leader of a NCAA Division I-A institution will tell you, a president ignores intercollegiate athletics only at great peril--both institutional and personal. There is an old saying in presidential circles that the university might be viewed as a very fragile academic entity, delicately balanced between the medical center at one end of the campus and the athletic department at the other. The former can sink it financially–the latter can sink it through public gaffs.

Although it is perhaps understandable that a large, successful program such as Michigan would dominate the local media, it also has more far-reaching visibility. Michigan receives far more ink in the national media–the New York Times or the Washington Post or even the Wall Street Journal–for its activities on the field that it ever did for its classroom or laboratory contributions. This media exposure is due in part to the University's long tradition of successful athletics programs of

Michigan takes the field!

high integrity. It also stems from the increasingly celebrity character of college sports: successful and quotable coaches such as Bo Schembechler and Jim Harbaugh, outstanding players such as Tom Brady, Desmond Howard, Cazzie Russell and Jaylen Rose, and flamboyant teams such as the Fab Five, and the extraordinary scale of Michigan athletics, with a football stadium averaging 110,000 spectators a game.

The popularity of Michigan athletics is a two-edged sword, however. While it certainly creates great visibility for the University–after each Rose Bowl or Final Four appearance, the number of applications for admission surges–it also has a very serious potential for instability. Every college athletic department, no matter how committed and vigilant its leadership, nevertheless can depend on an occasional misstep. After all, most college student-athletes are still in their teens; the great popularity of college sports attracts all hangers-on to key programs, some well-intentioned, some not; there is intense pressure from the sports media; and the NCAA rulebook is larger and more complex than the

United States Tax Code.

Perhaps far more serious is the extraordinary emotional attachment that ordinarily rational people can develop toward college sports–at least toward successful programs. We have all seen how fans behave at sporting events–not simply cheering the favored team on, but taunting the opposition, berating officials, and even occasionally booing their own players and coaches. For many, this emotional involvement extends far beyond simply the moment of athletic competition. After a series of disappointing seasons, boosters and alumni are not only likely to call for the firing of the coach, but for the athletic director and the president as well. Why not get rid of the whole @#$%& bunch?! And their one-dimensional view of the university through their sports binoculars is not only conveyed to other fans, but to legislators and regents as well–folks who have the power and sometimes the inclination to do really serious damage!

Corner any university president in a candid moment, and he or she will admit that many of the problems they have with the various internal and external constituencies of the university stem from athletics. Whether it is an appropriate concern about program integrity, or a booster-driven pressure for team success, or media pressure, or over-involvement by trustees, presidents are frequently placed in harm's way by athletics. As a result, whether they like it or not, most presidents learn quickly that they must become both knowledgeable and actively involved in their athletics programs. As Peter Flawn, former president of the University of Texas, put it in his wonderful "how-to" book on university leadership, "If you don't like or understand college football, learn how to fake it".

1960s

Far more histories have been written about Michigan athletics than have been written about the University itself. The names of Michigan's sports heroes—Yost, Crisler, Harmon—are better known than any members of Michigan's distinguished faculty or its presidents. Tellingly, most of these histories have been written by sportswriters, former athletic directors, coaches, or fans. Hence it seems both appropriate and amusing to provide a brief historical corrective from our perspective of long

time members of the UM community and service in an array of Michigan leadership roles.

Although the legends of the good old days of Michigan athletics make enjoyable reading, this purpose is better served by beginning somewhat later, in the mid-1960s, when Michigan athletics, and college sports more generally, began their mad dash toward the cliff of commercialization. During today's heady times of national championships and lucrative television and licensing contracts, Michigan fans sometimes forget that the University's athletics programs have not always been so dominant. During the 1960s, the Michigan football program had fallen on hard times, with typical stadium attendance averaging 60,000 to 70,000 per game (about two-thirds the capacity of Michigan Stadium). Michigan State University, just up the road, drew most of the attention with its powerful football teams—actually, this was part of President John Hannah's strategy to transform Michigan Agricultural College into a major university. Furthermore, student interest on activist campuses such as Michigan's had shifted during the 1960s from college athletics to political activism, with great causes such as racial discrimination and an unpopular war in Vietnam to protest.

There were, nevertheless, a few bright spots in Michigan's athletic fortunes. Michigan's basketball team had enjoyed considerable success in the mid-1960s, with Cazzie Russell leading the team to the NCAA championship game, only to lose to an upstart UCLA team (which would then dominate the sport for the next decade). Largely as a consequence of this success, the University used student-fee-financed bonds to build a new basketball arena, Crisler Arena, named after former football coach and athletic director Fritz Crisler. Actually, this facility was also known to many as simply "the house that Cazzie built."

Some of the other athletics programs were also successful. The ice hockey team won the national championship in 1964. Swimming began what was to become a three-decade long domination of the Big Ten Conference. There were considerable accomplishments in other sports such as wrestling, track, and gymnastics. But, at Michigan, football was king, and when the football fortunes were down, students and fans were apathetic about Michigan athletics.

Don Canham, defining the AD Czar

Coach Bo Schembechler

This began to change in the late 1960s. Although many attribute Michigan's turnaround to a new athletic director, Don Canham, reputed to be the shrewd marketing genius who transformed Michigan athletics into a commercial juggernaut, most of the faculty saw the situation somewhat different. Following the advice of the former football coach Bump Elliot, Canham recruited a talented young football coach, Bo Schembechler, who revitalized the Michigan program in his first year, beating Ohio State and going to the Rose Bowl. The sports scene in southeastern Michigan strongly supports winners, and within a couple of years, Michigan Stadium began to sell out on a regular basis. It doesn't take a rocket scientist—or a Michigan faculty member, for that matter—to realize that if one can regularly fill the largest football stadium in the country with paying customers, prosperity and success soon follow. And indeed it did, since year after year Michigan fielded nationally ranked football teams.

The annual matchup between Michigan and Ohio State, often personified as a battle between Bo Schembechler and Woody Hayes, soon grew to mythical proportions. Fans experienced some initial frustration because of a Big Ten Conference rule, which allowed only the conference champion to compete in a bowl game, the Rose Bowl. However the quality of the Michigan and Ohio State teams during the early 1970s soon forced the Big Ten to relax this rule, and Michigan began to add a bowl game to its schedule every year.

To be sure, Canham was inventive. He began to market Michigan football in sophisticated ways. For instance, he arranged for planes to pull banners advertising Michigan football over Detroit's Tiger Stadium during the 1968 World Series. He launched the practice of mass-mailed advertising and catalogs of souvenir items. Michigan athletics began to function more as a business, complete with marketing, advertising, and promotion, along with the development of new commercial activities. To many, Canham became the stereotype of the athletic director CEO-czar who would drive college sports into a commercial entertainment industry.

1970s-1980s

During the 1970s and 1980s, for all intents and purposes, Michigan athletics was a one-sport program. Football ruled the roost, and other sports were clearly secondary priorities. Taking a more objective look at this era, one cannot help but note that while several of the men's programs competed effectively within the Big Ten Conference, none were regarded as national leaders.

In fact, Michigan went twenty-five years without a national championship in any sport, from 1964 when Al Renfrew's hockey team won the national championship until 1989 when Steve Fisher's basketball team won the Final Four. Even the football team, generally nationally ranked during the season, always fell short by season's end, either losing to Ohio State in the season finale or in its annual bowl appearance.

While Michigan's leadership in commercializing college sports was successful in generating new revenues, this was not viewed as necessarily beneficial to the University's image and reputation, at least by the faculty. The Athletic Department's increasing autonomy largely eliminated any substantive role of the faculty in governing intercollegiate athletics. While other universities moved rapidly to introduce varsity programs for women, Michigan remained largely fossilized in a prehistoric state of football-dominated men's sports. In fact, in 1976, Michigan became a test case for gender discrimination in intercollegiate athletics under Title IX of the Higher Education Act. Indeed, it remained one of the few universities to field only male cheerleaders (other than Yale) well into the 1970s.

Although Michigan had long had a reputation for successful programs, there were warnings as early as the 1970s about systemic flaws in its Athletic Department. Although in theory the athletic director reported directly to the president, the Athletics Department used its proclaimed financial independence to skirt the usual regulations and policies of the university and operate according to its own rules and objectives, usually out of sight and out of mind of the university administration. Its financial success, due almost entirely to Schembechler's success in filling Michigan Stadium on football weekends in the fall, led to a mindset within the Department that it was administratively separate from the rest of the University and therefore not subject to the rules and policies governing other units. The Athletic Department routinely ignored University regulations and policies concerning personnel, financial accountability, and conflict of interest. Although criticized from time to time for the increasing independence and commercialism of Michigan athletics, Canham usually shrugged it off, pointing to Schembechler's winning football teams and

the department's financial health. Yet the "Michigan model," in which the revenues from the football program—due primarily to the gate receipts generated by the gigantic Michigan Stadium—would support all other athletic programs, would eventually collapse, as the need to add additional programs (e.g., women's sports), coupled with an unwillingness to control expenditures, led to financial disaster by the late 1990s.

The vast gulf between the Athletic Department and the University isolated student-athletes from academic life and coaches and staff from the rest of the University community. The recruiting philosophy of high visibility programs such as football and basketball shifted during the 1970s, away from recruiting strong students who were outstanding athletes to recruiting, instead, outstanding athletes with marginal academic ability, athletes who would "major in eligibility" as long as they could compete. While this generated winning programs, it would eventually erode the integrity of the department and lead to scandal. The University experienced one of its most serious rules violations in its modern history during the 1980s, with a major scandal in the baseball program involving slush funds, illegal payments to players, and recruiting violations, that led to the firing of the coach and the acceptance of NCAA sanctions. Further investigation of the Department at that time revealed numerous violations of University policies that arose from weak management and inadequate oversight.

Following a effort by basketball coach Bill Frieder to promise admissions to recruits with inadequate academic credentials that led to their rejection by the Office of Admissions, it was necessary to use the authority of the provost to reestablish control of admissions and academic eligibility for student athletes. As provost, Jim stepped in to negotiate new admissions constraints on the coaches of football, basketball, and hockey. But the high visibility of Michigan athletics and the myth of its financial wealth and autonomy could continue to haunt the university for years to come. This vast separation between Michigan athletics and the rest of the University posed a real challenge.

Hence in the late 1980s an effort was launched to "mainstream" Michigan athletics with the goals and culture of an academic institution. There was an important symbolism associated with the leadership for this effort coming from the Office of the Provost, since as the University's chief academic officer, the involvement of the provost made a strong statement that athletics should be related to the academic nature of the university. The effort began by arranging a series of events that brought together student-athletes and coaches in various academic settings—museums, concert halls, and such. The goal was to stress that student-athletes were students first, and that coaches were, in reality, teachers. In the process of arranging and hosting these events, it soon became apparent that the isolation among sports programs was just as serious as the chasm between the Athletic Department and the rest of the University. Students and coaches enjoyed the opportunity to meet participants from other sports programs. The effort led to stronger relationships between the administration and the coaches and Athletic Department staff, both through attending events and by meeting with them individually.

The efforts to strengthen relationships between the University leadership with student-athletes, coaches, and staff of the Athletic Department led to some strong friendships between the administration and the coaches, among them Bo Schembechler. In fact, in 1988 Bo made it a point to show up at the public interview for the University president. When the papers reported its selection by the Regents the next day, whose picture should be on the front page but Bo's, with the quote: "He was my choice!"

Yet the role of the university president relative to college sports was changing rapidly, driven by new pressures. The NCAA adopted a fundamental principle that institutional control and accountability of athletics rested with the presidents. The incorporation of the Big Ten Conference during the 1980s required that the university presidents serve as its board of directors. This new corporate conference structure demanded both policy and fiduciary oversight by the presidents, frequently in direct conflict with the athletic directors. It also demanded a great deal of time and effort, since the operations of the Big Ten Conference are more extensive than those of the professional athletic leagues. Many were the lonely, invisible battles Michigan presidents would fight for the university on such issues as sharing football gate revenue, conference expansion, and gender equity. Some were won. Some were lost. But most battles were unseen, unrecognized, and certainly unappreciated.

While such an active presidential role clearly provided additional powers to restore and maintain the integrity of Michigan athletics, it was sometimes not well understood or accepted by the old guard. Yet it was increasingly clear that the Athletic Department needed to be brought back into the mainstream of University life. By the late 1980s, it had also become clear that the days of the czar athletic director and the autonomy of Michigan athletics were coming to an end. Intercollegiate athletics activities were simply too visible and had too great an impact on the university to be left entirely to the direction of the athletics establishment, its values, and its culture. The administration faced the challenge of reining in the excesses of the Athletic Department during the days of two particularly powerful figures, athletic director Don Canham and football coach Bo Schembechler, both of whom were media celebrities adept at building booster and press support for their personal agendas.

Despite considerable resistance, President Harold Shapiro successfully negotiated Don Canham's retirement. Yet from the beginning of the athletic director search for a successor to Canham, it was clear to the chair of the search committee, President Emeritus Robben Fleming, that Bo Schembechler would not only be an important factor, but that he also would be considered as a serious candidate to succeed Don Canham. However, since the administration believed it would be very difficult for any mortal to hold both the jobs of head football coach and athletics director, Fleming came up with an ingenious idea. A long-serving and well-liked stalwart of the University, Associate Vice President for Business and Finance, Jack Weidenbach, was asked to serve as associate athletics director and handle the detailed management of the Department while Bo was involved in coaching duties.

Weidenbach was an outstanding choice. During the 1980s, as Canham had become less involved in the management of the Athletics Department, particularly during winter months spent in Florida, Jack has been assigned by the administration to handle many of its financial matters, a role that became even more important following the baseball scandals. Hence he already knew many of the key issues and was well

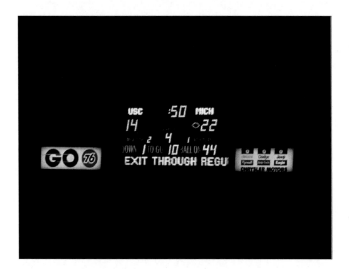

The success in Michigan athletics during the 1988-1989
provided an interesting first year in a new presidency

The new AD: Bo Schembechler
(and also stilll football coach)

Jack Weidenbach: Second in Command under Bo
and then Michigan's Athletic Director

known and respected by the staff and coaches of the Department. He was an athlete himself (a skier and distance runner) and had been long involved in the effort to build women's athletics at Michigan. Hence backing up Bo was a natural assignment for him.

1990s

After a year as football coach and athletics director, Bo decided to accept an offer from Tom Monahan to become president of the Detroit Tigers. After efforts to talk him out of it failed, he was given a year's leave of absence in the hopes he might later change his mind, and Jack Weidenbach was asked to serve as interim athletics director for this period. However, Weidenbach did such a spectacular job in the role that when Bo decided to stay with the Tigers, it was decided to dispense with a full search and obtain approval by the Regents to appoint him as the permanent athletic director. During his tenure, there were major changes facing college athletics at the conference and national level that required a close relationship between the athletics director and the president. Weidenbach had developed a close relationships with the Executive Officers and Regents over his many years of leadership at the University, and this enabled him to provide outstanding leadership for Michigan Athletics. In fact there is no other five-year

period in the history of Michigan athletics programs with more conference championships, bowl wins, Final Four appearances, and All-Americans–both athletic and academic. In addition, the financial structure of Michigan athletics was stabilized, its physical plant was rebuilt, and the coaches and student-athletes were more clearly integrated into the broader life of the campus community.

Unfortunately, Weidenbach was already close to retirement when he agreed to provide leadership for the Athletic Department. Hence in the 1990s the University was obliged to launch another major national search for his successor, chaired by VPCFO Farris Womack. The search identified several outstanding candidates and proceeded with early negotiations with the lead candidate. Unfortunately, the booster crowd got wind of the possibility that a "non-Michigan man" might be selected and began to apply pressure on the Regents to force the administration to turn away from external candidates and look inside the Department for a successor. The administration finally concluded that it was simply too dangerous to the University to continue the external search in the face of the pressure on both the University and the Regents. Instead, with the support of the search committee, Joe Roberson, then Director of the Campaign for Michigan, was persuaded to accept an appointment as athletic director. Actually,

Joe Roberson, another Michigan stalwart,
becomes Athletic Director.

Roberson's name had been considered as a top candidate early in the search, but his role as the director of the University's billion-dollar fund-raising campaign was felt to be more important. Yet the circumstances had changed, and his loyalty to the University led him to accept this call to duty.

Roberson's appointment was a surprise to outsiders. He was, however, a former college athlete and professional baseball player as a pitcher with the Los Angeles Dodgers. More important, he had served as both dean and interim chancellor of the UM-Flint campus. He was an individual of great integrity, with a strong sense of academic values in addition to his experience with both college and professional sports. Beyond his strong and wise leadership of the department, his long experience with students and academic life as a faculty member and academic leader enabled him to elevate the importance of young competitors as students first and athletes second, in priority, even in a highly competitive program such as Michigan. Certainly Joe Roberson had a better understanding of the mission and culture of an academic institution than any athletic director of his era. He was also an excellent leader. When he was finally pushed out by a new administration in 1997, he left the Athletics Department with a football program that would win the national championship in 1998

(the first in 50 years) and, moreover, an outstanding financial condition with reserves of over \$33 million.

However, the heightened public visibility of Michigan athletics, particularly in the marquee sports of football and men's basketball, accompanied by the ever-escalating expectations on the part of Michigan fans, put great pressure on both coaches and players alike. After five Big Ten championships in a row and the entrance of Penn State into the conference, the football team experienced a series of mediocre seasons (although "mediocre" for Michigan meant winning only eight or nine games a season and appearing in only a second-tier holiday bowl). In basketball, although Steve Fisher managed to continue to recruit top talent after the Fab Five, his teams never were able to win the Big Ten championship or return to the Final Four. Each misstep by a student athlete or coach, the inevitable defeats that characterize every leading program in off years or the loss of a key recruit resulted in a torrent of adverse media coverage. The sports media, which had been strong Michigan boosters during the championship years, were now viciously critical of these same programs and coaches as they struggled through occasionally mediocre seasons. The unrealistic expectations of Michigan fans, coupled with the ruthless criticism of the sports media, soon pushed both Michigan football and basketball to the crisis point.

Facing increasing pressure from fans, football coach Gary Moeller had an altercation with the police while at a Detroit nightclub that was captured on video by the media. Because of the intense public attention given the incident, Roberson asked Moeller to take a brief leave, but he decided instead to step down and exercise his retirement option. Lloyd Carr was later appointed as his successor, thereby maintaining the momentum of the program.

The high visibility of the "Fab Five" basketball team led to a continual onslaught of media attention, although without serious impact. However, unknown to Coach Fisher or anyone else in the University (including noted author, Mitch Albom, who wrote a book concerning the Fab Five) one of the players, Chris Webber, had received substantial payments from a local Detroit gambler. This serious violation by a player would be confirmed several years later resulting in major penalties. However, unlike earlier incidents in the 1980s that involved Athletics Department staff (e.g., the baseball coach), this violation was confined to three Michigan basketball players.

In summary, during the 1990s, working closely with the sequence of athletic directors who succeeded Canham—Bo Schembechler, Jack Weidenbach, and Joe Roberson—the University administration took a series of actions to better align athletics with the academic priorities of the University. It demanded that student-athletes receive the same educational and extracurricular opportunities as other Michigan students. Coaches were provided with more encouragement for their roles as teachers and more security as staff members. Clear policies were developed in a number of areas including admissions, academic standing, substance abuse, and student behavior that were consistent with the rest of the University.

At the same time, the University took a series of steps to secure the financial integrity of Michigan athletics. The Athletic Department began to apply cost-containment methods to its operations, and a major fund-raising program was launched. The department developed more sophisticated methods for licensing. Finally, the University invested in major improvements in the athletics facilities, including rebuilding Michigan Stadium (returning to natural grass and repairing the stadium infrastructure) and new facilities for swimming, gymnastics, ice hockey, tennis, track, and new fields for women's soccer, field hockey, and softball.

During this period the University finally began to take women's athletics seriously by providing women with the same opportunities for varsity competition as men. Major investments were made in existing women's programs as well as in the addition of new programs (women's soccer and women's rowing). In fact, despite decades of neglect, Michigan became one of the first major universities in the nation to make a public commitment to achieving full gender equity in intercollegiate athletics by the late 1990s.

There were also improvements in Michigan's overall competitiveness. While once Michigan had been content to be successful primarily in a single sport, football, during the 1990s it began to compete at the national level across its full array of 23 varsity programs. It began to rank each year among the top institutions nationwide for the national all-sports championship (the Sears Trophy). During the decade from 1988 to 1998, Michigan went to five Rose Bowls and won a national championship (1997) in football; three Final Fours and a national championship (1989) in men's basketball; and four hockey Final Fours and two NCAA championships in ice hockey (1996 and 1998). Michigan teams won over 50 Big 10 championships during this period, dominating the Big Ten in men's and women's swimming (including winning the NCAA championship in men's swimming), men's and women's cross-country, women's gymnastics, men's and women's track, and women's softball. Michigan athletes provided some of the most exciting moments in Michigan's long sports tradition, including two Heisman trophies (Desmond Howard and Charles Woodson) and a number of Olympians.

Despite the leadership and integrity of Athletic Director Joe Roberson, new president Lee Bollinger decided to replace him with Tom Goss, an executive with a soft drink company in California, who had been a former football player at Michigan. Goss, in turn, moved rapidly to fire Steve Fisher in the wake of the investigation of the relationship between Chris Webber and a Detroit gambler, Eddie Martin, although at the time there was no evidence of any wrong doing on Webber's part, and there never has been any indication that Fisher was as fault as coach. But the Regents were determined for change, and both Bollinger and Goss took their marching orders.

For a brief moment, the sun came out for Michigan, with a national championship in 1997 for Lloyd Carr's football team with an undefeated season and a victory over Washington State in the Rose Bowl (although Nebraska tied for the national championship with Michigan). The new administration embraced the event, and President Bollinger perched royally in a horse-drawn carriage in the Ann Arbor parade to celebrate the team, ignoring, of course, that both the appointment of Carr and the development of the team had been accomplished by Joe Roberson.

2000s

However with the changes at the helm, things soon began to go downhill. Goss appointed Fisher's assistant basketball coach as his successor, who was

Bollinger enjoyed the thrill of riding in the 1997 championship parade, but his attempt to place a "Halo" on Michigan Stadium fell flat.

clearly unqualified for the post, and the team rapidly collapsed. The financials of the Athletics Department were mismanaged and deficits began to appear, a first for Michigan. In fact, Bollinger agreed to put in $3 million from his "president's fund" (whatever that was) to plug the dike (or to make Bo happy, as some rumored). But Goss was a goner after another push from the Regents.

In searching for a successor, Bollinger tried to find an insider to do the job but after a couple probes without success, he was approached by Bill Martin, a local real estate developer, who offered his services. Although Martin had chaired a special committee to assess the financials of the Athletics Department after losses began to appear, his own experience was questionable. To be sure, he was a member of the U.S. Olympic Committee, but his sport was yachting, not college sports.

Martin was a business man and a real estate developer, and his goal was to embark on a massive renovation of Michigan Stadium to install skyboxes and premium facilities (dining, entertaining) characteristic of professional venues, financed by a dramatic increase in ticket prices and premium payments ("seat license" fees for the privileges to purchase season tickets in prime locations) that would support both the stadium renovation and the Department. Although this was highly controversial since it would essentially price Michigan football beyond levels affordable by most students, faculty, staff, townspeople, and long-time fans, transforming the stadium crowd into the high

roller (or obsessed) fans characteristic of a professional franchise, Bollinger, his successor Mary Sue Coleman, and the Regents nodded their approval, and it was off to the races. The Michigan Stadium project moved ahead, and ticket prices soared…from $25 per game to $75 plus the seat tax…to the point where the average ticket price, including seat tax, rose to $230 per game, and even student tickets were $50 per game, both the highest in the nation. Martin's experience as a real estate developer, builder, and businessman were strongly in evidence.

As we noted earlier, Martin and Bollinger also transformed the long-standing faculty Board in Control of Intercollegiate Athletics into an Advisory Board on Intercollegiate Athletics. Although this was intended to provide the Athletic Director with more power, it also decoupled the faculty from the University's athletic programs, thereby eroding the relationship between the academic mission of the institution and its athletic activities. Later Martin was to acknowledge that this was one of the most damaging decisions made during his tenure.

Martin's inexperience with college sports soon began to show in other areas. He hired a new basketball coach, Tommy Amaker, who had all the right credentials, smart, talented, and former player at Duke, but all the wrong cultural characteristics to handle the Big Ten. Amaker was soon replaced by John Belein, an experienced coach from West Virginia who would take Michigan to the Final Four, and Amaker went on to

Athletic Director David Brandon

The "Wow" Factor

success at Harvard.

But football became the Achilles heel. Whether pushed or pulled, Lloyd Carr stepped down after a long and successful tenure as football coach, and Martin launched a search that ended up with Rich Rodriguez, a successful coach at West Virginia, but a total misfit at Michigan, where both his personal style (about as anti-academic as one could find) and his flawed approach to Big Ten football left the team in a shambles, with losing seasons and strong fan disapproval. By this time, Martin's "my way or the highway" business approach to athletic leadership had worn thin, so he stepped down after ten years.

But if Martin was misaligned for athletic director, his successor, Dave Brandon, was even further removed, coming to the post from a career in advertising and serving as a former Regent of the University. Brandon did have some experience with Michigan athletics. He was walk-on quarterback for Schembechler in the 1980s, although he only made it into one game. Bo helped him get a job afterward with a large Detroit advertising company, and when Domino's Pizza was acquired by Bain Capital, they named him CEO where his marketing and advertising skills were valued (although the quality of the company's pizza deteriorated to the point at which Stephen Corbert suggested that it amounted to ketchup spread on cardboard).

Since Brandon had been instrumental in hiring Mary Sue Coleman when he was a Regent, nobody was particularly surprised when he was hired as Athletic Director. Unfortunately Brandon's background was in marketing, with no experience in managing college sports, so that is the tact that he took, pushing out over 143 long-standing employees (including 11 coaches) and replacing them with 200 new staff who were directed to "build the brand" of Michigan athletics and add the "Wow" factor to market it to the world. He moved quickly to fire Rodriguez, but strangely replaced him with an obscure coach, Brady Hoke, from San Diego State, who continued the malaise in the football program.

Ignoring the poor performance of the football program that was generating the revenue, Brandon continued to raise ticket prices and take on more debt with projects such as the renovation of the Crisler Arena (now renamed "Center") to resemble more of a department store with numerous shops along the entrances and concourses and a proposed $300 million investment in new facilities for the non-revenue sports. Advertising became the name of the game, with gigantic video displays not only inside Michigan Stadium but also outside to lure (and, more likely, distract) drivers as they approached the stadium. As the financial data indicates, the expenditures rose by over 50% during the Brandon years, mostly to fuel the rapid expansion of staffing (particularly in the marketing area) and debt service. Perhaps it is no surprise that student athletic support increased by only 10% during this period, clearly reflecting the new priorities.

Faculty influence was also essentially eliminated,

Michigan's new football coach Jim Harbaugh

Lloyd Carr, Jim Hackett, Jim
Harbaugh, and Gary Moeller

since as chair of the faculty Advisory Board on Intercollegiate Athletics, Brandon was able to schedule meetings with limited consequence. Furthermore, since few faculty members could afford the new ticket prices, they rapidly became disengaged with Michigan athletics, treating it largely with benign neglect.

Despite growing criticism from members of the University and Ann Arbor community who were priced out of Michigan football, basketball, and hockey events, Brandon was determined to continue his focus on elevating both the Michigan brand and its pricing, while aggressively pushing private fund raising in competition with the rest of the University. Michigan Athletics became increasingly a commercial entertainment company marketing primarily to the wealthy and effectively severed from the University. Yet Brandon also trampled on student interests by implementing a general admission policy that prevented them from sitting with their friends. Hence student attendance dropped in half, from 21,763 in 2012 to 11,569 in 2014, igniting student protest that eventually resulted in thousands of students descending on the President's House demanding that Brandon be fired.

The final straw was cast by a tragic incident , which occurred when the football coaches allowed a clearly injured quarterback to remain in a game with a concussion. The intense national exposure to this incident, shown live on a national television broadcast of the game, together with the growing frustration about Brandon's effort to sever the relationships with the University and the community through excessive ticket pricing and restrictive policies, finally exploded into calls for his firing. After performing extensive due diligence through discussions with many different perspectives, the University's new president, Mark Schlissel, concluded that Brandon's reign must come to an end, and he negotiated his "resignation" (at a cost of $3 million due to the excessive contract provided Brandon by Coleman early in his tenure).

Fortunately, the new president was able to persuade a former Michigan athlete, Jim Hackett, recently retired as CEO of Steelcase, to step in immediately as interim athletic director, and he demonstrated the skill of corporate recruiting by landing former UM quarterback Jim Harbaugh as the coach. Harbaugh's outstanding coaching records at San Diego, Stanford, and the San Francisco 49er's made him the top choice, and his acceptance of the offer created great excitement. Perhaps equally important, both Harbaugh and Hackett were shrewd enough to immediate open their arms to both former Michigan coaches and players and to the large community of football fans that had been pushed away by Brandon's escalating pricing and "wow" approach.

However, more broadly it was apparent that considerable rebuilding would be necessary after two decades of leadership from three different athletic directors with little experience with college sports.

The Michigan Marching Band apparently understood where college football was headed in 2010!

Over that period both the quality and the character of Michigan athletics have clearly deteriorated. Needless to say, the "leaders and best" had become anything but...

Of course, one could always blame this decline and fall on the presidents, as many do for other areas of institutional performance. But here it is important to realize that building a competitive athletics program requires many years, so that its performance in one era can usually be attributed to the era of one's predecessor. For example, the spectacular success of Michigan athletics in the 1990s, e.g., five Rose Bowl appearances and national championships in basketball, hockey, and swimming benefited from the development of these programs during the late 1980s. Similarly the football national championship won during Bollinger's first year was certainly not due to his administration but rather to the leadership of Joe Roberson as Athletic Director, Lloyd Carr as coach, and many others during the preceding years.

Lessons Learned

It is appropriate to conclude this chapter with some very personal and candid comments about the future of college sports, at least at the level of Michigan. Four decades as a college athlete, a faculty member, provost and president of the University of Michigan, and member and chair of the Presidents' Council of the Big Ten Conference, has led to several conclusions:

First, while most of intercollegiate athletics are both valuable and appropriate activities for our universities, big-time college football and basketball stand apart, since they have clearly become commercial entertainment businesses. Today they have little if any relevance to the academic mission of the university. Furthermore, they are based on a culture, a set of values that, while perhaps appropriate for show business, are viewed as highly corrupt by the academy and deemed corrosive to our academic mission.

Second, while one might be able make a case for

relevance of college sports to our educational mission to the extent that they provide a participatory activity for our students, there is no compelling reason why American universities should conduct intercollegiate athletics programs at the current highly commercialized, professionalized level of big-time college football and basketball simply for the entertainment of the American public, the financial benefit of coaches, athletic directors, conference commissioners, and NCAA executives, and the profit of television networks, sponsors, and sports apparel manufacturers.

One can argue that there are only three reasons why a university would want to conduct big-time college sports: i) because it benefits the student-athletes; ii) because it benefits the university (reputation, community, revenue); and iii) because it benefits the larger community. Big-time college football and basketball, as currently conducted, fail to meet any of these criteria.

Third, and most significantly, there is growing evidence that big-time college sports do far more damage to the university, to its students and faculty, its leadership, its reputation and credibility, that most realize--or at least are willing to admit. The evidence seems overwhelming:

Far too many of our athletics programs exploit young people, recruiting them with the promise of a college education—or a lucrative professional career—only to have the majority of Division 1-A football and basketball players achieve neither.

Furthermore, particularly in violent sports such as football and hockey, student-athletes are subjected to unacceptable health risks through injuries that could cripple them for life, without adequate protection or lifelong health security.

Scandals in intercollegiate athletics have damaged the reputations of many of our colleges and universities.

Big time college football and basketball have put inappropriate pressure on university governance, as boosters, politicians, and the media attempt to influence governing boards and university leadership.

The impact of intercollegiate athletics on university culture and values has been damaging, with poor behavior of both athletes and coaches, all too frequently tolerated and excused.

So too, the commercial culture of the entertainment industry that characterizes college football and basketball is not only orthogonal to academic values, but it is corrosive and corruptive to the academic enterprise

Some Myths and Realities of College Sports

Myth 1: Intercollegiate athletics are self-supporting.

Reality: No college programs in America today cover all their expenses (even those who claim to such as USC, U Texas, Ohio State, Michigan, and even Notre Dame). Athletic directors use flakey accounting methods that do not include full costs of capital expenditures, hidden subsidies such as instate tuition for out-of-state athletes, indirect costs born by the institution, fund-raising that competes with academic units, and, of course, the strange legislation that inserted a tax loophole that treats skybox rent and seat taxes as charitable "education" deductions. The NCAA estimates that in 2009 the total costs for intercollegiate athletics was $10.5 billion, while the total revenue was $5.6 billion (including ticket sales, television broadcasting, licensing, etc.). In reality the only people who make money –and big-time money, at that– from big time athletics are the coaches, athletic directors, NCAA brass, and the networks. But certainly not the "student athletes" and certainly not their host institutions.

In 2012 the media budget deficits for NCAA Division 1 programs averaged $9 million per year. From 2005 to 2009 athletics departments increased spending on student athletes by 50%, to $91,050 per athlete, while the increase for normal students was 20% to $13,470 per student.

Myth 2: Intercollegiate athletics are important for fund raising.

Reality: Donors who give because of winning teams give to wining programs, not to academic activities. But it gets even worse, since the tax-benefited "premium" payments for skyboxes and preferred seating generally come out of gifts that would otherwise have gone to academic purposes. At Michigan, our largest donors could not care less about college sports! They view it largely as a distraction from the primary mission of the University (except for Steve Ross, of course, who gave $100 million to the Athletics Department in 2013 to help

	FY07	FY08	FY09	FY10	FY11	FY12	FY13
Salaries	$26,845	$28,873	$30,860	$33,958	$35,703	$39,204	$44,235
Students	$14,411	$14,061	$15,129	$15,734	$16,206	$17,293	$18,348
Team/Game	$13,171	$13,871	$15,005	$15,791	$16,925	$18,109	$19,053
Facilities	$6,614	$7,264	$7,093	$7,580	$8,148	$9,834	$10,620
Def Main	$4,500	$4,500	$4,500	$4,500	$4,500	$4,500	$4,500
Other OpAd	$6,368	$6,878	$6,575	$5,923	$6,723	$7,674	$13,073
Debt Service	$2,575	$2,565	$1,029	$2,139	$11,254	$13,200	$14,688
	$74,474	$78,012	$80,191	$85,625	$100,307	$109,835	$124,517

	FY07	FY08	FY09	FY10	FY11	FY12	FY13
Tickets	$34,071	$38,642	$35,551	$37,714	$38,193	$45,588	$44,051
Big 10	$13,467	$17,267	$17,419	$18,305	$20,226	$21,948	$23,283
Seat Tax	$13,896	$15,138	$13,600	$13,600	$20,972	$26,153	$27,416
Corporate	$5,698	$8,065	$11,980	$13,760	$14,021	$14,328	$15,050
Facility Rent	$1,908	$1,934	$1,870	$1,774	$1,743	$1,825	$6,847
Licensing	$4,444	$2,221	$3,800	$4,100	$4,100	$4,774	$5,650
Investment	$5,320	$4,207	$3,444	$2,345	$2,700	$6,602	$8,025
	$83,926	$93,658	$90,461	$94,449	$105,038	$121,218	$130,322

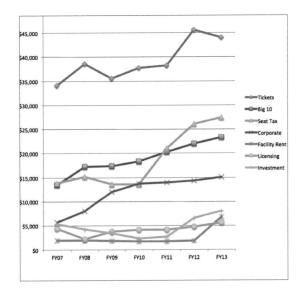

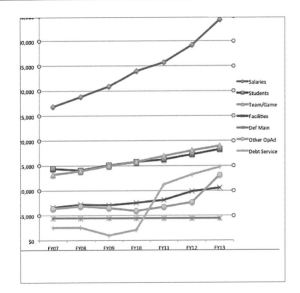

While the expenditures of the Athletics Department have almost doubled over the past seven year (driven tickets and seat taxes), most of this revenue has gone to salaries and not students.

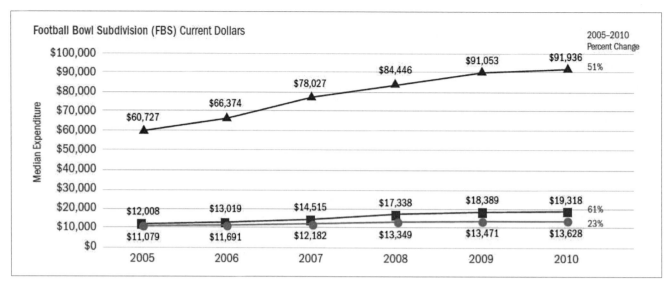

Football Bowl Subdivision (FBS) Current Dollars

2005–2010 Percent Change

The disparity between expenditures per student on athletics (upper curve) and academics (lower curves) continues to diverge, particularly in the leading confences and institutions.

build a "Walk of Champions", whatever that is).

Myth 3: All athletic facilities are self-financed.

Reality: Actually many require either institutional or public subsidy. But even those that are debt financed must pledge student tuition revenue for borrowing equity, not anticipated gate receipts or television revenue. They also depend on questionable tax practices such as being counted as 80% "charitable" deductions by the IRS despite the fact that they are quid pro quo required payments for benefits such as premium seating. If these tax loopholes disappear, many of the big stadium projects will collapse like a house of cards.

Myth 4: The power of the NCAA will protect the status quo.

Reality: Today the NCAA is in serious trouble and fighting for its survival. Its tax status is dependent upon rulings long ago that its primary purpose is educational. Yet grants-in-aid based on athletic performance could be ruled as "pay for play" and hence require employment rights for athletes (including unionization). The O'Bannon case could require payment to players for the use of their images for commercial purposes. Litigation associated with brain injuries or long-term health impact could cripple both the NCAA and universities. Finally, the compensation of coaches ($5 M and up), athletic directors ($1 M and up), and athletic staff (now several times that of faculty) is now so extreme that it

raises the threat of federal action.

Myth 5: Intercollegiate athletics is important for school spirit.

Reality: Sure, student applications do go up after a major championship. But the students attracted to an institution are not necessarily those most concerned about academic achievement. Besides, how important is athletics to the school spirit of institutions like Harvard, Yale...and Caltech? And how important is athletics to Penn State these days?

Myth 6: But we do pay student athletes! We give them valuable scholarships!

Reality: A quote from a recent book on college sports by Taylor Branch, the great historian on civil rights in America, puts this in an interesting context.

"'Scholarship athletes are already paid,' declared the Knight Commission members, in the most meaningful way possible: with a free education.' This evasion by prominent educators severed my last reluctant, emotional tie with imposed amateurism. I found it worse than self-serving. It echoes masters who once claimed that heavenly salvation would outweigh earthly injustice to slaves."

Myth 7: But we are preparing athletes for professional careers.

Reality: Michigan surveys indicate that most student

athletes realize their odds of making the pros are very remote. Instead they view their college experience as an opportunity to enter careers very similar to other students in fields such as business, law, and medicine. But after a few weeks on campus, many of the most vigorously recruited student athletes realize they are woefully academically unprepared and saddled with 50-60 hour/week "jobs" and lives controlled by coaches. Hence they are forced to shift to "majoring in eligibility", enrolling in cupcake majors (sports management, communications, general studies). The attrition rates are tragic, with 6-year graduate rates: less than 50% for football; 40% for basketball. Even those who graduate frequently have meaningless degrees (e.g., recreational sports, golf-course management).

What to do? The Traditional Approach

The actions suggested to protect student-athletes and their universities are both numerous and obvious:

Freshman Ineligibility: All freshmen in all sports should be ineligible for varsity competition. The first year should be a time for students to adjust intellectually and emotionally to the hectic pace of college life.

Financial Aid: Eliminate the "athletic scholarship" or "grant-in-aid" and replace it with need-based financial aid. Note this would not only substantially reduce the costs of college sports, but it would also eliminate the legal risks of continuing what has become, in effect, a "pay for play" system.

Mainstream Coaches: Throttle back the salaries of coaches, athletic directors, and other athletic department staff to levels comparable to faculty and other university staff. Subject coaches to the same conflict of interest policies that govern other faculty and staff (e.g., eliminating shoe contracts, prohibiting the use of the university's name and reputation for personal gain, etc.)

Mainstream the Administration of Intercollegiate Athletics: Intercollegiate athletics is a student extracurricular activity and, as such, should report to the vice president for student affairs. Academic matters such as student eligibility, counseling, and academic support should be the responsibility of the university's chief academic officer (e.g., the provost). Financial matters should be under the control of the university's chief financial officer. Medical issues should be under the control of staff from the university medical center or student health service.

Financial Support: We should adopt the principle that if intercollegiate athletics are of value to students, they should be subsidized by the General and Education budget of the university. To this end, we might consider putting athletics department salary lines (coaches and staff) on the academic budget and under the control of the provost. We could then use a counter flow of athletic department revenue into the General and Education budget to minimize the net subsidy of college sports.

Faculty control: We need to restructure faculty athletics boards so that they are no longer under control of athletic directors but instead represent true faculty participation. It is important to keep "jock" faculty off these boards and to give priority to those faculty with significant experience in undergraduate education. It is also important for faculty boards to understand and accept their responsibilities for seeing that academic priorities dominate competitive and commercial goals, while student welfare and institutional integrity are priorities.

Rigorous Independent Audits and Compliance Functions: Here we need a system for independent auditing of not simply compliance with NCAA and conference rules, but as well financial matters, student academic standing, progress toward degrees, and medical matters.

Limits on Schedules and Student Participation: We should confine all competitive schedules to a single academic term (e.g., football in fall, basketball, hockey in winter, etc.). Competitive schedules should be shortened to more reasonable levels (e.g., football back to 10 games, basketball to 20 games, etc.). We need to constrain competitive and travel schedules to be compatible with academic demands (e.g., no weekday competition). Student participation in mandatory, noncompetitive athletics activities during off-season should be severely limited (including eliminating spring football practice, summer conditioning requirements, etc.).

Throttle Back Commercialization: It is time to forget about the possibility of Division 1-A football playoffs and drastically reduce the number of post-season bowls. Perhaps we should return the NCAA Basketball Tournament to a two-week, conference champion only event. Furthermore, we need to stop this nonsense of negotiating every broadcasting contract as if dollars were the only objective and chase the sports press out of the locker rooms and lives of our students.

Of course, the first arguments launched against such reform proposals always have to do with money. College football and basketball are portrayed as the geese that lay the golden eggs for higher education. However these arguments, long accepted but rarely challenged, are flawed. Essentially all intercollegiate athletic programs are subsidized, to some degree, by the academic programs of the university (when all costs are included, such as amortization of facilities and administrative overhead.) Furthermore, in the scheme of things, the budgets of these programs are quite modest relative to other institutional activities (e.g., at Michigan, the $150 M/y budget of our athletic department is only about 2% of our total budget, and, more to the point, less than the amount of state support we have lost over the past three years!).

The current culture of college sports is driven by the belief that the team that spends the most wins the most. Not surprisingly, therefore, the more revenue athletic programs generate, the more they spend. Since most of the expenditures are in areas such as grants-in-aid, coaches and staff salaries, promotional activities, and facilities, many of the proposals in the previous section would dramatically reduce these costs.

More generally, the first step in reconnecting college sports to the academic enterprise is to stop treating our athletic departments, coaches, and student-athletes as special members of the university community, subject to different rules and procedures, policies and practices than the rest of university. The key to reform is to mainstream our athletics programs and their participants back into the university in three key areas: financial management, personnel policies, and educational practices.

Financial management: Athletics departments should be subject to the same financial controls, policies, and procedures as other university units. Their financial operations should report directly to the chief financial officer of the university and be subject to rigorous internal audit requirements and full public disclosure as an independent (rather than consolidated) financial unit. All external financial arrangements, including those with athletic organizations (e.g., conferences and the NCAA), commercial concerns (e.g., licensing, broadcasting, endorsements), and foundation/booster organizations should be under strict university controls. In that regard, it might be best to take the Sarbanes-Oxley approach, designed to eliminate abuses in the financial operations of publicly-held corporations, by requiring the Athletic Director, President, and chair of the Governing Board to sign annual financial statements and hold them legally accountable should these later be found to be fraudulent.

Possible Cost Reductions: There are many opportunities for significant cost reductions. For example, replacing the current system of grants-in-aid by need-based financial aid would reduce these costs by at least a factor of two. Throttling back the extravagant level of celebrity coaches salaries (and applying conflict of interest to eliminate excessive external income and perks) would do likewise. Demanding university control of all auxiliary activities such as broadcasting and licensing so that revenue flows to the institution and not to the coaches would also help. And reducing the expenditures required to mount big-time commercial entertainment events would also reduce costs, thereby compensating for lost broadcasting revenue.

Personnel: All athletics department staff (including coaches) should be subject to the same conflict-of-interest policies that apply to other university staff and faculty. For example, coaches should no longer be allowed to exploit the reputation of the university for personal gain through endorsements or special arrangements with commercial vendors (e.g., sports apparel companies, broadcasting, automobile dealers). Employment agreements for coaches should conform to those characterizing other staff and should be subject to review by university financial and personnel units. All personnel searches, including those for coaches, should comply fully with the policies and practices characterizing other staff (e.g., equal opportunity)

Who Should Take the Lead in Reform?

Several years ago, an invitation appeared from William Friday, former president of the University of

North Carolina, to testify before the Knight Commission on Intercollegiate Athletics. The book on college sports had just appeared, and they were interested in views on this complex subject. After stating several concerns, a possible approach to reform was suggested that began with the premier academic organization, the Association of American Universities (AAU). If these institutions were to adopt a series of reforms–a disarmament treaty, if you will– for their members, much of the rest of the higher education enterprise would soon follow. It was hoped that such an effort by the AAU would propagate rather rapidly throughout other organizations such as the National Association of State Universities and Land Grant Colleges and even the American Council on Education.

The testimony concluded by stressing the point that as higher education entered an era of great challenge and change, it was essential that we re-examine each and every one of our activities for their relevance and compatibility with our fundamental academic missions of teaching, learning, and serving society. From this perspective, there appeared to be little justification for the American university to mount and sustain big-time football and basketball programs at their current commercial and professional level simply to satisfy the public desire for entertainment and pursue the commercial goals of the marketplace. The damage to our academic values and integrity was simply too great. If intercollegiate athletics was to be retained as an appropriate university activity, it was essential to decouple our programs from the entertainment industry and reconnect them with the educational mission of our institutions.

After these remarks, the co-chair of the commission, Father Theodore Hesburg, former president of Notre Dame, was first to respond by stating that my concerns reinforced many of those of the Commission (after offering a prayer: "May God have mercy on your soul!")! He suggested that my comments had provided a first draft of the Commission's report. Of course, others on the Commission challenged some of the more outspoken conclusions and recommendations. But in the end, most of the conclusions seemed to stand, as evidenced by the strong statement in the final report of the Commission:

"After digesting the extensive testimony offered over some six months, the Commission is forced to reiterate its earlier conclusion that at their worst, big-time college athletics appear to have lost their bearings. Athletics continue to threaten to overwhelm the universities in whose name they were established. Indeed, we must report that the threat has grown rather than diminished. Higher education must draw together all of its strengths and assets to reassert the primary of the educational mission of the academy. The message that all parts of the higher education community must proclaim is emphatic: Together, we created today's disgraceful environment. Only by acting together can we clean it up."

A Call to Action: Reconnecting College Sports and Higher Education
The Knight Commission on Intercollegiate Athletics
June, 2001

Yet, in retrospect, it is now clear that while both this testimony and the Knight Commission report urgently portrayed the threat to American higher education posed by the ever-increasing commercialization and corruption of big-time college sports, neither proposed an effective method to deal with the problem. In fact, a major reason why the various efforts to reform college sports over the years have failed is because we continue to bet on the wrong horse. Reformers continue to propose that the university presidents take the lead into the reform of college sports, whether through academic organizations such as the AAU and ACE (my proposal) or the NCAA (the Knight Commission). And very little happens, and the mad rush toward more and more commercialism and corruption continues.

Perhaps this is not so surprising. After all, university presidents are usually trapped between a rock and a hard place: between a public demanding high quality entertainment from the commercial college sports industry they are paying for, and governing boards who have the capacity (and all too frequently the inclination) to fire presidents who rock the university boat too strenuously. It should be clear that few contemporary university presidents have the capacity, the will, or the appetite to lead a true reform movement in college sports.

Well, what about the faculty? Of course, in the end,

it is the governing faculty that is responsible for its academic integrity of a university. Faculty members have been given the ultimate protection, tenure, to enable them to confront the forces of darkness that would savage academic values. The serious nature of the threats posed to the university and its educational values by the commercialization and corruption of big-time college sports has been firmly established in recent years. It is now time to challenge the faculties of our universities, through their elected bodies such as faculty senates, to step up to their responsibility to defend the academic integrity of their institutions, by demanding substantive reform of intercollegiate athletics.

To their credit, several faculty groups have responded well to this challenge and stepped forward to propose a set of principles for the athletic programs conducted by their institutions. Beginning first in the Pac Ten Conference universities, then propagating to the Big Ten and Atlantic Coast Conferences, and most recently considered and adopted by the American Association of University Professors, such principles provide a firm foundation for true reform in college sports.

Yet as the influence of the faculty has been pushed out of intercollegiate athletics by eliminating oversight boards, as athletic departments have taken over control of academic counseling (and at some institutions, even admission and academic standing), and as even faculty participation as spectators has eroded due to premium pricing of tickets, little wonder that most faculty members treat the Athletics Department with benign neglect (at least until its missteps severely damage the integrity of their institution).

What about trustees? The next obvious step in this process is for the faculties to challenge the trustees of our universities, who in the end must be held accountable for the integrity of their institutions. To be sure, there will always be some trustees who are more beholding to the football coach than to academic values. But most university trustees are dedicated volunteers with deep commitments to their institutions and to the educational mission of the university. Furthermore, while some governing boards may inhibit the efforts of university presidents willing to challenge the sports establishment, few governing boards can withstand a concerted effort by their faculty to hold them accountable for the

integrity of their institution. In this spirit, several faculty groups have already begun this phase of the process by launching a dialogue with university trustees through the Association of Governing Boards.

Ironically, it could well be that the long American tradition of shared university governance, involving public oversight and trusteeship by governing boards of lay citizens, elected faculty governance, and experienced but generally short-term and usually amateur administrative leadership, will pose the ultimate challenge to big time college sports.

After all, even if university presidents are reluctant to challenge the status quo, the faculty has been provided with the both the responsibility and the status (e.g., tenure) to protect the academic values of the university and the integrity of its education programs. Furthermore, as trustees understand and accept their stewardship for welfare of their institutions, they will recognize that their clear financial, legal, and public accountability compels them to listen and respond to the challenge of academic integrity from their faculties.

What about a rising tide of public frustration? To be sure, many of those in charge of college athletics are unable (or unwilling) to understand the minefields that lie in the path of their plans. For example, the Big Ten leadership (conference commissioner and presidents) has largely destroyed the conference, adding new institutions that fail to meet the tests of geographical location, athletic competitiveness, or academic quality. As fans begin to realize that long-standing rivalries among academic peers (e.g., Michigan vs. Wisconsin) will largely disappear to satisfy the Big Ten Network, they could well abandon any loyalty to either teams or institutions. Of course, they could be replaced by new fans with interests more akin to professional sports such as automobile racing or boxing. After all, sports remain the "opiate of the masses".

Possible "Planet Killers" for College Sports

In summary, who will protect the interests of the student athletes?

Not the coaches or ADs or NCAA. They clearly have conflicts of interests.

What about faculty? They have been pushed to the

side.

What about university leaders like presidents or trustees? They clearly have abdicated all responsibility!!!

What about the government? They got us into this trouble!!!

What about...lawyers? Perhaps that is the only protection left!!!

There are still several possibilities on the horizon that could become "planet killers" for college sports as we know them today:

The federal government could finally step up to its responsibility to treat big-time athletics like other business enterprises, subjecting it to more reasonable treatment with respect to tax policy, employee treatment (meaning student-athletes), monopoly and cartel restrictions, and possibly even salary constraints.

The O'Bannon case has demonstrated that litigation may become a formidable force for changing college sports as we know it today. There are early signs that student-athletes may be given rights that protect them against exploitation by coaches and athletic departments, and others for personal gain.

But the most serious threat on the horizon is the increasing evidence of the damage that intensifying violent sports such as football, basketball, and hockey do to the health of young athletes. In recent years, there is growing medical evidence about the long-term impact of concussions and other trauma on longer-term illness such as dementia and Alzheimers. These concerns are broadening out to explore the epidemiology of longer health impact including life expectancy (now found to be as low as 57 for NFL players). Although most attention has been focused on the health implications of competition at the high school and professional level, it is only a matter of time before college sports falls under the microscope. Beyond the concerns about the impact of violent sports on the health of student athletes, these studies are likely to open up a Pandora's Box of litigation on issues such as institutional liability and requirements for the support of long-term health care that could financially cripple many institutions that insist on continuing to compete at the current level of intensity. In fact, the threat of litigation as class action suits could even eliminate violent sports such as football and hockey as we know them today at all but the professional levels.

A Magic Potion for Chasing Away the Commercialization of College Sports

Several years ago, a visit to give a major address to European university leaders at the University of Barcelona suggested another possible remedy. Across the street from the Barcelona campus was the incredible complex of FC Barcelona, one of Europe's most glamorous, successful, and profitable football clubs.

Check out their their website:

http://www.fcbarcelona.com/web/english/

and you'll find that FC Barcelona has essentially everything that Michigan Athletics desires: the excitement of a winning program, the exceptional loyalty of 150,000 members of the "football club", quality treatment of athletes, and high integrity. FC Barcelona also has not only a "football" club but also basketball and hockey programs, along with several "amateur" Olympic sports as part of the club. Its massive facilities, including Estadio Camp Mou, the largest stadium in Europe is adjacent to the University of Barcelona campus, but there is no direct relationship between the university and the football club.

There is one more characteristic of note: FC Barcelona's revenue in 2014 was over 600 million Euros ($700 million), far beyond that of Michigan, or any other college or professional sport in the United States. How, you might ask, can it achieve this? Because FC Barcelona is not a university or professional sports franchise but rather a corporation, with thousands of shareholders, and both a city (Barcelona) and region (Catalonia) of loyal fans.

So here is the proposal: How about conducting an IPO for the Michigan Wolverines? I'm sure that there would be hundreds of thousands of fans willing to participate in the initial stock offering. And the athletic directors are always looking for more revenue (and compensation, of course). The University could license to the new for-profit corporation, FC Michigan Wolverines, the trademark and lease them the stadium. With these funds, the University could return to truly amateur competition with REAL student participants and coaches as teachers, competing with other has-

Perhaps this is a model for the future of the Michigan Wolverines...

been big time programs that also sought escape from commercialism by taking their revenue-generating programs through a similar IPO process.

Seriously, this might be regarded as the way to finally separate "big time college sports" from the university, while maintaining a revenue flow to support "non-revenue" sports for students through licensing the UM "trademark" and renting its facilities. This might even be portrayed as "taking the Michigan Wolverines public" by enabling hundreds of thousands to become members of FC Michigan, even if they have never had a direct relationship with the University. (And of course it would also allow players, no longer necessarily students, to also benefit financially from the market for top talent...think Ronaldo or Beckham...)

Most important, it would allow the University to focus on its fundamental missions, teaching and research, while giving the public what it wants and eliminating the hypocrisy that now characterizes big time (and highly commercialized) college sports.

Perhaps this sounds crazy? But perhaps it also provides a future in which the commercial character of college sports is spun off to satisfy a sports craving public, leaving our universities to return to true amateur athletics with the fundamental purpose of student participation.

A Final Observation

Today there is a growing number of past and current university leaders who believe that higher education has entered an era of great challenge and change. Powerful social, economic, and technological forces are likely to change the university in very profound ways in the decades ahead. As our institutions enter this period of transformation, it is essential that we re-examine each and every one of our activities for their relevance and compatibility with our fundamental academic missions of teaching, research, and serving society.

If we are to retain intercollegiate athletics as appropriate university activities, it is essential we insist upon the primacy of academic over commercial values by decoupling our athletic programs from the entertainment industry and reconnecting them with the educational mission of our institutions.

The American university is simply too important to the future of this nation to be threatened by the ever increasing commercialization, professionalization, and corruption of college sports.

Is this a hopeless quest for change? Here one might recall a quote from Thomas Paine's Common Sense (February 14, 1776) that applies to this issue:

"Perhaps the sentiments contained in these pages are not yet sufficiently fashionable to procure them general favour; a long habit of not thinking a thing wrong, gives it a superficial appearance of being right, and raises at first a formidable outcry in defense of custom. But the tumult soon subsides. Time makes more converts than reason."

Returning Michigan Athletics to the People...

- Providing 25,000 students with free tickets to every game (cost: $7.4 million)
- Removing the seat license fee from all bleacher seats in the stadium (cost: $5 million)
- Reducing ticket prices for all bleacher seats to $50 (cost: $7.5 million)
- Retaining current pricing for all premium seating and skyboxes (no cost)
- Reducing athletic personnel by 100 staff (savings: $15 million)
- Reducing excessive coaches and AD salaries (savings: $6 million)

Another proposal for opening up Michigan Stadium once again to the "common man"

Oh, yes...there is one more observation about the success
of Michigan athletics over the past half-century...

1985	Michigan (#6)	27	Ohio State (#12)	17
1986	Michigan (#6)	26	Ohio State (#7)	24
1987	Michigan	20	Ohio State	23
1988	Michigan (#12)	34	Ohio State	31
1989	Michigan (#3)	28	Ohio State (#20)	18
1990	Michigan (#15)	16	Ohio State (#19)	13
1991	Michigan (#4)	31	Ohio State (#18)	3
1992	Michigan (#6)	13	Ohio State (#17)	13
1993	Michigan	28	Ohio State (#5)	0
1994	Michigan (#15)	6	Ohio State (#22)	22
1995	Michigan (#18)	31	Ohio State (#2)	23
1996	Michigan (#21)	13	Ohio State (#2)	9
1997	Michigan (#1)	20	Ohio State (#4)	14
1998	Michigan (#11)	16	Ohio State (#7)	31
1999	Michigan (#10)	24	Ohio State	17
2000	Michigan (#19)	38	Ohio State (#12)	26
2001	Michigan (#11)	20	Ohio State	26
2002	Michigan (#12)	9	Ohio State (#2)	14
2003	Michigan (#5)	35	Ohio State (#4)	21
2004	Michigan (#7)	21	Ohio State	37
2005	Michigan (#17)	21	Ohio State (#9)	25
2006	Michigan (#2)	39	Ohio State (#1)	42
2007	Michigan (#23)	3	Ohio State (#7)	14
2008	Michigan	7	Ohio State (#10)	42
2009	Michigan	10	Ohio State (#9)	21
2010[1]	Michigan	7	Ohio State (#12)	37
2011	Michigan (#15)	40	Ohio State	34
2012	Michigan (#20)	21	Ohio State (#4)	26
2013	Michigan	41	Ohio State (#3)	42
2014	Michigan	28	Ohio State (#6)	42
2015	Michigan (#12)	13	Ohio State (#8)	42

Year	Team	Score
1985	#3 Michigan	31–0
1986	#4 Michigan	27–6
1987	Michigan State	17–11
1988	#17 Michigan	17–3
1989	#5 Michigan	10–7
1990	Michigan State	28–27
1991	#5 Michigan	45–28
1992	#3 Michigan	35–10
1993	Michigan State	17–7
1994	#9 Michigan	40–20
1995	Michigan State	28–25
1996	#9 Michigan	45–29
1997	#5 Michigan	23–7
1998	Michigan	29–17
1999	#11 Michigan State	34–31
2000	#16 Michigan	14–0
2001	Michigan State	26–24
2002	#15 Michigan	49–3
2003	#13 Michigan	27–20
2004	#14 Michigan	45–37^{3OT}
2005	Michigan	34–31^{OT}
2006	#6 Michigan	31–13
2007	#14 Michigan	28–24
2008	Michigan State	35–21
2009	Michigan State	26–20^{OT}
2010	#17 Michigan State	34–17
2011	#23 Michigan State	28–14
2012	#23 Michigan	12–10
2013	#22 Michigan State	29–6
2014	#8 Michigan State	35–11
2015	#7 Michigan State	27–23

Michigan vs Ohio State and Michigan State Football Rivalries (season national ranking #)

Concerns

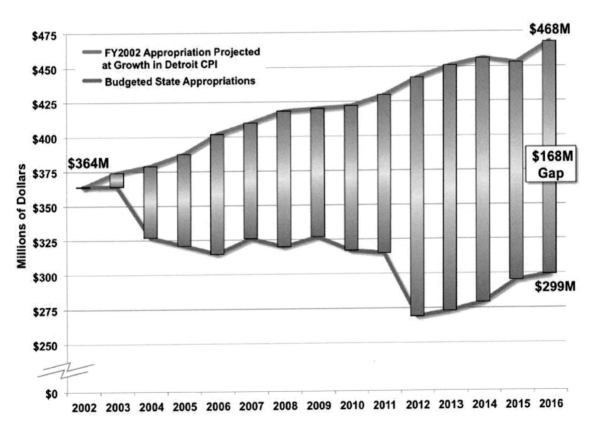

The Provost's "Jaws" Chart, showing the amount of annual State appropriation loss from inflation.

Chapter 18

Culture, Community, and Continuity

Beyond characteristics such as size, quality, and financial sustainability that can be tracked over time through quantitative data, there are other important characteristics of a university that require a more subjective approach. Universities are complex organizations that develop unique cultures over time not only influencing their fundamental missions of learning, discovery, and engagement with society, but also how they function as communities. In many cases these characteristics are not only unique to the institution but soon become evident to visitors, usually associated with the institutional "saga" of an institution, developing over a long period of time. (See Appendix.) Other characteristics such as how an institution accepts new members or sustains community activities or operates in making decisions or commitments are more subtle and can change significantly over a few years because of external or internal events.

In fact, we have noted that one of the core competencies of the University is its capacity to create learning communities. As a consequence there are many communities within the institution that are key to its intellectual, cultural, and social life. Some are organized along academic lines through faculty groups, institutes, centers, symposia, and salons. Others are organized about events, such as athletics and performing arts. Most require resources such as meeting places (e.g., Inglis Highlands), performance venues (e.g., Hill Auditorium, Power Center, Walgreen Center), and athletic complexes (...ah, yes...even the "Big House").

Changes in academic communities tend to occur slowly, particularly in the faculty, student, and staff cultures, because of its complexity and diversity. Fundamental academic values—academic freedom, intellectual integrity, striving for excellence—still dominate the faculty culture, as they must in any great university. Yet today fewer faculty members look to the University for long term academic careers and instead became nomadic, moving from institution to institution in an increasingly competitive academic marketplace.

Student communities change more rapidly, dependent in part on the nature of the student body. For example, fraternities and sororities have become more important as the student body has come from wealthier backgrounds (particularly those paying out-of-state tuition). So, too, student communities are more sensitive to challenges facing our society, e.g., conflicts, inequities, diversity, and the challenges of finding a job after graduation.

Radical changes in University communities can also happen due to "invasive species", new people joining the University with limited knowledge or respect for its long-standing traditions. For example, the Michigan Wolverines have always attracted an intensely loyal community of fans, consisting of students, alumni, and friends. Yet several years ago this was pushed aside by a new athletic director who proclaimed his intensely commercial approach as. "If it ain't broke, then break it!" He proceeded to break apart the loyal fan community by commercializing Michigan athletics to raise ticket prices so high that many students, faculty, staff, alumni, and loyal fans were pushed aside.

This philosophy of breaking apart communities that were certainly not broken has occurred in many other areas, usually by those unfamiliar or uncaring about University values and traditions. The academic and pastoral role of deans for the faculty community was broken apart by demanding highest priority given to the whims of wealthy donors. Resources that support faculty activities were discarded, such as replacing the University Club in the Michigan Union by an Au Bon Pan fast-food court and first restricting the Inglis

Highlands estate for fund-raising purposes and then attempting to sell it rather than return it to academic use. And, as we will demonstrate, the practice of "breaking the unbroken" continues and poses a constant threat and requires a sustained battle to protect important University traditions.

But first it is important to understand how these many communities had evolved as they were once nurtured.

University Families

The contemporary university is much like a city, comprised of a bewildering array of neighborhoods and communities. To the faculty, it has almost a feudal structure, divided up into highly specialized academic units, frequently with little interaction even with disciplinary neighbors, much less with the rest of the campus. To the student body, the university is an exciting, confusing, and sometimes frustrating complexity of challenges and opportunities, rules and regulations, drawing students together only in major events, such as fall football games or campus protests. To the staff, the university has a more subtle character, with the parts woven together by policies, procedures, and practices evolving over decades, all too frequently invisible or ignored by the students and faculty. In some ways, the modern university is so complex, so multifaceted, that it seems that the closer one is to it and the more intimately one is involved with its activities, the harder it is to understand its entirety and the more likely one is to miss the forest for the trees.

But a university is also a diverse community of many families: students, faculty, staff, and students; deans and executive officers; office staff and even presidents. While Michigan enjoys an intense loyalty among these families, it can also be a tough environment for many. It is a very large and complex institution, frequently immersed in controversial social and political issues. Senior academic and administrative leaders not only become members of these families but also must assume responsibilities to understand, support, encourage, and protect these communities, to understand their concerns and their aspirations, and to advance their causes.

Students, of course, comprise the most important family for the university, but they are also the most diverse, and for very large institutions such as Michigan, they are also the largest of our families. While one generally thinks of the student body as comprised of young high school graduates, roughly one third of the students in major research universities are adults engaged in graduate or professional study. In fact, an increasing number are adults with families and careers seeking further education. Hence both understanding and relating to this exceptionally diverse constituency can be a considerable challenge, particularly when it has a strongly activist nature such as Michigan.

The faculty–rather, the many faculties, since they are quite diverse–comprise another family, responsible not only for the intellectual life and impact of a university but also for its quality. Yet here too there is great diversity, from young scholars striving to achieve the quality of scholarship, teaching, and grantsmanship necessary for tenure, to more mature scholars commanding great respect and impact in the fields, to senior faculty approaching the end of careers and contemplating the endgame of retirement.

Students and faculty members tend to take the staff of a university pretty much for granted. While they understand these are the people who "keep the trains running on time" and who provide them with the environment they need for teaching and research, most view staff as only the supporting cast for the real stars, the faculty. When staff comes to mind at all, it is usually as a source of complaints. To many faculty members, such service units as the Plant Department, the Purchasing Department, and the Office of University Audits are sometimes viewed as obstacles to their interests rather than allies. Yet throughout the university, whether at the level of secretaries, custodians, or groundskeepers or the rarified heights of senior administrators for finance, hospital operations, or facilities construction and management, the quality of the university's staff, coupled with their commitment and dedication, is actually just as important as the faculty in making Michigan the remarkable institution it has become

The deans themselves form yet another family of the university, occasionally in competition with one another, more frequently working together, but always requiring the attention and the pastoral care of the president and the provost. Being a faculty member

248

Student events with the President and First Lady (the campus "mom and pop")

Pastoral care for the faculty family

Entertaining the deans

Entertaining the Executive Officers

Entertaining the Regents

Celebrating the staff

is the best job in a university (with the most prestige, the most freedom, and the most opportunity), but if one has to be an academic administrator, the next best role—at least at Michigan—is that of a dean. Although some of Michigan's academic units (e.g., the College of Literature, Science, and the Arts and the School of Medicine) rival major universities in their size, financial resources, and organizational complexity, both the size and the intellectual span of most UM schools and colleges is just about right to allow true academic leadership. To be sure, deans have to answer in both directions, to the provost from above and to their faculty from below. But their capacity to control both their own destiny and that of their school is far beyond that of most administrators.

The executive officers are also a family, although, quite unlike the deans, they are characterized by great diversity in roles and backgrounds. Although many of the executive officers at universities come from outside the academy (e.g., business and law), Michigan has usually benefited those few executive officers with academic roots, some even with faculty appointments and ongoing teaching and research responsibilities. This not only provides a leadership team with a deep understanding of academic issues, but it gives the University important flexibility in breaking down the usual bureaucracy to form multi executive officer teams to address key issues, such as federal research policy, fund-raising, resource allocation, and even academic policy—issues that would be constrained to administrative silos in other universities.

The UM Board of Regents comprises yet another family. Although most governing board members are dedicated public servants with a strong interest and loyalty to the university, as with any family, there are occasional disagreements—indeed, long-standing feuds—that might last months or even years. But this is not surprising for public governing boards that owe both their selection and support to highly partisan political constituencies.

There are many other University families beyond the campus, e.g., alumni, Ann Arbor citizens, and dedicated football fans. All are characterized by a respect for–indeed, a love of–at least some of the University's activities.

1960s to 1970s

When we first arrived in Ann Arbor, it was a time when low salaries priced many young faculty families out of the housing market. Hence the University allowed us to live for a bit in married student housing (Northwood IV), and this became our first introduction to the faculty family–at least those new faculty families who, like us, were sufficiently destitute to live in University housing. Yet among these early friends are several still at the University today, a half-century later, albeit in more pleasant surroundings and important roles.

The first exposure to academic communities was through the seminars, luncheons, and other events of a small Department of Nuclear Science and Engineering. Since the department conducted only graduate level programs in those early years, there was a strong bond between graduate students and the younger faculty. Students and faculty members played together (poker, basketball, baseball with the Nuclear Nine), went to the Old Heidelberg or Fraser's Pub after seminars, and celebrated each new PhD with a party hosted by each dissertation advisor. The chair of the Department and his spouse accepted major responsibilities for mentoring new faculty and hosting numerous events to entertain both faculty and students, a practice quite common throughout the University.

Fortunately, within a few weeks after our arrival, Anne encountered the first signs of the strong social network that had developed within the University through faculty spouses and women of the faculty. She was contacted by the leaders of the Newcomers Section of the Faculty Women's Club and invited both to join and to meet other new arrivals at a series of social get-togethers for the several hundred women joining the University faculty community each year.

Here it is important to stress just how important this community organization was to new faculty families. As noted earlier, the University is a very diverse and complex organization, broken up into smaller social groups usually aligned with academic departments or work areas. One can image the differences among academic units such as Law, Medicine, Engineering, and LS&A, or among the diverse departments and programs in each of these units. While most of these

1968 Department of Nuclear Science and Engineering

1970 Faculty Women's Club Newcomers

organizations made some effort to welcome and orient their new faculty members, their families were generally ignored.

In contrast, the Faculty Women's Club spanned the entire university, hosting an unusually broad set of activities and interest groups both for faculty partners and more broadly their families. In fact, since being launched by President Marion Burton's wife, Nina Burton, in the 1920s, it had become the primary social organization for pulling together faculty members and their families across the University. While many of the women in the Faculty Women's Club would remain active throughout their lives (including many of the wives of senior university leaders such as presidents and deans), the FWC Newcomers group played a particularly important role both in welcoming new arrivals to the University and providing them with opportunities to become engaged in its broad range of activities, both as members and as families.

Anne immediately joined the group and soon found herself not only with a host of new friends from other arriving faculty families, but also developing relationships with many of the women leaders of the University, including Sally Fleming and Alene Smith (both president's wives) and the spouses of leading faculty members such as Phyllis Wright, Sue Yohe, Betty Richart, and Florence Crane. Her participation in various Newcomers interest groups such as International Cooking, Parenting and Child Care, and Book Reviews gave both of us an immediate opportunity to meet other faculty families and make new friends across the

entire breadth of the University. In fact, Jim was almost overwhelmed when at one of Anne's events he found himself seated directly across from President Robben Fleming!!! Needless to say, for a brand-new assistant professor, this was a bit terrifying, until we learned just how warm and gracious the Flemings were. (As we will describe later, Robben and Sally Fleming were to become our primary tutors in learning the art of the university presidency during the brief several-month period when he became Interim President, just when we were thrust into the presidency as the successors to Harold and Vivian Shapiro.)

Of course, there were other opportunities for faculty members to come together, such as family events (school programs, summer activities), cultural events (performing arts), or "cosmic athletic events" (UM football and basketball), which usually appealed to particular interests or periods in family life (e.g., school-age children). There were also numerous cultural events such as the May Festival hosted by the University Musical Society and the array of performances by students and faculty of the School of Music.

All were important in sustaining community life in the University and Ann Arbor.

1970s

Our community activities shifted somewhat with the appointment to Dean of Engineering in 1981, since with the academic leadership role of the dean came an array of community building activities involving both

256

of us. As "Dean" and "Deanette", we were expected to host numerous events both for the department chairs and the Engineering faculty more broadly, organizing events to celebrate the beginning of the fall term, holiday season, and an array of special events for students and special visitors.

We found ourselves part of new communities such as the deans team (Chuck Vest, Dan Atkins, Scott Fogler, and later Lynn Conway and Walt Hancock), working closely with the provost (in this case, Billy Frye). In addition, we learned that the Dean of Engineering was part of a small informal committee of deans, the SOUP group (with the innocuous name of the "Seminar on University Priorities), which in fact served as the executive council of deans, working closely with the President and Provost on major strategic issues. Anne was particularly influential in using her long-standing friendships with the spouses of the deans of Michigan's other schools and colleges to provide a wonderful opportunity to build bonds with these units.

The role with the Faculty Women's Club also evolved, first as chair of the FWC Newcomers, and then as FWC President, in 1984 a role that provided not only leadership but also mentoring for the group. The presidency of the Faculty Women's Club strengthened these relations, forming a network of these women leaders that would prove invaluable as we moved up the ladder to more senior positions in the University.

While we very much enjoyed both the communities of faculty, students, and staff within the College, our responsibilities and hence activities necessarily broadened by the late 1980s with the appointment of Provost. Here our community building activities bumped up a notch to include all of the deans and many of the senior staff of the University. Once again, this required a very considerable effort both to strengthen and build new community bonds throughout the University. A series of monthly dinners held at Inglis House to bring together faculty couples from across the University. A tradition was launched to host an event in the Alumni Memorial Hall each spring to honor newly promoted faculty. An effort was even made to take on the challenge of "mainstreaming" Michigan athletics by arranging events where student-athletes and coaches were brought together in various academic settings–e.g., museums and concert halls. We wanted to stress that student-athletes were students first, and that coaches were, in reality, teachers.

1990s

Our community roles changed once again with the appointment as President in 1988. It had long been a tradition that the "First Family" of the University played a key role both in building and sustaining its various communities for its faculty, students, and staff. Here we accepted a responsibility for several new communities. The Executive Officers were a particularly important team, and numerous events were arranged and hosted including a Fall Kickoff picnic, holiday dinners, and a spring "Thank heavens the term is ending!" celebration. We also accepted responsibility for another more challenging community, the University's Board of Regents, hosting them for their monthly meetings and arranging for their care during special events such as the Rose Bowl and Final Four Championship.

We also found ourselves involved in numerous external communities, e.g., the presidents and spouses of those universities belonging to the Association of American Universities, the elite institutions in the Tanner Trust, the Business Higher Education Forum–all organizations in which the dual nature of the university presidency, president and spouse, was recognized and valued.

In our role in the presidency, Anne inherited an important legacy from the contributions of early first ladies of the university. Each had brought to the University a unique style, but all had been totally committed to this important role. Early in the our tenure, she took on the challenge of major renovation of the two primary ceremonial facilities of the University, the President's House and the Inglis Highlands estate.

The President's House had been home for all of the University's presidents since 1852. Its location in the center of the campus gave it a special symbolism, much as the White House in Washington. Furthermore, as the oldest building on the campus, it was of major historical significance. When the decision was made to modernize the mechanical systems of the President's House during the last year of the Shapiro presidency, it was also recognized that such a massive system replacement would require as well significant renovation of the

The President's House

The Inglis Highlands Estate

interior design. Funding was set aside so that carpets could be replaced, walls could be painted, and plaster repaired. However, when we assumed the presidency in the midst of this project, Anne suggested a different direction. Rather than simply replacing the existing carpets and decoration details, she instead worked within the original project budget to restore many of the house's original features.

A similar opportunity soon presented itself with the Inglis Highlands estate, which had long provided not only a guest house for distinguished visitors to the University, but more important as a heavily used meeting facility for academic groups. Again, the driving factor was another project, in this case the need to replace the massive slate roof of the manor house, which was in danger of collapse. It was soon realized that the cost of renovating the interior of the house could be accomplished through only a small addition to the original project cost. Again, Anne took responsibility for both the design and the renovation project. And again, working closely with the gardening staff, the formal gardens and grounds of the Inglis Highlands estate were totally replanted and nurtured back to their original elegance.

There were other facilities important to University community life that required attention. Anne worked closely with the staff of the Athletics Department and the University Plant staff to redesign the entertaining areas in Michigan Stadium, including major redesigns of the reception and seating areas in the press box. She also was involved in the design of additional

entertaining areas in the University Golf Course Club House.

Beyond the array of facilities development, Anne also built a strong staff that supported her many activities to build communities throughout the University. And, as the quality of the events hosted by the President and executive officers increased, there was a strong ripple effect across the campus, resulting in an increase in quality in all areas. Yet, even as the standards for the quality of University events increased, Anne also was unrelenting in her expectation that costs be kept under control. She sought these same objectives–excellence and efficiency–in a broad range of other projects: presidential events, football weekends, bowl events, fund-raising, etc.

Finally, it was first in this role that Anne launched a major effort to recapture the history of the University. She was instrumental in creating the University History and Traditions Committee and the position of University Historian, first occupied by Robert Warner, Dean of the School of Library and former United States Archivist. She worked with numerous University faculty and staff on projects ranging from the restoration of the Detroit Observatory (led by Sandy Whitesell) to producing a series of publications on the history of the University. These historical activities would continue long after our presidency.

Throughout our years in the presidency, we sought not only to lead the University but to create a broad understanding that we viewed this as a "public calling", a role through which we served those varied

258

Planning for the Inauguration

Sandy Whitesell and Anne

History and Traditions Committee

Reconnecting the University with its past

communities of faculty, students, and staff that comprised the institution. In a sense, we tried to make it clear to everyone that we worked for them, that they could trust us, and that we were determined both to protect and advance our institution, the University of Michigan. We were very much servants of the University.

2000s

Of course, with new leadership comes new ideas, priorities, agendas, and people, which over time leads to the appearance of new cultures and characteristics. This was certainly true for the administrations of the post-2000 years, which established new priorities and practices for engagement and outreach that created new communities while casting aside others.

Many of the events designed to build leadership teams among the deans, Executive Officers, and Regents

disappeared during the early years of the new century. No longer do the Regents and executive officers gather for dinner and discussions at Inglis House during their monthly meetings. So too, the fall, holiday, and spring events for the deans and executive officers hosted by the president have disappeared. With the withdrawal of Inglis House for faculty and academic events during the fund-raising campaigns of the 2000s, the monthly faculty dinners by the provosts and the many events to honor distinguished achievements by faculty have also vanished.

While there are still faculty social communities within various departments or smaller schools, many of the University-wide faculty activities have weakened. The University's faculty governance through the Senate Assembly and Senate Advisory Committee on University Affairs has assumed more of an advisory role, in contrast to the strong working relationship that existed with the president and executive officers in the

After locking faculty events out of Inglis House for fund-raising, the administration tried to sell the estate!

The UM Economic Dinner Group was forced to meet at Washtenaw Community College!

1960s to 1990s. Its role as the voice of the faculty, once symbolized by its meetings in the amplitheater of the Rackham Hall of Graduate studies, has been muted by moving its meetings to the Palmer Commons. While there remain numerous committees and boards seeking faculty members, there also has been a long-standing suspicion that when the administration wants to avoid action, it appoints yet another committee which tends to discourage faculty participation.

For most of its history the senior faculty has enjoyed a number of clubs for both scholarly conversation and social engagement. Many of these clubs, dating from the 19th Century, such as the Apostles and Church Wardens and the Catholespistimead have long since disappeared. However several still remain: the Scientific Club (now comprised of faculty from any of the University disciplines), the Azazels (a Hebrew word for scapegoat), and the Economics Dinner Group (containing both faculty and business leaders) still are active, their composition has become older and their meetings more difficult to organize.

Unlike many other universities, Michigan has not had a University-wide faculty club for many years. Decades ago the Michigan Union had provided not only a University Club but also a bar and tap room, but today these spaces have been transformed into an Au Bon Pain food court. Efforts to build faculty support for such facilities or perhaps even a club for emeritus faculty have failed to receive strong support from either faculty or the University leadership.

While the Faculty Women's Club met in the University of Michigan Depression Center!

The Faculty Women's Club, founded by Nina Burton in the 1920s, remains quite active and includes both faculty wives and women faculty. But like the other clubs, its membership has declined significantly over the past several decades, although it continues to perform valuable services for the University.

There are several possible reasons for the decline of interest in these clubs. With the increasing number of two-career couples and the limited time for family activities, these clubs are clearly not the priority for the limited free time of faculty. The increasing cost of housing in Ann Arbor have pushed many faculty families into neighboring communities such as Saline, Dexter, and Chelsea, where they form their social groups.

The Inglis Highlands estate was kept in excellent condition and used heavily by academic units, Regents, and visitors to the University until 2011 when the administration ceased allowing access.

In 2011 the estate was closed, the maintenance of the house and grounds abandoned, and much of its furniture moved over into the President's House. Even the memorial to the Duderstadts was dismantled.

Students leaving "broken" Michigan Stadium.

It is also the case, however, that in recent years the leadership of the University has simply not given these groups the attention of earlier presidents. Although the Faculty Women's Club still holds a holiday reception in the Presidents House, a tradition throughout its history, the president stopped attending years ago and, in fact, charges the group thousands of dollars each year for this affair. The Inglis Highlands estate, which has long been the meeting place for important groups such as the Economics Dinner Group, the Henry Russell Lecturers, and the Faculty Women's Club, as well as faculty meetings with the provost and other executive officers (not to mention fund-raising activities) has been withdrawn from University use with the intent to sell the nine acre estate given to the University for use by the president in the 1950s, for commercial development, a short-sighted decision to the extreme. These groups now must meet in off-campus space such as local restaurants and Washtenaw Community College, an embarrassing experience for a great University!

There are few opportunities for members of the University community–students, faculty, staff, alumni– to join together for major events. Over the long history of the University, athletic events (particularly football, basketball, and hockey) and musical and theatrical performances (both the University Musical Society and the School of Music) have provided these.

Yet, driven by aggressive new leadership of the Athletic Department in 2010, Michigan athletics became more focused on achieving national leadership in revenues and expenditures (already doubling budgets to rank 2nd in the nation) rather than building winning programs or serving University needs.It raised ticket prices beyond the range of all but the wealthiest fans. Few faculty members, staff, or even Ann Arbor township people could afford the ticket prices characterizing Michigan Stadium (averaging $230 per game, including premium and seat license fees). Student ticket prices rose to the highest in the nation. And, as a result, the crowds attending events in Michigan Stadium and the Crisler Center and the "wow" entertainment provided to them became more typical of professional athletics. (This was not surprising, since many of the new staff hired by Michigan Athletics come with experience in professional sports including promotion and marketing.)

Unfortunately, the May Festival has disappeared. While the extraordinary quality of the events hosted by the University Musical Society provides a wonderful community experience for a great many members of the Ann Arbor community, the rising prices of these events are a challenge for many. Perhaps here the solution is not through pricing, which is driven by a broader commercial market, but rather more strongly promoting the availability of the extraordinarily diverse array of student and faculty performances provided at modest cost (or indeed free) by the School of Music. It is also important that both the University Musical Society and School of Music better coordinate and promote their activities and avoid competing for either audiences or donors.

Longer Term Concerns

From Serving the "Common Man" to Pampering the "Uncommonly Rich"

The University moved rapidly to develop effective fund-raising and alumni relations activities during the 1980s and 1990s to respond to declining state support, although it continued without restraint to make massive investments in staffing and funding development, communications, and marketing efforts that would seriously distort the culture of the University by the early 2000s, essentially selling both the name and purpose of the institution to the highest bidder. As one by one, ambitious development staff sold the names of the schools and buildings to rich donors (who only contributed a modest amount to their construction or operation), it was only natural to wonder whether they were selling the University's visibility as well. After all, how many outsiders would know from their new names that the Taubman School of Architecture, the Penny Stamps School of Art and Design, and the Ross School of Business Administration were really part of the University of Michigan.

We have noted earlier the increasing degree to which the University of Michigan has become "an engine of inequality" as it enrolled an increasing number of high income out-of-state students while the enrollment of students from low-income backgrounds dropped to among the lowest level of any many public university. But this is only one of many signs of the degree to which the University is not only increasingly dependent upon but also shifting its focus to serving the wealthy. As we have noted, few can afford the soaring costs of tickets imposed by Michigan Athletics. University Musical Society events are following a similar commercial trend in price escalation, albeit with the School of Music continuing to provide a very high quality but remarkably low price alternative.

As bit by bit the University has been selling its resources to the highest bidder–student enrollments, the names of programs and places, access to athletic and cultural events, etc.–faculty, staff, and indeed many students are beginning to feel no longer welcome or even tolerated by the armies of new staff now determined to redefine and market the "brand" of the university.

This bias increasingly toward the wealthy has also influenced University staff policies. As noted earlier there has been an extraordinary growth in both staffing of the central administration and compensation provided to senior administrators at a time when faculty and staff compensation has been relatively stagnant. Through the use of hidden devices such as one-time bonuses, deferred compensation, or incentive awards, the compensation of executives in the central administration and selected deans and directors is now considerably above that of most other public universities and challenging some of the leading private universities. While such executive compensation is usually argued as driven by market considerations both by leadership

and compensation, it must be kept in mind that nonprofit organizations such as universities should not be driven by corporate models. Furthermore, unlike the compensation of corporate executives, which require a rigorous incentive compensation policy consistent with accounting practices and public disclosure, university compensation is all too often determined by ad hoc decisions made by senior administrators rather than adhering to rigorous, public salary structures.

While executive search consultants love to stress the importance of competitive compensation (after all, there fees are frequently based on this), one should be very skeptical of just how important compensation is at this level. Instead, most senior academic leaders are rarely lured by the dollars. To be sure, a competitive salary is viewed by some candidates as a measure of how much you want them. But it is rarely the deciding factor. Far more important is the challenge, opportunity, and prestige of building a top-ranked academic program.

Many candidates are seeking new opportunities because they have been blocked by the narrowing pyramid of the academic hierarchy in their own institution. Some are after wealth and fame, not from the university, but rather from outside their academic appointment through corporate boards, national commissions, or other opportunities. Some actually view academic leadership as a "higher calling", with emotional rewards and satisfaction that simply cannot be quantified in terms of compensation. In fact, some actually have acquired a sense of loyalty to a university and view such assignments as a duty of service.

Anyone doubting this should just look at the list of institutions with the highest executive salaries. Usually these are places you have to pay people to go, not at the very best institutions!

The Erosion of the Michigan Saga

It has been suggested that a key feature of the Michigan saga, its particular character and impact, over most of its history has been its role as a pathfinder for higher education. It has leveraged its unusual combination of quality, breadth, scale, and risk-taking spirit to blaze new trails for learning, discovery, and engagement to serve society. In fact, this pathfinding role has occasionally been so profound that it has changed the world itself.

Recently the University has seemed more content to follow the lead of others, to embrace more common themes in higher education such as "interdisciplinarity", "engaged learning", and "entrepreneurism". Its pioneering spirit seems to be lagging. The novelty is missing in its initiatives. To be sure, the financial challenges faced by the University with the loss of much of its state support have required attention by both the University's leadership and its Regents. It is also the case that over the past 15 years many of the key leadership and administrative positions have been intentionally filled through external appointments of those unfamiliar with the University's history, weakening somewhat the corporate memory and, indeed, corporate culture of the University. Indeed, there are many signs that they have been slowly decoupling the University from its past, just as did the disruptions of the protest movements of the 1960s. In fact, long-standing programs such as the University's History and Traditions Committee have been ignored and then abandoned. The opportunity to utilize the Bicentennial Year to understand and recommit the University to the spirit that led to two centuries of leadership for not only higher education but for the world now seems to be set aside in favor of using this moment to push yet another fund-raising campaign.

As many of the priorities of the University have shifted to activities such as development, public relations, marketing, and promoting the University by those from the commercial world with little experience with academe, it has become increasingly evident that the first years of the new century have become yet another "lost" decade similar to the 1970s when little of the traditional pathfinding achievements of University leadership occurred.

Whatever the reason, it is clear that this new culture of defining and promoting the "brand" of the University through slogans such as "Victors for Michigan", by those with little understanding of either its academic character, history, or saga will seriously undermine the leadership role it has played in higher education over the years if allowed to continue. Put another way, a culture which transforms one of the great universities of the world into a follower rather than a pathfinder should be strongly resisted by those who understand and value Michigan's remarkable contributions to the state, the nation, and the world throughout its long history.

The Road Ahead

So, how might the University begin to rebuild some of the communities and resources that have disappeared over the past two decades? Put another way, how might they glue back together broken communities?

First, it is important to counter those practices that tend to compete with academic communities, such as:

Allowing wealthy donors to distort both the priorities and traditions of the University (particularly through "naming" gifts).

Stressing once again that the primary role of chairs and deans is not fund-raising but rather academic leadership, and the constituencies they serve are students and faculty, not wealthy donors.

Seeking a better balance between external and internal appointments for key leadership positions (e.g., chairs, deans, executive officers, and president), perhaps by countering the external bias of search consultants.

Achieving a better balance between the attention given to the priorities of academic and auxiliary units. To be sure, units such as the University Medical Center, University Housing, and the Athletics Department do have access to vast resources. But the heart and purpose of a university are learning and scholarship, and whether prosperous or not, these activities and their associated communities involving faculty and students must be given the priority.

It is also critical to recommit the University to both the maintenance and community use of key facilities such as the President's House, the Inglis Highlands estate, the Michigan Union, and the Michigan League.

The importance of long-standing organizations such as the Faculty Women's Club and the Economics Dinner Group should be both recognized and supported through University policies and resources (e.g., Inglis Highlands).

The degree to which commercialism has fractured the community of long-standing fans of Michigan

Athletics, a community including not only students, alumni, and fans but also faculty and staff, must be addressed. There needs to be a significant restructuring of both costs and pricing, as well as positioning the University once more as a leader in reforming college sports rather than exemplar in their excesses.

Finally new communities should be considered. For example, there is a need for new faculty clubs for senior faculty similar to those longstanding historical groups such as the Scientific Club and the Azazels. The possibility of clubs for faculty couples should be considered, perhaps modeled after several of the Interest Sections of the Faculty Women's Club.

Strong consideration should be given about the possibility of a faculty club for emeritus faculty members. Since faculty retirement is increasingly accompanied by a strong desire to retain some level of intellectual, cultural, and social interaction with the University community, Michigan should join many other institutions in providing resources to support this continued engagement.

Here we might note that the University used to have such clubs. Alumni Memorial Hall, which was built by the Alumni as a War Memorial to honor fallen University of Michigan students, faculty, staff and alumni, was completed in 1910, dedicated a large room in the basement was used for the University Club, a faculty organization.

When the Michigan Union was expanded in 1936, it provided space for a new University Club for the faculty.

Alumni Memorial Hall

University Club Faculty Lounge
Michigan Union

Faculty Recreation Room
Michigan Union

Appendix

Weakening of Key Assets and Cultures
The University of Michigan, Circa 2015

Continuities

"An uncommon education for the common man"
...Loss of student economic and social diversity
...Loss of leadership diversity
...UM today is pandering primarily to the rich
....Over commercialization of athletics, UMS,...

The Michigan Saga
...leadership of past two decades failed to honor the UM saga as pathfinder
...tendency to neither appreciate nor honor UM history
...grasping at the straws of "me-too isms"

Weakening of Historical Assets
...Limited priority given by the Bentley Library
...Elimination of History and Traditions Committee
...Elimination of University Historian
...Failure to take advantage of UM 2017
...Limited role of UM Press in UM History projects
...Disappearance of UM courses on University History (particularly the Stenecks course in LS&A)

Erosion or Loss of Major UM Assets
...Inglis Highlands Estate
...Ford Fairlane Estate
...Historical Role of Bentley and UM Press
...Ford Nuclear Reactor and Phoenix Project
...Alumni Memorial Hall

Culture

Faculty activism and engagement
...erosion of SACUA and Senate Assembly influence
...muzzling by leadership
..."Board in Control" to "Advisory Board" for Intercollegiate Athletics

Overrun by administration
...shared services
...growth in central administration

Migratory nature of faculty
...no longer committed to livelong UM careers
...responsive to market pressures

Staff Pressures
...lowering priorities given staff
...layoffs, weak compensation
...shared services, IT rationalization

Decentralization vs Centralization

Weakening of Deans
...Loss of teamwork
...Disappearance of SOUP group
...Dominated by outsiders (13 to 6)
...Overwhelmed by fund-raising pressures
...Inadequate support by administration
...Intentional weakening by provost and president

Lack of EOs with faculty experience
...EO "faculty": president, provost, VPR, VPHA

Student activism
...wealthy students are "paying for the party"
...erosion of student diversity and inclusion
...disappearance of "common man" priority

Governance
...What is the priority of the Regents? To act as trustees to protect the University, or as governors to demand its near-term service to state?
...Commitment to fiduciary responsibilities?
...Inadequate interaction with UM administration

Community

Weakening of key social organizations
...Faculty Women's Club
...Senior Faculty Clubs
...Decline of EO, Dean social events for faculty
...Loss of Inglis House for faculty groups
...Pricing of athletics and performance venues

Chapter 19

A Tough Neighborhood

The University of Michigan, highlighted for its free and liberal spirit during its early years, has a long history of activism on the part of its students, faculty, and alumni. Student and faculty concerns upon and extending beyond the University's campus have frequently not only addressed but also influenced major national issues, such as civil rights and the Teach-Ins against the war in Vietnam in the 1960s, the environmental movement of the 1970s, and in the 1980s and 1990s, the University's leadership in helping reaffirm the importance of diversity to higher education. Of course this sometimes runs against the grain of political opinion in the community, state government, or the public at large. But the University's constitutional autonomy, coupled with the long-standing principle of academic freedom, gave it both the capacity and the responsibility to challenge the norms and beliefs of society from time to time.

While Ann Arbor may be a small Midwestern community, the University itself has always had more of the hard edge characterizing the urban centers of the Northeast. Although sports fans might suggest this flows naturally from Michigan's reputation in violent sports such as football and hockey, in reality it has evolved as a defensive mechanism to protect the University against the reality of its harsh political environment. In a sense, the University of Michigan grew up in a rough neighborhood and had to become lean and mean and capable of looking out for itself.

Michigan is a state characterized by confrontational politics. It was long dominated by the automobile industry–big companies, big labor unions, and big state government. During the last half of the 20th century, as the state's economy and population faced the challenges and hardships driven by global competition and poverty in its industrial cities, this political

atmosphere has become more strident, with organized labor fighting to retain its control of the Democratic party while the conservative communities of western Michigan, dominated by the religious right, now control the Republican party and State government.

In many ways, Ann Arbor is an oasis, a liberal eastern community planted in the center of a tough Midwestern state. The politics of the city of Ann Arbor still reflect the rebellious spirit of the protest days of the 1960s (declaring itself in the 1980s as "a nuclear free zone"!). The community continues to this day to mark its history of civil disobedience by celebrating each April 1 with the annual Hash Bash, where thousands come to promote and experience the evil weed, uninhibited by Ann Arbor's pot law, a $5 fine for possession of marijuana.

The relationship between public universities and their states varies significantly. Some universities are structurally organized as components of state government, subject to the same hiring and business practices characterizing other state agencies. Others possess a certain autonomy from state government through constitutional provision or statute. All are influenced by the power of the public purse--by the nature and degree of state support.

Although the University of Michigan faced many of the challenges experienced by other state universities, declining state appropriations, intrusive sunshine laws, over-regulation, politically motivated competition among state institutions, and a politically determined governing board–there are two characteristics of our relationship with the state that are quite unique. First, as noted earlier the University was given unusual autonomy in the state constitution, autonomy comparable to that of the Legislature, Executive, and Judicial branches. While it was certainly subject to state funding decisions and regulations, the University's elected Board of Regents possessed exceptionally strong constitutionally derived powers over all academic activities of the institution. Second, both because of the University's autonomy and its long history, first as a territorial institution and then later, in effect, as a national university–and today, one might argue, a world university–it was determined to do whatever was necessary to protect both the quality of and access to its academic programs.

In particular, the University refused to allow the quality of its academic programs to be determined by state appropriations or policies, which were usually insufficient to support a world-class institution. Instead it developed an array of alternative resources to supplement state support, including student tuition, federal research support, private giving, endowment earnings, and auxiliary activities such as clinical care. Furthermore, it used its constitutional autonomy to defend its commitment to serving a diverse population, reaching out not only to underserved minority communities and students from low income families, but also to students from across the nation and around the world. While this philosophy of independence was key to the quality of the University and its ability to serve not simply the people of the state, but those of the nation and the world, it did not always endear the University to state government, which tended to equate the University's independence with arrogance.

Political winds shift over time, and this has certainly been the case for the political fortunes of the University of Michigan. For its first century, the University enjoyed a privileged position. Many of its alumni were in the state legislature and in key positions in government and communities across the state. Political parties were disciplined, and special interests had not yet splintered party solidarity. In that environment the University had little need to cultivate public understanding or grassroots support. A few leaders from the University met each year with the governor and leaders of the legislature to negotiate our appropriation (rumored to be in a duck blind…). That was it. The University was valued and appreciated. There was a historic and intense public commitment to the support of public higher education that had characterized the founders of the University of Michigan and the generations of

immigrants who followed, sacrificing to provide quality public education as the key to their children's future.

But, as we shall see, this broad public support for a world class public research university is a far cry from the political cauldron in which flagship public universities find themselves today.

1950s - 1970s

This University of Michigan's privileged position and broad support changed dramatically in the 1950s and 1960s, both because of the aggressive ambition of the other state colleges and universities and the detached and occasionally arrogant attitude of the University of Michigan. In the early 1950s, Michigan State's legendary president John Hannah transformed that institution from an agricultural college into a major research university, relying both on his own political skill and UM's missteps. Hannah began, ironically enough, with football, by maneuvering Michigan State into the opening left by the University of Chicago's departure from big-time football and the Big Ten Conference. With this visibility, he then persuaded the State Legislature to change the name of his institution to Michigan State University and later added professional schools such as medicine and law. The University of Michigan adamantly and unsuccessfully opposed each of these steps, finally attempting to save face by capitalizing the word "The" in its own title. (We ended this arrogant practice during the 1990s.) These unsuccessful battles firmly established UM's reputation for arrogance in Lansing, as in, "those arrogant asses from Ann Arbor."

A story contrasting the styles of the presidents of the two universities at the time illustrates the challenge: Michigan's president, Harlan Hatcher, a tall and distinguished scholar, used to arrive to visit legislators in Lansing driving up in his chauffeur-driven Lincoln. John Hannah, in shirtsleeves, would drive himself over in his Ford pickup to make the case to legislators more typically from outstate farm country than big-city Detroit. A second Hannah story: during the 1950s and 1960s, the Michigan State campus was pockmarked with construction projects. The legend was that Hannah would get funds from the legislature for a single building, and then use the funds to dig the

President John Hannah

President Harlan Hatcher

foundations of several more buildings, and then turn to the legislature for the funds to fill all those holes in the ground with new buildings.

A long-time leader of the state legislature portrayed Michigan during this period of its history as a university led by a distinguished but conservative president and moneyed Republican Regents determined to hang onto the past. They were surprised when the state legislature not only labeled Michigan as arrogant but actually took great delight in disadvantaging it relative to other public universities. The student protests on campus during the 1960s provided even more ammunition to those who wanted to attack Michigan for political reasons. The University entered the 1970s with both a bruised ego and a damaged reputation–at least in Lansing.

Slowly the University began to realize that the world had changed, and that it no longer had monopoly on state support. The state was in the midst of a profound economic transformation that was driving change in the political environment. Political parties declined in influence. Special-interest constituencies proliferated and organized to make their needs known and influence felt. Even as the University became more central in responding to the needs of the state, it was also held more accountable to its many publics.

Driving the complexity of this situation was a growing socioeconomic shift in priorities at both the state and federal level. In Michigan, as in many other states, priorities shifted from investment in the future through strong support of education to a shorter-term focus, as represented by the growing expenditures for prisons, social services, and federal mandates such as Medicaid, even as conservative administrations cut taxes in the

1990s. This was compounded by legislation that earmarked a portion of the state budget for K-12 education, leaving higher education to compete with corrections and social services for limited discretionary tax dollars. As a result, the state's support for higher education declined rapidly in real terms during the early 1980s and continued to drop, relative to inflation, throughout the remainder of the decade.

In summary, during the last half of the 20th century the University of Michigan's political influence in Lansing plummeted. Although changing external factors such as the rise of populism, changing demographics, and the rise of the religious right in western Michigan were key factors, the University's presidents had been largely ineffective in reversing the situation since the 1940s. Ruthven's declining health prevented his active role in Lansing. Hatcher was effective with moneyed Republicans, but he was a poor match for John Hannah's shirtsleeve approach. Fleming relied heavily on others, keeping his powder dry for the periodic crises erupting on the campus during the volatile protest years of the 1960s and 1970s. Shapiro was dedicated and tireless, but the sharp mismatch of his thoughtful style with the crude populism and paranoia of legislative was simply too great.

The key factor allowing the University to sustain its quality during this difficult period was its constitutional autonomy. Relying heavily on this autonomy to control its own destiny, the University began to increase both its tuition and its nonresident enrollments to compensate for the loss of state support. Yet even the constitutional autonomy of the University faced formidable challenges from legislative efforts to control admissions, gubernatorial efforts to freeze tuition, and even onslaught from the media under the guise of the state's sunshine laws to control everything from presidential searches to Regental elections.

The situation was quite different in the University's relationships with the federal government. Although the United States leaves most of the responsibility for higher education to the states and the private sector, the federal government does have a considerable influence on higher education, both through federal policies, in areas such as student financial aid and through the direct support of campus activities such as research and health care. In fact some would maintain that the most transformative changes in American higher education have usually been triggered by federal actions such as the Land Grant Acts of the 19th Century, the G. I. Bill and government-university research partnership (Vannevar Bush's Science, the Endless Frontier) following World War II, and the Higher Education Acts of the 1960s.

As Washington became convinced that higher education was important to the future of the nation in the decades after World War II, the federal government began to provide funding to colleges and universities in support of research, housing, student financial aid, and key professional programs such as medicine and engineering. Of course, with significant federal support also came massive federal bureaucracy. Universities were forced to build large administrative organizations just to interact with the large administrative bureaucracies in Washington. Federal rules and regulations snared universities in a web of red tape that not only constrained their activities but became important cost drivers. Universities were frequently whipsawed about by the unpredictable changes in Washington's stance toward higher education as the political winds shifted direction each election year. Yet, it was strong federal support rather than state support or philanthropy that transformed universities like Michigan into global leaders as research universities.

1980s

Despite the changing nature of its economic and politics, the State of Michigan was characterized very much by a blue-collar mentality in the 1980s, perhaps best illustrated by a comment by a senior executive of General Motors during a visit to GM headquarters: "As long as we can put a car on the showroom floor for fewer dollars per pound than anybody else, we will dominate the global marketplace!" Of course, the Japanese demonstrated convincingly that people no longer bought cars by the pound–they chose quality instead. Similarly, in the global, knowledge-driven economy of the 21st Century, it was the quality of a workforce that counts, as evidenced by the increasing tendency of American companies to outsource–rather, offshore, in contemporary language–not only unskilled labor but high-skilled activities such as software engineering. Higher education in Michigan tended to be treated at best with benign neglect and at worst as a convenient political whipping boy.

The 1980s began with a deep national recession–read "depression" in Michigan, since when the nation gets a cold, Michigan catches pneumonia because of the sensitivity of the automobile industry to the national economy. Although the University of Michigan was not singled out for abuse, it suffered greatly along with the rest of higher education. It also faced an unusual alignment of the political planets when legislative champions for Michigan State University and Wayne State University assumed the chairs of the key higher education appropriation committees, along with two-decade long succession of Michigan State alumni as governors.

There were many theories about what was actually happening. Despite the fact that the state's governors paid lip service to the unique role of the University of Michigan as the state's flagship university, none lifted a finger to help the University if political capital were at stake. As William Hubbard, former UM dean of medicine and UpJohn CEO, put it, the state was cursed with an "extreme intolerance of extraordinary excellence." And it was certainly true that an angry strain of populism ran throughout the state. As one key legislator summarized the situation: "It is no longer possible for a kid like me to go to the University of Michigan. The University's prospects in Lansing are at a low point. The Senate is controlled by MSU Republicans more interested in agriculture and boosting their alma mater. The Democrats are simply not very effective, dominated by the Detroit Black Caucus. The key legislators are simply no longer swayed by public pressure. They cannot be intimidated, since they cannot be beaten in their gerrymandered districts."

With fewer and fewer Michigan graduates in influential positions in state government, it was questionable whether a traditional approach to lobbying legislators would be effective. There were those who believed the UM bashing had become a popular sport in Lansing because the University no longer had allies with sufficient power or commitment to threaten retaliation. The University was drifting politically without a plan of attack or even an effective defense. Another Lansing observer put it this way: "Michigan is big, vulnerable, and it doesn't dance very well!"

Much of the University of Michigan's political challenge was stimulated by its very success as one of the nation's leading research universities. Its aspirations for excellence frequently were met by state government and the public at large with questions of "Excellence for whom?" and "Excellence for what purpose?", assuming that excellence really meant an elitism that would exclude their constituents. Furthermore, as one of the largest and most prominent universities in the nation, Michigan was frequently targeted by those in the federal government hoping to use it as a lynchpin for driving broader change in higher education. Since the University operates one of the nation's largest and financially most successful university medical centers, it was understandable that Michigan would be the target for federal efforts to reduce health care reimbursement and funding for medical training. The University's national leadership in sponsored research also made it an attractive target for the same congressional investigations that trampled Stanford in the early 1990s, ironically led by Michigan's own Congressman John Dingell. However unlike Stanford, we were prepared and immediately responded to the Congressional attack not only with a strong public defense led by alumnus Mike Wallace, but also back-channel conversations with the Congressman that successfully deflected the attack.

There were other factors that frequently placed the University in the political bull's-eye. The success and visibility of the University's athletic programs–particularly its football team–made the University a primary target for the enforcement of gender equity through Title IX in the 1970s. As the largest employer in Ann Arbor, with vast assets in the billions of dollars, it was also natural that Michigan would become a popular target of litigation on almost every issue imaginable from those plaintiffs and lawyers who were hoping that the institution's deep pockets would lead to a quick settlement, regardless of the merits of the case.

The University's public purpose, "an uncommon education for the common man", and its success in leading the struggle for campus diversity through efforts such as the Michigan Mandate, which doubled minority student and faculty representation on campus during the early 1990s, gave the University even more prominence. Hence it was not surprising that the institution would become a target for conservative groups seeking to challenge and roll back affirmative action policies in college admissions, an effort which would lead to the important Supreme Court decision of 2003.

As an interim strategy, the University lowered its sights from hogging the entire trough of state support to simply trying to stay even with Michigan State. But even this proved to be a formidable challenge, with Michigan State alumni as governors (James Blanchard and John Engler) in the 1980s and 1990s. Although the University of Michigan at least managed to avoid being low man on the totem pole during the latter part of the 1970s, the University's Replacement Hospital Project exhausted the state's discretionary capacity to fund higher education capital facilities. The cupboard was bare.

The 1980s started off positively enough for the University when the new Blanchard administration made a special effort to recognize the impact of the research universities on the state's economy through the Research Excellence Fund, a special $30 million annual appropriation for campus-based research. The College of Engineering was able to capture roughly $11 million/year of this annual appropriation flowing to the University. But this effort to differentiate among institutions and mission soon ran afoul of Lansing politics, and eventually the special funding for research disappeared.

Blanchard's second term became a disaster for higher education when he realized through polling that he could get more votes by attacking the rising tuition levels of public universities–a consequence of inadequate state support–than investing in their capacity. The governor launched a major effort to constrain tuition as a cheaper political alternative to providing adequate support for the state's universities in gaining political popularity. In parallel, the state established a prepaid tuition plan, the Michigan Education Trust, that portrayed itself as a state-guaranteed program to help parents meet the cost of a college education–although, in reality, it provided no real guarantee and was constructed as a Ponzi scheme, in which the unrealistic price of early contracts would be compensated by later participants. Since the financial–and political–integrity of the Trust was heavily dependent on tuition levels, the governor launched a major effort to force universities to freeze tuition increases.

This was the challenging political environment the University faced in the late 1980s. It had to resist the state's effort to dictate tuition, since these resources represented the only real alternative to maintaining the quality and health of higher education in Michigan during a time in which state support was declining. The President's Council of Public Universities waged a bitter yet successful struggle to resist the governor's efforts to control tuition. We also fought hard to maintain the University's autonomy in areas such as the admission of out-of-state students. State funding for higher education dropped from 12% to less than 8% of the state's budget during the decade. Even more dramatically, the state of Michigan fell into the bottom quartile in its support of higher education, dropping as low as 45th in the nation at one point.

Fortunately, the University had a top-notch state-relations team with experience on both sides of the aisle. Although we soon reaffirmed the pragmatic conclusion of our predecessors that it was unlikely that the University would ever again benefit from its flagship status in Lansing, we also realized that we were destined to continue to lose in state politics as long as we stayed on the defensive, simply reacting to whatever trumped-up charge–out-of-state enrollments, high tuition, racism on campus, whatever–that our enemies used to disadvantage us with respect to other state universities.

Instead, we adopted a quite different strategy by forming a bond with the presidents of Michigan State and Wayne State to build a team of the leaders of the

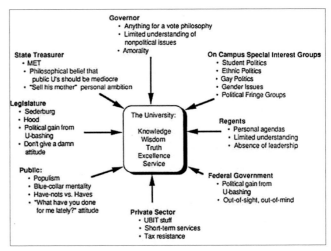

Charting the "forces of darkness" threatening the university.

state's public universities that would both advocate for stronger support of higher education and resist efforts to challenge our constitutional autonomy by controlling issues such as enrollments, tuitions, and academic priorities. In particular, we visited most of the major cities in the state, holding press conferences for visibility and hosting numerous receptions to recruit our alumni who were in leadership roles in communities throughout the state–in business, the professions, and public service-to assist in this efforts. This "treetops" strategy was extremely effective, and not only beat back the efforts of the Blanchard administration to control our institutions, but was a factor in electing his successor, John Engler, as "the education governor"!

1990s

Higher education faced a paradoxical situation as it approached the 1990s. On the one hand, it was clear that the universities were becoming more critical players in a society increasingly dependent upon knowledge, upon educated people and their ideas. They were not only more important to society than ever, but they were more deeply engaged through a broad range of activities ranging from education to health care to public entertainment (through athletics). Yet, even as the university moved front and center stage, it also came under attack from many directions: the cost of education, political activities on campus, student and faculty behavior, and racial diversity and affirmative action. The American university became for many just another arena for the exercise of political power, an arena for the conflict of fragmented interests, a bone of contention for proliferating constituencies. It was increasingly the focus of concern for both the powerful and the powerless.

One of the most important roles of a university president is to protect the university from hostile political forces, both internal and external, that could cause it great harm. At the beginning of each academic year our leadership team of executive officers would meet together for a risk-assessment session, to predict the most political significant threats to the University and develop strategies for its defense. We actually developed a threat chart identifying the greatest concerns for the year ahead. At the top of the chart would usually be the governor, since whether by opportunistic intent or just neglect, this state leader was frequently the source of many of the woes facing higher education in the state. Close behind was the state legislature, dominated during the 1980s by graduates of Michigan State University, who took great delight in thrashing that arrogant institution in Ann Arbor.

Washington also posed an ongoing threat, usually through the meddling of federal agencies or Congressional action. There were times when even members of our own Michigan Congressional delegation would make the list, for example, when manipulated by their staff into taking positions hostile to the University in order to win political influence or visibility at the national level.

Next on the chart would be the Fifth Estate, particularly the hometown newspapers—which, in Michigan's case, included not only the Ann Arbor News but also the Detroit papers. While most hometown newspaper editors soon realize that university controversies stimulate interest and advertising sales, the Ann Arbor paper often was led by those who actually carried a chip on their shoulders about the University—perhaps because Michigan was perceived as elitist and arrogant, or because of rocky town-gown relations, or even because we refused to invest heavily in building degree programs in journalism (flames occasionally fanned by several of our own faculty members). We usually didn't bother listing the student newspaper, the Michigan Daily, as a major threat since

it was usually more preoccupied with college sports or student causes such as disciplinary policies.

We never included any students, faculty, or staff on our threat chart. We believed that student activism, while occasionally annoying to administrators, was nevertheless an important and positive element of the Michigan saga. To be sure, Michigan had its share of outspoken students and faculty members, some enjoying the spotlight of campus politics, some as squeaky wheels pushing one personal agenda or another, and some speaking out on issues of considerable importance to the institution or broader society. But generally we regarded this as a normal–indeed desirable–characteristic of a campus with an activist tradition. We preferred to not only tolerate but actually encourage such behavior, even when, in one case, it led to the Supreme Court case on affirmative action. Although we occasionally had outspoken staff members as well, particularly on union issues, most staff were intensely loyal university citizens and were viewed as strong allies rather than threats.

We did include on our threat chart an occasional member of our Board of Regents, however. We viewed most members of the board as conscientious public servants, basically supportive of the University, although some had their particular hang-ups such as football, campus architecture, or student rights. However, we always had one or two regents who were renegades, frequently seizing on opportunities to embarrass or even disrupt the University to promote their personal visibility and political agenda.

Finally, there was the usual array of special-interest groups, some on campus, some off, inclined to use the University as a convenient and highly visible target to further their particular cause. Here the list was very long and ever changing, spanning the political spectrum from the Marxist left to the Genghis Khan right.

To test our assumptions, we decided to conduct a reality check with a number of the state's political and corporate leaders. Each was asked to challenge the following assumptions: First, because of the limited will and capacity to support higher education, and in the face of a weakened economy and other social needs, the state would, at best, be able to support higher education at the level of a regional four-year college—not at the level of a world-class research university. Second, political pressures would make it increasingly difficult for state leaders to give priority to state support for flagship institutions. Instead, strong political forces would drive a leveling process in which state appropriations per student would equalize across all state universities.

In the end, few of these leaders disagreed with our premises. Furthermore, all believed that the University's only prudent course was to assume that state support would continue to deteriorate throughout the 1990s. Consistent with the University's long-standing philosophy of refusing to let the state control our quality, we continued Harold Shapiro's strategy: i) to build alternative revenue streams (tuition, federal grants and contracts, auxiliary enterprises, private giving, and building endowment through wise investment strategies) to levels sufficient to compensate for the loss in state support; ii) to deploy our resources far more effectively than the University had in the past by focusing on quality at the possible expense of breadth and capacity, while striving to improve efficiency and productivity; and iii) to enhance the University's ability to control its own destiny by defending our constitutional autonomy, building strong political support for our independence, and strengthening the quality of the university's Board of Regents.

Yet it was clear that the University of Michigan was a creature of the state constitution, and it was unlikely that it could ever separate itself from this constraint. Yet it was also the case that the political realities of the past several decades had shifted the University's Lansing strategy from offense, e.g., maximizing state support, to defense, i.e., minimizing the damage to the University from state government. We needed a new and more aggressive strategy to move toward operating more like a private institution while becoming less dependent on the state. With a new Republican administration coming to power in the early 1990s, the pressure on controlling university tuition and enrollments subsided somewhat–although state support continued to decline.

A similar shift was also occurring in federal support of higher education. There were signs that the nation was no longer willing to invest in research performed by universities, at least at the same level and with a similar willingness to support basic research. Furthermore, even the basic principles of this extraordinarily productive research partnership began to unravel, changing from a partnership to a procurement process. This view unleashed on the research university an army of government staff, accountants, and lawyers all claiming as their mission that of making certain that the university meets every detail of its agreements with the government.

To address this, during the 1990s we substantially increased the University's presence in Washington by establishing a permanent office on Capital Hill, significantly expanding our federal relations staff, and mobilizing our extensive army of alumni in the Washington area. We strongly encouraged University faculty members to become actively involved in federal policy activities, providing support through our Washington office and federal relations team. Perhaps most important, however, was our acceptance of a major role in acting on behalf of all of higher education on important issues ranging from research policy to student financial aid to health care to diversity. We encouraged our federal relations team to work closely with the various national higher education associations. This spirit of building alliances was very similar to that we had employed in our state-relations efforts, since we realized that the interests of the University of Michigan were best served when we helped advance the interests of all of higher education.

Michigan's very success in rising to a position of national leadership in attracting federal support for its research activities placed it at considerable risk during this period of shifting federal priorities and attitudes. As one of America's leading research universities, it generally was targeted by every federal effort to restructure the long-standing partnership between the nation and its universities. For example, although Stanford University was the primary target of the vicious attacks on research grant overhead charges by Congressman John Dingell's powerful investigative committee, Michigan also was attacked by committee staff members. Efforts to transfer more of the expense of federally procured research to universities through artificial constraints on overhead payments or excessive cost-sharing requirements hit Michigan harder than most institutions.

The University continued to experience the usual ups and downs in its relationships with the city of Ann

Senator Don Riegle and Tom Butts

UM Congressional Breakfast

Congressman Bob Carr

Congressman Bill Schutte

Senator Carl Levin

Pollster Bob Teeter

Governor John Engler

VP Dan Quale and Gov Engler

Governor John Engler

Senator Lana Pollack and
Governor James Blanchard

Hearing with
Senator Joe Schwartz

Testifying with
Gil Whitaker

There were times when we went to higher authorities...the 60 Minutes cast and the Dalai Lama!

Arbor that had characterized not only its history but town-gown relations in other campus communities. The factors causing tensions between the University and the city were also not surprising: rowdy students, traffic, competition for housing, and removing property from the tax roles. The efforts taken by the University to work more closely with fraternities and sororities to address neighborhood concerns had a positive impact. There was a genuine effort to strengthen relationships between the University leadership, city government, and leaders of the local business community, and overall there was progress in improving town-gown relations.

The University also intensified its outreach efforts with other Michigan communities. Its Schools of Education, Public Health, and Social Work intensified their activities with the metropolitan Detroit area. Many other units and individual faculty became engaged in research and service in Detroit and worked to strengthen relations with the city's leadership. Efforts with other Michigan cities also gained momentum. Of particular note here were the efforts of UM-Flint and UM-Ann Arbor to work closely with city government, industry, labor, private foundations, and private leadership to address a wide range of issues facing the City of Flint, including education, public health, and economic development.

The University also took important steps to improve its relationship with the media. It appointed Walt Harrison, the former head of a major national public relations firm, to the post of Vice President for University Relations, and he moved ahead rapidly to build a strong communications program capable of supporting all of the University's external relations activities.

In summary, much of the attention of the administration during the 1990s was directed at building far stronger relationships with the multitude of external constituencies served by and supporting the University. Efforts were made to strengthen bonds with both state and federal government, ranging from systemic initiatives such as opening and staffing new offices in Lansing and Washington to developing personal relationships with key public leaders (e.g., the Governor, the White House). A parallel effort was made to develop more effective relationships with the media at the local, state, and national level. These included major media campaigns such as the Big Ten public service announcements and national organizations such as the Science Coalition. Additional efforts were directed toward strengthening relationships with key communities including Ann Arbor, Detroit, and Flint.

2000

The nature of Michigan's relationships with its various constituencies began to shift yet again during the first decade of the 21st century. Although Republican John Engler was succeeded by a Democrat, Jennifer Granholm, who had long standing relationships with several Regents, the erosion of state support dropped even more precipitously. In later interviews, Granholm explained that whenever she put a list of state priorities such as crime (build more prisons), the economy (cut more taxes), and education (K-12 comes first) in front of audiences, higher education always came up last, so this is what she decided to sacrifice. Of course, since she had attended UC Berkeley and Harvard herself, she should have understood well the importance for the long term in investing in higher education, but instead she took a "let them eat cake" approach and sacrificed university funding.

One might ask where was the University of Michigan during this period. After all, the University had led a successful effort in the 1990s by uniting all of the public universities in the state to galvanize their leading alumni ("the treetops" strategy) to beat back a similar effort to cut higher education funding while freezing tuition by Democratic Governor James Blanchard. Of course, one explanation for Michigan's failure to get off the bench and get back in the game of state relations during the past decade involves the degree to which Michigan shifted more of its attention on private fund-raising. However there was also a serious failure to make adequate investment in its state relations activities, with only a small office and one part-time state relations staff member based in Lansing, in contrast to the well-staffed effort of the 1990s. This neglect of state relations would become even more damaging when the University failed to beat back a petition drive that successfully led to a state constitutional amendment to ban affirmative action in college admissions, depressing the enrollment of underrepresented minorities at the University even further.

While the University had a more effective relationship with the federal government, with a well-staffed office on Capital Hill, perhaps its most influential role was through a number of its faculty who served in leadership roles in government agencies and advisory groups. In fact, this breadth of involvement of Michigan faculty at the highest level of the federal government and its various advisory bodies (NSF, NIH, DOE, NASA, DOEd, National Science Board, National Academies, American Association for the Advancement of Science) was one of the reasons that the University had created its program in Science, Technology and Public Policy.

Interactions with the City of Ann Arbor were largely characterized by benign neglect. Since this relationship only became awkward when students misbehaved or the athletics director irritated the city by disrupting traffic or mounting a gigantic video sign to blast advertising along the main thoroughfare running by Michigan Stadium, they simply assigned a staff member to calm down the mayor (who occasionally taught at the University anyway). (Of course, the president didn't help matters by suggesting that citizens concerned about the gigantic video sign should "drive responsibly and not be distracted by it".

While the interactions with the media had always been a major priority of the University, particularly when facing vigorous investigative journalism, the demise of the Ann Arbor News, coupled with the shift in the interest of the Detroit papers from statewide interests to the collapse of the City of Detroit, left only the Michigan Daily as a truly independent source of news. This erosion of the fourth estate was intensified by a massive increase in the communications, marketing, and public relations activities of the University, that took over control of most of the information flow both within the University and to the media. When electronic news media began to appear, such as MLive.com, their staff was easily co-opted by controlling their access to University sources (particularly Michigan Athletics) based on their behavior toward the University. That left only the blogosphere as independent critics of the institution. The refusal of the University to respond to requests for information, even when accompanied by formal FIOA searches became a problem. The windowless character of the Fleming Building that houses the central administration became reflective of the attitude of the University toward controlling all communications activity.

Today's Challenges

Some of the most significant short-term pressure for change in universities is driven by a converging political agenda at every level with multiple, not always compatible goals: to limit educational costs, even at the expense of quality; to make education ever more widely available; to draw back from the national commitment to research support, at least in the forms and amounts we have depended on since World War II;

and to accelerate institutional transformation through application of information technology.

Running counter to these goals are a few troublesome trends already affecting our universities. Public funding for higher education has been declining in a climate where education is seen increasingly as a personal economic benefit rather than as a public good in and of itself. Long-standing policies such as affirmative action, which represented earlier commitments to equity and social justice, are now being challenged by governing bodies, in the courts, and through public referenda. The allocation of research funding is increasingly driven by those with great skepticism (or fear) of scientific reasoning, particularly in areas such as the social sciences and climate change. Our curriculum is deformed by the competitiveness and vocational demands of students whose debt load impels them toward excessive careerism, even as other voices call for a return to an idealized "classical" curriculum based on the great works of Western civilization.

Of particular concern is the intrusion of political forces in nearly every aspect of university governance and mission. State and federal government seek to regulate admissions decisions and financial aid. There are egregious examples of political or judicial intrusion in the research process itself, for example, Star Chamber hearings before government bodies investigating scholarly research integrity or the expenditure of research funds. We are only beginning to feel the crippling effects of open-meetings requirements on the conduct of business and on hiring. We are over regulated, and the costs of accountability are excessive both in dollars and in administrative burden. Governance of public institutions is too often in the hands of people selected for partisan political reasons rather than for their understanding and support of higher education. Most distressing, there is an increasing tendency by ambitious politicians to use the university as a whipping boy for personal political gain. These trends, symptomatic of the erosion of public confidence in universities, parallel the loss of trust in our institutions across the board.

Not that we in universities are blameless. We too often have been reactive rather than proactive in responding to demands from students, faculty, government, politicians, patrons, ideologues, and demagogues who distort or undermine our fundamental values and purposes. Academic structures are too rigid to accommodate the realities of our rapidly expanding and interconnected base of knowledge and practice. Higher education as a whole has been divided and competitive at times when we need to speak with a single unequivocal voice. Our entrenched interests block the path to innovation and creativity. Perhaps, most dismaying, we have yet to come forth with a convincing case for ourselves, a vision for our future, and an effective strategy for achieving it.

The fortunes of higher education in America seem to ebb and flow from generation to generation. The principal themes of America's colleges and universities during the latter half of the 20th Century have been diversification and growth. In the three decades following World War II, strong public investments allowed our system of higher education to expand rapidly to keep pace with expanding populations and growing aspirations. The research university became the cornerstone of our national effort to sustain American leadership in science and technology, thereby ensuring both our economic prosperity and military security. The triad mission of our colleges—teaching, research, and service—acquired a degree of prestige and public support unprecedented in our history.

Today, higher education faces a much different world with its own unique challenges. In many parts of the country, the pool of college-bound students graduating from high school has been declining for two decades, as the surge of post-war baby boomers has swept through. Although we will hit the bottom of this demographic dip this decade, growth in this traditional source of college students will remain modest for at least another decade, with the exception of sunbelt states experiencing the impact of immigration. Yet at the same time, the increasing skill and education requirements of the high performance workplace are spurring a rapid growth in the number of adult college students. Universities are also facing both the challenge and the uncertainty of an aging professoriate, no longer compelled to retire after the removal of mandatory retirement caps and increasingly posing a logjam for younger academicians.

Public support of higher education has leveled off in the face of other competing social needs. As the share of college costs financed by both state and federal governments has fallen, the share borne by families has inevitably increased. And as families have been asked to bear a larger share of the costs of educating their offspring, the outcry about the "excessive" cost of a college education has reached a crescendo.

Yet there has also never been a time when the university was the target of greater concern and more criticism from our society, ranging from elected public officials and corporate leaders to the press and members of the public at large. While we may disagree with many of our critics, we should nevertheless listen carefully to them, consider, and respond. Many of the concerns voiced by our multiple constituencies contain a good deal of truth. Others, while perhaps not on target, may reveal deeper concerns worthy of attention.

Among this array of criticisms, one in particular stands out: the growing frustration of society with the hesitancy or reluctance of the university to face up to the challenge of change. In our rapidly changing world, corporations have undergone restructuring and re-engineering. Governments and other public bodies are being overhauled, streamlined, and made more responsive. More individuals are facing a future of impermanence, in their employment, in their homes, even in their families. Even the nation-state itself has become less relevant and permanent in an increasingly interconnected world.

Yet, at least according to our critics, the university has responded to the needs of a changing society largely by defending the status quo. Change has usually occurred in higher education on glacial time scales—not surprising since the career of a tenured faculty member typically spans three decades or more. Even in the late 20th Century, when our society, our nation, and the world itself are changing rapidly, the university tends to frame its contemporary roles largely within traditional paradigms. It resists any major changes in curricula or pedagogy. Students continue to be evaluated and credentialed relative to "seat time" or course credit hours rather than learning outcomes. The technology that is changing our world has largely bounced off the classroom, which continues to function largely as it has since the 19th Century. Tenure is seen not as a protection for academic freedom but rather as a perquisite that shields the faculty from accountability

and change.

At times we are tempted to respond to our critics: "We agree with you. Our universities are not good enough, not accountable enough, and not smart enough. But they are the best in the world." And in fact, the American university is the envy of the world, both as attested by the multitude of foreign students seeking education in our institutions and by the effort of other nations to imitate the American approach to higher education. But this argument may no longer suffice, particularly if the university should become more detached from a changing world or should other social institutions compete more effectively for our roles.

The Road Ahead

Many of the most powerful forces driving change in higher education come from the marketplace, driven by new societal needs, the limited availability of resources, rapidly evolving technologies, and the emergence of new competitors such as for-profit ventures. Clearly, in such a rapidly changing environment, agility and adaptability become important attributes of successful institutions.

Unfortunately, the governance of public universities, whether at the level of state government or institutional governing boards, is more inclined to protect the past than prepare for the future. Furthermore, all of higher education faces a certain dilemma related to its being far easier for a university to take on new missions and activities in response to societal demand than to shed missions as they become inappropriate, distracting, or too costly. This is a particularly difficult matter for public universities because of intense public and political pressures that require these institutions to continue to accumulate missions, each with an associated risk, without a corresponding capacity to refine and focus activities to avoid risk. Examples here would include pressures to launch expensive new academic programs in areas such as medicine or engineering without adequate resources or to embark on high-risk economic development activities through university-business partnerships that may be incompatible with the academic culture. Furthermore there are many demands from state and federal government, governing boards, and public opinion for increasing accessibility, decreasing costs, and accountability for learning outcomes. All of these forces have long constrained the agility of public universities.

Little wonder that one finds an increase in the efforts of public research universities to free themselves from the constraints of politically-determined governing boards, the tyranny of university systems, and the intrusive regulation of state government in the hope of achieving the autonomy and agility to adapt to a future with limited state support. Steps should be taken to ensure that during a time of great financial stress on flagship public universities, they are provided with the autonomy and agility to restructure their operations to enable them to survive with their quality intact what is likely to be a generation-long period of inadequate state support. After all, should the states intentionally allow their public research universities to decline significantly in quality and capacity, it would be a major blow to the nation's prosperity and security since public universities are the primary source of advanced degrees and basic research for the United States. Put another way, states should be warned not to add insult to injury by strangling their research universities with unnecessary regulation or intrusion on sensitive political issues such as climate change or gay rights, even as they starve them with inadequate support.

The challenges in the state of Michigan today are obvious. We have experienced decades of eroding state support without much hope of turning this around significantly (Delphi, GM, Ford, …and an entire industry will continue to decline). It has been over a decade since Michigan has had a significant capital outlay bill for academic facilities. Recent polling suggests that many (most?) Michigan parents still think their children can find decent jobs with only a high school diploma, while even Michigan CEOs view lowering taxes as more important than raising the quality of Michigan's workforce (a rather alarming perspective at odds with almost every other state). Numerous conversations suggest that much of the state's business leadership really does not understand or appreciate the University of Michigan. And, there is almost total public ignorance (including politicians, business leaders, and the media) about Michigan's real problems–a 1950s tax structure, ignoring the inevitability of the "creative destruction" necessary to grow new economic activity, …all of the

other flat world issues.

In looking back over the past five decades, the University has been most effective in stimulating new state investments when the times are the toughest. In the early 1980s, after we had lost roughly one-third of our state support, Harold Shapiro was able to leverage his "smaller but better" philosophy into a strategic effort to restore state funding of operations and capital facilities along with unusual programs such as the Research Excellence Fund, which gave highest priority to the state's research universities. Then again, at the bottom of a similar trough in the state's economy in 1990, we were able to unite PCSUM (and particularly UM, MSU, and WSU) in a "treetops" alumni strategy, activating key alumni leadership across the state, protecting institutional autonomy (meaning tuition control), triggering capital outlay support, and electing a new governor more supportive of higher education.

This spirit of "when the going gets tough, the tough get going" seems highly appropriate today. There is ample evidence from years past that the University of Michigan is almost unique in its capacity to lead this effort.

Yet for much of the post-2000 years, higher education had been largely invisible in Lansing, even as the State Legislature has cut its support by over 50% per student. The absence of such efforts by higher education stands in sharp contrast to the late 1980s and early 1990s when the University of Michigan had led a strong coalition of public university presidents using a "treetops" strategy to bring political pressure to resist such budget cuts.

The growing concerns in Lansing about the failure of the University of Michigan to lead an effort by the state's universities to make the case for higher education suggests the following strategy for the University: The University of Michigan needs to develop and then provide strong leadership for a full-court press effort aimed at public education that will likely take several years to have the desired effect. While the president of the University will play the key role as public spokesperson for this effort, it is important to leverage leadership with a carefully designed and highly strategic communications effort. Put most simply, the University's communications operation must become much more of the type of a marketing effort one would find in a political campaign, complete with sophisticated polling, market segmentation, and a highly strategic media plan. Our state relations operation should operate more like a development campaign, identifying and cultivating key alumni in each legislative district focused on political influence–akin to the NRA. In fact, the similarity of the effort to a development campaign suggests that our own development staff might well be a third member of this team.

Possible elements of such an effort would include:

1. First, forming a high-level executive officer team to design and implement the strategy.

2. Getting MSU and WSU on board (although recognizing that they are likely to remain far behind the front lines as UM marches into battle until they see what is in it for themselves).

3.At some point the Presidents Council of State Universities of Michigan (PCSUM) needs to be pulled into this, although perhaps only in with a view that "a rising tide raises all boats".

4. Sophisticated polling is a critical element, since we really do not understand very well what various segments of the public thinks about higher education and the future of the state–much less the University of Michigan, for that matter. Perhaps ISR can help, although experience suggests we might be better off getting a professional such as Market Opinion Research involved.

5. Building the necessary alumni leadership networks (the "treetops" strategy) will be key and likely involve some degree of segmentation–UM, UM+MSU+WSU, and PCSUM. Here a network of development volunteers will be essential.

6. Defining the message will be critical. Here the Ford School can help, but there are others across the University who can be of assistance. Key issues will be tax policy, the state budget, the importance of education–>higher education–>research universities–>and the UM, R&D and tech transfer, etc.

7. Media outreach and cultivation in every major

population center of the state will be essential. Again, this should be less of a "public relations" effort and more a "political campaign".

8. Advertising might be a possibility. Here we might use some of the material that Leo Burnett produced for the Big Ten advertising campaign of the mid-1990s, "Higher Education Makes Dreams Come True", when we used our free institutional advertising time on football and basketball broadcasts to promote higher ed.

9. Truth squads: Again, consistent with the political campaign theme, we will occasionally need tiger teams to counter falsehoods (e.g., the recent media stories on waste in higher education or the attack on sabbaticals). We will probably also need spear chuckers and spear catchers.

Finally, it is important to stress once again that such an effort will take time to build and even more time to have an impact. But in a region likely to continue to have serious economic difficulties for the foreseeable future, such a long-term effort seems essential both for the welfare of the state and the University of Michigan.

One Final Possibility

An important theme throughout the history of American higher education has been the evolution of the public university. The nation's vision and commitment to create public universities competitive in quality with the best universities in the world were a reflection of the democratic spirit of a young America. With an expanding population, a prosperous economy, and imperatives such as national security and industrial competitiveness, the public was willing to make massive investments in higher education. While elite private universities were important in setting the standards and character of higher education in America, it was the public university that provided the capacity and diversity to meet our nation's vast needs for post-secondary education and research.

Today, however, in the face of limited resources and the pressing social priorities of aging populations, this expansion of public support of higher education has slowed. While the needs of our society for advanced education and research will only intensify as we continue to evolve into a knowledge-driven global society, it is not evident that these needs will be met by further expansion of our existing system of state universities. The terms of the social contract that led to these institutions are changing rapidly. The principle of general tax support for public higher education as a public good and the partnership between the states, the federal government, and the universities for the conduct of basic research and education, established in 1862 by the Morrill Act and reaffirmed a century later by post-WWII research policies, are both at risk.

These forces are already driving major change in the nature of the nation's public research universities. One obvious consequence of declining state support has been the degree to which many leading public universities may increasingly resemble private universities in the way they are financed, managed, and governed, even as they strive to retain their public character. Public universities forced to undergo this privatization transition–or, in more politically acceptable language, "self-sufficiency"–in financing must appeal to a broader array of constituencies at the national—indeed, international—level, while continuing to exhibit a strong mission focused on state needs. In the same way as private universities, they must earn the majority of their support in the competitive marketplace, that is, via tuition, research grants, and private giving, and this will require actions that come into conflict from time to time with state priorities. Hence, the autonomy of the public university will become one of its most critical assets, perhaps even more critical than state support for many institutions.

Yet such efforts to portray these financial transitions in the face of declining state support as "privatizing" the public university is a flawed concept. The public character of state research universities runs far deeper than financing and governance and involves characteristics such as their large size, disciplinary breadth, and deep engagement with society through public service. These universities were created as, and today remain, public institutions with a strong public purpose and character. Hence the issue is not whether the public research university can evolve from a "public" to a "private" institution, or even a "privately funded but publicly committed" university. Rather, the issue is a dramatic broadening of the "publics" that these institutions serve, are supported by, and become accountable to, as state support declines to minimal levels.

In view of this natural broadening of the institutional mission, coupled with the increasing inability (or unwillingness) of states to support their public research universities at world-class levels, it is even possible to conclude that the world-class "state" research university may have become an obsolete concept. Instead, many of America's leading public research universities may evolve rapidly into "regional," "national," or even "global" universities with a public purpose to serve far broader constituencies than simply the citizens of a particular state who no longer are able or willing to provide sufficient support to sustain their programs at world-class levels. In fact, one might well argue that states today would be better off if they encouraged their flagship public research universities to evolve into institutions with far broader missions (and support), capable of accessing global economic and human capital markets to attract the talent and wealth of the world to their regions.

Today public research universities have become critical to the national interests such as security, prosperity, and public welfare. Yet the states have not only cut dramatically their support of these institutions and then attacked them for the consequent rise in tuitions as the state subsidy has been withdrawn. Today many state leaders have actually attacked their public universities for personal political gain. Clearly it is necessary to alert the body politic concerning what is at risk in this environment. As the states turn their backs on their public universities, they are ignoring the needs of the nation during a time of great challenge to America.

Chapter 20

Public Purpose

The University of Michigan was established in 1817 in the village of Detroit by an act of the Northwest Territorial government and financed through the sale of Indian lands granted by the United States Congress. Since it benefited from this territorial land grant, the new university was subject to the Enlightenment themes of the Northwest Ordinance guaranteeing civil rights and religious freedom. Envisioned by the people of the Michigan Territory as truly public, Michigan became the first university in America to successfully resist sectarian control. Buoyed by committed students, faculty, staff, and the citizens of our state, the University of Michigan has consistently been at the forefront of higher education, grappling with the difficult issues of plurality and promoting equality.

In many ways, it was at the University of Michigan that Thomas Jefferson's statement of the principles of the Enlightenment in his proposition for the nation, "We hold these truths to be self-evident: That all men are created equal", was most fully embraced and realized. Whether characterized by gender, race, religion, socioeconomic background, ethnicity, or nationality–not to mention academic interests or political persuasion–the university has always taken great pride in the diversity of its students, faculty, and programs.

Particularly notable here was the role of Michigan President James Angell in articulating the importance of Michigan's commitment to provide "an uncommon education for the common man" while challenging the aristocratic notion of leaders of the colonial colleges such as Charles Eliot of Harvard. Angell argued that Americans should be given opportunities to develop talent and character to the fullest. He portrayed the state university as the bulwark against the aristocracy of wealth. However the journey to achieve Angell's vision of the University's public purpose did not come easily.

As with most of higher education, the history of diversity at Michigan has been complex and often contradictory. There have been many times when the institution seemed to take a step forward, only to be followed by two steps backward. Michigan was one of the earliest universities to admit African-Americans and women in the late 19th century. At our founding, we attracted students

President James Angell

from a broad range of European ethnic backgrounds. In the early 1800s, the population of the state swelled with new immigrants from the rest of the country and across the European continent. The University took pride in its large enrollments of international students at a time when the state itself was decidedly insular. By 1860, the Regents referred "with partiality," to the "list of foreign students drawn thither from every section of our country." Forty-six percent of our students then came from other states and foreign countries. Today more than one hundred nations are represented at Michigan.

In contrast, our record regarding Native Americans has been disappointing. In 1817, in the treaty of Fort Meigs, local tribes became the first major donors when they ceded 1,920 acres of land for "a college at Detroit." A month later the Territorial Legislature formed the "university of Michigania," and accepted the land gift in the college's name. Today, although the number of Native American students enrolled is very low, they continue to make vital cultural and intellectual contributions to the University.

The first African American students arrived on campus in 1868, without official notice. In the years following Reconstruction, however, discrimination increased. Black students joined together to support each other early in the century and staged restaurant sit-ins in the 1920s. It was not until the 1960s that racial unrest finally exploded into campus-wide concerted action.

Michigan's history with respect to gender is also very mixed. Michigan was the first large university in America to admit women. At the time, the rest of the nation looked on with a critical eye. Many were certain that the "experiment" would fail. The first women who arrived in 1870 were true pioneers, the objects of intense scrutiny and resentment. For many years, women had separate and unequal access to facilities and organizations. Yet, in the remaining decades of the 19th Century, the University of Michigan provided strong leadership for the nation. Indeed, by 1898, the enrollment of women had increased to the point where they received 53 percent of Michigan's undergraduate degrees. However, during the early part of the 20th Century, and even more with the returning veterans after World War I, the representation of women in the student body declined significantly. It only began to climb again during the 1970s and 1980s and, for the first time in almost a century, once again exceeded that of men in 1996. During the past several decades, the University took a number of steps to recruit, promote, and support women staff and faculty, modifying University policies to better address their needs. True equality has come slowly, driven by the efforts of many courageous and energetic women.

1960-1970s

The University of Michigan faltered badly in its public purpose of achieving a campus characterized by the diversity of the society it served in the post-WWII years. As minority enrollments languished and racial tensions flared in the 1960s and 1970s, it was student activism that finally stimulated action. Although the University had made efforts to become a more diverse institution, both black and white students, frustrated by the slow movement, organized into the first Black Action Movement (BAM) in 1970, which demanded that the University commit to achieving 10% black enrollments. The administration building was occupied and students boycotted classes. Yet many positive advances came from this outpouring of student solidarity. The number of African American faculty and students on campus increased during the 1970s, new programs were initiated and old programs were funded.

Yet after only a few years, minority enrollments began to fall once again and funding waned by the late 1970s. Two more student movements (BAM II and III) formed in an effort to stimulate the University to once again take a systematic look at the difficult problems of race on campus. While the University renewed its efforts to achieve diversity and the enrollment of underrepresented minorities began to increase, this soon envolved into a largely bureaucratic effort based on affirmative action and equal opportunity policies, and minority enrollments continued to decline. Although there were occasional expressions of concern about the lack of University progress on these fronts, these were not sufficient to reorder University priorities until the late 1980s.

1980s

Throughout the 1980s there were increasing signs of a reoccurrence of racial tensions on several of the more politically active campuses across the country. Both UC Berkeley and Columbia had experienced the first signs of a new generation of student activism along racial lines. By the late 1980s concern about minority affairs had also appeared at Michigan through a movement known as the Free South Africa Coordinating Committee, or FSACC, led by a small group of graduate students in the social sciences. Although the group initially built most of their activism around the case for divestment of University holdings in firms doing business in apartheid South Africa, there were a series of other issues including demands that the University establish Martin Luther King Day as an official University holiday, that it re-evaluate the manner in which tenure was provided to minority faculty, and that it discard the normal admissions requirements such as the use of standardized test scores. Although such activism continued at a fairly vocal level, it was stable and did not escalate until a series of racist events occurred in early 1987. This activism was generally manifested in occasional rallies on the Diag, angry testimony to the

Protest Shanties on the Diag

Protests in the President's Office

Regents at public comments sessions, or letters to the editor of the Michigan Daily.

Nevertheless, there were other signs that all was not well within the University. The University was subject to occasional attacks from both of the Detroit newspapers about its lack of success in achieving racial diversity. It was clear that the effort to recruit minority students was not a top University priority in the late 1970s and early 1980s, and minority student enrollment declined throughout this period. Furthermore, the number of minority faculty had leveled off and began to decline; indeed, there were losses of key minority faculty throughout the 1980s. This led to a growing sense of frustration on the part of a number of minority faculty and staff.

Early in 1987, student activism shifted from divestment to focus instead on racism as its rallying cry. FSACC was renamed the United Coalition Against Racism, or UCAR, and the rallies on the Diag began to address incidents of racism on campus. Coincidentally, the number of charges of racist incidents began to increase, including the appearance of racist flyers in dormitories and complaints about racist slurs directed against minority students. Needless to say, these charges attracted great attention from the Detroit papers, which had become almost fixated on the subject of racism because of the increasing racial polarization of that city.

1990s

By the late 1980s, it had become apparent that the university had made inadequate progress in its goal to reflect the rich diversity of our nation and our world among its faculty, students and staff. In assessing this situation, the new administration concluded that although the University had approached the challenge of serving an increasingly diverse population with the best of intentions, it simply had not developed and executed a plan capable of achieving sustainable results. More significantly, we believed that achieving our goals for a diverse campus would require a very major change in the institution itself.

It was the long-term strategic focus of our planning that proved to be critical, because universities do not change quickly and easily any more than do the societies of which they are a part. Michigan would have to leave behind many reactive and uncoordinated efforts that had characterized its past and move toward a more strategic approach designed to achieve long-term systemic change. Sacrifices would be necessary as traditional roles and privileges were challenged. In particular, we understood the limitations of focusing only on affirmative action; that is, on access, retention, and representation. The key would be to focus instead on the success of underrepresented minorities on our campus, as students, as faculty, and as leaders. We believed that without deeper, more fundamental institutional change these efforts by themselves would inevitably fail–as they had throughout the 1970s and 1980s.

The challenge was to persuade the university community that there was a real stake for everyone in seizing the moment to chart a more diverse future. People needed to believe that the gains to be achieved through diversity would more than compensate for the necessary sacrifices. The first and most important step was to link diversity and excellence as the two most compel-

The Michigan Mandate: MLK Day Unity March, addressing student and alumni groups, Professor Bunyon Bryant, Professor Charles Moody (with President Ford), Dean Rhetaugh Dumas, Associate Vice Provost Lester Monts, toasting the heros of the successful Michigan Mandate.

ling goals before the institution, recognizing that these goals were not only complementary but would be tightly linked in the multicultural society characterizing our nation and the world in the future. As we moved ahead, we began to refer to the plan as The Michigan Mandate: A Strategic Linking of Academic Excellence and Social Diversity.

Over the first two years, hundreds of discussions with groups both on and off campus were held. We reached out to alumni, donors, and civic and political leaders and groups, while meeting with countless student faculty and staff groups. Great care was taken to convey the same message to everyone as a means of establishing credibility and building trust among all constituencies. Meetings were sometimes contentious, often enlightening, but rarely acrimonious. Gradually

understanding increased and support grew. Although the plan itself came from the administration, it would be individuals and units that would devise most of the detailed plans for carrying it forward. University publications, administrators' speeches and meetings, Faculty Senate deliberations, all carried the message: Diversity would become the cornerstone in the University's efforts to achieve excellence in teaching, research, and service in the multicultural nation and world in which it would exist.

The mission and goals of the Michigan Mandate were stated quite simply: 1) To recognize that diversity and excellence are complementary and compelling goals for the university and to make a firm commitment to their achievement. 2) To commit to the recruitment, support, and success of members of historically underrepresented groups among our students, faculty, staff, and leadership. 3) To build on our campus an environment that sought, nourished, and sustained diversity and pluralism and that valued and respected the dignity and worth of every individual.

Associated with these general goals were more specific objectives:

1) Faculty recruitment and development: To substantially increase the number of tenure-track faculty in each underrepresented minority group; to increase the success of minority faculty in the achievement of professional fulfillment, promotion, and tenure; to increase the number of underrepresented minority faculty in leadership positions.

2) Student recruitment, achievement, and outreach: To achieve increases in the number of entering underrepresented minority students as well as in total underrepresented minority enrollment; to establish and achieve specific minority enrollment targets in all schools and colleges; to increase minority graduation rates; to develop new programs to attract back to campus minority students who have withdrawn from our academic programs; to design new and strengthen existing outreach programs that have demonstrable impact on the pool of minority applicants to undergraduate, graduate, and professional programs.

3) Staff recruitment and development: To focus on the achievement of affirmative action goals in all job categories; to increase the number of underrepresented minorities in key University leadership positions; to strengthen support systems and services for minority staff.

4) Improving the environment for diversity: To foster a culturally diverse environment; to significantly reduce the number of incidents of racism and prejudice on campus; to increase community-wide commitment to diversity and involvement in diversity initiatives among students, faculty, and staff; to broaden the base of diversity initiatives; to assure the compatibility of University policies, procedures, and practice with the goal of a multicultural community; to improve communications and interactions with and among all groups; and to provide more opportunities for minorities to communicate their needs and experiences and to contribute directly to the change process.

A series of carefully focused strategic actions was developed to move the University toward these objectives. These actions were framed by the values and traditions of the University, an understanding of our unique culture characterized by a high degree of faculty and unit freedom and autonomy, and animated by a highly competitive and entrepreneurial spirit. The strategy was both complex and pervasive, involving not only a considerable commitment of resources (e.g., fully funding all financial aid for minority graduate students) but also some highly innovative programs.

To cite just one highly successful example, the University established what was called the Target of Opportunity Program aimed at increasing the number of minority faculty at all ranks. Traditionally, university faculty searches were driven by a concern for academic specialization within their respective disciplines. Too often in recent years the University had seen faculty searches that were literally "replacement" searches rather than "enhancement" searches. To achieve the goals of the Michigan Mandate, the University had to free itself from the constraints of this traditional perspective. Therefore, the administration sent out the following message to the academic units: be vigorous and creative in identifying minority teachers/scholars who can enrich the activities of your unit. Do not be limited by concerns relating to narrow specialization; do not be concerned about the availability of a faculty slot within the unit. The principal criterion for the recruitment of a minority faculty member is whether the individual can enhance the department. If so, resources will be made available to recruit that person to the University of Michigan.

By the mid 1990s Michigan could point to significant progress in achieving diversity. The representation of underrepresented minority students, faculty, and staff more than doubled over the decade-long effort. But, perhaps even more significantly, the success of underrepresented minorities at the University improved even more remarkably, with graduation rates rising to the highest level among public universities, promotion and tenure success of minority faculty members becoming comparable to their majority colleagues, and a growing number of appointments of minorities to leadership positions in the University. The campus climate not only became more accepting and supportive of diversi-

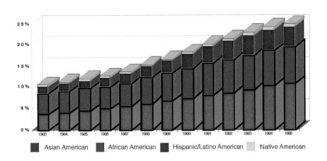

Minority student enrollments (percentages)

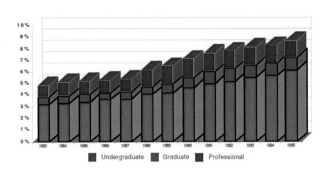

African-American student enrollments (percentages)

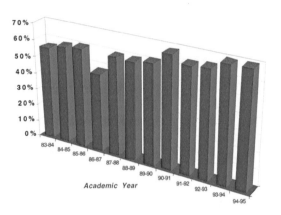

Graduation rates of African-American student cohorts six years afer initial entry

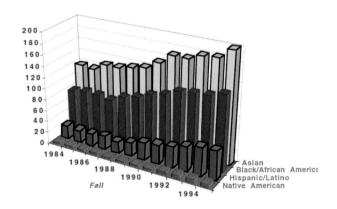

Number of minority tenured and tenure-track faculty

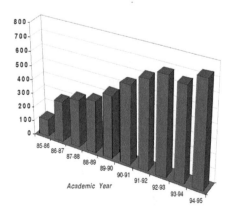

Number of university minority graduate fellowships

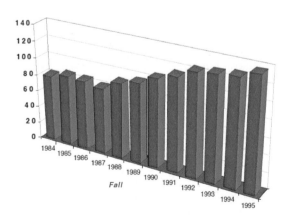

Number of African-American faculty

Student Access and Success
    Undergraduate Student Access
        Wade McCree Incentive Scholarship
        King/Chavez/Parks Program
        Summer programs (e.g., DAPCEP)
        College Day visitation for families
        Tuition grants to all Native American students
            from Michigan.
    Special Undergraduate Programs
        Undergraduate Research Opportunity Program
        21st Century Program
        CRLT Programs
        Leadership 2017
        Office of Academic Multicultural Initiatives
    Graduate Student Support
        Fully funding minority graduate support
        Rackham Graduate Merit Fellowship Program
Special Programs
    Tapped grass-roots creativity and energy using
        $ 1 M/y Presidential Initiatives Funds tor
        competitive proposals from faculty and
        student groups.

Results
    Enrollments:
        83% increase in students of color (to 28%)
        90% increase in underrep min (to 15%)
        57% increase in AA (to 2,715 or 9.1%)
        126% increase of Latinos (to 4.3%)
        100% increase in Native Americans (to 1.1%)
    Graduation rates for African Americans highest
        among public universities.
    UM ranked 27th in nation in minority BA/BS
        8th for M.S. degrees, 7th for PhD degrees
        1st in African American PhDs (non HBCU's)
    Graduate education
        Increased minority fellowships by 118%
        Of 734 Rackham Fellows in 1994,
            51% were African American,
            29% were Latino
    Professional Schools:
    Business: 12% AA, 28% color
    Medicine: 11% AA, 39% color
    Law: 10% AA, 21% color

Faculty
    Target of Opportunity Program
    Faculty Development (Faculty Awards Program for
        minority faculty)
    Cluster hiring
    Creating a welcoming and supportive culture (net-
        works, centers, surveys)
    Enlarging candidate pool by increasing PhD enroll-
        ments

Results
    +62% for African Americans (128)
    +117% for Latinos (52)
    +75% for Native Americans (7)
    Senior academic leadership (URM): from 14 to 25

Staff
    Demanded accountability in hiring and promotion
    Human Resources and Affirmative Action pro-
        grams
    Consultation and Conciliation Services

Results
    Top managers: +100% (to 10% of management)
    P&A: +80 (from 449 to 816)
More Generally
    Building University-wide commitments
    Office of Minority Affairs, Vice-Provost for Minor-
        ity Affairs
    Demanding accountability
    Included in compensation review
    Included in budget review
    Included in appointment review
Leadership
    Half of Executive Officers were African American
    Executive VP Medical Center (Rita Dumas)
    Secretary of University (Harold Johnson)
    VP Research (Homer Neal)
    UM Flint Chancellor Charlie Nelms
    UM Dearborn Chancellor James Renick
JJD's Successor was African American (Homer Neal)

Some Actions and Results of the Michigan Mandate by 1996

Listening, learning, planning, and selling the Michigan Agenda for Women

ty, but students and faculty began to come to Michigan because of its growing reputation for a diverse campus.

Perhaps most significantly, as the campus became more racially and ethnically diverse, the quality of the students, faculty, and academic programs of the University increased to the highest level in the institution's history. This latter fact reinforced our contention that the aspirations of diversity and excellence were not only compatible but, in fact, highly correlated. By every measure, the Michigan Mandate was a remarkable success, moving the University beyond the original goals of a more diverse campus.

Even while pursuing the racial diversity goals of the Michigan Mandate, we realized we could not ignore another glaring inequity in campus life. If we meant to embrace diversity in its full meaning, we had to attend to the long-standing concerns of women faculty, students, and staff. Here, once again, it took time–and con-

siderable effort by many women colleagues to educate the administration to the point where we began to understand that the university simply had not succeeded in including and empowering women as full and equal partners in all aspects of its life and leadership.

In faculty hiring and retention, despite the increasing pools of women in many fields, the number of new hires of women had changed only slowly during the late twentieth century in most research universities. In some disciplines such as the physical sciences and engineering, the shortages were particularly acute. We continued to suffer from the "glass ceiling" phenomenon: that is, because of hidden prejudice women were unable to break through to the ranks of senior faculty and administrators, though no formal constraints prohibited their advancement. The proportion of women decreased steadily as one moved up the academic ladder. Additionally, there appeared to be an increasing

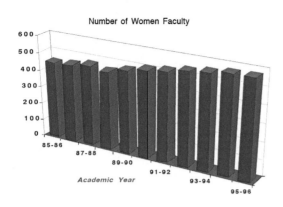

Number of women faculty

tendency to hire women off the tenure track as post-doctoral scholars, lecturers, clinicians, or research scientists. The rigid division among various faculty appointments offered little or no opportunity for these women to move into tenured faculty positions.

Many of our concerns derived from the extreme concentration of women in positions of lower status and power—as students, lower-paid staff, and junior faculty. The most effective lever for change might well be a rapid increase in the number of women holding positions of high status, visibility, and power. This would not only change the balance of power in decision-making, but it would also change the perception of who and what matters in the university. Finally, we needed to bring university policies and practices into better alignment with the needs and concerns of women students in a number of areas including campus safety, student housing, student life, financial aid, and childcare.

To address these challenges, the university developed and executed a second strategic effort known as the Michigan Agenda for Women. With the assistance of the President's Advisory Council on Women's Issues (PACWI), chaired by Carol Hollenshead, director of the Center for Women, a broad agenda was developed. While the actions proposed were intended to address the concerns of women students, faculty, and staff, many of them benefited men as well. In developing the Michigan Agenda, we knew that different strategies were necessary for different parts of the university. Academic units varied enormously in the degree to which women participated as faculty, staff, and students. What might work in one area could fail miserably in another. Some fields, such as the physical sciences, had very few

women represented among their students and faculty. For them, it was necessary to design and implement a strategy which spanned the entire pipeline, from K-12 outreach to undergraduate and graduate education, to faculty recruiting and development. For others such as the social sciences or law, there already was a strong pool of women students, and the challenge became one of attracting women from this pool into graduate and professional studies and eventually into academe. Still other units such as education and many departments in humanities and sciences had strong participation of women among students and junior faculty, but suffered from low participation in the senior ranks and in leadership roles.

Like the Michigan Mandate, the vision was again both simple yet compelling: that by the year 2000 the university would become the leader among American universities in promoting and achieving the success of women as faculty, students, and staff. Again the president took on a highly personal role in this effort, meeting with hundreds of groups on and off campus, to listen to their concerns and invite their participation in the initiative. Rapidly there was again significant progress on many fronts for women students, faculty, and staff, including the appointment of a number of senior women faculty and administrators as deans and executive officers, improvement in campus safety, and improvement of family care policies and child care resources. In 1988 Michigan appointed its first woman Dean of LS&A, Edie Goldenberg, in 1993 our first Vice Provost for Health Affairs, Rhetaugh Dumas, and in 1997 our first woman provost, Nancy Cantor. Finally, in 2002, the University of Michigan named its first woman president, Mary Sue Coleman.

The University also took steps to eliminate those factors that prevented other groups from participating fully in its activities. For example, we extended our anti-discrimination policies to encompass sexual orientation and extended staff benefits and housing opportunities to same-sex couples. This was a particularly controversial action because it was strongly opposed not only by the religious right but also by several of the University's Regents. Yet, this was also an issue of equity, deeply frustrating to many faculty, staff, and students, which required attention.

Harold Shapiro had tried on several occasions to

persuade the regents to extend its anti-discrimination policies to include the gay community, without success. Finally, with a supportive, albeit short-lived, Democratic majority among the Regents, we decided to move ahead rapidly to put in the policy while there was still political support, no matter how slim. The anticipated negative reaction was rapid and angry–an attempt by the Legislature to deduct from our appropriation the estimated cost of the same-sex couple benefits (effectively blocked by our constitutional autonomy), a personal phone call to the president from our Republican governor (although it was a call he did not want to make, and he did not insist upon any particular action), and a concerted and successful effort to place two conservative Republican candidates on our Board of Regents in the next election (resulting in the horror of a 4-4 divided board during the administration's last two years).

We were determined to defend this action, however, as part of a broader strategy. We had become convinced that the university had both a compelling interest in and responsibility to create a welcoming community, encouraging respect for diversity in all of the characteristics that can be used to describe humankind: age, race, ethnicity, nationality, gender, religious belief, sexual orientation, political beliefs, economic background, geographical background.

2000s

But, of course, this story does not end with the successful achievements of the Michigan Mandate in 1996. Beginning first with litigation in Texas (the Hopwood decision) and then successful referendum efforts in California and Washington, conservative groups such as the Center for Individual Rights began to attack policies such as the use of race in college admissions. Perhaps because of Michigan's success with the Michigan Mandate, the University soon became a target for those groups seeking to reverse affirmative action with two cases filed against the University in 1997, one challenging the admissions policies of undergraduates, and the second challenging those in our Law School.

Even as the new Bollinger administration launched the expensive legal battle to defend the use of race in college admissions, it discontinued most of the effective policies and programs created by the Michigan

A quilt assembled from student T-shirts reflecting the University's diversity in 1996 presented by student government to the Duderstadts.

Mandate, in part out of concern these might complicate the litigation battle, but also because such action was no longer a priority of the new administration. Indeed, even the mention of the Michigan Mandate became a forbidden phrase in its effort to erase the past.

As a consequence, the enrollment of underrepresented minorities began almost immediately to drop at Michigan, eventually declining from 1997 to 2010 by over 50% for African American students overall and by as much as 80% in some of UM's professional schools. In 1996 half (5) of the Executive Officers were minority, but by the early 2000s, only one out of 11 executive officers and one out of 18 deans in the new administration were underrepresented minorities.

Although the 2003 Supreme Court decisions were split, supporting the use of race in the admissions policies of our Law School and opposing the formula-based approach used for undergraduate admissions, the most important ruling in both cases stated, in the words of the court: "Student body diversity is a compelling state interest that can justify the use of race in university admission. When race-based action is necessary to further a compelling governmental interest, such action does

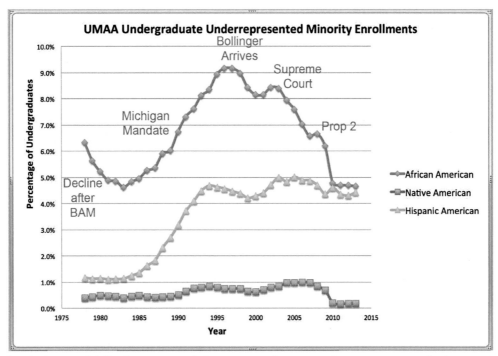

The decline and fall of UM's racial diversity with a new administration in the late 1990s.

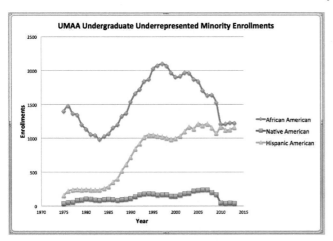

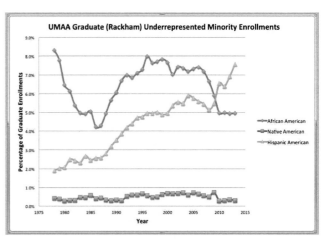

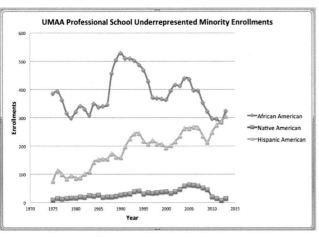

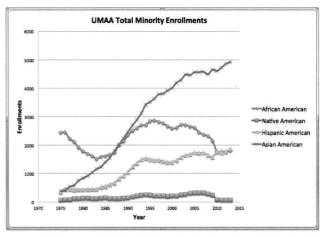

Changes in minority enrollments over past four decades

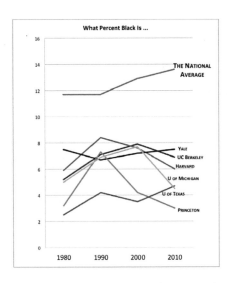

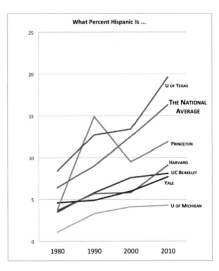

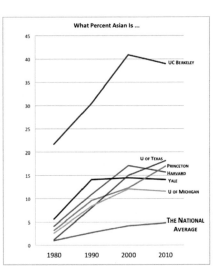

A comparison of Michigan with other peer institutions demonstrates the catastrophic decline in minority enrollments that began at UM in the late 1990s and continued for the next 15 years. (Atlantic, 2014)

not violate the constitutional guarantee of equal protection so long as the narrow-tailoring requirement is also satisfied." Hence, the Supreme Court decisions on the Michigan cases reaffirmed those policies and practices long used by most selective colleges and universities throughout the United States. But more significantly, it reaffirmed both the importance of diversity in higher education and established the principle that, appropriately designed, race could be used as a factor in programs aimed at achieving diverse campuses. Hence the battle was won, the principle was firmly established by the highest court of the land. We had won. Or so we thought...

While an important battle had been won with the Supreme Court ruling, we soon learned that the war for diversity in higher education was far from over. As university lawyers across the nation began to ponder over the court ruling, they persuaded their institutions to accept a very narrow interpretation of the Supreme Court decisions as the safest course. Actually, this pattern began to appear at the University of Michigan during the early stages of the litigation process. Although the Supreme Court decision supported the use of affirmative action (if "narrowly tailored"), many universities began to back away from programs aimed at recruitment, financial aid, and academic enrichment for minority undergraduate students, either eliminating entirely such programs or opening them up to non-minority students from low-income households. Threats of further litiga-

tion by conservative groups have intensified this retrenchment.

After the years of effort in building successful programs such as the Michigan Mandate and defending the importance of diversity in higher education all the way to the Supreme Court, the tentative nature of the decision ("narrowly tailored race considerations") probably caused more harm than good by unleashing the lawyers on our campuses to block successful efforts to broaden educational opportunity and advance the cause of social justice. Ironically, the uses of affirmative action (and programs that involved racial preference) actually were not high on the agenda of the Michigan Mandate. Rather our success involved commitment, engagement, and accountability for results.

Minority enrollments continued to decline at Michigan throughout the 2010s as the new priority became attracting large numbers of wealthy out-of-state students capable of paying high tuition and generating the revenue to compensate for the loss of state support. No effort was made to resume those programs that had been so successful in the 1990s under the Michigan Mandate. As the charts above indicate, Michigan's decline in diversity ranked among the most precipitous among its peers during this period.

In 2006, Michigan voters approved a constitutional referendum similar to that of California's Proposition 209 to ban the use of affirmative action in public institutions. Although most of the decline in minority

Change in Minority Enrollments

Minority	1996	2015	Change
African Am	2,824	1,801	-36%
Hispanic	1,473	2,018	+37%
Native Am	227	92	-60%
Underrep	4,524	3,921	-14%

Change in Minority Percentages

Minority	1996	2015	Change
African Am	9.3%	4.8%	-48%
Hispanic	4.5%	5.4%	+20%
Native Am	0.7%	0.25%	-64%
Asian Am	11.6%	13.5%	+13%
Underrep	14.1%	10.1%	-32%
Fresh AA	9.3%	5.1%	-45%

The drop in underrepresented minorities
over the past 20 years.

enrollments had occurred by this time, this referendum prevented Michigan colleges and universities from using even the narrowly tailored prescriptions of the 2003 Supreme Court decision, and the decline in the enrollments of underrepresented minority students continued, erasing most of the gains with the Michigan Mandate strategy in the 1990s and returning this measure of diversity to the levels of the 1960s. More specifically (as shown in several charts depicting the enrollments of underrepresented minorities over the past 40 years), enrollments of underrepresented minority students dropped from 14% of all students in 1996 to 10% in 2015. African American enrollments have dropped from a peak of 9.3% in 1996 to 4.8% in 2015. While nce Michigan's professional schools were leaders in minority enrollments (with Medicine, Business, and Law at 10% to 12% African American enrollments in the 1990s); today they have fallen badly to levels of 5% or less. ,

While the very recent decline may be attributable in part to the impact of the State of Michigan's Proposition 2 passed in 2006 that restricted the use of affirmative action, racial diversity on campus has actually been declining for well over a decade, suggesting more fundamental concerns about the University's commitment to diversity. It clearly began when a new admin-

istration in the late 1990s halted all of the programs of the Michigan Mandate, and then continued to fall rapidly following the 2003 Supreme Court decision, when University attorneys cautioned against reinstating the aggressing programs of the 1990s because of concerns about the ambiguity of the Supreme Court decision. While racial diversity remained a goal of the University, few programs were put in place to achieve it, and accountability for progress weakened. Ironically, instead the priority was given to a rapid expansion of students from affluent backgrounds capable of paying the high tuition necessary to generate revenues to compensate for the loss of state support.

Economic Diversity

Throughout the last decade, there has been an increasing concern that many public universities, particularly flagship research universities such as Michigan, were also losing the economic diversity that characterized their public purpose. A 2010 report by the Education Trust, *Opportunity Adrift*, stated: "Founded to provide 'an uncommon education for the common man', many flagship universities have drifted away from their historic mission". (Haycock, 2010) Analyzing measures such as access for low-income and underrepresented minority students and the relative success of these groups in earning diplomas, they found that the University of Michigan and the University of Indiana received the lowest overall marks for both progress and current performance among all major public universities in these measures of public purpose. For example, Michigan's percentage of Pell Grant students in its freshman class (the most common measure of access for low-income students) has fallen to 11%, well below most other public universities including Michigan State (23%) and the University of California (32%); it even lags behind several of the most expensive private universities including Harvard, MIT, and Stanford. (Campbell, 2015)

Yet, another important measure of the degree to which public universities fulfill their important mission of providing educational opportunities to a broad range of society is the degree to which they enroll first generation college students. It is disturbing that today less than 6% of the University's enrollment consists of

	Percent of undergrads with Pell grants
AAU Privates (average)	15%
AAU Publics (average, excluding U-M)	23%
University of California-San Diego	40%
University of California-Davis	36%
University of California-Los Angeles	34%
Stony Brook University	33%
University of California-Berkeley	32%
University of California-Santa Barbara	31%
University of California-Irvine	30%
University of Florida	28%
University at Buffalo	28%
University of Arizona	27%
Rutgers University	27%
Syracuse University	25%
University of Texas at Austin	24%
Michigan State University	23%
Iowa State University	22%
University of Oregon	22%
Ohio State University	21%
University of Minnesota	21%
University of Washington	20%
New York University	20%
University of Nebraska	20%
Texas A & M University	19%
Purdue University	19%
University of Missouri	19%
University of Kansas	19%
Emory University	19%
University of Rochester	19%
Massachusetts Institute of Technology	19%

	Percent of undergrads with Pell grants
University of Illinois	18%
University of North Carolina	18%
University of Southern California	18%
Columbia University	18%
Tulane University of Louisiana	18%
Pennsylvania State University	17%
Indiana University	17%
University of Maryland	17%
University of Iowa	17%
University of Pittsburgh	17%
University of Chicago	17%
Brandeis University	17%
University of Colorado	16%
Georgia Institute of Technology	16%
Stanford University	16%
University of Wisconsin	15%
Cornell University	15%
Rice University	15%
Carnegie Mellon University	14%
Vanderbilt University	13%
Brown University	13%
Johns Hopkins University	13%
Yale University	13%
Duke University	12%
UNIVERSITY OF MICHIGAN	11%
University of Pennsylvania	11%
Northwestern University	11%
Princeton University	11%
California Institute of Technology	11%
Harvard University	10%
Washington University	6%

SOURCE: Integrated Postsecondary Education Data System (IPEDS).

Michigan's ranking in Pell Grant students lags badly behind other public universities.

such students, compared to 16% by its public university peers and 14% of the enrollments of highly selective private universities.

What was happening? To be sure, the State of Michigan ranks at the bottom of the states in the amount of need-based financial aid it provides to college students, requiring the University to make these commitments from its own internal funds. But it is also due to the decision made in the late 1990s to compensate for the loss of state support by dramatically increasing enrollments with a bias toward out-of-state students who generate new revenues with high tuition. Clearly students who can pay annual tuition-room & board at the out-of-state rates of $60,000 come from highly affluent families. Indeed, the average family income of Michigan under-

graduates now exceeds $150,000 per year, more characteristic of the "top 1%" than the "common man".

Lessons Learned

It seems appropriate to end this chapter on the University's public purpose with several conclusions: First, we must always keep in mind that the University of Michigan is a public university, created as the first such institution in a young nation, evolving in size, breadth, and quality, but always committed to a truly public purpose of "providing an uncommon education for the common man".

Today there is an even more urgent reason why the University must once again elevate diversity to a higher

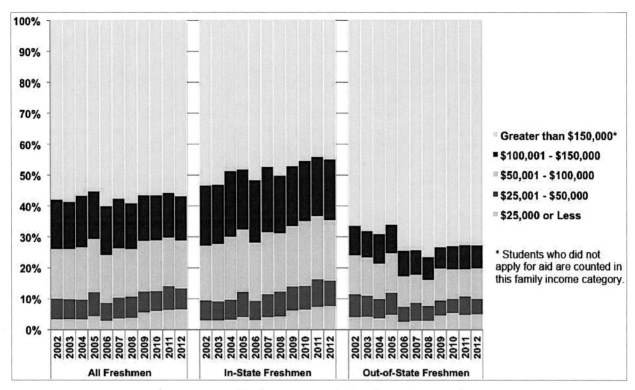

Legend:
- Greater than $150,000*
- $100,001 - $150,000
- $50,001 - $100,000
- $25,001 - $50,000
- $25,000 or Less

* Students who did not apply for aid are counted in this family income category.

The majority of both in-state and out-of-state UM Freshman now come from families with incomes greater than $150,000.

priority as it looks toward the future: the rapidly changing demographics of America. The populations of most developed nations in North America, Europe, and Asia are aging rapidly. In our nation today there are already more people over the age of 65 than teenagers, and this situation will continue for decades to come. Over the next decade the percentage of the population over 60 will grow to over 30% to 40% in the United States, and this aging population will increasingly shift social priorities to the needs and desires of the elderly (e.g., retirement security, health care, safety from crime and terrorism, and tax relief) rather than investing in the future through education and innovation.

However, the United States stands apart from the aging populations of Europe and Asia for one very important reason: our openness to immigration. In fact, over the past decade, immigration from Latin America and Asia contributed 53% of the growth in the United States population, exceeding that provided by births (National Information Center, 2006). This is expected to drive continued growth in our population from 300 million today to over 450 million by 2050, augmenting our aging population and stimulating productivity

with new and young workers. As it has been so many times in its past, America is once again becoming a nation of immigrants, benefiting greatly from their energy, talents, and hope, even as such mobility changes the ethnic character of our nation. By the year 2030 current projections suggest that approximately 40% of Americans will be members of minority groups; by mid-century we will cease to have any single majority ethnic group. By any measure, we are evolving rapidly into a truly multicultural society with a remarkable cultural, racial, and ethnic diversity. This demographic revolution is taking place within the context of the continuing globalization of the world's economy and society that requires Americans to interact with people from every country of the world.

The increasing diversity of the American population with respect to culture, race, ethnicity, and nationality is both one of our greatest strengths and most serious challenges as a nation. A diverse population gives us great vitality. However, the challenge of increasing diversity is complicated by social and economic factors. Today, far from evolving toward one America, our society continues to be hindered by the segregation and

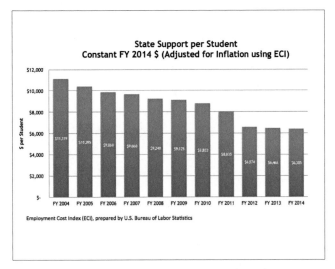

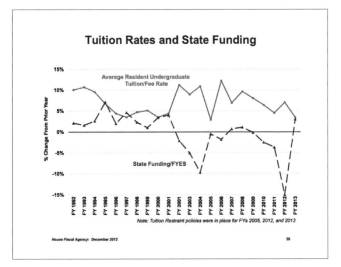

Two tragic realities: 1) Michigan tuition is determined largely by state support.

non-assimilation of minority and immigrant cultures. If we do not create a nation that mobilizes the talents of all of our citizens, we are destined for a diminished role in the global community and increased social turbulence. Higher education plays an important role both in identifying and developing this talent. And the University of Michigan faces once again a major challenge in reclaiming its leadership in building a diverse campus.

To be sure, there is ample evidence today from states such as California and Texas that a restriction to race-neutral policies will limit the ability of elite programs and institutions to achieve diversity across all underrepresented groups. In fact, many of the approaches used by the University of California in the wake of Proposition 209 have been considered by Michigan. The UC reached out to low-performing high schools, making it possible for students achieving at top levels in these schools would not be penalized in admission decisions for the weaknesses of their schools. They changed its standardized test requirements to put primary emphasis on achievements tests rather than aptitude tests. They sought to look more carefully at applicants to identify those who had overcome serious obstacles in preparing themselves for higher education. They worked with K-12 schools and community colleges to strengthen the preparation for under represented minority students. They launched a major effort to let students, parents, and counselors know about the opportunities UC provided in financial aid, broadened applications, and preparation for attendance.

Yet, as former UC President Richard Atkinson and his colleagues concluded, "Today if we look at enrollment overall, racial and ethnic diversity at the University of California is in great trouble. A decade later, the legacy of Proposition 209 is clear. Despite enormous efforts, we have failed badly to achieve the goal of a student body that encompasses California's diverse population. The evidence suggests that–without attention to race and ethnicity–this goal will ultimately recede into impossibility." Today the University of Michigan provides further evidence from the collapse of its minority enrollments of the difficulty of achieving a diverse campus in the wake of Proposal 2.

However, when one turns to economic diversity, the University of California provides a sharp contrast to the University of Michigan. Today 42% of all UC undergraduates are Pell Grant eligible, compared to 12% at UM. 46% of UC's entering California residents come from families where neither parent graduated from college, compared to 6% for UM. Approximately 25% of undergraduates come from underrepresented minority populations (African American, Chicano/Latino, and Native American) compared to 12% at UM (although this later comparison is due in part to the very large growth in the Latino population of California). Key to the UC's success in achieving this remarkable economic diversity have been two key factors: i) the importance of the state's Cal Grant program providing need-based financial aid that essentially doubles the support of Pell Grant eligible students, and ii) a strategic relationship

Fiscal Year	Budget	% Change
FY 2006	$51,531,977	11.6%
FY 2007	$55,506,768	7.7%
FY 2008	$61,873,699	11.5%
FY 2009	$68,550,532	10.8%
FY 2010	$76,560,562	11.7%
FY 2011	$84,681,931	10.6%
FY 2012	$93,903,679	10.9%
FY 2013	$103,414,892	10.1%
FY 2014	$117,570,894	13.7%

The majority of this aid is <u>need-based grants</u>.
Other sources of institutional undergraduate financial aid: Endowed Scholarships; School/College aid (both General Fund and non-General Fund).

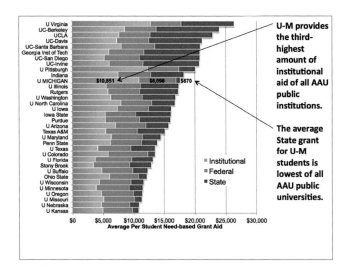

2) Although the University makes a substantial commitment to need-based financial aid, it is unable to compensate for the absence of a meaningful state need-based financial aid program in Michigan.

between California's community colleges and the University of California, carefully articulated in the California master plan, that enables their associated degrees to serve as stepping stones from secondary school into baccalaureate programs at UC.

In sharp contrast, the State of Michigan during the 2000s eliminated essentially all state need-based financial aid. Furthermore, the autonomy granted Michigan's community colleges allows them to focus more on providing more adult education programs in their communities rather than serving as "junior colleges" to prepare students for admission to university programs.

To be sure, rising tuition levels in Michigan's public universities have also been a factor. However this has not been the fault of higher education in the state, since there is strong evidence that the actual cost of its educational programs has increased only at the inflation rate. Instead, the real blame for the increasing costs seen by parents must fall on the State of Michigan, which has dramatically cut its support of higher education. In fact, a chart comparing state appropriations with University tuition and fees demonstrates that almost all of the increase in the costs faced by students and parents has been driven by the erosion of the state subsidy through appropriations. Hence restoring the University's economic diversity will require action along several fronts.

Of highest immediate priority is restoring a significant need-based financial aid program at the state level capable of augmenting the modest Pell Grants received by low income students to enable them to attend col-

lege. Next, there needs to be serious effort to better define the mission of the state's community colleges in preparing students for further university education and developing appropriate articulation agreements to support this transition. Finally, it is absolutely essential to the future of the State of Michigan and the welfare of its people that it begin to restore adequate support for higher education. Michigan's ranking in the bottom 10% in its ranking of state support for higher education is not only embarrassing but also indicative of why the state's economic performance today and in the future will similarly lag the rest of the nation.

Hence achieving the University's objectives for diversity will require not only a serious restructuring of Michigan's financial strategies, but even more important, a renewed commitment to the fundamental public purpose that has guided the University for almost two centuries. While the University of Michigan's concerted effort to generate support from other patrons, particularly through private giving and sponsored research, it simply must realize that these will never be sufficient to support a world-class university of this size, breadth, or impact. Without substantial public support, it is unrealistic to expect that public universities can fulfill their public purpose.

Hence the highest priority should be to re-engage with the people of Michigan to convince them of the importance of investing in public higher education and unleashing the constraints that prevent higher education from serving all of the people of this state. This must become a primary responsibility of not only the leadership of the University, but its Regents, faculty, students, staff, alumni, and those Michigan citizens who depend so heavily on the services provided by one of the great universities of the world.

Returning again to President Atkinson's analysis, he suggests "We need a strategy that recognizes the continuing corrosive force of racial inequality but does not stop there. We need a strategy grounded in the broad American tradition of opportunity because opportunity is a value that Americans understand and support. We need a strategy that makes it clear that our society has a stake in ensuring that every American has an opportunity to succeed—and every American, in turn, has a stake in our society. Race still matters. Yet we need to move toward another kind of affirmative action, one in which the emphasis is on opportunity and the goal is educational equity in the broadest possible sense. The ultimate test of a democracy is its willingness to do whatever it takes to create the aristocracy of talent that Thomas Jefferson saw as indispensable to a free society. It is a test we cannot afford to fail."

The Road Ahead

Hence perhaps we need a bolder approach, similar to that when in 1862 President Lincoln signed the Morrill Act to create the land-grant colleges to serve both the working class and build an industrial nation. Or perhaps better yet, when President Roosevelt signed the G.I. Bill in 1944 or President Johnson signed the Higher Education Act in 1965. In this spirit, then, consider the following three recommendations, drawn from the work of the 2007 National Commission on the Future of Higher Education (Miller, 2006).

Learn Grants for the Millennium Generation

Many disadvantaged students (and parents) do not see higher education as an option open to them, but rather as a privilege for the more affluent. As a result, these students do not have the incentive to perform well in K-12 (nor do their parents have the incentive to support them), hence falling behind early or dropping out of the college-bound ranks. To provide strong incentives, the idea would be to provide EVERY student with a "529 college savings account", a "Learn-Grant", when they begin kindergarten. Although this account would be owned by the students, its funds would be managed by an independent agency and could only be used for postsecondary education upon the successful completion of a high school college-preparatory program. Each year students (and their parents) would receive a statement of the accumulation in their account, with a reminder that this is their money, but it can only be used for their college education (or other postsecondary education). An initial contribution of, say, $10,000 (say, a $5,000 federal grant with a state $5,000 match) would accumulate over their K-12 education to an amount that, when coupled with other financial aid, would likely be sufficient for a four-year college education at a public college or university.

Beyond serving as an important source of financial aid, the Learn Grants would in themselves be a critical incentive for succeeding in K-12 and preparing for a college education. The program might be funded from any of a number of sources, e.g., from a federal plus state match. Learn Grants would be provided to all students when entering K-12 (in order to earn broad political support) and could be augmented with additional contributions from public, private, or parental sources during their pre-college years. As to cost, if we assume roughly 4.5 million children enter K-12 each year (the estimate for 2010), then at $10,000 per student, this would cost $40 billion annually ($20 billion each to the states and the federal government). While such a sum is, in fact, immense, it is about the cost of one year of K-12 education (or college education, on the average). It also should be compared to other public expenditures (Medicaid, corrections, defense, and even student financial aid). From this broader perspective, it really does notseem excessive when viewed as an investment in the future of the nation.

Building a Society of Learning through a National Commitment to Lifelong Learning

The nation would commit itself to the goal of providing universal access to lifelong learning opportunities to all its citizens, thereby enabling participation in the world's most advanced knowledge and learning society. While the ability to take advantage of educational opportunity always depends on the need, aptitude, aspirations, and motivation of the student, it should not depend on one's socioeconomic status. Access to lifelong learning opportunities should be a <u>civil right</u> for all rather than a privilege for the few if the nation is to achieve prosperity, security, and social well being in the global, knowledge- and value-based economy of the 21st century. Perhaps no other recommendation, if implemented, would drive a greater transformation in higher education in America, changing very dramatically whom it serves, how it is financed, and how it is provided. It would clearly transform higher education into a resource capable of serving a 21st century nation in a global, knowledge economy.

A Final Appeal to "Us"...the "Me" Generation

When we joined the University of Michigan community in the late 1960s, our parents' generation was in the final stages of a massive effort to provide educational opportunities for all Americans. Returning veterans funded through the GI bill had doubled college enrollments, particularly at large public universities such as Michigan. The post-WWII research strategy developed by the federal government was transforming flagship institutions such as Michigan into research universities responsible for most of the nation's basic research. The Truman Commission had proposed that all Americans should have the opportunity of a college education, and California responded with its Master Plan, which would expand the opportunities for providing "an uncommon education for the common man" at great public universities such as the University of Michigan.

Our nation–and, indeed, the world–benefited greatly from these efforts both to provide the educational opportunity and new knowledge necessary for economic prosperity, social well being, and national security. We saw spectacular achievements such as sending men to the Moon, decoding the human genome, and, of course, creating the Internet and the digital age. Although our generation of baby boomers benefited greatly from the commitments of the "Greatest Generation", our priorities in the 1960s lay elsewhere–protesting the war in Vietnam, fighting for civil rights, saving the environment, and, of course challenging the establishment.

Yet, fast-forwarding to today, fifty years later, our generation has clearly failed to embrace the commitments made by our parents to educational opportunity. The quality of our primary and secondary schools lags many other nations as K-12 teaching has been transformed into a blue-collar profession. Over the past decade, state support of our public universities has dropped by roughly 35%, with the University of Michigan regarded as the poster child as its state appropriations dropped from 80% of our academic budget in 1960 to less than 8% in 2015. Perhaps most telling of all are the extraordinary inequities characterizing educational opportunity today. As one of our colleagues has put it: "If you are poor and smart, today you have only a one-in-ten chance of obtaining a college degree. In contrast, if you are dumb and rich, your odds rise to nine-in-ten!" Something has gone terribly wrong!

Both the tragedy and irony of this situation flows from the realization that today our world has entered a period of rapid and profound economic, social, and political transformation driven by knowledge and innovation. It has become increasingly apparent that the strength, prosperity, and welfare of region or nation in a global knowledge economy will demand a highly educated citizenry enabled by development of a strong system of education at all levels. It will also require institutions with the ability to discover new knowledge, develop innovative applications of these discoveries, and transfer them into the marketplace through entrepreneurial activities.

Now more than ever, people see education as their hope for leading meaningful and fulfilling lives. Just as a high school diploma became the passport to participation in the industrial age, today, a century later, a college education has become the requirement for economic security in the age of knowledge. Furthermore, with the ever-expanding knowledge base of many fields, along with the longer life span and working careers of our aging population, the need for intellectual retooling will become even more significant. Even those with advanced degrees will soon find that their continued employability requires lifelong learning.

Education in America has been particularly responsive to the changing needs of society during early periods of major transformation, e.g., the transition from a frontier to an agrarian society, then to an industrial society, through the Cold War tensions, and to today's global, knowledge-driven economy. As our society changed, so too did the necessary skills and knowledge of our citizens: from growing to making, from making to serving, from serving to creating, and today from creating to innovating. With each social transformation, an increasingly sophisticated world required a higher level of cognitive ability, from manual skills to knowledge management, analysis to synthesis, reductionism to the integration of knowledge, invention to research, and today innovation, and entrepreneurship.

So what can our generation do to address these challenges, much as our parents and our ancestors did for us? After all, the generation–protested as students during the 1960s and 1970s, demanded less government and lower taxes in the 1980s and 1990s, and today are embracing a "Let's eat dessert first since life is uncertain!" attitude, even while denying the impact that their way of life poses to future generations

Perhaps it is time as we enter our "golden years" that we should be challenged to finally step forward to accept a greater degree of generational responsibility for the educational opportunities that we provide our descendants. Perhaps it is time that we use our influence, our wisdom, and for many, our considerable wealth, to make our own bold commitments for the educational resources that will be needed by future generations.

Today a rapidly changing world demands a new level of knowledge, skills, and abilities on the part of our citizens. Just as in earlier critical moments in our nation's history when its prosperity and security was achieved through broadening and enhancing educational opportunity, it is time once again to seek a bold expansion of educational opportunity. But this time we should set as the goal providing all American citizens with universal access to lifelong learning opportunities, thereby enabling participation in the world's most advanced knowledge and learning society.

Let us suggest that perhaps it should be our generation's legacy to ensure that our nation accepts a responsibility as a democratic society to provide all of its citizens with the educational, learning, and training opportunities they need and deserve, throughout their lives, thereby enabling both individuals and the nation itself to prosper in an ever more competitive global economy. While the ability to take advantage of educational opportunity will always depend on the need, aptitude, aspirations, and motivation of the student, it should not depend on one's socioeconomic status. Access to livelong learning opportunities should be a right for all rather than a privilege for the few if the nation is to achieve prosperity, security, and social well being in the global, knowledge- and value-based economy of the 21st century.

Several of the many awards received by the University
for its national leadership role in achieving diversity during the 1990s

Chapter 21

The University of Michigan Circa 2017

Today, much of American higher education is still recovering from the impact of the Great Recession of 2008 and 2009. Endowments are growing again, but state support remains at the lowest levels in decades and faculty and staff layoffs are still all too common. Yet, the University of Michigan appears to be enjoying a period of relative peace, prosperity, and growth. New buildings are appearing across the campus–the new Mott Pediatrics Hospital, a new graduate student residence hall, a massive expansion of the Athletics Campus, new buildings for the Ross Business School, the Law School, and the School of Nursing, a major new complex for the biological sciences, and a $650 million renovation of most of the student residence halls.

In contrast to the rest of higher education, Michigan seems financially secure, completing a $3.2 billion fundraising campaign in the 2000s and today in the midst of an even larger $4 billion campaign. Student applications and enrollments continue to grow, as do research expenditures, now exceeding $1.3 billion per year. The University's endowment has topped $10 billion. To be sure, some highly visible University programs have been enduring hard times, e.g., the first losing seasons of the Michigan football teams in over half a century and the athletic dominance over the Wolverines by Ohio State and–even worse–Michigan State. But an exciting new football coach (Jim Harbaugh) has arrived and a highly competent athletics director (Jim Hackett) has taken over, putting Michigan Athletics once again on the upswing. The spirit of the campus seems upbeat, confident, and secure. Or at least so we are told by the ever-optimistic and ever-present communications machinery of the University.

Yet, if one looks more closely, there are numerous warning signs that suggest that below the surface the University community should not be so sanguine. State support per student remains at its lowest levels since the 1960s. While there has been significant new debt-financed construction in auxiliary units (notably the Medical Center, student housing, and athletics), academic units have seen only a handful of projects financed by gifts, debt financing, or reallocation, but none with significant state support. Much of cost savings has come from constrained faculty/staff salaries and benefits programs (although certainly not for senior administrators whose compensation has soared to the levels of private universities) and assigned cost cutting targets for academic units. While research expenditures continue to lead the nation, externally sponsored research has declined while University subsidies of sponsored research projects have now grown to over 30% of research volume. Student applications have increased largely because of the Common Application now used in higher education, but the University's yield rate from admitted students remains lower than many of its peer universities. Faculty quality has been challenged by the University's struggle to retain top faculty in the face of increasing instructional loads, modest compensation, and aggressive offers from competing institutions. In recent years the University has suffered a serious erosion in its public purpose with the tragic decline in enrollments of underrepresented minority and low income students. Compared to earlier decades, the University's pathfinding achievements appear to be lagging both in number and impact.

Beyond these signals of possible problems, a more thorough investigation suggests that Michigan is clearly facing many of the challenges currently experienced by the rest of higher education, e.g., the unsustainability of its traditional sources of financial support, the increasing competition for the best students and faculty, and mission creep in auxiliary activities that dilutes the priority given to the academic core of the university. Cracks are beginning to appear in our façade of confidence. There is a growing fear we may be whistling through the graveyard, ignoring serious issues and concerns that could threaten our most fundamental goals of quality, public purpose, leadership, and even our institutional saga as a pathfinder for American higher education.

Through the lessons learned from our exercise in tracking the ebb and flow of various characteristics of the University of Michigan over the past half-century, we have identified a number of current concerns. We summarize them in this chapter and then suggest possible remedies in the next.

Growth

The rapid growth in student enrollments coupled with the unbridled expansion of auxiliary activities (hospitals, housing, and athletics) has triggered concern that the University is on a determined path toward becoming big, bigger, and biggest at the expense of both quality of its academic programs and the quality of life both on campus and beyond. While growth brings opportunities (and pride), it also brings challenges such as financing and managing such a gigantic complex. Overwhelming size commands respect, but we have many disturbing examples of how size and complexity can lead to disaster, e.g., the dinosaurs and General Motors.

Quality

Michigan's character as leader through its path-finding and trailblazing required it to build spires of excellence in key fields, rather than trying to achieve a uniform level of lesser quality across all of its activities. Only by attempting to be the best in these fields can we develop in our students, faculty, and staff the necessary intensity and commitment to excellence. Furthermore, only by competing with the best can Michigan establish appropriate levels of expectation and achievement.

The University culture has traditionally operated by placing very large bets in high-risk ventures involving our very best people at the grass roots level. Few of these have been top-down from the University's leadership but rather from the willingness to work hard to prospect, identify, and support major opportunities among its faculty, students, and staff.

Here a particular warning flag should be raised

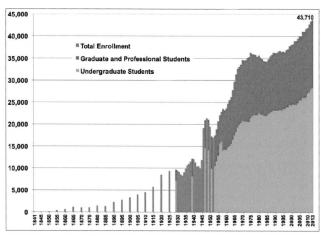

Over the last 15 years UM enrollments have increased by 10,000 students (25%).

Another demonstration of enrollment growth.

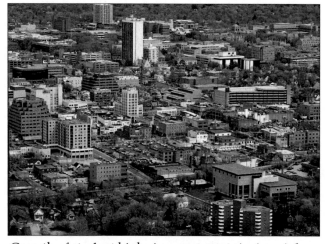

Growth of student high-rise apartments in Ann Arbor.

about the use of initiatives at the presidential or executive officer level to lead or steer the university, since Michigan throughout its history has been very much a bottom-up driven institution. It is not just that most top-down initiatives are soon rejected by the Michigan grassroots culture and fade away into obscurity, but more important, the true creativity, wisdom, and drive flourishes best at the grass-roots level with outstanding faculty members, students, and staff rather than administrators.

Balance (Academics vs. Auxiliaries)

Although the academic activities of the University remain key to its reputation and impact, the attention of recent University administrations and Regents has increasingly been focused on nonacademic opportunities. During the first decades of the new century there has been a growing faculty concern that the rapid growth of the Michigan's auxiliary activities (hospitals, housing, and athletics), now comprising almost 50% of the University's budget, has driven an increased focus on these activities by the leadership and governance of the institution to the neglect of academic programs. To be sure, the auxiliary units operate in markets that are relatively insensitive to pricing compared to the tuition constraints and limited public support of academic units. But there is growing concern that this rapid growth is also driven by unusually aggressive leadership of auxiliary units as well as the priority given by the University's leadership and governance. There is also the related issue as to whether the aggressive growth of the auxiliary units actually completes with and draws resources away from the academic core.

This concern about academic priorities applies not only to resource allocation but also to the attention of governance (the Regents), leadership (the Executive Officers), and management (central administration functions such as development and communications). Too many universities have seen the quality of their academic programs deteriorate through the distraction of important but clearly secondary activities such as fund-raising (e.g., donor cultivation and influence), the management of billion-dollar enterprises such as health systems, the public visibility of intercollegiate athletics,

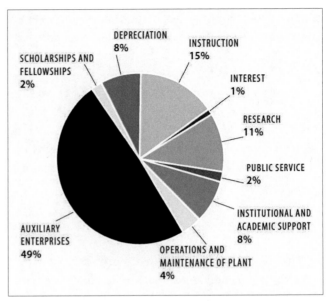

The 2015 UM Budget demonstrating the balance between academics and auxiliary activities.

and the misguided efforts to force upon universities many of the inappropriate practices of business and commerce (e.g., "shared services").

While much of this is driven both by the differing financial opportunities and challenges facing academic, auxiliary, and administrative activities, it is also due to an erosion of the academic voice in University leadership. Michigan provides a disturbing example of the impact of the increasingly "corporate" nature of large research university, with an increasing fraction of its central administration comprised of staff with little experience in higher education, and decision making largely detached from academic considerations. Here we must note again the efforts to recentralize resource control, weakening the power of deans and directors, launching new initiatives from the central administration rather than harvesting them from faculty and students, and imposing upon faculty and academic programs a corporate bureaucracy that is orthogonal to the spirit of academic freedom and creativity.

Pathfinding Leadership

It has been suggested that a key feature of the Michigan saga, its particular character and impact, over most of its history has been its role as a pathfinder for higher education. It has leveraged its unusual combination of quality, breadth, scale, and risk-taking spirit to blaze new trails for learning, discovery, and engagement to serve society. In fact, this pathfinding role has occasionally been so profound that it has changed the world itself.

Yet in recent years the University has seemed more content to follow the lead of others, to embrace more common themes in higher education such as "interdisciplinarity", "engaged learning", and "entrepreneurism". Its pioneering spirit seems to be lagging. The novelty is missing in its initiatives. To be sure, the financial challenges faced by the University with the loss of much of its state support have required attention by both the University's leadership and its Regents. It is also the case that over the past 15 years many of the key leadership and administrative positions have been filled through external appointments of those unfamiliar with the University's history, weakening somewhat the corporate memory and corporate culture of the University. Indeed, there are many signs that they have been slowly decoupling the University from its past, just as did the disruptions of the protest movements of the 1960s.

As many of the priorities of the University have shifted to activities such as development, public relations, marketing, and promoting the University by those from the commercial world with little experience with academe, it has become increasingly evident that the 2010s became a "lost" decade similar to the 1970s when little of the traditional pathfinding role of the University occurred.

Whatever the reason, it is clear that this new culture of defining and promoting the "brand" of the University through slogans such as "Victors for Michigan", by those with little understanding of either its academic character, history, or saga will seriously undermine the leadership role it has played in higher education over the years if allowed to continue. Put another way, a culture which transforms one of the great universities of the world into a follower rather than a pathfinder should be strongly resisted by those who understand and value Michigan's remarkable contributions to the state, the nation, and the world throughout its long history.

Students

Of particular note here has been the growing concern about the increase in student enrollments, from 35,000 in the 1990s to almost 44,000 today, a 25% growth occurring mostly at the undergraduate level with a particular emphasis on enrolling wealthy out-of-state students in an effort to increase tuition revenue to compensate for the loss of state support. This enrollment growth has had a significant impact both on the character of the University's academic programs and the nature of the University community. Since tenure-track faculty size has increased only modestly in those units undergoing major expansion (e.g., LS&A and Engineering), this has shifted lower division instruction toward an increasing dependence on part-time or nontenure-track faculty (who now provide over 50% of lower division undergraduate instruction). Teaching loads, as measured by students per full-time faculty member, are the highest in the University's history.

There is also a concern about the significant growth in students from high income backgrounds (with family incomes now averaging over $150,000/year) are distorting the culture of the student body, attending Michigan more in the spirit of "paying for the party" (fraternities and sororities, big-time athletics, sushi bars in the residence hall dining) than academic challenge and excellence. In fact, there is considerable evidence that the University is no longer honoring its long-standing public purpose of providing "an uncommon education for the common man".

Tragically, the University's leadership in providing exceptional educational opportunities to low income and underrepresented minority students has declined as its state support has eroded. More specifically, the percentage of Pell Grant students enrolled at UM Ann Arbor (the standard measure used by higher education of measuring enrollment by low income students) has dropped to 11% (compared to an average among flagship public universities of 22%), while its fraction of underrepresented minorities is now down to 10% (low again compared to an average of 25%). It is also disturbing that its percentage of first generation college students has now dropped to less than 6% compared to 16% of its public university peers and 14% of the

	Percent of undergrads with Pell grants
AAU Privates (average)	15%
AAU Publics (average, excluding U-M)	23%
University of California-San Diego	40%
University of California-Davis	36%
University of California-Los Angeles	34%
Stony Brook University	33%
University of California-Berkeley	32%
University of California-Santa Barbara	31%
University of California-Irvine	30%
University of Florida	28%
University at Buffalo	28%
University of Arizona	27%
Rutgers University	27%
Syracuse University	25%
University of Texas at Austin	24%
Michigan State University	23%
Iowa State University	22%
University of Oregon	22%
Ohio State University	21%
University of Minnesota	21%
University of Washington	20%
New York University	20%
University of Nebraska	20%
Texas A & M University	19%
Purdue University	19%
University of Missouri	19%
University of Kansas	19%
Emory University	19%
University of Rochester	19%
Massachusetts Institute of Technology	19%

	Percent of undergrads with Pell grants
University of Illinois	18%
University of North Carolina	18%
University of Southern California	18%
Columbia University	18%
Tulane University of Louisiana	18%
Pennsylvania State University	17%
Indiana University	17%
University of Maryland	17%
University of Iowa	17%
University of Pittsburgh	17%
University of Chicago	17%
Brandeis University	17%
University of Colorado	16%
Georgia Institute of Technology	16%
Stanford University	16%
University of Wisconsin	15%
Cornell University	15%
Rice University	15%
Carnegie Mellon University	14%
Vanderbilt University	13%
Brown University	13%
Johns Hopkins University	13%
Yale University	13%
Duke University	12%
UNIVERSITY OF MICHIGAN	11%
University of Pennsylvania	11%
Northwestern University	11%
Princeton University	11%
California Institute of Technology	11%
Harvard University	10%
Washington University	6%

SOURCE: Integrated Postsecondary Education Data System (IPEDS).

Michigan's poor ranking in Pell Grant recepients

enrollment of highly selective private universities. In fact, a 2010 report by the Education Trust, Opportunity Adrift, stated: "Founded to provide 'an uncommon education for the common man', many flagship universities have drifted away from their historic mission". (Haycock, 2010) Analyzing measures such as access for low-income and underrepresented minority students and the relative success of these groups in earning diplomas, they found that the University of Michigan and the University of Indiana received the lowest overall marks for both progress and current performance among all major public universities in these measures of public purpose.

To be sure, the State of Michigan ranks at the bottom of the states in the amount of need-based financial aid it provides to college students, requiring the University to make these commitments from its own internal funds. But it is also due to the decision made in the late 1990s to compensate for the loss of state support by dramatically increasing enrollments with a bias toward out-of-state students who generate new revenues with high tuition. Clearly students who can pay annual tuition-room & board at the out-of-state rates of $60,000 come from highly affluent families. Indeed, the average family income of Michigan undergraduates now exceeds $150,000 per year, more characteristic of the

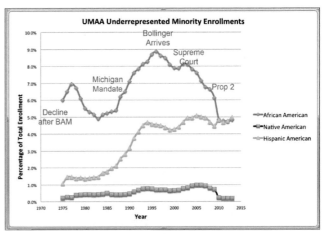

Following the major growth during the 1990s, minority enrollments have been dropping precipitously.

"top 1%" than the "common man".

Of comparable concern is the significant drop in enrollments of underrepresented minority students, dropping from 14% of enrollments in 1996 (including 9.4% African American) to 10% in 2015 (4.8% African American). Once Michigan's professional schools were leaders in minority enrollments (with Medicine, Business, and Law at 12% African American enrollments in the 1990s); today they have fallen badly to levels of 5% or less. Although this dramatic decline is usually blamed on the state's adoption in 2006 of a constitutional amendment banning affirmative action in college admissions, it actually began in the late 1990s when a new administration abandoned the successful programs of the Michigan Mandate. Minority enrollments continued to decline throughout the 2010s, even with the positive Supreme Court decision of 2003, declining to levels even below those of the 1960s. It was clear that the University leadership no longer gave diversity the priority that it had received in 1990s.

This decline was particularly tragic since during the 1990s the University led the nation in its efforts to achieve diversity through efforts such as the Michigan Mandate, which doubled the population of underrepresented minority students, faculty, and staff. But, perhaps even more significantly, during the 1990s, the success of underrepresented minorities at the University improved even more remarkably, with graduation rates rising to the highest level among public universities, promotion and tenure success of minority faculty members becoming comparable to

Change in Minority Enrollments

Minority	1996	2015	Change
African Am	2,824	1,801	-36%
Hispanic	1,473	2,018	+37%
Native Am	227	92	-60%
Underrep	4,524	3,921	-14%

Change in Minority Percentages

Minority	1996	2015	Change
African Am	9.3%	4.8%	-48%
Hispanic	4.5%	5.4%	+20%
Native Am	0.7%	0.25%	-64%
Asian Am	11.6%	13.5%	+13%
Underrep	14.1%	10.1%	-32%
Fresh AA	9.3%	5.1%	-45%

The drop in underrepresented minorities
over the past 15 years.

their majority colleagues, and a growing number of appointments of minorities to leadership positions in the University. The campus climate not only became more accepting and supportive of diversity, but students and faculty were attracted to Michigan because of its growing reputation for a diverse campus. Perhaps most significantly, as the campus became more racially and ethnically diverse, the quality of the students, faculty, and academic programs of the University increased to the highest level in the institution's history. This fact reinforced the premise of the Michigan Mandate that the aspirations of diversity and excellence were not only compatible but, in fact, highly correlated. By every measure, the Michigan Mandate was a remarkable success, moving the University beyond our original goals of a more diverse campus while enhancing its excellence and achievement.

Faculty and Staff

Looking back over the past 50 years, it is clear that the career trajectories of the faculty have changed significantly. No longer do young faculty expect a career at a single institution, but they anticipate more of a nomadic path moving from institution to institution in order to rise up the promotion ladder. Yet, of even

more concern, the opportunities for establishing an academic career are dwindling, with non-tenure track appointments as post-doctoral scholars, lecturers, and adjunct faculty now providing the majority of lower division instruction, a feature driven by the efforts of universities to cut costs and improve productivity with a more flexible faculty workforce. As a consequence, today less than 50% of the instructional staff is comprised of tenured or tenure-track faculty.

The marketplace has become even more intense as faculty careers span multiple institutions, now remaining less than a decade at each waystation on their route to a professorial chair or administrative position. New elements have been added to the package of negotiations, including not only promotion, salary increases, startup funding, and perhaps an endowed chair, but now dual-career family placement, more generous sabbatical leaves, lower teaching assignments, and even signing bonuses. The competition among institutions has become ever more intense.

The analysis of faculty attrition during the past 15 years finds that the loss of Michigan faculty to other institutions has been unusually high among junior faculty, and particularly among women and minorities. Although some of this is due to the long-standing process of tenure evaluation, the number of young faculty with distinguished records who leave the University for appointments at peer institutions (e.g., Harvard, MIT, Yale, Stanford, University of California) is cause for concern.

But it also must be recognized that despite rhetoric to the contrary, faculty salaries simply have not been a priority of the University administration in recent years. Recent comparative analyses of faculty and staff salaries found the average salary of full professors at Michigan not only fall 20% below those of private universities but also lag many public universities. In sharp contrast the compensation of senior administrators (Executive Officers, deans, and senior financial administrators) are 30% to 40% higher than all other peer public universities, and when undisclosed bonuses are included, rank at the top of all institutions, public and private. The impact on faculty morale of excessive compensation of senior administrators has been considerable.

Adopting such corporate approaches to university management and leadership is not only orthogonal to

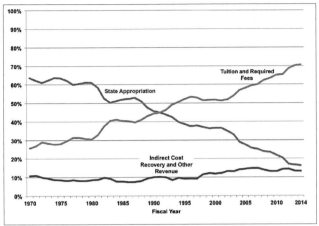

General contribution of state support to
the UMAA General Fund budget

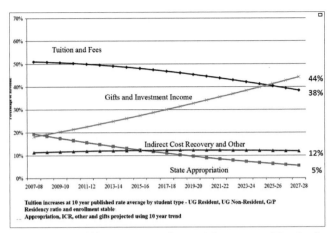

Projections of longer term financial support (Hanlon)

the spirit of academic freedom and creativity. But when coupled with the nomadic life it imposes upon today's faculty members, such actions also seriously damage faculty loyalty to institutions. Little wonder than many of Michigan's most accomplished and distinguished faculty members have largely stepped back from efforts to influence the future of the University through service in a faculty governance role with little power or through initiatives that are usually ignored or overwhelmed by the public relations efforts of the central administration. In a very real sense, perhaps one of the greatest challenges to the University of Michigan today, as it is to other great public research universities, is to find a way to empower once again those faculty members whose contributions in teaching, scholarship, and service have been the key factor in establishing and sustaining the reputation of the University.

Yet in the same way that an increasingly corporate approach to University management and decision-making now threatens academic priorities, it also puts talented staff at great risk, as evidenced by the degree to which cost-saving ventures such as administrative shared services and reduction in benefits all too frequently have their most negative impact on the staff. The significant growth of high salary staff in the central administration has raised many concerns, since many of these new staff not only enjoy salaries far above those of the faculty, but also benefit from undisclosed bonus and deferred compensation that boost their salaries even higher (amounting to more than $46 million in 2013), while many staff members in academic units are seriously under paid. Despite the critical role they play

in teaching and research, their colleagues in roles such as branding. marketing, and fund raising in the central administration enjoy compensation far beyond that they would merit in business or industry.

Financials

The highly competitive nature of higher education in America has created an intensely Darwinian winner-take-all ecosystem in which the strongest and wealthiest institutions become predators, raiding the best faculty and students of the less generously supported and more constrained public universities and manipulating federal research and financial policies to sustain a system in which the rich get richer and the poor get devoured. These institutions now find themselves caught with declining state support and the predatory wealthy private universities competing for the best students, faculty, and support.

So how might we assess the financial state of the University over the past 50 years? As state support declined over the past five decades, the University of Michigan found itself a predominantly "privately-supported" public university, in the sense that roughly 95% of its revenues now come from non-state sources such as student tuition, clinical fees, research grants, and private gifts that are determined by competitive markets.

While the loss of state support has largely been compensated by ramping up enrollments of students paying nonresident tuition, this remedy has approached a ceiling. Today the current out-of-state undergraduate tuition of $45,000 has caught up with leading private universities such as Harvard and Stanford. Furthermore although there are strong pressures to continue to grow enrollment, while holding permanent faculty lines relatively constant, the increasing instructional load in UM's large undergraduate colleges, LS&A and Engineering, are already becoming unbearable for many faculty members.

While private support is important, frequently these funds are heavily constrained by donor intent and unavailable to meet the highest priorities of the University. Furthermore, although the University's current development and marketing staffing is several times that of the 1990s, it has failed to achieve any real growth in annual giving, ranking below many other public and private universities.

The one bright spot is the impressive growth in Michigan's endowment, due largely to the extraordinary success in creating a $2.5 billion endowment during the 1990s. Yet, although Michigan's $10 billion endowment today appears impressive, paticularly for a public institution, the University's endowment-per-student is only one-tenth the level of leading private institutions.

While research expenditures have continued to grow, maintaining the University's position as the nation's leader by this measure, the fact that over 30% of UM research expenditures are now provided from institutional funds such as tuition revenue and clinical fees suggest that plugging the hole in eroding federal sponsorship of research with University funds may also be distorting institutional priorities. Yet it is also clear that the financial dependence on such growth creates a dependence that makes it hard to reverse.

On the other side of the ledger, the University has launched an ambitious cost reduction effort during the past decade, with the goal of trimming roughly 1.5% to 2.0% each year of annual expenditures. While this has resulted in part from more efficient management of energy and supply acquisition and administration, much of the highly touted recent "savings" of the University have come out of faculty-staff benefits. Furthermore faculty and staff compensation has been modest, dropping 20% below its private university peers and lagging behind several other leading public universities. Hence there is a serious concern that further cuts in benefits could cripple UM's efforts to attract outstanding faculty and staff.

To be sure, the University has survived in the face of losing over 50% of its state support, with its reputation largely intact. Yet, from the late 1990s to the 2010s, a series of short term actions have been taken that may have walked the University out on a financial limb. In recent years faculty surveys suggest growing concerns about whether the current financial strategy of the University is capable of sustaining both the quality and the public purpose of the institution.

Facilities

The University of Michigan campus has continued to evolve over the past two decades, despite the disappearance of state support for capital facilities. The two major complexes designed by architect Robert Stern, Weill Hall (for the Ford School) and North Quad, provide elegant entrances to the Central Campus, albeit at very considerable cost. The major buildings of the Ross School of Business Administration and expansion of the Law School are also important academic projects. While Venturi's Life Sciences complex is actually a somewhat smaller version of a buildings he designed for Yale and UCLA, the biomedical research complex on Huron and Observatory is important for the continued expansion of research activity in the life sciences, as well as the recently acquired North Campus Research Center (the former Pfizer R&D Center).

The University has taken advantage of exceptionally low interest rates to launch a massive series of renovations of residence halls ($650 million) that will be important for the growing student enrollment. The addition of skyboxes and club facilities has brought in additional revenue for Michigan athletics, albeit at possible risk because of its dependence on generous federal tax treatment and its serious impact on the morale of long-time campus and community fans who can no longer afford to attend events. Finally, the clinical facilities for the University Hospitals have grown very significantly with the addition of the Frankel Cardiovascular Center and the new Mott Pediatrics Hospital, along with planned expansion of the Medical School, although there are already warning signs about the costs of these very large new clinical facilities in view of the current health care market in Michigan and

North Quad

Weill Hall

Life Sciences Institute

Biomedical Sciences Building

Ross School of Business Administration

Law School South Hall

North Campus Research Center

Michigan Energy Institute

Mott Children's Hospital

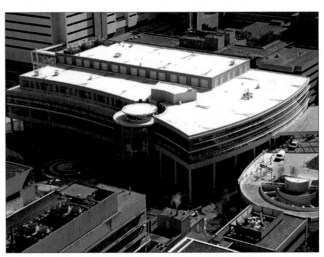

Frankel Cardiovascular Center

Hill Dining Hall

Munger Graduate Residence Hall

Michigan Stadium Expansion

Chrisler Center Expansion

the future restructuring of federal health care policies such as the Affordable Care Act (with recent operating losses in the $100 million to $200 million per year).

Yet, here there are also more general concerns. Most of the campus growth (75%), at least in terms of investment ($4 billion), has occurred in auxiliary units (i.e., clinical activities, housing, athletics) and are funded by auxiliary revenue streams, albeit with debt secured by student fee revenues. Those buildings responding to academic needs have generally depended upon anticipated federal research support (e.g., Public Health Annex), private funding (Ross Business School, Weill Hall), or debt-financing (Biosciences Center). This raises a serious question as to just how, in the absence of state support, the University will meet the future capital facilities needs of those academic units that have no donors or other external revenue sources (e.g., federal R&D).

The budget growth of auxiliary units (hospitals, housing, athletics) also raises the important issue of university priorities and balance. At Michigan there is some truth to the old saying that the academic core of the contemporary university is a quite fragile institution struggling to survive between the pressures exerted by the football stadium on one end of the campus and the university hospital on the other. But more serious is the issue of how one sustains the highest priority for the academic core of the university in an increasingly resource-driven (and for many academic units, resource-starved) environment constrained by "fund accounting", in which it is increasingly difficult to provide cross-subsidies from one unit to another (and particularly from auxiliary units to academic units).

Technology

The primary missions of the University, its teaching, research, and service activities (or alternatively, its activities of learning, discovery, and engagement with society) are increasingly dependent on cyberinfrastructure, i.e., information and communications technology. The rapid advances in these technologies are not only reshaping but creating entirely new paradigms for research, education, and application not only in science and engineering but in all of the academic and professional disciplines. It has been clear for some time that to maintain world-class academic programs, the University must also achieve leadership in the quality and relevance of the cyberinfrastructure it provides at the level of each of its highly diverse teaching and research programs.

This is particularly challenging since the features of information technology such as processing speed, memory, and bandwidth, have been increasing in power at rates of 100 to 1,000 fold per decade since WWII. This is one of the major reasons for the continued surprises we get from the emergence of new applications–the Internet, social networks, big data, machine learning– appearing in unexpected ways at a hyper exponential pace. We have learned time and time again that it makes little sense to simply extrapolate the present into the future to predict or even understand the next

The Univerity provides a rich cyberinfrastructure environment for students and faculty.

"tech turn". These are not only highly disruptive technologies, but they are highly unpredictable. Ten years ago nobody would have imagined Google, Facebook, Twitter, etc., and today, nobody really can predict what will be a dominant technology even five years ahead, much less ten!

Too much of the current focus is shaped by today's technologies, not tomorrow's, e.g., cloud services, big data, analytics. Again, overdependence on commodity products, particularly to the degree we constrain the cyber environments of academic units through policies such as purchasing and shared services, will harm the loosely coupled adaptive culture of the university that is one of our greatest strengths. This is particularly dangerous if we become overly dependent on particular vendors because of top-down rather than bottom-up forces. The reality is (and always has been) that it has been our faculty, staff, and students who spot the next big trends in technology and then drive change upward through the institution.

The tension between centralization of technology (or "rationalization", the term used by University consultant Accenture) and decentralization (where cacophony leads to innovation) can be very threatening, particularly to those parts of the University that need to make the trains run on time (e.g., financial services, hospitals, etc.) Fortunately, in the past, the wisdom of maintaining a loosely coupled adaptive system at the academic level finally bubbles up to the leadership of the institution, and academic units are set free once again. To be sure, the University has important responsibilities that require mission critical computing. But it is at the level of academic units rather than the enterprise level where innovation and leadership must occur. Why? Because they are driven by learning and discovery, by experimentation, by tolerance for failure, and by extraordinarily talented faculty, students, and particularly, staff.

Leadership and Governance

One of the most serious recent trends in University leadership has been the erosion of the power of the deans and directors. As we have noted, the strength of the University's academic programs has been due in large measure to the quality of the leadership of the deans. The deans are the key line officers of the University. They are also the ones most responsible for maintaining its academic priorities and quality. Great deans create and lead great schools and colleges, not to mention generating over 90% of the resources of the University.

Yet in recent years there is some evidence that the traditional roles and power of the deans have been weakened. The rigid application of 10 year limits on the appointments of deans, with little attention given to easing their transitions to "life after leadership", has been very discouraging and led to the departure of several of the University's most talented leaders. So too, there has been a clear trend to fill most open dean positions with outsiders with little experience with decentralized management.

The long-standing practice of achieving a balance between the appointment of internal and external candidates for senior leadership positions such as deans seems to have been abandoned. During the 1970s through the 1990s, the majority of the deans came from internal appointments of outstanding faculty. In recent years there has been a very significant preference for external candidates, now comprising over two-thirds of the deans and the majority of the executive officers. Indeed, by 2015, 13 of 19 dean positions had been filled with external candidates. When comprised with the 10-year limit on deans service, the influence of the deans on University-wide issues has been substantially weakened.

This is an important issue since there has been a long University tradition of making certain that the University's distributed academic leadership is well balanced between long-time members of the University faculty who understand the unique Michigan culture of pathfinding and innovation and those newcomers to the University who may not understand its culture initially but bring in new ideas and insights. Such a balance is able to preserve the University's long role as a pathfinder, not a follower. But perhaps the most worrisome trend has been the weakening of the voice and influence of the University's deans in recent years. The deans and department chairs are the key players in such pathfinding ventures. They are the ones who understand best both the quality of their faculty and the unusual nature of the Michigan culture. Hence throughout the history of the University, the deans have been given extraordinary authority, accompanied by responsibility, in providing the leadership necessary to build and sustain outstanding program.

There has been similar erosion in both the academic credentials and experience of the executive officers. In the past, most of the University's senior leadership team had sufficient academic experience to merit faculty appointments in addition to their administrative assignments. Today, however, only four executive officers (president, provost, VP Research, and EVP Health System) have faculty credentials. The recent trend to appoint senior officers without academic background or experience has decoupled the central administration from the academic core of the University to an alarming degree.

Michigan has also seen some change in its shared governance involving faculty, trustees, and administration. Such a system represents the effort to achieve a balance among academic priorities, public purpose, and operating imperatives such as financial solvency, institutional reputation, and public accountability. Quality universities require quality leadership and governance. Nothing is more critical than attracting experienced and dedicated citizens in standing for election to Michigan's Board of Regents and attracting distinguished faculty members into leadership positions in faculty governance.

But here the University of Michigan system of faculty governance is somewhat different than most institutions. Its Senate Assembly, the campus-wide, elected faculty governance, is primarily advisory in nature, in contrast to the strong executive committee structures at the department, school, and college level. Hence while the faculty is strong at the school and college level, it is relatively weak on University-wide issues.

Since the influence of faculty governance at the University is primarily concentrated in powerful elected faculty executive committees at the school, college, and department level rather than with a University-wide faculty senate, the deans also have primary responsibility for making certain that academic priorities dominate the attention of the University administration and governing board. To weaken the access and influence of the deans relative to both the Executive Officers and Regents of the University is tantamount to weakening the academic priorities of the institution.

Here the deans must play an important role, since the decentralized nature of the University allocates to them not only the power of resource control but also the responsibility for defending University-wide academic priorities. When the deans are strong, this checks-and-balance system works well. When they are weak or myopically focused on their own academic units, the university becomes vulnerable to political forces.

Organization and Management

Today, the primary missions of the University, its teaching, research, and service to society, are characterized by extraordinary scale and complexity. To accommodate the necessary financial restructuring and growth of the University during the 1980s and 1990s, the University of Michigan began a decade-long effort to decentralize both authority and responsibility to the level of its academic and auxiliary operating units, with the deans and directors assuming the role of distributed management responsibility for both revenue generation and expenditure controls. This system allowed the University not only to adapt and maintain academic priorities and quality, but its "loosely coupled adaptive ecosystem" structure has enabled it to withstand stresses that might cripple smaller institutions.

Unfortunately, as the University entered a new century, the recruitment of new deans and senior administrators from institutions with more centralized cultures has stimulated efforts to recentralize the institution, leading to major growth in both the numbers and compensation of administrators. It also resulted in efforts to apply corporate management styles, complete with the demands to centralize and standardize services, bonus-based compensation systems, and excessive investment in corporate-like functions (e.g., marketing, branding, advertising, and other forms of "institutional advancement"). Such attempts to recentralize the institution's management have encountered strong faculty opposition because of the threat of damage to the core academic mission by such a corporate-style central administration.

Here, Michigan provides a disturbing example of the impact of the increasingly "corporate" nature of large research university, with an increasing fraction of its central administration comprised of staff with little if any experience in higher education, and decision making largely detached from academic considerations (e.g., the efforts to recentralize resource control, weakening the power of deans and directors, launching new initiatives from the central administration rather than harvesting them from faculty and students, and imposing upon faculty and academic programs a corporate bureaucracy

Missions

One of the greatest challenges to the modern research university is balancing its various complex roles, even as these roles are rapidly changing. How does one achieve an optimum balance between teaching and research? Public service versus our role as an independent critic of society? The liberal arts and the professions? The tensions among these various roles occur in part because of the incompatibility in the needs, values, and expectations of the various constituencies served by higher education.

The basic functions of the university continue to be its core academic activities. Other major activities of the university gain legitimacy only to the degree that they are linked with education and scholarship. In this sense, public service that is based on teaching and research is not a function but one of a number of principles that animate and guide the basic work of a university.

Efforts to respond to unrealistic public aspirations and expectations by attempting to be all things to all people, higher education has whetted an insatiable public appetite for a host of service activities of marginal relevance to its academic mission. A quick glance around any community with a local university provides numerous examples of this, from extension offices for continuing education to medical clinics to incubation centers for high-tech business formation to athletic camps for K-12 students.

Yet such responsiveness to the needs—indeed, even the whims—of society by higher education may, in the long run, be counterproductive. Not only has it fueled an inaccurate public perception of the primary mission of a university and an unrealistic expectation of its role in public service, but it has also stimulated an increasingly narrow public attitude toward the support of higher education. A "What-have-you-done-for-me-lately?"attitude now permeates federal, state, and local government. This fuels powerful forces of parochialism that force institutions to spread themselves ever more thinly as they scramble to justify themselves to their elected public officials.

Perhaps the most extreme example of such misguided "public service" is the entertainment most large universities like Michigan are expected to provide through intercollegiate athletics. While many of the University's athletic programs provide valuable and appropriate learning experiences for student, its football and basketball programs have clearly become commercial entertainment businesses. They have evolved to the point where they no longer have relevance to the academic mission of the university. Furthermore, they are based on a culture, a set of values that, while perhaps appropriate for show business, are viewed as highly corrupt by the academy and deemed corrosive to our academic mission. It is increasing clear that "big-time" college sports exploit not only the health but also the educational opportunity of young students primarily to generate the revenues necessary to make a very small number of people fabulously wealthy, namely coaches, athletic directors, conference commissioners, and NCAA executives. Put another way, there is growing evidence that big-time college sports do far more damage to the university, to its students and faculty, its leadership, its reputation and credibility, that most realize--or at least are willing to admit. The evidence seems overwhelming:

Far too many of our athletics programs exploit young people, recruiting them with the promise of a college education—or a lucrative professional career—only to have the majority of Division 1-A football and basketball players achieve neither. Furthermore, particularly in violent sports such as football and hockey, student-athletes are subjected to unacceptable health risks through injuries that could cripple them for life, without adequate protection or lifelong health security.

Scandals in intercollegiate athletics have damaged the reputations of many of our colleges and universities. Big time college football and basketball have put inappropriate pressure on university governance, as boosters, politicians, and the media attempt to influence governing boards and university leadership. The impact of intercollegiate athletics on university culture and values has been damaging, with inappropriate behavior of both athletes and coaches, all too frequently tolerated and excused.

In summary, today at Michigan the commercial culture of the entertainment industry that characterizes college football and basketball is not only orthogonal to academic values, but it is corrosive and corruptive to the academic enterprise. It is clearly damaging to the institution, its students, its reputation, and its integrity.

Community

We have noted earlier the increasing degree to which the University of Michigan has become "an engine of inequality" as it enrolled an increasing number of high income out-of-state students while the enrollment of students from low-income backgrounds dropped to among the lowest level of any public university. But this is only one of many signs of the degree to which the University is not only increasingly dependent upon but also shifting its focus to serving the wealthy. As bit by bit the University has been selling its resources to the highest bidder (e.g., student enrollments, the names of programs and places, access to athletic and cultural events, etc). Faculty, staff, and indeed many students are beginning to feel no longer welcome or even tolerated by the armies of new staff now determined to redefine and market the "brand" of the university.

This bias increasingly toward serving the wealthy has also influenced University staff policies. As noted earlier there has been an extraordinary growth in both staffing of the central administration and compensation provided to senior administrators at a time when faculty and staff compensation has been relatively stagnant. Through the use of hidden devices such as one-time bonuses, deferred compensation, or incentive awards, the compensation of executives in the central administration and selected deans and directors is now considerably above that of most other public universities and challenging some of the leading private universities. While such executive compensation is usually argued as driven by market considerations both by leadership and compensation consultants, it m,ust be kept in mind that nonprofit organizations such as universities should not be driven by corporate models. Furthermore, unlike the compensation of corporate executives, which require a rigorous incentive compensation policy consistent with accounting practices and public disclosure, university compensation is all too often determined by ad hoc decisions made by senior administrators rather than adhering to rigorous, public salary structures.

University faculty, staff, and students are being priced out of community events.

Political Challenges

Yet today universities are trapped by a converging political agenda at every level with multiple, not always compatible goals: to limit educational costs, even at the expense of quality; to make education ever more widely available; to draw back from the national commitment to research support, at least in the forms and amounts we have depended on since World War II; and to accelerate institutional transformation through application of information technology.

Running counter to these goals are a few troublesome trends already affecting our universities. Public funding for higher education has been declining in a climate where education is seen increasingly as a personal economic benefit rather than as a public good in and of itself. Long-standing policies such as affirmative action, which represented earlier commitments to equity and social justice, are now being challenged by governing bodies, in the courts, and through public referenda. The allocation of research funding is increasingly driven by those with great skepticism (or fear) of scientific reasoning, particularly in areas such as the social sciences. Our curriculum is deformed by the competitiveness and vocational demands of students whose debt load impels them toward excessive careerism, even as other voices call for a return to an idealized "classical" curriculum based on the great works of Western civilization.

Of particular concern is the intrusion of political forces in nearly every aspect of university governance and mission. State and federal government seek to regulate admissions decisions and financial aid. There are egregious examples of political or judicial intrusion in the research process itself, for example, Star Chamber hearings before government bodies investigating scholarly research integrity or the expenditure of research funds. We are only beginning to feel the crippling effects of open-meetings requirements on the conduct of business and on hiring. Today higher education is over regulated, and the costs of accountability are excessive both in dollars and in administrative burden. Governance of public institutions is too often in the hands of people selected for partisan political reasons rather than for their understanding and support of higher education. Most distressing, there is an increasing tendency by ambitious politicians to use the university as a whipping boy for personal political gain. These trends, symptomatic of the erosion of public confidence in universities, parallel the loss of trust in our institutions across the board.

Not that we in universities are blameless. We too often have been reactive rather than proactive in responding to demands from students, faculty, government, politicians, patrons, ideologues, and demagogues who distort or undermine our fundamental values and purposes. Academic structures are too rigid to accommodate the realities of our rapidly expanding and interconnected base of knowledge and practice. Higher education as a whole has been divided and competitive at times when we need to speak with a single unequivocal voice. Our entrenched interests block the path to innovation and creativity. Perhaps, most dismaying, we have yet to come forth with a convincing case for ourselves, a vision for our future, and an effective strategy for achieving it.

Hence the University of Michigan should be challenged to should be to re-engage with its many publics–the people of Michigan, the nation, indeed, the world–to convince them of the importance of investing in higher education to provide its two great services, education and scholarship, "light and truth" or *lux et veritas*, to all who need and seek them. This must become a primary responsibility of not only the leadership of the University, but its Regents, faculty, students, staff, alumni, and those citizens who depend so heavily on the services provided by one of the great universities of the world.

Lingering Questions

During the past half century the University has continued to demonstrate significant pathfinding leadership, e.g., building the nation's leading programs in the quantitative social sciences, building and managing the Internet, pioneering the early development of genetic medicine, creating the world's largest digital libraries (JSTOR and the HathiTrust) and becoming a leader in the peaceful appplications of atomic energy. The challenge today is how to sustain such pathfinding efforts in the century ahead.

From this brief review of the current status and the challenges facing the University of Michigan, a number of more general questions have arisen that should be considered by both the University's leadership and governance:

Question 1: What is the fundamental role of the university in modern society? What are its core values to society? If the issue is to get back to fundamentals, to reorganize the institution according to our basic values, then how and where do we begin?

Question 2: How does one preserve the public character of an increasingly privately financed university? How does a "state-related" or "hybrid state-national-global" university adequately represent the varied interests of its majority shareholders (e.g.,

students, parents, patients, federal agencies, private donors)? Can one sustain an institution the size and breadth of the University of Michigan on self-generated revenues (e.g., tuition, federal grants and contracts, private gifts, auxiliary revenues) alone?

Question 3: Should our balance of missions shift among teaching, research, and service? Among undergraduate, graduate, and professional education? Among service to state, nation, and world?

Question 4: What is the proper balance between disciplinary and interdisciplinary activity? How can we encourage more people to work in truly innovative areas without unduly jeopardizing their academic careers? How can we stimulate a greater risk-taking intellectual culture in which people are encouraged to take bold initiatives?

Question 5: We have an unparalleled opportunity to shape the academy for the future through this generation of graduate students. How should we meet this responsibility? Is the Ph.D. degree the appropriate training for the broadly educated, change-tolerant faculty needed by today's universities?

Question 6: As Michigan enters its third century, it will be facing a major number of faculty retirements, thereby providing the opportunity to attract bright young faculty to the University. How should we select new faculty for brilliance and creativity? Do our present traditions and practices in faculty selection allow us to select genius? How do we assess and enhance teaching ability? How do we evaluate and reward service activities? Indeed, what is the appropriate form of service in the research university?

Question 7: How do we enable the University to flourish during a period of very rapid change?

Question 8: How do we best protect the University's capacity to control its own destiny?

Provocative questions, indeed. And both challenging and appropriate for today if we are to prepare for tomorrow.

Yesterday	Today
UM Values	Publically committed?
	Privately supported?
Excellence	State governed (lay, politically governed)
Leadership	Nationally supported
Critical Inquiry	Decentralized, distributed leadership
Liberal Learning	Misunderstood (from within, from without)
Diversity	Ponderous, risk adverse
Innovation	Distracted (lost in forest for the trees)
Excitement	Trapped in sinking state
Spirit	Large, larger, largest in the land
	Campus
Characteristics	Budget
	Michigan Stadium
Leaders and Best	Medical Center
Control of its destiny (constitutional autonomy)	Trajectories
Freedom and responsibility	UG up
Broad and Liberal Spirit	Out-of-state up
Critical inquiry and learning	Rich students up
Diverse in character, united in spirit	Research volume up
Uncommon education for the common man	Graduate education down
Critic and servant of society	Tenure-track faculty declining
Relish for innovation and excitement	Part-time faculty up
Pathfinder, Trailblazer, Pioneer	Priorities
	Academic programs benign neglect
	Quantity up
	Quality down
	Auxiliaries up
	Medical Center up
	Housing up
	Athletics way up
	Resources
	State ignored
	Federal leveraged
	Donors up (but inadequate)
	Investments stable

A summary of assessments of the University of Michigan expressed in faculty workshops held in 2011-2012.

Appendices to Chapter 21
A Summary of UM Concerns

UM Appears to be doing just fine...
> UM appears to be enjoying a period of relative peace, prosperity, and growth.
> Lots of new buildings North Quad, Law School, Ross School, Munger Hall, Pediatrics Hospital, Athletics
> Completed a $3.2 B campaign and launching a $4 B effort
> Leading the nation with $1.32 B in research funding
> New revenue plus cost control plus AAa ratings
> (Not all good news: lost to Ohio State 12 out of last 14 games and Michigan State 6 out of last 7 games...)

But is UM whistling through graveyard?
> Unsustainability of its traditional sources of financial support
> Increasing competition for the best students and faculty
> Mission creep in auxiliaries that dilutes the priority given to the academic core of the university
> Are we ignoring serious issues and concerns that could threaten our most fundamental goals of quality, public purpose, leadership, and even our institutional saga as a pathfinder for American higher education?
> Cracks are beginning to appear in our façade of confidence.

Threats to student quality
> Common Application Online process creates a false sense of student demand
> Student selectivity: Instate: 60%; Outstate: 40%
> Student yield: Instate: 70%; Outstate: 25%
> It is clear that Michigan is still a "safety" school for out-of-state students.
> Many out-of-state students come from very affluent families and are "paying for the party" rather than a rigorous education
> Sharp drop in low-income and underrepresented minority students

Threats to faculty quality
> Heavy instructional loads and weaker salaries have caused both attrition and hiring problems.
> Michigan is winning only 50% of the battles to keep key faculty from being raided
> Losses over past 7 years: 55 to Harvard, 54 to UCBerkeley, 46 to Stanford, 46 to Chicago, 37 to UTexas, 25 to Columbia...AND 23 to Ohio State!
> Of particular concern is the loss of over 600 junior faculty over the past decade, many just after achieving tenure at Michigan.

Threats to public purpose
> Founded to provide "an uncommon education for the common man", many flagship universities have drifted away from their historic mission (Haycock's *Engines of Inequality*)
> Pell Grant percentage: 11% (22% pub U average)
> First generation college students: 6% (down from 14%)
> Underrepresented minorities: 10% (pub U 25% average)
> African American enrollments: 4.3% (down from 9.4% in 1996)

Problems of scale
> Enrollments are up 10,000 students (25%) over the past two decades!
> Good news: tuition revenue up by $400 M/y, roughly comparable to state support.
> Bad News: so are teaching loads, student misbehavior, and student high-rise slums (e.g., wealthy students "Paying for the Party")
> Fund raising is up! Well...kind of...since annual giving, campaign yields, and endowment are really just extrapolations of activity during the 1990s, but with five times the number of staff (500 in development, 600 in communications)
> UM is also being pressured to accept and partially fund projects of low priority, e.g., Munger Hall, "The Walk of Champions"
> And the deans and chairs are now spending much of their time on the road begging for dollars rather than providing academic leadership

Research is up!
> Michigan is still the leader in research dollars.
> However we are also the leaders in how much we are spending from institutional funds (e.g., $380 M out of $1.32 B, or 30% of our research activity, compared to 20% for most universities).
> Note that much of this subsidy comes from student tuition and patient fees.

Other problems with scale

    Increasing concerns that we may not have the management talent to handle such a gigantic enterprise… (e.g., shared services, IT rationalization…)

    We may also not understand the risk of launching larger and larger projects (e.g., Mott Pediatrics Hospital ($760 M) , Michigan Wolverines, Inc. ($152 M/y),

    Remember, we have a dramatic nearby examples of the dangers of scale: General Motors and Chrysler…

Past decade of campus evolution

    New academic buildings: Weill Hall, Ross Hall, Law School, LS&A Bioscience Building.

    New/Renovated auxiliary buildings: Pediatrics Hospital, Cardiovascular Hospital, Hill Dorms, North Quad, East Quad, South Quad, West Quad, Munger Hall, Michigan Stadium, Crisler Arena, …

    NOTE: Most capital expansion has been in auxiliaries (hospitals, housing, athletics). Relatively little has been invested in academic facilities.

Culture

    What has happened to Michigan's "public purpose", its "uncommon education for the common man"?

    The University has been selling it to the highest bidder!!!

    Students who can afford $60,000 per year…

    Spectators who can pay on the average $230 per game to sit in Michigan Stadium, and students who can afford $50 per game

    Donors who can buy almost anything they desire (including a monstrous dormitory with 7-student "suites", few windows, and no parking)

    And perhaps a reputation that took two centuries to build!

A summary of the past two decades

    Collapse of state with little change of near-term recovery

    Unconstrained UM growth threatening academic mission

    Driven by auxiliary activities and whims

    Inability to focus on academic priorities

    Possible erosion of quality and public purpose

    Managing and reacting rather than visioning and leading

The University of Michigan Today

    Publicly committed, yet privately supported

    State governed, yet nationally supported

    Priorities: UG up, Grad down; sponsored research up (albeit with University subsidy way up)

    Academic reputation (and faculty quality) up? down?

    Big, bigger, biggest: budget, campus, stadium

    Leadership: decentralized, reactive, or strategic

    Who is shaping UM's future? Faculty? EOs? Regents? Donors?

    Is UM climbing, cruising in level flight, or on a downward glide path?

Major faculty concerns 1

    Lack of priority for academic core

    Imbalance in priorities (academics vs. auxiliaries)

    Erosion of quality (preoccupation with growth, mission creep)

    UM's public purpose in jeopardy

    "Common man" has been replaced by "uncommonly rich man"

    Diversity is dropping rapidly

    Unsustainable financial models

    Trapped in a sinking state (for at least a generation)

Major faculty concerns 2

    Campus culture: complacent, detached, malaise?

    Where is the excitement? The creativity? The innovation?

    Where is the vision? The strategy? The strategic intent?

    Are we drifting away from our heritage?

        Uncommon education for the common man?

        Leaders and best?

        Broad and liberal spirit?

        Pathfinder and trailblazer?

        UM's ability to change the world?

324

Vulnerabilities

Financial sustainability

Out-of-state tuition is approaching a ceiling (e.g., at Ivy League levels); instate tuition is still limited by Regents

States continue to be under pressure for health care, corrections, retirement, and tax relief

Federal research support has been eroding (and the costs of research increasing)

Endowments track with equity markets...up AND down

Competition for gifts is becoming more aggressive

Health care revenues will be affected by Obamacare

Intensifying competitive forces

An intensely Darwinian winner-take-all ecosystem in which the strongest and wealthiest institutions become predators, raiding the best faculty and students of the less generously supported and more constrained public universities and manipulating federal research and financial policies to sustain a system in which the rich get richer and the poor get devoured.

Over the next decade, Harvard's endowment will grow to almost $100 B and Stanford to $50 B. (Michigan's will be at $20 B)

Cultural changes with scale

UM --> MSU, OSU, UT,...???

Auxiliaries increasingly dominate academics

Management increasingly dominates faculty

Leadership (EOs, Deans, Chairs) increasingly distracted by fund-raising

Technology increasingly dominates campuses (MOOCs, connected learning, cognitive tutors, fiber to the forehead)

Intercollegiate athletics increasing dominates both university values and academic integrity (as well as common sense...)

Public Purpose

The current size, financial model, leadership, and governance of the University is incompatible with its public purpose.

Without the restoration of some level of public support and the commitment of governance and leadership, there is simply no way that the University can achieve an acceptable level of participation by low-income and underrepresented minority students.

We will become increasingly a university for the rich...

Academic priorities

The past decade has seen an increasing dominance by auxiliary activities over academic programs, driven both by the revenues available to these enterprises and by exceptionally aggressive leadership.

The voice of the faculty has been weak, particularly at the level of University governance.

The concept of a dean-driven institution has largely been weakened by both inadequate authority and the distraction of deans by fund-raising demands.

Disconnection with UM's saga

From time to time the University of Michigan has become disconnected from its history as "leader and best", a pathfinder for higher education.

During the 1960s, activism and protest destroyed much of the awareness, leading to a "lost decade" of the 1970s, when little of note happened, other than keeping the campus stable.

Fortunately, the 1980s and 190s administration was populated with long-time Michigan faculty and staff who not only understood the importance of Michigan's historical roles but were determined to restore it.

In recent years this tradition of continuity has been seriously weakened.

The recent effort to replace much of the University leadership team (EOs, Deans, key administrators) with the recruiting of an increasing number of outsiders into key university positions threatens the University once again with the loss of connection to its history.

In a very real sense, this could well become another lost decade, as we abandon our heritage as both a pathfinder and leader.

University of Michigan SWOT Analysis

As a final consideration, we have reassembled the various challenges, responsibilities, and opportunities facing the University of Michigan today into a Strengths, Weaknesses, Opportunities, and Threats analysis contained in an appendix to this chapter.

Strengths
Quality
Intellectual breadth and comprehensiveness
Scale
Spirit
Risk-tolerance
Loosely coupled, adaptive, entrepreneurial system
Constitutional autonomy
Decentralization
Pathfinder saga

Weaknesses
Public support
Public governance
Faculty governance (U wide)
Obsolete (unsustainable) financial models
Obsolete public policies (state, federal)
Mission creep
Unconstrained growth of auxiliaries threatening
    academic priorities
Erosion of
    Public Purpose ("common man")
    Public Character (enrollment, athletics, etc.)
    Community activities
    Student activism
    Academic effort, "paying for the party"
    Racial diversity
    First generation college students
Inadequate capacity for strategic change and
    transformation

Opportunities
Need for UM's leadership as pathfinder
Rebalance competition and cooperation
Redefine core mission
Explore new paradigms
Leadership in key areas of vision
    Open Learning

Connectivity
Open Knowledge
Renaissance Campus

Threats
Warning Signs
    Quality
    Erosion of public purpose
    Unbridled (non-strategic) growth
    Financial challenges
    Priorities
        Cloud > core
        Auxiliary > academic;
    Campus evolution
Trapped in a sinking state next to a sinking city
Political hostility, intrusion, manipulation
Public perception
Aggressiveness of auxiliaries (particularly
        Athletics, UMMC, Housing)
Loss of influence of the deans
Opportunistic rather than strategic growth
Disruptive technologies
Public/political awareness
Taken over by PR and marketing; promoting
        myth over reality

What does the SWOT analysis suggest?
Smaller but better?
Restructuring governance, management, leadership
Moving to a federalist model
    Regents --> senate
    Faculty --> house
    EOs --> executive branch
    Deans --> governors
Note: This would require a new constitution!

A summary of the past two decades
Collapse of state with little change of near-term
        recovery
Unconstrained UM growth threatening
        academic mission
Driven by auxiliary activities and whims
Inability to focus on academic priorities
Possible erosion of quality and public purpose
Managing and reacting rather than visioning
        and leading

Chapter 22

The Road Ahead

In considering how the University of Michigan has evolved over the past half-century, the events that have occurred, the actions that have been taken, and the challenges that remain today, a number of possible options for the future have become apparent. In this chapter we pull these ideas together for each of the topics considered earlier to suggest a possible roadmap to the University of Michigan's future.

Growth

It is critical that the University develop a more strategic approach to growth. One of the problems with a loosely coupled adaptive ecosystem is how to control growth, e.g., to prevent explosive growth in some components at the expense of others or even the entire organism. A key is communication among components and across the institution. When such communication is artificially limited or distorted (whether intentional or not), instabilities can set in.

Hence it is important to use a multiplicity of networks both to monitor growth and subject it to assessments of its relationship to University priorities such as quality, financial sustainability, and impact. Bigger is not always better!

Here an excellent example is enrollment growth. Although this allows the University to serve more students, the dramatic growth over the past two decades (over 10,000 students) was clearly driven not by a desire to broaden the University's impact but rather to increase tuition revenue to compensate, in part, for the loss of state support. However in the process enrollment growth has clearly overloaded both faculty and facilities resources, shifting much of instruction to the use of part-time or non-tenure-track faculty and driving the priorities for capital facilities. It has also driven a major private construction boom of high-cost apartment complexes designed for the

The importance of controlling growth

expanding student population.

Hence any strategy for enrollment growth must take into account the impact on faculty, staff, facilities, campus infrastructucture, and the city of Ann Arbor, itself, in addition to priorities such as quality and mission. The desire for additional tuition revenue through enrollment growth should also consider other options such as year-round operation, distance learning, and other forms of Internet-based academic services such as collaboratories and virtual organizations.

Quality

The quality of the University of Michigan academic programs is the most fundamental determinant of its ability to develop and maintain leadership. However, a comprehensive and diverse array of intellectual, social, and cultural experiences is also important for its leadership role in higher education. The scale of our programs not only contributes to the richness and quality of the University (e.g., the size and quality of central resources such as libraries, computing networks, and athletic facilities), but it also determines its potential impact on society. Rather than viewing the quality, breadth, and scale of the University as competing objectives–or possibly even as constraints on what it can accomplish within a world of limited resources–instead these characteristics, when linked together creatively, can provide an unusual opportunity.

Michigan's character as leader through its pathfinding and trailblazing requires it to build "spires of excellence" in key fields, rather than trying to settle for a uniform level of simply good quality across all of its activities. Only by attempting to be the very best in these fields can we develop in our students, faculty, and staff the necessary intensity and commitment to excellence. Furthermore, only by competing with the best can it establish appropriate levels of expectation and achievement.

The theme of pathfinding leadership influences the focus of emphasis within Michigan's traditional endeavors of education, scholarship, and service. On the one hand, the strength of its professional schools and the strong research and scholarly orientation of our faculties should not be compromised. On the other hand, the University needs to generate a fresh commitment to cultivating a spirit of liberal learning among its undergraduates and its faculties, to encourage major efforts to improve the quality of teaching and learning.

In order to develop leaders among its faculties, at least some fraction of its scholarship needs to be shifted to venturesome intellectual activities at the cutting edge of inquiry. Faculty members should also be encouraged to work in seminal, cross-disciplinary areas where extraordinary insight and intellectual breadth can lead to the creation of entirely new fields of knowledge.

The development of leaders among students demands challenging intellectual experiences, both in formal instruction and in the extracurricular environment. Key in these endeavors is the importance of a liberal education. Today's students will enter an increasingly complex, changing, and fragmented world. Too many undergraduates channel their energies into pre-professional and more narrowly vocational directions. The challenge is to cultivate among undergraduates a greater willingness to explore and to discover–to assist undergraduates to develop critical, disciplined, and inquiring minds.

Finally we must again stress the importance of

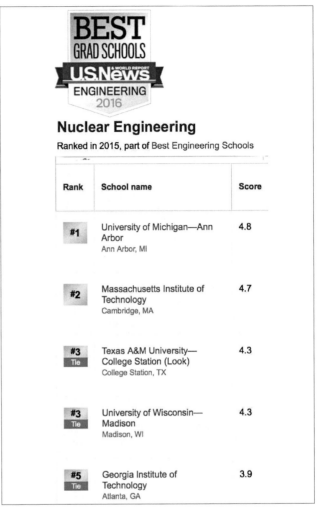

One of UM's true spires of excellence for 50 years!

understanding the history of the University, the nature of our past achievements of academic quality and leadership, and our unique institutional culture. The University's unusual combination of quality, breadth, scale, and spirit not only allow it, but actually *compel* it to provide leadership for higher education through risk taking, path finding, and trail blazing. To this leadership character, one must add the importance of recognizing that the true source of Michigan's excellence and leadership rests with the quality, spirit, and innovation of its people–its faculty, students, and staff–and decidedly not with its administrative leadership or governance. It thrives as a loosely coupled, adaptive organization, drawing its strength, innovation, and vision from the grass roots, from the faculty, students, and staff who embrace deep commitments to academic priorities.

While ingrained in the culture of the institution and shaping the perspective and achievements of its people, such a high degree of decentralization of authority can be a threatening characteristic to those new to the University–particularly to those recruited into leadership positions as deans or executive officers or elected to serve on the University's Board of Regents. Hence the challenge is both to make certain that the selection of University leadership at all levels is balanced among insiders both knowledgeable and committed to the unique history and culture of the University, and those recruited from outside into leadership positions adequately informed and committed to sustaining this culture and its academic priorities.

Balance (Academics vs. Auxiliaries)

Careful consideration should be given to strategic issues of institutional balance and priorities. While the relative scale of different academic programs such as schools and colleges is an important issue for University leadership and governance, perhaps even more so is the balance among academic and auxiliary activities. For example, auxiliary activities such as clinical services, student housing, and intercollegiate athletics have increased in scale (by any measure–financial, personnel, visibility) at a rate considerably faster than that characterizing the core academic activities of the University. While such auxiliary activities certainly are responding to demand, they also have been benefiting from lucrative markets that are relatively price insensitive, thereby fueling substantial growth.

To this end, the University needs to address in a more strategic fashion whether it is appropriate for an academic institution to be responsible for a health system that has already become comparable in size to the academic institution itself (e.g., $3.0 billion/year compared to $3.4 billion/year) or an intercollegiate athletic program that has clearly evolved into a $150 million/year commercial enterprise rather than a student activity. Perhaps the time is approaching for a serious consideration of exploring a different organizational structures (e.g., a holding company of relatively autonomous financial and management units) to govern and manage such rapidly growing auxiliary enterprises so different in character from the academic core of the University.

More generally, how does one sustain the quality and leadership of academic programs in an unusually large and complex institution such as the University of Michigan that is continually challenged to balance rapidly changing challenges, responsibilities, and opportunities? For example, highly selective private institutions sometimes sacrifice breadth and size in an effort to achieve absolute excellence in a small number of fields. This results in institutions highly focused in an intellectual sense, which while certainly capable of conducting very distinguished academic programs, are nevertheless unable to provide the rich array of opportunities and diverse experiences of "multiversities" such as Michigan. At the other end of the spectrum, the University can also set itself apart from many other large, comprehensive public universities by the degree to which it chooses to focus its resources on academic quality.

Students

It is important to achieve the proper balance among undergraduate, graduate, and professional student

The University as a fragile organization balanced between the university hospital and football stadium

Achieving a better balance between "paying for the party" against student service activities

enrollments that characterizes the world's leading research universities. Over the past 15 years enrollments have grown 25% to almost 44,000. However essentially all of this growth has been at the undergraduate level, while graduate and professional enrollment has stayed relatively constant. This major shift in student composition deserves serious strategic attention, since it has strained the faculty and facilities resources that support our graduate and professional programs.

The emphasis on attracting more out-of-state students capable of paying $60,000 for tuition, room and board has generated very substantial new resources, it has also shifted somewhat the student culture, away from the historic mission of "providing an uncommon education for the common man" and, instead, attracting more students from wealthy backgrounds, many of whom selected Michigan as a "safety school" backup to Ivy League applications or have chosen Michigan for its extracurricular life (i.e., have come "paying for the party").

It is important to emphasize here the concern about the low enrollments of students from low-income backgrounds. Much of Michigan's impact in the past came from students from working class families from the state's farms and factories who saw attending the University as a great opportunity to do something important with their lives, provided they worked hard enough. To serve more of these students, once the backbone of its student body, the University must restructure its admissions policies, financial aid, and outreach.

The University also needs to throttle back its reputation as a party school and instead rebrand it as an institution determined to demand the student academic effort required for leadership roles later in life. Although *in loco parentis* disappeared decades ago, the University has learned that it simply cannot ignore the behavior of students beyond the classroom. While most communities of young people experience the challenges of excessive alcohol consumption, drugs, and sexual misconduct and assault, large university communities are particularly vulnerable to these, as evidenced by Michigan's "leadership" in various national polls attempting to rate institutions as "party schools" or tragically, "sexual assault and misconduct". While the University has taken major steps toward addressing these concerns, the very scale and diversity of its many student communities will likely require new approaches.

Here particular attention must be given to "Greek life" on campus, since the unusually large number of students belonging to unregulated fraternities leads to a serious issue of adequate controls, as evidenced by the frequent instances of serious misbehavior and, indeed, even criminal conduct by fraternity members. While there is always a danger to the University in exposing itself to liability in becoming too engaged with these organizations, their damage to the University has been and remains today simply too great to ignore. While it is unrealistic to ban fraternities entirely as some

330

Respecting student activism and protest against injustice

institutions have done, the University must reinforce demands for appropriate behavior with strong penalties for misconduct, both for students as well as for the fraternities as organizations.

Furthermore, the University should urge faculty to challenge, in turn, our students through demanding academic programs. Here a goal might be set of demanding that through course assignments, students spend a minimum of two hours of effort for every one hour of class time, a metric used at leading universities through much of the last century. We also need to provide more opportunities for student engagement with faculty in research, service, and professional activities. Here technology might help, since social networking has largely decoupled such engagement and interactions from space and time constraints.

Finally, on a more positive note, Michigan's long history of student activism, while occasionally challenging to the University's leadership and governance, is an activity of great importance because of its social impact. Michigan must not only tolerate such student activities, including occasional disruption of University activities, but actually encourage it and remain attentive and responsive to student issues. Here, particular concern should be given to maintaining the University's long tradition of "truth and light", by throttling back efforts to manage information flow throughout the institution so that bad news is disguised and good news is marketed heavily. Students deserve the truth, the whole truth, and nothing but the truth from the institution responsible for their education.

The role and experiences of graduate and professional students also deserves attention. In particular, the various concerns of graduate teaching assistants and postdoctoral scholars, raised both by oncampus organizations and national studies such as those conducted by the National Academies, requires attention both at Michigan and at the national level. The fundamental principle is that these members of the University community must be regarded as students and future scholars first, and not just simply as a cost-effective way to conduct instruction and research. Similarly, the nature of professional education is changing rapidly in many fields such as the health sciences, law, education, and business, and once again, Michigan must continue to not only provide leadership as these instructional paradigms shift, but also be attentive to the demands they place among students.

Faculty

Department chairs and deans spend much of their time recruiting new faculty (and persuading their best faculty not to leave). However this amount of faculty retention and recruiting effort is difficult to assess at the University level. To be sure, a provost is usually sensitive to the "wins" and "losses" of a school or college when evaluating deans, but the broader University and its faculty are usually not aware of how the institution is doing in this competition for faculty. To this end, it might be useful to adopt a practice of the 1990s by creating each spring an "Ebb and Flows" chart identifying new faculty hires and losses at the department level, including where the gains came from and where the losses went. This would be analogous to a "business dashboard" exercise in the corporate world.

While the overall strength of the faculty in departments and schools is of great importance to the University, determining the strength of its teaching and research, the visibility of the institution is frequently determined by truly exceptional individuals, so-called "essential singularities", whose intellectual impact is immense. At a large pubic university such as Michigan, these exceptional faculty members usually are first discovered as young hires, before their work has reached the attention of competing institutions. However once their work becomes visible, they are aggressively recruited by many other institutions, particularly leading private institutions such as the Ivy League, MIT, or Stanford, who can focus great resources to recruit them away from Michigan.

The University should think very strategically about how to provide a supportive environment for their unusual brilliance (not the easiest challenge in a community of outstanding scholars) and move them rapidly through the ranks in an effort to hold them to Michigan. At the highest level, the University might consider the creation of professorial chairs with institution-wide appointments, such as the University Professors at the University of California or the Institute Professors at MIT. These provide exceptional faculty members with appointments in all academic units (and campuses in the case of Michigan), funded centrally by the institution, so that they have maximum flexibility for their research and teaching interests.

The disappearance of mandatory retirement age and the vulnerability of defined contribution retirement plans in a fluctuating economy have had a major impact on faculty retirement planning. While financial security certainly influences the retirement plans of faculty members, surveys have indicated many senior faculty also seek some level of continued engagement with their University following retirement, since their intellectual, cultural, and social lives have been shaped by these institutions. Today faculty retirement considerations require more flexibility through options such as phased retirement or part-time appointments. Many universities have developed

specific policies to encourage the engagement of senior faculty in productive roles, such as emeritus-in-service appointments providing them with the opportunity to continue teaching, research, and service at reduced appoint levels.

While the desire to recapture faculty positions for new younger faculty from retiring faculty members within the current environment of limited funding remains a priority for most deans, it is important to recognize that many emeritus faculty members remain among the University's most distinguished, dedicated, and capable teachers and scholars. Hence the emeritus faculty cadre should be viewed as an important asset of the University from a strategic viewpoint.

Finally, it is important to understand that the national leadership of the University of Michigan is due primarily to the national leadership and influence achieved by members of its faculty in several areas:

Intellectual Leadership: e.g., stimulating, defining, and leading a particular field

Teaching Leadership: e.g., developing new pedagogy or reshaping a field through textbooks

Leadership in practice or application of knowledge: e.g., leading in a field of practice such as law or medicine or building a company through technology transfer

Academic leadership: e.g., achieving recognition as a department chair, dean, or university president

There are many paths to such leadership achievements, e.g., through research and scholarship, entrepreneurial activities, pedagogical development (e.g., award winning textbooks that dominate a field, intellectual leadership (e.g., election to a National Academy), and broader academic leadership (as chairs, deans, executive officers, and university presidents). However all of these paths to consequential leadership require not only talent, effort, and persistence, but they also require a supportive environment in the University and influence beyond its campus. Hence the University not only needs to better encourage and recognize the national leadership of its faculty members, but it also needs to create an environment that supports such efforts, identifies and promotes opportunities, and remove barriers to such activities beyond the campus.

Giving higher priority to faculty leadership at the national level

Staff

Throughout the university, whether at the level of secretaries, custodians, or groundskeepers or the rarified heights of senior administrators for finance, hospital operations, or facilities construction and management, the quality of the university's staff, coupled with their commitment and dedication, was actually just as important as the faculty in making Michigan the remarkable institution it has become. In some ways, it has been even more so, since unlike many faculty members, who view their first responsibilities as to their discipline or perhaps their careers, most staff members are true professionals, deeply committed to the welfare of the university as their highest priority, many dedicating their entire careers to the institution. Most staff members serve the university far longer than the faculty, who tend to be lured away by the marketplace.

It is important that the University implement employee development programs comparable in scale and quality. While it is certainly true that many staff members develop unique skills of great value to the University, this should not be used as an excuse to lock them in place. Instead, they should be provided with the opportunity to develop new skills and explore new employment roles. The current University policy of allowing staff to take courses while employed is important to such career advancement.

Although the unique roles of staff throughout such a large, diverse, and highly decentralized organization should be respected, there needs to be a thorough review of salary practices to achieve equity across the institution. There have been too many examples of inexperienced management providing inappropriate compensation through the undisclosed use of bonuses and other forms of one-time compensation, particularly at the central administration level. While making the total compensation of all employees of the University openly available for comparison, it is also appropriate to implement an ongoing compensation review to ascertain inequities that may arise across the university for similar staff roles. Furthermore, the University should move away from the ad-hoc approaches relying on individual management decisions (or higher education compensation consultants) and instead adopt the more rigorous approach to compensation policies demanded by the SEC of Fortune 500 companies by developing, in advance, formula-based compensation policies and then disclosing.

Financials

Clearly, because of the impact of aging populations and the global financial crisis on state and federal budgets and hence on support for higher education, the nation's colleges and universities must intensify their efforts to increase efficiency and productivity in all of their activities. In particular, they should set bold goals for reducing the costs of their ongoing activities. While universities have many differences from business corporations–for example, cost reductions do not

The University must always remember the critical importance of its staff!!!

drop to the bottom line of profits–there is likely a very considerable opportunity for process restructuring in both administrative and academic activities.

Of course, in the face of deep cuts in state appropriations, most public research universities have already been engaged in intense cost-cutting efforts, particularly in non-academic areas such as financial management, procurement, energy conservation, competitive bidding of services, and eliminating unnecessary regulation and duplication. But many have also chosen to limit employee compensation and throttle back staff benefits as a tempting target, although this has put at risk their capacity to attract and retain outstanding faculty and staff.

Furthermore, many universities have chosen to implement actions recommended by consultants and adopted from the corporate world without due regard to the unique character of the university environment, thereby disrupting the academic mission and damaging employee morale. Rather than distracting Michigan with such penny-wise and pound-foolish actions such as "shared services" (that will undercut the staff support of our teaching and research) or IT "rationalization" (that will stifle the innovation and creativity in our academic units), while achieving only marginal savings (less than 1% on the average), we should consider "pound-wise and penny-foolish" approaches that would have very major impact on the University.

1. Re-establish the control of the Provost over budgets, expenditures, and financial discipline by recreating the Committee on Budget Administration and the Budget Priorities Committee, both chaired or reporting to the Provost.

From 1970 to 2000, the authority as chief budget officer of the Provost was sustained by the Executive Officers convened as the Committee on Budget Administration and chaired by the Provost and by the Budget Priorities Committee, a blue-ribbon body comprised of faculty, staff, deans, and executive officers reporting to the Provost. Note the Provost maintained control over all operating and capital expenditures through these mechanisms, a control and discipline authority that is clearly missing today.

2. Build a network of experienced financial managers throughout the University with dotted line reporting relationships to the EVPCFO to maintain both reliability and consistency in financial controls.

The role of experienced financial managers in each of the many academic units is critical since most deans and chairs come from the ranks of faculty rather inexperienced in such management and financial roles. The EVPCFO should not only maintain a network of contacts with these managers at the unit level, capable of providing assistance or warnings when necessary, but should also be involved to some degree in both the appointment and evaluation of these staff. As noted, it is this informal network of experienced management staff in the units linking to the EVPCFO that is the key

334

Building stronger relations between EOs and Regents

Moving to year-round operation including summers

to the financial integrity of such a massive and highly decentralized institution.

3. The Provost and EVPCFO should implement a series of actions to establish greater discipline and cost containment.

All capital projects that are either not fully funded (for BOTH capital expenditures and operating costs) or central to the academic programs of the University should be carefully re-evaluated. Similarly, private gifts that either do not address significant University priorities or entail significant additional expenditures should be declined. It is absolutely essential that the Executive Officers constrain those activities that convey a false impression of the University's prosperity or compete with the academic core for resources. Any auxiliary or University-related activities that compete directly with academic units for private giving or University subsidy should be constrained. Finally, the salaries of senior administrators, including the President, should be clearly linked to faculty and staff salaries rather than simply market-driven (which is largely a fictitious rationale for compensating what are "public callings" similar to many government positions).

4. Moving to year-round operation

It is time that the University seriously considered moving to year-round operation at full capacity. One

can no longer justify the idle use of expensive fixed-cost capital facilities for instruction or student residence during the spring-summer months, particularly since these have now been renovated to handle year-round operation. Furthermore, since today state support provides for only 8% of instructional activities, it is no longer necessary for expanding the instructional calendar to subsidize the spring-summer months. Indeed, with over 50,000 applications for admission to the University, there is ample demand capable of generating adequate student tuition and fees to support year round activity.

Moving to a three-term year-round calendar would provide students additional flexibility in how they schedule their instructional program. In fact, students entering with advanced placement credits could conceivably earn a bachelor's degree in two years by enrolling year-round, thereby providing as well very considerable savings in the cost of their education (particularly through both living costs and additional employment opportunities).

While it is true that many faculty members use the spring-summer term for research, the University could rely on senior and/or emeritus faculty as the major teaching staff for the summer (perhaps negotiating a reduced salary).

5. Tax auxiliary units to support the academic core

The auxiliary units of the University, i.e., hospitals,

Take care to avoid the "edifice complex" and demand full funding of donor-initiated facilities

student housing, intercollegiate athletics, depend heavily on the reputation and capacity of the academic core of the institution. Furthermore the auxiliaries currently operate in a less price sensitive market and are less constrained by political issues than tuition (e.g., Regents).

Hence it seems perfectly appropriate (albeit controversial) to "tax" the expenditures of the auxiliary units to help support the academic core. Indeed, such a tax on expenditures might provide an additional brake on unnecessary spending, such as capital facilities expansion.

6. Implement a statewide effort to restore state higher education appropriations

During the 1980s and 1990s the University successfully led a statewide coalition of public universities and their most influential alumni to make the case for state support (the so-called "treetops" strategy). During the past decade there has been little effort to build such a unified approach. It is clearly time to repeat the "treetops" strategy of the 1990s to restore state appropriations to earlier inflation-adjusted levels. (A detailed plan is suggested later in this chapter.)

Facilities

While capital facilities (or bricks and mortar) are necessary and important assets for the teaching,

research, and service activities of a university, they also have other characteristics that can pose risks. For example, they sometimes have a monumental character, symbolizing the history and tradition of an institution. Hence they provide an important objective for university leaders, from deans to presidents to trustees, to build something designed by a "big name architect" to symbolize the impact of their leadership. In a similar way, many donors have an edifice complex, designing to mark the campus with a major facility bearing their name. It is perhaps not surprising that these other objectives sometimes conflict with the actual need for the building or the serious consideration of its construction and long-term operating costs.

Here the recommendation is that the University should think very carefully about the financial burden it is assuming by building an edifice for a donor. It should at least demand a gift in excess of 50% of the actual construction costs in constant dollars. It might even consider seeking an additional endowment to provide further support for the operations of the facility.

Name-brand architects are another problem, since they are interested in making a statement just as a dean or president or governing board is. And the result can be an expensive facility that will haunt further leadership and governance of the institution for years to come. Such commissions should be seriously considered and balanced against the costs of using local architect-engineering services.

Technology

The University of Michigan has been able to respond to rapid technological change in the past–and, indeed, achieved leadership–because it has functioned as a loosely coupled adaptive system with many of our academic units given not only the freedom, but also the encouragement, to experiment and to try new things. We have intentionally avoided the dangers of centralizing these activities.

To be sure, the tension between centralization (commodity technology and "rationalization") and decentralization (where cacophony leads to innovation) can be very threatening, particularly to those parts of the University that need to make the trains run on time (e.g., financial services, hospitals, etc.) Fortunately, in the past, the wisdom of maintaining a loosely coupled adaptive system at the academic level finally bubbles up to the leadership of the institution, and the IT efforts academic units are set free once again.

It is important not to attempt to standardize the campus cyberinfrastructure environment. The university in general–and Michigan in particular–is one of the most intellectual diverse organizations in the world. In fact, its great strength and contribution to society arises from this very unusual diversity in ideas, experiences, and people. Again, this argues for a much more organic plan, essentially a diverse ecosystem that will continue to mutate and evolve in ways that we cannot anticipate. While dependence on commodity services, particularly those provided through the cloud, can be cost-effective, it can also become highly constraining for the creative enterprise characterizing research universities. Overdependence on commodity products can become debilitating to the academic process, particularly to the degree we constrain the cyber environments of academic units through policies such as purchasing and shared services, that can harm the loosely coupled adaptive culture of the university that is one of our greatest strengths.

To be sure, the University has important responsibilities that require mission critical computing. But it is at the level of academic units rather than the enterprise level where innovation and leadership must occur. Why? Because they are driven by learning and discovery, by experimentation, by tolerance for failure, and by extraordinarily talented faculty, students, and particularly, staff.

Leadership

The role of leaders in a major public research university such as Michigan is complicated by its scale and diversity, comparable to that of global corporations or government agencies. Today's university conducts many activities, some nonprofit, some publicly regulated, and some operating in intensely competitive marketplaces. Universities teach students, conduct research for various clients, provide health care, engage in economic development, stimulate social change, and provide mass entertainment (e.g., college sports). Of course the university also has higher purposes such as preserving our cultural heritage, challenging the norms and beliefs of our society, and preparing the educated citizens necessary to sustain our democracy.

Few university leaders are powerful enough to change the culture of their institution much less its historical saga, since both have evolved over generations of students, faculty, staff, and leaders. Indeed, institutions such as Michigan tend to shape its leadership rather than vice versa, and if leaders fail to adjust to its culture, they are usually repelled or at least sequestered so they can do little harm.

To be sure, it is important to seek a balance in leadership, bringing in leaders from outside for new ideas and energy while relying on internal appointments to sustain important traditions and values. When this balance is distorted, perhaps due to complacency with the status quo, or more serious, an effort by newcomers, frustrated with the Universilyty's resistance to change, to bring in too many outsiders in key roles as deans or executive officers in an effort to change the culture of the institutions. Fortunately, the decentralized organization of the University is not only capable of responding to a changing environment but also repelling invasive species that attempt dramatic change.

So what balance should be sought? Certainly the majority of deans should be chosen from inside, perhaps in a ratio of two to one over outsiders. To be sure this is difficult in an era in which universities are increasingly dependent upon executive search consultants, tempted to push their existing stable of external candidates

The importance of building a close relationship between Deans and Regents

and motivated by compensation indexed to the compensation negotiated by selected candidates. At the executive officer level, perhaps a balance closer to 50%-50% seems best, balancing internal and external experiences.

It is important in these days of increasing public concerns about the costs of higher education, that the role of the university president be clearly defined as one of public service rather than corporate leadership and compensated accordingly. Leading an academic institution should be characterized as a duty similar to those of other public leadership roles such as mayors, governors, and, indeed, United States presidents. It is a high calling to service, and to allow aggressive search consultants, ambitious candidates, or inexperienced boards to suggest otherwise in determining excessive compensation puts American higher education at considerable risk. Instead presidential and executive compensation should be closely linked to faculty salaries. (And, of coursre, the same can be recommended for coaches and athletic directors...)

Finally it is very important to view leadership development as a strategic issue for the University. Every effort should be made to encourage and support such activities, providing opportunities for further leadership experiences, albeit with strong evaluation of leadership ability. Interestingly enough, since such leadership usually requires not only time and effort, but also sacrificing one's scholarly activity, such willingness to participate in faculty service should be recognized as a sign of possible leadership interest.

Governance

The contemporary university has many activities, many responsibilities, many constituencies, and many overlapping lines of authority, and from this perspective, shared governance models still have much to recommend them: a tradition of public oversight and trusteeship, shared collegial internal governance of academic matters, and, experienced administrative leadership. But it also seems clear that the university of the twenty-first century will require new forms of governance and leadership capable of responding to the changing needs and emerging challenges of our society and its educational institutions. Governing board members should be selected for their expertise and commitment and then held accountable for their performance and the welfare of their institutions. Faculty governance should focus on those issues of most direct concern to academic programs, and faculty members should be held accountable for their decisions. Our institutions must not only develop a tolerance for strong presidential leadership; they should demand it.

As the contemporary university becomes more complex and accountable, it may even be time to set aside the quaint American practice of governing universities with boards comprised of lay citizens, with their limited expertise and all too frequently political character, and instead shift to true boards of directors similar to those used in the private sector. Although it may sound strange in these times of scandal and corruption in corporate management,

338

there is increasing evidence today that university governing boards should function with a structure and a process that reflects the best practices of corporate boards. Corporate board members are selected for their particular expertise in areas such as business practices, finance, or legal matters. They are held accountable to the shareholders for the performance of the corporation. Their performance is reviewed at regular intervals, both within the board itself and through more external measures such as company financial performance. Clearly, directors can be removed either through action of the board or shareholder vote. Furthermore, they can be held legally and financially liable for the quality of their decisions–a far cry from the limited accountability of the members of most governing boards for public universities.

The key to effective faculty governance is to provide faculty bodies with true executive powers rather than merely advisory authority, thereby earning the active participation of the university's leading faculty members. Advisory bodies, paid only lip service by the administration or the board of trustees, rarely attract the attention or the participation of those faculty most actively engaged in scholarship and teaching. The faculty should become a true participant in the academic decision process rather than simply a watchdog on the administration or defenders of the status quo. Faculty governance should focus on those issues of most direct concern to academic programs, and faculty members should be held accountable for their decisions. Faculties also need to accept and acknowledge that strong leadership, whether from chairs, deans, or presidents, is important if their institution is to flourish, particularly during a time of rapid social change.

Because of the unusual nature of faculty governance at Michigan, vested in both university-wide structures such as the Senate Assembly and school and department level executive committees, some specific suggestions are appropriate for our University. First it is essential that the voice of the faculty on both academic and institutional matters be strengthened by restoring the executive powers of school and college executive committees.To this end, it is important that newly appointed deans understand both the bylaws and past practices that have granted and recognized the executive powers characterizing these bodies.

Consideration should also be given to strengthening the Senate Assembly and the Senate Advisory Committee on University Affairs, both by providing some degree of executive authority and perhaps a new structure capable of attracting the engagement of the University's most distinguished faculty members into service on these bodies. One possiblity would be to move to a bicameral organization comprised of both elected faculty members from general ranks ("the house") and a "senate" of appointed senior faculty with endowed or honorific chairs.

More generally, it is appropriate to question whether the key participants in shared governance– the lay governing board, elected faculty governance, and academic administrators–have the expertise, the discipline, and the authority, not to mention the accountability, necessary to cope with the powerful social, economic, and technological forces driving change in our society and its institutions. More specifically, is it realistic to expect that the shared governance mechanisms developed decades (or, in some cases, centuries) ago can serve well the contemporary university or the society dependent upon its activities? Can boards comprised of lay citizens, with little knowledge either of academic matters or the complex financial, management, and legal affairs of the university be expected to provide competent oversight for the large, complex institutions characterizing American higher education? What is the appropriate role for the faculty in university governance, and is this adequately addressed by the current determination and conduct of faculty governing bodies? Can academics with limited experience in management serve as competent administrators (deans, provosts, presidents)? And, finally (and most speculatively), what works, what does not, and what to do about it?

The complexity of the contemporary university and the forces acting upon it have outstripped the ability of the current shared governance system of lay boards, elected faculty bodies, and academic administrators to govern, lead, and manage. It is simply unrealistic to expect that the governance mechanisms developed decades or even centuries ago are appropriate for the contemporary university. To blind ourselves to these realities is to perpetuate a disservice to those whom we serve, both present and future generations.

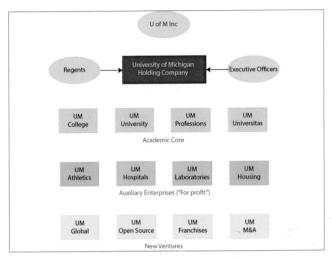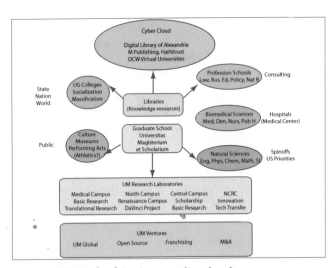

Any new organizations and management must respect UM's highly decentralized culture

Organization and Management

While the decentralization of authority and accountability throughout the University was radical when introduced in the 1980s and 1990s in response to the decline in centrally obtained resources such as state support, it aligned well with the increasing complexity and scale of the University that evolved beyond centralized control. The trail-blazer character of the Michigan saga demands a risk-tolerant environment in which initiatives are encouraged at all levels among students, faculty, and staff. For example, the university intentionally distributes resources among a number of pots, so that entrepreneurial faculty with good ideas rarely have to accept "no" as an answer but instead can simply turn to another potential source of support.

Hence, the message that today should be provided to all new leadership recruited from outside is that "Michigan exists today and must remain highly decentralized in authority, and its evolution must be driven by the talent, achievements, and goals of faculty, students, and staff at the grass-roots level. Don't attempt to challenge this. Learn how to live with it!"

From this discussion, it should be apparent that a top-down leadership style is quite incompatible with the Michigan culture. Those presidents who have chosen to ignore this reality or attempted to reign in this distributed power, to tame the Michigan anarchy, have inevitably failed, suffering a short tenure with inconsequential impact. Not to suggest that Michigan

will tolerate a weak president. Presidents unable to adapt to the Michigan trailblazing saga, who are hesitant to push all the chips into the center of the table on a major initiative or incapable of keeping pace with the high energy level of the campus, will soon be rejected–or at least ignored–by the faculty. Michigan embraces bold visions, and without these, effective leadership is simply impossible.

Yet, as the influence of powerful forces such as the changing needs of society, globalization, and technology reshape the activities of the university, one can expect its organization and structure to continue to evolve, albeit while preserving its decentralized character. Many research universities are already evolving into so-called "core in cloud" organizations in which academic departments or schools conducting elite education and basic research, are surrounded by a constellation of quasi-academic organizations—research institutes, think tanks, corporate R&D centers—that draw intellectual strength from the core university and provide important financial, human, and physical resources in return. Such a structure reflects the blurring of basic and applied research, education and training, the university and broader society.

Missions

Education

Today the university is caught between the contradictory forces of responding to more pragmatic

340

The University's primary activities must remain learning and scholarship, e.g., lux et veritas (shown here with Governor Rick Snyder and Professor Gary Was in his laboratory).

goals of students and employers while providing the liberal education that provides a student with the broader skills important for good citizenship and a meaningful life. Furthermore, in a world of ever-changing needs, one objective of an undergraduate education certainly must be to prepare a student for a lifetime of learning. The old saying that the purpose of a college education is not to prepare a student for their first job but rather their last job still has a ring of truth.

Today's college graduates will face a future in which perpetual education will become a lifetime necessity since they are likely to change jobs, even careers, many times during their lives. To prepare for such a future, students need to acquire the ability and the desire to continue to learn, to become comfortable with change and diversity, and to appreciate both the values and wisdom of the past while creating and adapting to the new ideas and forms of the future. These objectives are, of course, those that one generally associates with a liberal education.

There is a certain irony here. The contemporary university provides one of the most remarkable learning environments in our society—an extraordinary array of diverse people with diverse ideas supported by an exceptionally rich array of intellectual and cultural resources. Yet we tend to focus most of our efforts to improve undergraduate education on traditional academic programs, on the classroom and the curriculum. In the process, we may have overlooked the most important learning experiences in the university.

There seems little doubt that the undergraduate experience needs to be reconsidered from a far broader perspective. Better alignment with the multiple missions of the university—providing undergraduates with education through teaching, research, and service—would seem an appropriate goal for most universities. All too frequently each of the missions of the university is associated with a different component—a liberal education and teaching with the undergraduate program, research with the graduate school, and practical service with professional schools. However, in reality, all components of the university should be involved in all of its missions—particularly undergraduate education.

Research

A decade into the 21st century, a resurgent America must stimulate its economy, address new threats, and position itself in a competitive world transformed by technology, global competitiveness, and geopolitical change. Educated people, the knowledge they produce, and the innovation and entrepreneurial skills they possess, particularly in the fields of science and engineering, have become key to America's future.

Restoring the nation's research capacity will require a balanced set of commitments by each of the partners–federal government, state governments, research universities, and business and industry–to provide leadership for the nation in a knowledge-intensive world and to develop and implement enlightened policies, efficient operating practices, and necessary investments.

The federal government must re-establish campus based research as a national priority, honoring earlier commitments such as the America COMPETES Act and doubling the support of NIH, reducing unnecessary regulations that increase administrative costs, impede research productivity, and deflect creativity energy without substantially improving the research environment.

Over the past two decades, in the face of shifting public priorities and weak economies, states have decimated the support of their public research universities, cutting appropriations per enrolled student by an average of 35 percent, totaling more than $15 billion each year nationally. As the leader of one prominent private university put it, "The states are methodically dismantling their public universities where the majority of the nation's campus research is conducted and two-thirds of its scientists, engineers, physicians, teachers, and other knowledge professionals are produced."

Hence, the nation must challenge the states to recognize that the devastating cuts and meddlesome regulations imposed on their public research universities is not only harming their own future, but also putting at great risk the nation's prosperity, health, and security. While strongly encouraging the states to begin to restore adequate support of these institutions as the economy improves, they should also be urged to move rapidly to provide their public research universities with sufficient autonomy and agility to navigate an extended period with limited state support.

It is important that the relationship between business and higher education should shift from that of a customer-supplier—of graduates and intellectual property—to a peer-to-peer partnership nature, stressing collaboration in areas of joint interest and requiring joint commitment of resources.

Although universities seek high efficiency in their teaching and research–particularly public universities in the face of eroding state support, it is essential that the nation's research universities strive even harder to address the concerns of the American public that their costs are out of control. To this end,

universities should set and achieve bold goals in cost-containment, efficiency, and productivity. They should strive to constrain the cost escalation of all continuing activities—academic and auxiliary—to the national inflation rate or less through improved efficiency and productivity. This will require the development of more powerful, strategic tools for financial management and cost accounting, tools that better enable universities to determine the most effective methods for containing costs and increasing productivity and efficiency. It is essential that universities, working together with key constituencies, intensify efforts to educate people about the distinct character of American research universities and cease promoting activities that create a public sense of unbridled excess on campuses.

Service

Our institutions need a continually refreshed vision of their role that responds to the ever-changing needs of the society we serve. As we evolve along with broader society, the linkages between us become more varied, complex, and interrelated. Within this context of change, it is clear that public service must continue to be an important responsibility of the American university. Yet it is important to always remember that education and scholarship are the primary functions of a university, its primary contributions to society, and hence the most significant roles of the faculty. When universities become overly distracted by other activities, they not only compromise this core mission but they also erode their priorities within our society.

Community

So, how might the University begin to rebuild some of the communities and resources that have disappeared over the past two decades? Put another way, how might they glue back together broken communities? First, it is important to counter those practices that tend to compete with academic communities, such as:

Stressing once again that the primary role of chairs and deans is not fund-raising but rather academic leadership, and the constituencies they serve are students and faculty, not wealthy donors.

342

Seeking a better balance between external and internal appointments for key leadership positions (e.g., chairs, deans, executive officers, and president), perhaps by countering the external bias of search consultants.

Achieving a better balance between the attention given to the priorities of academic and auxiliary units. To be sure, units such as the University Medical Center, University Housing, and the Athletics Department do have access to vast resources. But the heart and purpose of a university are learning and scholarship, and whether prosperous or not, these activities and their associated communities involing faculty and students must be given the priority.

Placing a much higher priority on creating and sustaining places where communities of students, faculty, staff, and leaders can regularly meet and discuss key issues, e.g., the Inglis House estate, the Michigan Union, and perhaps an emeritus faculty club.

Neighborhood

Many of the most powerful forces driving change in higher education come from the marketplace, driven by new societal needs, the limited availability of resources, rapidly evolving technologies, and the emergence of new competitors such as for-profit ventures. Clearly, in such a rapidly changing environment, agility and adaptability become important attributes of successful institutions.

In looking back over the past five decades, the University has been most effective in stimulating new state investments when the times are the toughest. In the early 1980s, after Michigan had lost roughly one-third of its state support, Harold Shapiro was able to leverage his "smaller but better" philosophy into a strategic effort to restore state funding of operations and capital facilities along with unusual programs such as the Research Excellence Fund, which gave highest priority to the state's research universities. Then again, at the bottom of a similar trough in the state's economy in 1990, Michigan was able to unite the state's public universities (and particularly UM, MSU, and WSU) in a "treetops" alumni strategy, activating key alumni leadership across the state, protecting institutional autonomy (meaning tuition control), triggering capital outlay support, and electing a new governor more supportive of higher education.

The University of Michigan needs to develop and then provide strong leadership for a full-court press effort aimed at public education that will likely take several years to have the desired effect. While the president of the University will play the key role as public spokesperson for this effort, it is important to leverage leadership with a carefully designed and highly strategic communications effort. Put most simply, the University's communications operation must become much more of the type of a marketing effort one would find in a political campaign, complete with sophisticated polling, market segmentation, and a highly strategic media plan. Our state relations operation should operate more like a development campaign, identifying and cultivating key alumni in each legislative district focused on political influence–akin to the NRA. In fact, the similarity of the effort to a development campaign suggests that our own development staff might well be a third member of this team.

Public Purpose

We must always keep in mind that the University of Michigan is a public university, created as the first such institution in a young nation, evolving in size, breadth, and quality, but always committed to a truly public purpose of "providing an uncommon education for the common man". Today there is an even more urgent reason why the University must once again elevate diversity to a higher priority as it looks toward the future: the rapidly changing demographics of America

The increasing diversity of the American population with respect to culture, race, ethnicity, and nationality is both one of our greatest strengths and most serious challenges as a nation. A diverse population gives us great vitality. However, the challenge of increasing diversity is complicated by social and economic factors. Today, far from evolving toward one America, our society continues to be hindered by the segregation and non-assimilation of minority and immigrant cultures. If we do not create a nation that mobilizes the talents of all of our citizens, we are destined for a diminished

An interesting contrast between the car of one of our "paying for the party" students and a reception for the new HAIL program aimed at recruiting low-income students!

role in the global community and increased social turbulence. Higher education plays an important role both in identifying and developing this talent. And the University of Michigan faces once again a major challenge in reclaiming its leadership in building a diverse campus.

The most immediate challenge is to restore a significant need-based financial aid program at the state level capable of augmenting the modest Pell Grants received by low income students to enable them to attend college. Next, there needs to be serious effort to better define the mission of the state's community colleges in preparing students for further university education and developing appropriate articulation agreements to support this transition. Finally, it is absolutely essential to the future of the State of Michigan and the welfare of its people that it begin to restore adequate support for higher education. Michigan's ranking in the bottom 10% in its ranking of state support for higher education is not only embarrassing but also indicative of why the state's economic performance today and in the future will similarly lag the rest of the nation.

Restoring the University's diversity will require not only a serious restructuring of Michigan's financial strategies, but even more important, a renewed commitment to the fundamental public purpose that has guided the University for almost two centuries. While the University of Michigan's concerted effort to generate support from other patrons, particularly through private giving and sponsored research, it

simply must realize that these will never be sufficient to support a world-class university of this size, breadth, or impact. Without substantial public support, it is unrealistic to expect that public universities can fulfill their public purpose.

Hence the highest priority should be to re-engage with the people of Michigan to convince them of the importance of investing in public higher education and unleashing the constraints that prevent higher education from serving all of the people of this state. This must become a primary responsibility of not only the leadership of the University, but its Regents, faculty, students, staff, alumni, and those Michigan citizens who depend so heavily on the services provided by one of the great universities of the world.

Of particular interest are several new approaches:

Learn Grants: To provide strong incentives, the idea would be to provide EVERY student with a "529 college savings account", a "Learn-Grant", when they begin kindergarten. An initial contribution of, say, $10,000 (say, a $5,000 federal grant with a state $5,000 match) would accumulate over their K-12 education to an amount that when coupled with other financial aid would likely be sufficient for their college education at a public college or university. The Learn Grants would in themselves provide a critical incentive for succeeding in K-12 and preparing for a college education.

A National Commitment to Livelong Learning: The nation would commit itself to the goal of providing universal access to lifelong learning opportunities to all its citizens, thereby enabling participation in the world's most advanced knowledge and learning society. While the ability to take advantage of educational opportunity always depends on the need, aptitude, aspirations, and motivation of the student, it should not depend on one's socioeconomic status. Access to lifelong learning opportunities should be a *civil right* for all rather than a privilege for the few if the nation is to achieve prosperity, security, and social well being in the global, knowledge-and value-based economy of the 21st century.

A Call for Generational Responsibility: It should be the baby-boomers generation legacy to ensure that our nation accepts a responsibility as a democratic society to provide all of its citizens with the educational, learning, and training opportunities they need and deserve, throughout their lives, thereby enabling both individuals and the nation itself to prosper in an ever more competitive global economy. While the ability to take advantage of educational opportunity will always depend on the need, aptitude, aspirations, and motivation of the student, it should not depend on one's socioeconomic status.

Chapter 23

The Third Century

Throughout this book we have drawn on an array of personal experiences, memories, perceptions, and perhaps a few misunderstandings from our years at University of Michigan. This effort was motivated in part by the fact that as the University celebrates its Bicentennial in 2017, the Duderstadts will reach their 50th year of service to the institution. Hence it seemed like an interesting exercise to chart the course of the University over this period in an effort to develop a few ideas about the road ahead. In this final chapter we turn from the past to the future, to possible themes for the University of Michigan's third century.

Of course, developing a vision for the future of the University of Michigan is a challenging exercise, even for the two of us who have personally experienced a quarter of its history. The unusual size, breadth, and complexity of the institution and the important leadership role it has played in American higher education make any such visioning effort complex indeed.

Yet today we believe the University of Michigan faces a pivotal moment in its history, a fork in the road. Taking one path can, with dedication and commitment, preserve the University as a distinguished–indeed, a great–university, but only one among many such institutions. We believe, however, there is another path, a path that will require a bold vision, courage, and creativity in addition to dedication and commitment. By taking this second path, the University can seek not only to sustain its quality and distinction, but it would seek to embrace its long history as a leader–indeed, a pathfinder–for not simply higher education but for the nation and the world at large.

The Foundations of a Vision for the University of Michigan's Future

To develop a suitable vision for this planning effort we have begun with the most important values of the institution, for example, quality, academic priority, leadership, liberal learning, diversity, critical and rational inquiry, caring, commitment, and community. We have also kept in mind the key characteristics of the University over its history, as framed by descriptors such as "the leaders and best", "an uncommon education for the common man", "a broad and liberal spirit", "diverse, yet united in a commitment to academic excellence and public service", "a center of critical inquiry and learning", "an independent critic and servant of society", "a relish for innovation and excitement", "control of our own destiny comparable to private universities", and "freedom with responsibility for students and faculty". Finally we have extensively surveyed the powerful forces driving change in our world and higher education and evaluated the position of the University of Michigan within this framework for the decades ahead.

And, like Michigan's earlier visions, a vision for

The Knowledge Economy
Demographic Change
Globalization
Technology
Innovation
Global Sustainability

→

Societal Needs
Technology Drivers
Financial Imperatives
Market Forces

→

Evolution?
Revolution?
Extinction?

The forces driving change in higher education

Developing a vision for a hazy future

the University's third century should flow up from the imagination and inspiration of the faculty, students, and staff who are deeply engaged in the University's academic mission.

The Theme for the Near Term: Reflection

For the near term, from now until the Bicentennial Year 2017-2018, we suggest the University of Michigan would benefit from a period of reflection upon its remarkable history and accomplishments. The University community should not simply prepare to celebrate two centuries of leadership in higher education, but it first should strive to understand and secure those values and characteristics that have played such an important role throughout its history:

Academic quality: The reputation of Michigan as one of the world's great universities has been based primarily on the quality of its academic programs. While there are many sources of superficial rankings (e.g., US News & World Report, the London Times, Shanghai Jaio Tong, and the QS World Rankings), it would seem appropriate for the University to attempt a more rigorous and sustained assessment of its quality, analogous to the important resource provided by the Michigan Almanac or perhaps even similar to a "business dashboard". Of course, key in this effort would be not only an ongoing assessment of the quality of students, faculty, and academic programs, but also major contributions of the University.

Establishing and sustaining the academic core of the University as its highest priority: Sometimes in the face of the substantial assets and growth characterizing auxiliary activities of the University (e.g., hospitals, housing, athletics), it is all to easy to forget that Michigan's impact on the state, nation, and world is determined primarily by the quality of its academic programs and the achievements of its faculties. This must always be clearly established and understood as the University's highest priority. The University of Michigan is not primarily a hospital, a hotel, or a football team. It is one of the great learning institutions of the world.

Diversity: The University has long been distinguished by its strong and sustained commitment to providing educational and faculty opportunities to underrepresented racial and ethnic populations. From its earliest efforts to enroll minority students in the 19th century to the BAM activism of the 1960s, to the Michigan Mandate of the 1990s, the University has long been viewed as, and must remain a national leader in the achievement of diversity. Despite the challenges it faces, the University simply must renew its commitment to regain this leadership. Failure is not an option.

Public Purpose: So too, the University's long-standing commitment to providing "an uncommon education for the common man" demands that it provide educational opportunities for students from all economic circumstances. While this has become increasingly difficult in the face of eroding state support, it nevertheless is both a core value of the University and a critical element of its public purpose. It simply must take those actions necessary to restore a more equitable socioeconomic balance in its student body.

Spirit: Michigan's "broad and liberal spirit" has been an important characteristic of our students, faculty, and staff. While this may at times annoy or antagonize the politics that swirl about the institution, such activism is not only an important element of our heritage but at times represents the conscience of the nation on controversial issues. This spirit must always be not only respected and tolerated but furthermore encouraged on the part of the University community.

Leadership: The University of Michigan has long taken pride in its "leaders and best" heritage, seeking both leadership and excellence in its achievements. Key in establishing and sustaining this element of our character is setting bold goals where the University not only aspires to excellence but can have great impact on society, where it can change the world!

The Michigan Saga: Finally, the role of the University in serving as both a pathfinder and trailblazer for all of higher education remains one of its most important roles. To sustain this role requires attracting to the University students, faculty, staff, and leadership of unusual initiative, creativity, and determination.

While renewing the effort (or restoring our commitment) to achieve these characteristics seems obvious, particularly as we prepare for the University's bicentennial by reviewing its history and honoring its heritage and saga, it is nevertheless in the spirit of the near term vision that we suggest the University should set out to challenge itself.

The Theme for the Next Generation: *Renaissance*

The world is changing rapidly, driven by the role played by educated people, new knowledge, innovation, and entrepreneurial skill. While these forces challenge us and our social institutions, they also contain the elements of what could become a *renaissance* of creativity and innovation in the 21st century. Since universities will play a critical role as the source of these assets of the age of knowledge, our vision for the early 21st century involves stressing similar characteristics among our people and our programs, e.g., creativity, innovation, ingenuity, invention, and entrepreneurial zeal. Put another way, the future university must add to its traditional motto of *lux et veritas*, the scholarly to discover *truth* and the learning to *enlighten* society, the mission of *genius* itself, of the creativity demanded by an ever changing world.

Of course while learning and scholarship have long been viewed as missions of the university, so too has been the creation of new knowledge across all intellectual and professional disciplines. Developing new approaches to scholarship, great works in literature and the arts, ingenious approaches to investigating physical and social phenomenon, these have long been the goal of most scholars. Not just to preserve and transmit knowledge, but to actually create it.

In fact, Ralph Waldo Emerson suggested the importance of creativity to the university's mission almost two centuries ago in his 1837 Address to Phi Beta Kappa that to the traditional missions of veritas (the search for truth) and *lux* (the enlightenment provided by learning), one should add *genius*, the power of creativity:

> *"Colleges have their indispensable office, to teach elements. But they can only serve us when they aim not to drill but to create; when they gather from far every ray of various genius to their hospitable halls, and by the concentrated fires, set the hearts of their youth aflame.."*.

The professions that have dominated the late 20th Century—and to some degree, the late 20th Century university—have been those which manipulate and rearrange knowledge and wealth rather than create it; professions such as law, business, accounting, and politics. Yet it is becoming increasingly clear that the driving intellectual activity of the 21st Century will be the act of creation itself, as suggested by Jacques Attali in his provocative forecasts for the 21st century at the turn of the Millennium:

> "The winners of this new era will be creators, and it is to them that power and wealth will flow. The need to shape, to invent, and to create will blur the border between production and consumption. Creation will not be a form of consumption anymore, but will become work itself, work that will be rewarded handsomely. The creator who turns dreams into reality will be considered as workers who deserve prestige and society's gratitude and remuneration." (Jacques Attali, 2000)

But today the new tools of creativity are appearing characterized by extraordinary power. We have the capacity to create new objects literally atom by atom. With new methods in molecular biology such as CRISPR and gene drive, we can not only precisely modify the

DNA code for a living organism, but actually cause it to propagate through a species to change future generations (a frightening thought when human gene editiing is considered). The dramatic pace of evolution of information technology shows no sign of slowing, continuing to advance in power from 100 to 1000 fold a decade, enabling not only new forms of analysis such augmenting the traditional tools of experiment and theory with the sophisticated tools of data analysis (big data). Indeed, the tools of artificial intelligence not only are rapidly progress but have stimulate fears of eventual sentient behavior of machines. These tools also have changed the opportunities available in literature, performace, and art, with powerful tools of investigation and display (e.g., the CGI techniques increasingly dominating the film industry.)

Already we are seeing the spontaneous emergence of new forms of creative activities, e.g., the "maker" fairs providing opportunities to showcase forms of artistic, recreational, and commercial activity; the use of "additive manufacturing" to build new products and processes atomic layer by atomic layer; and the growing use of the "app" culture to empower an immense marketplace of small software development companies. In fact, some suggest that our civilization may experience a renaissance-like awakening of creative activities in the 21st century similar to that occurring in 16th century Europe.

Since universities will play such a critical role as the source of these assets of the age of knowledge, perhaps the university of the 21st century will also shift its intellectual focus and priority from the preservation or transmission of knowledge to the process of creation itself. A determining characteristic of the university of the 21st Century may be a shift in intellectual focus, from the preservation or transmission of knowledge, to the process of creation itself. Thus, our vision for the early 21st century should stress the following characteristics among our people and our programs:

Creativity
Innovation
Ingenuity and Invention
Entrepreneurial Zeal

But here lies a great challenge. As noted earlier, creativity and innovation are key not only to problem solving but more generally to achieving economic prosperity, social well being, and national security in a global, knowledge-driven economy. Yet, while universities are experienced in teaching the skills of analysis, we have far less understanding of the intellectual activities associated with creativity. In fact, the current disciplinary culture of our campuses sometimes discriminates against those who are truly creative, those who do not fit well into our stereotypes of students and faculty.

The university may need to reorganize itself quite differently, stressing forms of pedagogy and extracurricular experiences to nurture and teach the art and skill of creation and innovation. This would probably imply a shift away from highly specialized disciplines and degree programs to programs placing more emphasis on integrating knowledge. There is clearly a need to better integrate the educational mission of the university with the research and service activities of the faculty by ripping instruction out of the classroom–or at least the lecture hall–and placing it instead in the discovery and tinkering environment of studios or workshops or "hacker havens".

Actually, as John Seely Brown points out, today's students are already using technology to function much like artists – disciplined, focused, pushing boundaries, challenging assumptions and creating meaning. (Brown, 2009) They are willing to engage with multiple viewpoints before synthesizing their own. But beyond that, they look for meaning not just in what they create or own but in addition through what they contribute back to society-at-large. They are engaged, first and foremost, in fostering what might be called the creative class. Not only do they want to create for themselves, but they also want others to build on their creations.

The platforms they use are mostly digital: instant messaging to keep in constant contact with one's own intimate community; blogging to let one experiment by exposing their ideas to others and getting rapid feedback; by participating in the rapidly expanding worlds of open source, open content (e.g., Wikipedia), and remixing the work of others; rich media capable of expressing complex ideas; and a vast network characterizing cyberinfrastructure that lets one access communities, instruments, and databases all over the

The Renaissance Campus: Music, Art, Architecture, and Engineering

world (an infrastructure that the University of Michigan has played a key role in creating). These are the power tools of the Net Generation.

Here, the University of Michigan provides an interesting example of how academic programs characterized by technology-driven creative activities might evolve. On the University's North Campus, we already are fortunate to have several schools—music, dance, and the performing arts; art and design; architecture; and engineering—that focus on the creative activities that increasingly require new tools, . The Media Union (aka Duderstadt Center) and Walgreen Center on the North Campus provide unique "commons" facilities, gathering places that support interdisciplinary activities in "making things"—3-D objects, virtual reality simulations, new art forms, CGI-based performances, responding to a growing need for both student learning and faculty participation in such activities. It is important to recapture the original vision of the Media Union as an innovation commons or creation space where students, faculty, and staff from multiple disciplines gather to create, invent, design, and even make things (whether objects of art, performances, buildings, or new technologies). In fact, the four deans of these schools who created the concepts for the Media Union and Walgreen Center used to refer to the North Campus as the University's "Renaissance Campus".

Drawing together aspects of hardware and software, inquiry and discovery, tinkering and invention, and creativity and innovation, experimentation and performance, the Duderstadt Center and Walgreen Center provide tremendous interactive playground for imaginative scholars and students. The tools in these facilities are so easy to use that ideally they become natural extensions to everyday activity. For example, an artist , an engineer, and a choreographer should be able to think up a new staging for a performance together, sketch it out in three dimensions on a computer, then show it off and discuss it in real time with colleagues both here and across the world, all without noticing the complex technology that allows them to collaborate.

This model of "creativity and innovation" commons facilities that enable faculty members and students from diverse schools to work together is now being propagaged to other parts of the University, including the arts and humanities and social sciences of the Central Campus and the natural science and biomedical programs.

This vision of renaissance aligns well with several other aspects of the University's institutional saga such as its commitment to excellence and leadership and its belief that this rests upon building diverse learning communities. But achieving such a vision will also likely require a culture change that encourages risk taking and tolerates occasional failure as the price one must frequently pay for setting and accomplishing challenging goals.

To adapt its pedagogy to the challenge of a

350

School of Music, Theatre, and Dance

College of Engineering

Duderstadt Center.

Walgreen Center

School of Architecture and Urban Planning

School of Art and Design

"renaissance" education, universities may form strategic alliances with other groups, organizations, or institutions in our society whose activities are characterized by great creativity, for example, the art world, the performing arts, and high-tech industry.

Particularly key in this effort is the earlier goal of diversity. As Tom Friedman noted in a New York Times column, "The sheer creative energy that comes when you mix all our diverse people and cultures together. We live in an age when the most valuable asset any economy can have is the ability to be creative–to spark and imagine new ideas, be they Broadway tunes, great books, iPads, or new cancer drugs. And where does creativity come from?" As Newsweek described it, 'To be creative requires divergent thinking (generating many unique ideas) and then convergent thinking (combining those ideas into the best result)." And where does divergent thinking come from? It comes from being exposed to divergent ideas and cultures and people and intellectual disciplines. (Friedman, 2011)

Just what a world-class research university characterized by great socioeconomic diversity such as the University of Michigan can offer!

The Theme for the Third Century: Enlightenment

Any vision proposed for the University of Michigan's third century must consider the extraordinary changes and uncertainties of a future driven by exponentially evolving information and communications technology. The extraordinary connectivity provided by the Internet already links together the majority of the world's population. To this, one can add the emerging capacity to capture and distribute the accumulated knowledge of our civilization in digital form and provide opportunities for learning through new paradigms such as MOOCS and cognitive tutors. This suggests the possible emergence of a new global society no longer constrained by space, time, monopoly, or archaic laws and instead even more dependent upon the generation of new knowledge and the education of world citizens. In such an era of rapid change, it has become the responsibility of democratic societies to provide their citizens with the learning opportunities they need throughout their lives, at costs they can afford, as a right rather than a privilege.

More generally, what the nation (and also the world) needs today is a 21st century version of the Enlightenment movement of the 17th and 18th century that swept aside the divine authority of kings by educating and empowering the public, stimulating revolution, and creating the liberal democracies that now characterize most developed nations. Our nation and our world needs once again the "illumination" provided by distributing "the light of learning and knowledge" to counter the ignorance (e.g., today's "denier" culture) and address the challenges of our times.

More specifically, the goals of the Enlightenment were to provide for a rational distribution of freedom, universal access to knowledge, and the formation of learning communities. Rational and critical thought was regarded as central to freedom and democracy. Knowledge and learning were regarded as public goods, to be made available through communities such as salons, seminars, and academies. These dreams of the universal and the collective, *Liberte, Egalite, and Fraternite* for the French Revolution–or perhaps better articulated by Jefferson's opening words from our Declaration of Independence: "We hold these truths to be self-evident, that all men are created equal, that they are endowed by their Creator with certain unalienable Rights, that among these are Life, Liberty and the pursuit of Happiness."–remain as important today as they were three centuries ago.

Today, the educational institution most capable of launching a new "age of Enlightenment" is the "university", with its dual missions of creating "unions" of scholars and learners and providing "universal" access to knowledge. In a sense, the word "university" itself conveys the elements of this vision: both the sense of a "union" or community of learners (i.e., *universitas magistrorum et scholarium*) and the "universality" or totality of knowledge and learning as the key to social well-being in an age of knowledge. Furthermore, since these have been regarded as public goods, one might even suggest that the public universities have a particular responsibility in providing these.

Our proposition is that the Enlightenment theme would be a particularly compelling and appropriate goal for the University of Michigan's third century. After all, our future will continue to be one in which

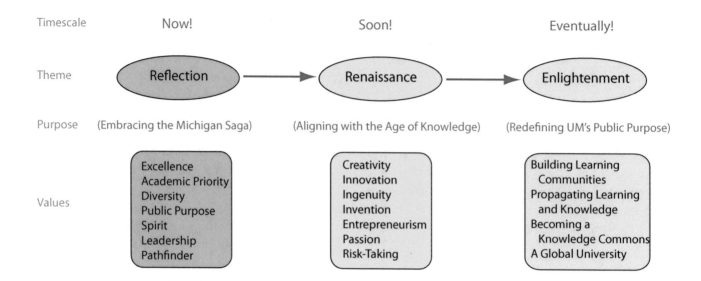

Timescale	Now!	Soon!	Eventually!

Theme: Reflection → Renaissance → Enlightenment

Purpose: (Embracing the Michigan Saga) — (Aligning with the Age of Knowledge) — (Redefining UM's Public Purpose)

Values:

| Excellence
Academic Priority
Diversity
Public Purpose
Spirit
Leadership
Pathfinder | Creativity
Innovation
Ingenuity
Invention
Entrepreneurism
Passion
Risk-Taking | Building Learning
  Communities
Propagating Learning
  and Knowledge
Becoming a
  Knowledge Commons
A Global University |

A Vision for the Third Century of the University of Michigan

freedom and prosperity depend upon widespread distribution of "the light of learning and knowledge", and hence this should become a key component of our extended public purpose.

Actually, this theme traces its origin to the earliest days of the University of Michigan, since its original incarnation as "the Catholepistemiad or University of Michigania" was a utopian vision stimulated by the principles of the Enlightenment that undergirded the Northwest Ordinance of 1787, e.g., "religion, morality, and knowledge being necessary to good government and the happiness of mankind, schools and the means of education shall forever be encouraged". Michigan's early evolution was heavily influenced by Henry Tappan's efforts to build a true university, based not simply on learning but on scholarship laid the foundation for the research university in America. And, perhaps most important, its public character was shaped by the Jeffersonian ideal of education for all to the extent of the individual's capacity, i.e., "providing an uncommon education for the common man". These fundamental principles, along with its unusual secular character, established Michigan as one of the nation's first and most prominent "public" "research" universities and continues to define its public purpose today in terms of both creating and distributing learning and knowledge to society. Hence, it is most appropriate

that any vision for the University's future embrace and extend its character as a truly "public university" to address the nature of our changing world.

But while the Enlightenment of the 18th century was concerned with "celebrating the luminosity of knowledge shining through the written word", today knowledge comes in many forms–words, images, immersive environments, "sim-stim". And learning communities are no longer constrained by space and time but rather propagated instantaneously by rapidly evolving technologies (e.g., cyberinfrastrucure) and practices (e.g., open source, open knowledge). The ancient vision of the Library of Alexandria to collect all of the books of the world in one place is rapidly becoming true–except the "place" has now become a cloud in cyberspace. Learning communities are evolving into knowledge generating communities–wikis, crowd sourcing, hive cultures that span the globe.

William Germano suggests yet another argument for such a theme as the possible next stage in speculating about the evolution of the "book", from the invention of writing to the codex to the printed volume to the digital revolution. As he explains:

"Right now we are walking through two great dreams that are shaping the future of scholarship, even the very idea of scholarship and the role "the book"

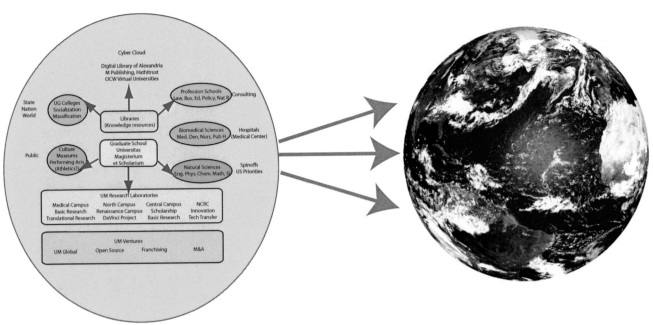

A Public Purpose for the Third Century: Providing the light of knowledge and learning to the world!

should play within it. Great Dream No. 1 is universal access to knowledge. This dream means many things to many people, but for knowledge workers it means that scholarly books and journals can, and therefore should, be made available to all users. New technologies make that possible for the first time in human history, and as the argument goes, the existence of such possibilities obligates us to use them. Great Dream No. 2 is the ideal of knowledge building as a self-correcting, collective exercise. Twenty years ago, nobody had Wikipedia, but when it arrived it took over the hearts and laptops for undergraduates and then of everyone else in the education business. Professional academic life would be poorer, or at least much slower, without it. The central premise of Wikipedia isn't speed but infinite self-correction, perpetually fine-tuning what we know. In our second dream, we expand our aggregated knowledge quantitatively and qualitatively". (Germano, 2010)

Germano continues on to suggest that "these two dreams–the universal and the collective–should sound very familiar since they are fundamentally the latest entries in Western culture's utopian tradition."

In a sense, then, the concept of a 21st century analog to the Enlightenment combines several themes that we suggested earlier might characterize the university of the future:

The emergence of a *Universitas Magistrorum et Scholarium* in cyberspace.

The power of network architectures in distributing knowledge and learning

The increasing access to knowledge and learning resources through the massive digitization and access to printed materials and other sources of information

The perspective of learning organizations as ecologies that evolve and mutate into new forms

The university as the prototype of an emergent global civilization

Today, the University of Michigan is already playing a leadership role in achieving just such a vision. Its efforts during the 1980s (together with IBM and MCI) to build and manage the backbone of the Internet, its role in creating Internet2, and most recently the early effort to create a "national learning, research, and innovation network" linking together the nation's research universities, national laboratories, federal agencies, and industry with advanced cyberinfrastructure all provide strong evidence of the leadership role it plays in linking together people and institutions around the world.

The University of Michigan has also played a leadership role in redefining the nature of the "library" for a digitally connected world, first with the NSF digital library project in the 1990s–a consortium of universities that stimulated the development of the Page Rank search algorithm and the creation of Google, and helping to build the JSTOR project, the first major effort to digitize a massive collection of scholarly publications in disciplines such as economics and history. Today, Michigan serves as the lead partner in the Google Books project, to provide search access to the printed knowledge of the world, and the HathiTrust, a collection of 60 leading libraries with the futher goal of providing full-text access to large inventories of scholarly materials. Furthermore, as a participant in the OpenCourseWare and MOOC movements to provide global access to learning resources, the University has firmly established its leadership role in providing both knowledge and learning on an unprecedented global scale. Its leadership in promoting open access to research data and intellectual property through efforts such as the Creative Commons has potential for redefining the public university as a "knowledge commons" serving the world.

Hence, it is appropriate and perhaps provocative) to suggest that the University is well-positioned to participate in a contemporary version of the Enlightenment, spreading knowledge and learning throughout the world. We suggest that this might even become the primary mission of the University for its Third Century!

Achieving the Vision

We have suggested three visions for the future of the University of Michigan:

A vision for today of *Reflection* upon the past accomplishments, values, and key characteristics of the University's institutional saga;

A near-term vision of a *Renaissance* as the University aligns itself to better engage with a world dependent upon learning, knowledge, creativity, and innovation, a world by spanning the broad range of learning from simply "to know", "to do", "to create" and "to become; and

A longer term vision of *Enlightenment* as it commits itself to expand its public purpose to provide "the light of learning and knowledge" to the world in the new forms enabled by rapidly evolving information and communications technologies.

Although bold, we believe these visions to be consistent both with the University's heritage and challenges and opportunities it will face as it begins its third century.

Of course there are always those who believe that Michigan should settle for achieving excellence and leadership within the confines of the current American research university paradigm. The University of Michigan, they argue, should take the necessary steps to preserve its options, to create flexibility, to develop the capacity to adapt to and control change, and to open up opportunities during the decades. They prefer more modest strategies to clearly identify the goals that would enable the University of Michigan to adapt to a changing world in a far more organic, evolutionary manner.

But such a laissez-faire approach to the future is not the Michigan style. The University tends to flourish when it has been enlivened and emboldened by challenging visions of the future. While acknowledging the difficulties and the risks inherent in long-range planning exercises, the University's heritage as a leader in higher education demands the development and articulation of a bold vision for the third century. It is a fitting exercise for an institution aspiring to become "the leader and best."

We contend that as the University approaches its third century, it should embrace once again its heritage as a pathfinder for higher education, a saga established two centuries ago in the 19th century when the University of Michigan became a primary source for much of the innovation and leadership for higher education. Once again Michigan has the opportunity to influence the emergence of a new paradigm of what the university must become in our 21st Century world to respond to the changing needs of our society.

This, then, is the particular challenge and opportunity for the University of Michigan. As it has so many times in its past, the University of Michigan must embrace yet again its historic role of leadership for a future characterized by great challenges, immense responsibilities, and exciting opportunities.

Appendix

The Michigan Saga

Universities are based on long-standing traditions and continuity, evolving over many generations (in some cases, even centuries), with very particular sets of values, traditions, and practices. Historians of higher education usually focus on the broader forms of universities over the centuries, such as the emergence of the *Universitas Magistrorum et Scholarium* or "union of masters and scholars" in medieval times to the vocational Ecoles that augmented more traditional universities in France in the late 18th century to the emergence of wissenschaft, lernfreiheit, and lehrfreiheit (scholarship coupled with the freedom to learn and freedom to teach) characterizing the German universities based on the principles of von Humboldt in the early 19th century. The early American colleges were based on the objectives of character building and elitism of the British universities such as Oxford and Cambridge, but would later evolve into a more unique merger of several European forms in the mid-19th century that combined the instruction of young students, graduate students in the learned professions, and faculty scholarship.

But there are other characteristics that have shaped, distinguished, and sustained the universities of our times. Burton R. Clark, a noted sociologist and scholar of higher education, introduced the concept of "organizational legend " or "institutional saga," to refer to those long-standing characteristics that determine the distinctiveness of a college or university. (Clark, 1970) Clark's view is that "an organizational legend (or saga), located between ideology and religion, partakes of an appealing logic on one hand and sentiments similar to the spiritual on the other"; that universities "develop over time such an intentionality about institutional life, a saga, which then results in unifying the institution and shaping its purpose." Clark notes: "An institutional saga may be found in many forms, through mottoes,

traditions, and ethos. It might consist of long-standing practices or unique roles played by an institution, or even in the images held in the minds (and hearts) of students, faculty, and alumni. Sagas can provide a sense of romance and even mystery that turn a cold organization into a beloved social institution, capturing the allegiance of its members and even defining the identity of its communities."

All colleges and universities have a social purpose, but for some, these responsibilities and roles have actually shaped their evolution and determined their character. The appearance of a distinct institutional saga involves many elements—visionary leadership; strong faculty and student cultures; unique programs; ideologies; and, of course, the time to accumulate the events, achievements, legends, and mythology that characterize long-standing institutions. For example, the saga of my alma mater, Yale University, was shaped over the centuries by old-boy traditions, such as secret societies (e.g., Skull and Bones); literature (from dime-novel heroes, such as Frank Merriwell and Dink Stover, to Buckley's God and Man at Yale); and national leadership (William H. Taft, George H. Bush, Bill Clinton, George W. Bush, and Gerald R. Ford—although the latter was first and foremost a Michigan man). Harvard's saga is perhaps best captured by the response of a former Harvard president who, when asked what it takes to build a great institution like Harvard, responded simply, "Three hundred years!" Notre Dame draws its saga from the legends of the gridiron, that is, Knute Rockne, the Four Horsemen, and the Subway Alumni. Big Ten universities also have their symbols: fraternity and sorority life, campus protests, and gigantic football stadiums.

While institutional sagas are easy to identify for older universities (e.g., North Carolina, Virginia, and

John Harvard's statue (350 years old?)

Yale's Skull and Bones

Virginia's Academical Village

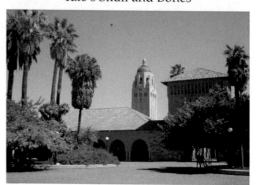

The "farm" at Stanford

Notre Dame's "Touchdown Jesus"

Michigan's Powerplant Smokestack

Michigan among the publics; Harvard, Yale, and Princeton among the privates), they can sometimes be problematic to institutions rising rapidly to prominence. During the controversy over inappropriate use of government research funds at Stanford during the 1990s, the late Roger Heyns—former Michigan dean; chancellor at the University of California, Berkeley; and then president of the Hewlett Foundation, adjacent to the Stanford campus—once observed to me that Stanford faced a particular challenge in becoming too good too fast.[4] Prior to World War II, its reputation as "the farm" was well deserved. Stanford was peaceful, pastoral, and conservative. The extraordinary reputation it achieved first in the sciences and then across all the disciplines in the latter half of the twentieth century came on so abruptly that the institution sometimes found it difficult to live with its newfound prestige and visibility, as its inquisition by a congressional inquiry into misuse of research funds in the 1990s demonstrated.

Again to quote Burton Clark: "The institutional saga is a historically based, somewhat embellished understanding of a unique organization development. Colleges are prone to a remembrance of things past and a symbolism of uniqueness. The more special the his-

Michigan Images (clockwise): Hill Auditorium, MLK Day March, Jonas Salk,
University Hospital, Apollo 15 (all Michigan crew), Go Blue, Angell Hall (center)

tory or the more forceful the claim to a place in history, the more intensively cultivated are the ways of sharing memory and symbolizing the institution."[5] A visit to the campuses of one of our distinguished private universities conveys just such an impression of history and tradition. Their ancient ivy-covered buildings and their statues, plaques, and monuments attesting to important people and events of the past convey a sense that these institutions have evolved slowly over the centuries—in careful and methodical ways—to achieve their present forms and define their institutional saga.

In contrast, a visit to the campus of one of our great state universities conveys more of a sense of dynamism and impermanence. Most of the buildings look new, even hastily constructed to accommodate rapid growth. The icons of the public university tend to be their football stadiums or the smokestacks of their central power plants, rather than ivy-covered buildings or monuments. In talking with campus leaders at public universities, one gets little sense that the history of these institutions is valued or recognized. Perhaps this is due to their egalitarian nature or, conversely, to the political (and politicized) process that structures their governance and all too frequently informs their

358

choice of leadership. The consequence is that the public university evolves through geological layers, each generation paving over or obliterating the artifacts and achievements of its predecessors with a new layer of structures, programs, and practices. Hence, the first task of a new president of such an institution is that of unearthing and understanding its institutional saga.

Continuing in this spirit, then, what are the first images that come to mind when one mentions the University of Michigan? Academic activities such as students listening attentively to brilliant faculty in the lecture hall or studying in the library? Scientists toiling away late in the evenings in the laboratory, striving to understand the universe; or scholars pouring over ancient manuscripts, rediscovering our human heritage? Not likely.

The University of Michigan is many things to many people, but its images are rarely stimulated by its core missions of teaching and scholarship. To some, the university's image is its football team, the Michigan Wolverines, decked out in those ferocious winged helmets as it stampedes into Michigan Stadium before a crowd of 110,000, rising to sing the Michigan fight song, Hail to the Victors. Others think first of a Michigan of the arts, where the world's leading orchestras and artists come to perform in Hill Auditorium, one of the great concert halls of the world.

For some, Michigan represents the youthful conscience of a nation—the birthplace of the teach-in protests against an unpopular war in Vietnam, site of the first Earth Day, and home of the century-old Michigan Daily, with student engagement in so many of the critical issues of the day. There is also the caring Michigan, as experienced by millions of patients who have been treated by the University of Michigan Medical Center, one of the nation's great centers of medical research, teaching, and clinical care.

Then there is the Michigan of the cutting-edge research that so improves the quality of our lives. For example, it was at Michigan, in 1952, that the clinical trials were conducted for the Salk polio vaccine. It was at Michigan that the gene responsible for cystic fibrosis was identified and cloned in the 1990s. And although others may have "invented" the Internet, it was Michigan (together with another "big blue" partner, IBM) that built and managed the Internet backbone for the

nation during the 1980s and early 1990s.

Michigan can also be seen as a university of the world, long renowned as a truly international center of learning. If you walk down the streets of any capital city in the world, you will encounter Michigan graduates, often in positions of leadership. Indeed, Michigan is even a university of the universe, with the establishment of the first lunar chapter of the UM Alumni Association by the all-Michigan crew of Apollo 15.

These activities may serve as images of the university for many. I would suggest, however, that they are less a conveyance of the nature of Michigan's institutional saga than a consequence of its more fundamental traditions and character. To truly understand Michigan's saga, one must go back in time almost two centuries ago, to the university's founding in frontier America.

A University on the Frontier

It can be argued that it was in the Midwest, in frontier towns such as Ann Arbor and Madison, that true universities first appeared in America. By augmenting the traditional mission of educating the young with faculty scholarship and public service to society, the emerging public state universities created a uniquely American university capable of responding to the needs of a rapidly changing nation in the 19th Century and that still dominates higher education today.

The University of Michigan was established in 1817 in the village of Detroit by an act of the Northwest Territorial government and financed through the sale of Indian lands granted by the United States Congress. (Price, 2003) Since it benefited from this territorial land grant, the new university was subject to the Enlightenment themes of the Northwest Ordinance guaranteeing civil rights and religious freedom. But equally significant for our purposes was the Northwest Ordinance's statement of the importance of education in the new territories: "Religion, morality, and knowledge being necessary to good government and the happiness of mankind, schools and the means of education shall forever be encouraged." (Northwest Ordinance, 1909)

The University of Michigan traces its earliest heritage to two quite different models of higher education in 19th century Europe. Actually, the first incarnation of the University of Michigan proposed by Augus-

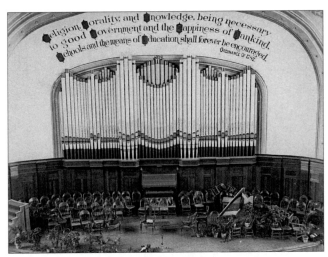

The words of the Northwest Ordinance
in the auditorium of old University Hall

The original building of the Catholepistemiad
or University of Michigania in Detroit, 1817

tus Woodward, Secretary and later Governor of the Michigan Territory, was not a university but rather a centralized system of schools, libraries, and other cultural institutions borrowing its model from the *Universite Imperiale de France* founded by Napoleon a decade earlier. (Ruegg, 1996) Named "the Catholepistemiad or University of Michigania" by Woodward, this was actually an extraordinary vision for the times. It proposed an intellectual breadth far beyond the classical curriculum of the colonial colleges that would be run by the professors rather than boards of churchman and denominations like other American colleges of the early 19th century. Woodward also proposed that it would be supported by taxation so that its primary schools were free and its higher education programs would require only a modest tuition from students.

It was only after the State of Michigan entered the Union in 1837 that a new plan was adopted to focus the University on higher education, establishing it as a "state" university after the Prussian system, with programs in literature, science and arts; medicine; and law–the first three academic departments of the new university. The new Michigan State Legislature authorized funds to purchase a campus for the University, and an enterprising group of citizens from Ann Arbor offered a 40 acre site in their community. (Actually, the group first wanted to attract the state capital, but that went to Lansing. Then they considered going after the state prison before finally offering the site for a university.)

Because the University had already been in existence for two decades before the State of Michigan entered the Union in 1837, and because of the frontier society's deep distrust of politics and politicians, the new state's early constitution (1851) granted the University an unusual degree of autonomy as a "coordinate branch of state government," with full powers over all University matters granted to its governing board of regents, although surprisingly enough it did not state the purpose of the University. This constitutional autonomy, together with the fact that the University traces its origins to an act of Congress rather than a state legislature, has shaped an important feature of the University's character. In financial terms, the University of Michigan was actually a United States land grant university supported entirely by the sale of its federal lands and student fees rather than state resources until after the Civil War. Hence throughout its history the University has regarded itself as much as a national university as a state university, albeit with some discretion when dealing with the Michigan State Legislature.

Implicit in the new constitution was also a provision that the University's regents be determined by state-wide popular election, again reflecting public dissatisfaction with both the selection and performance of the early-appointed regents. (The last appointed board retaliated by firing the professors at the University.) The constitution also provided for the University to be led by a president, who would preside over the meetings of the regents (without vote). Hence the first assignment of the newly elected board was to select a president for the University (after inviting back the fired professors).

After an extensive search, they elected Henry Philip Tappan, a broadly educated professor of philosophy from New York, as the first president of the reconfigured University.

Under Tappan's leadership, the University rapidly began to evolve into yet a third European form with the appointment of its first president. In fact, one can make a strong case that with Tappan's arrival, the University of Michigan became the first attempt in America to build a true university. At a time when the colonial colleges were teaching young boys the classical curriculum of Greek, Latin, and rhetoric using the scholastic methods to "transform savages into gentlemen", much as the British public school, Tappan brought to Ann Arbor a vision of building a true university in the European sense, one which would not only conduct instruction and advanced scholarship, but also respond to popular needs. He was strongly influenced by European leaders such as Wilhelm von Humboldt, Prussian minister of education and founder of the University of Berlin, who stressed the importance of combining specialized research with humanistic teaching to define the intellectual structure of the university. (Ruegg, 2004; Clark, 2006)

Tappan articulated a vision of the university as a capstone of civilization, a repository for the accumulated knowledge of mankind, and a home for scholars dedicated to the expansion of human understanding. In his words, "a university is the highest possible form of an institution of learning. It embraces every branch of knowledge and all possible means of making new investigations and thus advancing knowledge."(Tappan, 1851) He aimed to develop "an institution that would cultivate the originality and genius of those seeking knowledge beyond the traditional curriculum, with a graduate school in which diligent and responsible students could pursue their studies and research under the eye of learned scholars in an environment of enormous resources in books, laboratories, and museums". (Peckham, 1963)

Henry Tappan's concept for the University wove together the classical curriculum and mental discipline of the collegiate model, the utilitarian emphasis of the newly emerging state universities, and the Ger-

President Henry Tappan

man university emphasis on pure scholarship. (Thelin, 2004) During his tenure, the University of Michigan broadened the classical curriculum to include the sciences, planted the early seeds for a graduate school to distinguish postgraduate professional studies from undergraduate education, and introduced the seminar model of instruction for graduate education. (Peckham, 1963) Furthermore Michigan faculty members carried this broader concept of the university with them as they moved on to leadership roles at other institutions (e.g., Andrew Dixon White at Cornell, Charles Kendall Adams at Cornell and Wisconsin, and Erastus Haven at Northwestern). (Rudolph, 1962)

Although premature for a frontier state, Tappan's vision for the University of Michigan in the 1850s and 1860s provided the first American model of a modern university. Hence from its founding, the University of Michigan has been identified with the most progressive forces in American higher education. The early colonial colleges served the aristocracy of colonial society, stressing moral development over a liberal education, much as the English public schools, and based on a classical curriculum in subjects such as Greek, Latin, and rhetoric. In contrast, Michigan blended the classical curriculum with the European model that stressed faculty involvement in research and dedication to the preparation of future scholars. Michigan hired as its first professors not classicists but a zoologist and a geologist. Unlike other institutions of the time, Michigan added instruction in the sciences to the humanistic curriculum, creating a hybrid that drew on the best of both a "liberal" and a "utilitarian" education. (Turner, 1988)

The University of Michigan's campus in 1852 (Cropsey Painting)

The University of Michigan can also claim to be one of the first truly public universities in America, created by the Northwest Territorial government in a nonsectarian spirit 20 years before Michigan was admitted to the Union. (Technically, the Universities of Georgia and North Carolina were the first state universities, but since they were highly influenced by the church–think "Chapel Hill"–they could not strictly be regarded as "public" in character.) (Thelin, 2004)

One might also consider the University of Michigan as one of the earliest examples of the American research university, with its construction of one of the three largest telescopes in the world, the first teaching laboratory building for chemistry, and the first courses in new disciplines such as bacteriology, forestry, meteorology, sociology, modern history, journalism, and American literature. In fact, almost every American intellectual movement from the mid-19th century onward must include some mention of Michigan. Beyond its impact on the traditional literature, arts, and science, the University led in the creation of many new disciplines such as the quantitative social sciences, biomedical disciplines, engineering sciences, and policy disciplines. (Turner, 1988)

The influence of the University on the professions has also been immense. Michigan was the first university in the West to pursue professional education, establishing its medical school in 1850, engineering courses in 1854, and a law school in 1859. Michigan joined with Columbia and Penn in creating the paradigm for medical practice and education by defining the M.D. as a graduate degree, introducing laboratory science in the curriculum, and opening the first university hospital for clinical training. Decades later, this model would be adopted to transform the rest of medicine through the Flexner Report of 1910. (Flexner, 1910) Moreover through the efforts of Henry Frieze, Michigan stimulated the development of secondary education (high schools) throughout the Midwest.

An Uncommon Education for the Common Man

By the late 19th Century, Michigan was recognized, to quote *Harper's Weekly*, as "an institution in whose progress not a single State alone, but the whole country as well, may claim an interest". (*Harper's Weekly*, 1887) The magazine went on to note: "The most striking feature of the University is the broad and liberal spirit in which it does its work. Students are allowed the widest freedom consistent with sound scholarship in pursuing the studies of their choice. Women are admitted to all departments on equal terms with men; the doors of the University are open to all applicants who are properly qualified, from whatever part of the world they may come."

Particularly notable here was the role of Michigan President James Angell in articulating the importance of Michigan's commitment to provide "an uncommon education for the common man" while challenging the aristocratic notion of leaders of the colonial colleges such as Charles Eliot of Harvard. (Rudolph, 1962) Angell argued that Americans should be given opportunities to develop talent and character to the fullest. He portrayed the state university as the bulwark against

The University of Michigan in 1887, as depicted in the famous article in Harper's Weekly

the aristocracy of wealth. This commitment continues today, when even in an era of severe fiscal constraints, the University still meets the full financial need of every Michigan student enrolling in its programs.

The University has long placed high value on the diversity of its student body, both because of its commitment to serve all of society, and because of its perception that such diversity enhanced the quality of its educational programs. From its earliest years, Michigan sought to attract students from a broad range of ethnic and geographic backgrounds. In 1860, the regents referred "with partiality" to the "list of foreign students drawn thither from every section of our country." Forty-six percent of the University's students then came from other states and foreign countries. Although the Michigan legislature occasionally objected to this high out-of-state enrollment, the Regents reminded state government that the University had not been founded by state action or money but by a grant of land from the United States Congress, which support rendered its obligations at the national level. President Haven noted that the larger fees from out-of-state students provided much of the University's income that subsidized in part the education of Michigan residents (a situation that continues today).

The first African American students arrived on campus in 1868. Michigan was one of the first large universities in America to admit women in 1870. At the time, the rest of the nation looked on with a critical eye, certain that the experiment of co-education would fail. Although the first women students were true pioneers, the objects of intense scrutiny and some resentment, by 1898 the enrollment of women had increased to the point where they received 53 percent of Michigan's undergraduate degrees. The University's constitutional autonomy enabled it to defend this commitment to diversity in the face of considerable political resistance to challenging the status quo, eventually taking the battle for diversity and equality of opportunity all the way to the United States Supreme Court in the landmark cases of 2003. In more contemporary terms, it seems clear that an important facet of the institutional saga of the University of Michigan would be its achievement of excellence through diversity.

Michigan's international presence in both students and activities has also been unusual for public univer-

Spring Commencement on the Diag
gives a sense of Michigan's massive scale

sities. The University awarded the first doctorate to a Japanese citizen who later was instrumental in founding the University of Tokyo. President Angell's service in 1880-82 as United States Envoy to China established further the university's great influence in Asia, including providing the resources to establish Tsinghua University from the reparations from the Boxer Rebellion.

Hence in many ways, it was at the University of Michigan that Thomas Jefferson's embrace of the principles of the Enlightenment in his proposition for nation, "We hold these truths to be self-evident: That all men are created equal", was most fully embraced and realized. Whether characterized by gender, race, religion, socioeconomic background, ethnicity, or nationality—not to mention academic interests or political persuasion—the University has always taken great pride in the diversity of its students, faculty, and programs.

The Biggest in the Land

Throughout its history, the University of Michigan has also been one of the nation's largest universities, vying with the largest private universities such as Harvard and Columbia during the 19th and early 20th centuries, and then holding this position of national leadership until the emergence of the statewide public university systems (e.g., the University of California and the University of Texas) in the post-WWII years. Perhaps this addiction to growth is best explained by Michigan's president during the 1920s, Marion Burton, when he concluded that, "A state university must accept happily the conclusion that it is destined to be large. If its state grows and prospers, it will naturally reflect those conditions." (Peckham, 1963)

Although growth stabilized during the Depression years of the 1930s, enrollments exploded once again following World War II, growing to 20,000 in 1947, of whom 11,000 were returning veterans. To accommodate the growth of the campus, the Regents first purchased 300 acres north of the Huron River as a North Campus, then later agreed to attach upper division senior colleges to the junior colleges in Flint and Dearborn to accommodate the post-war baby boom population explosion. In 1971, these senior colleges were separated off and given full four-year academic programs as regional campuses of the University. Growth of the Ann Arbor campus began to slow during the 1970s and 1980s, stabilizing at 35,000 students in the mid-1990s. But as state support continued to deteriorate, the University launched yet another major expansion over the first decade of the new century, expanding to 44,000 students in an effort to capture the higher tuition revenue provided by major growth in out-of-state and international students, while maintaining its commitment to serve Michigan resident students regardless of need.

Today the Ann Arbor campus is the largest in the nation–indeed, in the world–in facilities (34 million gsf), budget ($7 billion/year), and research activity ($1.3 billion/year). The University continues to benefit from one of the largest alumni bodies in higher education, with over 500,000 living alumni. Michigan sends more of its graduates into professional study in fields such as law, medicine, engineering, and business than any other university in the nation. Michigan graduates are well represented in leadership roles in both the public and private sector and in most of the learned professions. The University's influence on the nation and the world has been immense, both through the achievements of the faculty and staff on its campus and of its graduates as they continue on to roles in commerce, service, and leadership.

Michigan Does Big Things!

Michigan students have often stimulated change in our society through their social activism and academic achievements. From the teach-ins against the Vietnam War in the 1960s to Earth Day in the 1970s, to the Michigan Mandate in the 1980s, Michigan student activism has often been the catalyst for national movements. In a similar fashion, Michigan played a leadership role in public service, from John Kennedy's announcement of the Peace Corps on the steps of the Michigan Union in 1960 to the AmeriCorps in 1994. Its classrooms have often been battlegrounds over what colleges will teach, from challenges to the Great Books canon to more recent confrontations over diversity and social inclusion. This spirit of democracy and tolerance for diverse views among its students and faculty continues today.

Nothing could be more natural to the University of Michigan than challenging the status quo. Change has always been an important part of the University's tradition. Michigan has long defined the model of the large, comprehensive, public research university, with a serious commitment to scholarship and progress. It has been distinguished by unusual breadth, a rich diversity of academic disciplines, professional schools, social and cultural activities, and intellectual pluralism. The late Clark Kerr, the president of the University of California, once referred to the University of Michigan as "the mother of state universities," noting it was the first to prove that a high-quality education could be delivered at a publicly funded institution of higher learning. (Kerr, 1963)

This unrelenting commitment to academic excellence, broad student access, and public service continues today. In virtually all national and international surveys, the University's programs rank among the very best, with most of its schools, colleges, and departments ranking in quality among the top ten nationally and with several regarded as the leading programs in the nation. Other state universities have had far more generous state support than the University of Michigan. Others have had a more favorable geographical location than "good, gray Michigan." But it was Michigan's unusual commitment to provide a college education of the highest possible quality to an increasingly diverse society–regardless of state support, policy, or politics–that might be viewed as one of the University's most important characteristics. The rapid expansion and growth of the nation during the late 19th and early 20th centuries demanded colleges and universities capable of serving all of its population rather than simply the

One of the world's largest telescopes

The nation's first instructional chemistry laboratory

The nation's first university hospital

The world's first academic programs in atomic energy

Apollo 15, the All-Michigan mission to the moon

Michigan's leadership in developing the Internet

Michigan is one of the few universities capable of changing the world.

elite as the key to a democratic society. Here Michigan led the way in both its commitment to wide access and equality and in the leadership it provided for higher education in America.

A list of many of the ways that the University of Michigan has contributed to society–on occasion even changing the world, is provided at the end of this chapter.

The Key to Michigan's Leadership

Interestingly enough, both the University's growth and success in building an unusually broad array of world-class programs had little to do with the generosity of state support. For the first half-century following its founding in 1817, the University was supported entirely from its federal land grant endowment and the fees derived from students. During these early years, state government both mismanaged and then misappropriated the funds from the Congressional land grants intended to support the University. (Peckham, 1963) The University did not receive direct state appropriations until 1867, and for most of its history, state support has actually been quite modest relative to many other states. Although there were periods during which state support matched those for other public universities, such as the 1920s and 1960s when both adequate appropriations and support for facilities became available, these were followed by long periods of deteriorating state support (e.g. the Depression years of the 1930s and then the recessions of the 1970s , 1980s, and 2000s).

More specifically, the strong support of both operating appropriations and capital facilities enabling strong growth of the Ann Arbor campus during the post-WWII years began to slow in the 1960s. The efforts of state government to take over direct control of all campus construction in direct conflict with Regental authority led to a moratorium in state-funded campus construction during the late 1960s and much of the 1970s. The impact of the OPEC oil embargo and the emergence of strong competition from the Japanese auto industry weakened state tax revenues. Although the University and the state shared in the support of the Replacement Hospital Project in the early 1980s, the drain of this mammoth project on the state funds once again severely limited state support for capital facilities.

President Harold Shapiro

President Harold Shapiro understood well the longer-term implications of weakening state support (dropping from 65% to less than 30% of the academic budget during his tenure). He moved in the 1980s to put in place a series of major financial measures to sustain the quality and capacity of the University. First a more conservative financial management and investment strategy was implemented, making tough decisions to set priorities, focusing resources to achieve excellence, and beginning a major decentralization of authority and responsibility for resource decisions that was better aligned with both revenue generation and cost containment. As the state subsidy of the costs of educational programs declined, it was necessary to compensate with major increases in tuition, highly differentiated between Michigan resident and out-of-state students. Finally, aggressive fund-raising efforts were launched with campaigns raising over $300 million during the 1980s and $1.4 billion in the 1990s. More aggressive efforts were taken to actively manage the University's endowment, increasing it from a modest $250 million during the 1980s to over $3 billion by the late 1990s.

As a consequence of these actions, the financial strength of the University rose dramatically even as state support declined to less than 10% of its total operating budget. In fact by 1997 the University of Michigan earned Wall Street's highest AAa credit rating, joining the University of Texas (with its rich oil assets) as the only public universities to achieve this. It would be this unusually high credit rating that would allow the University to borrow at minimum interest rates the resources to sustain further campus facility expansion and renovation despite the fact that the state support would continue to decline to one of the lowest levels in the nation (dropping to 47th among the states by 2010). Yet even as the University became predominantly supported by private resources (tuition and gifts) and federal grants (for research and student financial aid), it was able to sustain its strong commitment to serve the needs of the state. As Frank Rhodes, a former Michigan dean and provost before becoming president of Cornell put it, Michigan had become the prototype of a "privately financed but publicly committed" university, a description that characterizes many of the nation's leading public research universities today.

The real key to the University's quality and impact over its two centuries of history has certainly not been support by the State of Michigan, but rather the very unusual autonomy granted the institution by the state constitution of 1851 as a "coordinate branch of state government". This unusual characteristic of constitutional autonomy for the young university not only arose from the concerns of a frontier state about the role of government but also reflected the importance of freedom as a key Enlightenment theme embraced by Jefferson and his colleagues in defining the early structure of the republic and later became an important founding principle of the Northwest Ordinance that led to the creation of the University.

This constitutional autonomy, together with the fact that the University traces its origins to an act of Congress rather than a state legislature, has shaped an important feature of the University's character. Throughout its history the University has regarded itself as much as a national university as a state university, as exemplified by the declaration of its early Regents:

"The University of Michigan is indebted for its existence of the munificence of Congress, in the redemption of its solemn pledge given to the whole Northwest that 'schools and the means of education should forever be encouraged', and to keep up the mutual good feeling between our State and the General Government in which the endowment of the University originated. The doors of all its Departments are open to students from every State in the Union, upon the same terms as to those of our own State; so that it may, in some sense, with propriety, be styled a National Institution, and every State in the Union has an interest in its prosperity." (Regents Minutes, 1859)

Furthermore, Michigan's constitutional autonomy, periodically reaffirmed through court tests and constitutional conventions, has enabled the University to have much more control over its own destiny than most other public universities. (Peckham, 1963)

The University has always been able to set its own goals for the quality of its programs rather than allowing these to be dictated by the vicissitudes of state policy, support, or public opinion. Put another way, although the University is legally "owned" by the people of the state, it has never been obligated to adhere to the priorities or whims of a particular generation of Michigan citizens. Rather, it has been viewed as an enduring social institution with a duty of stewardship to commitments made by generations past and a compelling obligation to take whatever actions were necessary to build and protect its capacity to serve future generations. Even though these actions might conflict from time to time with public opinion or the prevailing political winds of state government, the University's constitutional autonomy clearly gave it the ability to set its own course. When it came to objectives such as program quality or access to educational opportunity, the University of Michigan has always viewed this as an institutional decision rather than succumbing to public or political pressures.

The Michigan Saga

What might be suggested for the University of Michigan institutional saga in view of the University's history, its traditions and roles, and its leadership over the years? Among the possible candidates from Michigan's history are the following characteristics:

The Catholepistemiad or University of Michigania (the capstone of a system of public education)

The flagship of public universities or "mother of state universities"

A commitment to providing "an uncommon education for the common man"

The "broad and liberal spirit" of its students and faculty

The University's control of its own destiny, due to its constitutional autonomy providing political independence as a state university and to an unusually well-balanced portfolio of assets providing independence from the usual financial constraints on a public university

An institution diverse in character yet unified in values

A relish for innovation and excitement

A center of critical inquiry and learning

A tradition of student and faculty activism

A heritage of leadership

The leaders and best" (to borrow a phrase from Michigan's fight song, *The Victors*)

But one more element of the Michigan saga seems particularly appropriate during these times of challenge and change in higher education. It is certainly true that the vast wealth of several of the nation's elite private universities–e.g., Harvard, Yale, Princeton, and Stanford–can focus investments in particular academic areas far beyond anything that Michigan or almost any other university in the nation can achieve. They are capable of attracting faculty and students of extraordinary quality and supporting them with vast resources.

Yet, Michigan has one asset that these universities will never be able to match: its unique combination of quality, breadth, scale, and spirit. This enables Michigan to take risks far beyond anything that could be matched by a private university. Because of their relatively modest size, most elite private universities tend to take a rather conservative approach to academic programs and appointments, since a mistake could seriously damage a small academic unit. Michigan's vast size and breadth allows it to experiment and innovate on a scale far beyond that tolerated by most institutions, as evidenced by its long history of leadership in higher education. It can easily recover from any failures it encounters on its journeys along high-risk paths. This ability to take risks, to experiment and innovate, to explore various new directions in teaching, research, and service, enables Michigan's unique role in American higher education. During a time of great change in society, Michigan's most important institutional saga is

that of a pathfinder and a trailblazer, building on its tradition of leadership and relying on its unusual combination of quality, capacity, and breadth, to reinvent the university, again and again, for new times, new needs, and new worlds.

Here, perhaps we should be more precise in our choice of descriptors: *pathfinders* are those who identify new directions; *trailblazers* explore the new pathways; *pioneers* build the roads along the new paths that others can follow; and *settlers* occupy the new territory. (Cheri Pancake, 2003) Hence we suggest that Michigan should be viewed first and foremost both as a pathfinder and a trail-blazer, identifying possible paths into new territory and blazing a trail for others to follow. Michigan has also been at times a pioneer, building roads that others could follow (e.g., the Internet).

Whether in academic innovation (e.g., the quantitative social sciences), social responsiveness (e.g., its early admission of women, minorities, and international students), or its willingness to challenge the status quo (e.g., teach-ins, Earth Day, and the Michigan Mandate), Michigan's history reveals this pathfinding and trailblazing character time and time again. Recently, when Michigan won the 2003 Supreme Court case concerning the use of race in college admissions, the general reaction of other colleges and universities was "Well, that's what we expect of Michigan. They carry the water for us on these issues." When Michigan, together with IBM and MCI, built NSFnet during the 1980s and expanded it into the Internet, this again was the type of leadership the nation expected from the University.

Continuing with the frontier analogy, while Michigan has a long history of success as a pathfinder, trailblazer, and occasional pioneer, it has usually stumbled as a settler, that is, in attempting to follow the paths blazed by others. All too often this leads to complacency and even stagnation at an institution like Michigan. The University almost never makes progress by simply trying to catch up with others.

Michigan travelers in Europe and Asia usually encounter great interest in what is happening in Ann Arbor, in part because universities around the world see the University of Michigan as a possible model for their own future. Certainly they respect—indeed, envy—distinguished private universities, such as Harvard and Stanford. But as public institutions themselves, they realize that they will never be able to amass the wealth of these elite private institutions. Instead, they see Michigan as the model of an innovative university, straddling the characteristics of leading public and private universities.

Time and time again colleagues mention the "Michigan model" or the "Michigan mystique." Of course, people mean many different things by these phrases: the University's unusually strong and successful commitment to diversity; its hybrid funding model combining the best of both public and private universities; its strong autonomy from government interference; or perhaps the unusual combination of quality, breadth, and capacity that gives Michigan the capacity to be innovative, to take risks. Of course, all these multiple perspectives illustrate particular facets of what it means to be "the leaders and best."

The institutional saga of the University of Michigan involves a combination of quality, size, breadth, innovation, and pioneering spirit. The University has never aspired to be Harvard or the University of California, although it greatly admires these institutions. Rather, Michigan possesses a unique combination of characteristics, particularly well suited to exploring and charting the course for higher education as it evolves to serve a changing world.

And it is this unique character as a pathfinder, trailblazer, and pioneer that should shape the University's mission, vision, and goals for the future. Such bold efforts both capture and enliven the institutional saga of the University of Michigan. And these are the traits that must be recognized, honored, and preserved as the University enters its third century.

370

References

Adelman, Clifford. *The Bologna Process for U.S. Eyes: Relearning Higher Education in the Age of Convergence.* San Jose, CA: Institute for Higher Education Policy, 2009.

America COMPETES Act. America Creating Opportunities to Meaningfully Promote Excellence in Technology, Education, and Science Act, Public Law No. 110-69 (reauthorized 2010).

Armstrong, Elizabeth and Laura Hamilton, *Paying for the Party: How College Maintains Inequality,* Harvard University Press, 2013.

Atkins, Daniel E. (chair). *Revolutionizing Science and Engineering Through Cyberinfrastructure.* Report of the National Science Foundation Blue-Ribbon Advisory Panel on Cyberinfrastructure. Washington, DC: National Science Foundation, 2003.

Atkins, Daniel E., John Seely Brown and Allen L Hammond. *External Review of the Hewlett Foundation's Open Educational Resources (OER) Program: Achievements, Challenges, and Opportunities.* Menlo Park, CA: Hewlett Foundation, February, 2007.

Augustine, Norman (chair). *Rising Above the Gathering Storm: Energizing and Employing America for a Brighter Economic Future.* National Academies Committee on Prospering in the Global Economy of the 21st Century. Washington, DC: National Academies Press, 2005.

Bement, Arden L. "Cyberinfrastructure: The Second Revolution", *The Chronicle of Higher Education,* January, 2007.

Berdahl, Robert. "Maintaining America's Competitive Edge: Revitalizing the Nation's Research University". Testimony to the National Academies Committee on Research Universities. Washington, DC: Association of American Universities, 2010.

Bok, Derek. *Our Underachieving Colleges.* Princeton, NJ: Princeton University Press, 2006.

Bok, Derek. "The Ambiguous Role of Money in Higher Education", Commentary, Chronicle of Higher Education, August 12, 2013.

Borgman, Christine L. (chair). Fostering Learning in the Networked World: The Cyberlearning Opportunity and Challenge. Report of the NSF Task Force on Cyberlearning. Washington, D.C.: National Science Foundation, 2008.

Boulos, Michael. "Bill Gates and a Prescription for
Breneman, David. "Peering Around the Bend: The Leadership Challenges of Privatization, Accountability, and Market-Based State Policy". *Association of Governing Boards,* Washington, DC, 2005.

Bowen, William G. "Walk Deliberately, Don't Run, Toward Online Education". Chronicle of Higher Education. March 25, 2013; See also William G. Bowen, Higher Education in the Digital Age. Princeton, NJ: Princeton University Press, 2013.

Bowen, William G., Matthew M. Chingos, Kelly A. Lack, and Thomas I. Nygren. Interactive Learning Online at Public Universities: Evidence from Randomized Trials. Ithaka, May 22, 2012, available on the ITHAKA website: http://www.sr.ithaka.org

Breneman, David. *Are the States and Public Higher Education Striking a New Bargain? Public Policy Paper Series.* Washington, DC: Association of Governing Boards and Colleges, 2005.

Brown, John Seely. "Minds on Fire", Educause, January/February 2009.

Brown, John Seely and Paul Duguid. *The Social Life of Information.* Cambridge, MA: Harvard Business School Press, 2000.

Brownstein, Ronald. "The Generational Mismatch", *National Journal,* July, 2010.

Carnegie Higher Education Reporter, *The Big Picture: Assessing the Future of Higher Education,* Winter, 2014.

Christensen, Clayton M. *The Innovator's Dilemma*. Cambridge, MA: Harvard Business School Press, 1997.

Chronicle of Higher Education. "State Appropriations for Higher Education". *Chronicle of Higher Education,* January 11, 2008.

Clark, Burton R. *The Distinctive College: Antioch, Reed, and Swarthmore*. Chicago: Aldine, 1970.

Clark, William. *Academic Chrisma and the Origins of the Research University*. Chicago: University of Chicago Press, 2006.

Cole, Jonathan R. The Great American University. New York, NY: Public Affairs, 2009.

Council for Aid to Education, "College Fund Raising Rankings in 2013", February 24, 2014.

Delta Project, *Academic Spending vs Athletic Spending: Who Wins*, January, 2013.

Delta Project, *Labor Intensive or Labor Expensive: Changing Staffing and Compensation Patterns in Higher Education*, February, 2014.

Detesiewicz, William, "The Miseducation of America", Chronical Review, July 4, 2014.

Drucker, Peter. "A Better Way to Pay for College". *Wall Street Journal*, A14, May 9, 1991.

Drucker, Peter. "Beyond the Information Revolution". *Atlantic Monthly*, 284:4, October, 1999.

Duderstadt, James J., Daniel E. Atkins and Douglas Van Houweling. *Higher Education Faces the Digital Age: Technology Issues and Strategies for American Colleges and Universities*. Washington, DC: American Council on Education, 2002.

Duderstadt, James J. (chair). *Preparing for the Revolution: Information Technology and the Future of the University*. Washington, DC: National Academies Press, 2003.
http://www.nap.edu

Duderstadt, James J., William A. Wulf, and Robert Zemsky. "Envisioning a Transformed University", *Issues in Science and Technology,* 22(1), 35-41, Washington, DC: National Academy Press, 2005.

Duderstadt, James J. *A Case Study in University Transformation: Positioning the University of Michigan for the New Millennium* (Ann Arbor: University of Michigan, Millennium Project, 1999), http://milproj.dc.umich.edu/publications/strategy.

Duderstadt, James J. *A University for the 21st Century*. Ann Arbor, MI: University of Michigan Press, 2001.

Duderstadt, James J. and Farris W. Womack. *The Future of the Public University in America: Beyond the Crossroads*. Baltimore, MD: Johns Hopkins University Press, 2002.

Duderstadt, James J. *The View from the Helm: Leading the American University During an Era of Change*. Ann Arbor, MI: University of Michigan Press, 2007.

Duderstadt, James J., Aligning American Higher Education with a Twenty-first-century Public Agenda". *Higher Education in Europe*, Vol 34, No. 3-4, 2009.

The Economist. "The Brains Business: A Survey of Higher Education". *The Economist*, September 10, 2005.

The Economist. "The Search for Talent: The World's Most Valuable Commodity Is Getting Harder to Find". *The Economist*, October 2006.

The Economist. "Now for the Reckoning—Corporate America's Legacy Costs". *The Economist*, October 15, 2005.

The Economist. "Special Report: Blacks in America". *The Economist*, August 6, 2005.

The Economist. "Detroitosaurus Wrecks: The lessons for America and the car industry from the biggest industrial collapse ever". *The Economist*, June 4, 2009.

The Economist. "A Ponzi scheme that works". *The Economist*, December 19, 2009.

Editorial, "Fat-Cat Administrators at the Top 25", New York Times, May 23, 2014

Finley, Nolan. "Attitude May Make Michigan the New Mississippi". *Detroit News*, May 1, 2005.
See also Finley, Nolan. *Detroit News*, December 9, 2007.

Flexner, Abraham. *Medical Education in the United States and Canada*. New York: Carnegie Foundation for the Advancement of Teaching, 2010.

Frey, William H, "Five Myths about the 2010 Census and the U.S. Population", Brookings Institute Report, 2010.

Friedman, Thomas. *The World Is Flat: A Brief History of the 21st Century*. New York, NY: Farrar, Strauss, and Giroux, 2005.

Garcia, M.L. and O.H. Bray. *Fundamentals of Technology Roadmapping*. Albuquerque, NM: Sandia National Laboratory, 1997.

Germano, William. "What Are Books Good For?" *The Key Reporter*, Phi Beta Kappa Society, Winter, 2010, p. 8.

Gibson, William. *Neuromancer*. New York: Ace Books, 1984.

Glazer, Louis. *A New Agenda for Michigan*. Ann Arbor, MI: Michigan Future, 2007. http://www.michiganfuture.org

Glazer, Louis and Donald Grimes. *Michigan's Transition to a Knowledge-Based Economy, Annual Progress Reports, 2008, 2009, 2010*. Ann Arbor, MI: Michigan Future, Inc., 2010.

Google Books, http://books.google.com/, 2011

Gratz v. Bollinger, Docket 02–516, 539 U.S. 244 (2003), Decision: June 23, 2003; *Grutter v. Bollinger,* Docket 02–241, 539 U.S. 306 (2003), Decision: June 23, 2003

Harpers Magazine, 1887.

HathiTrust, http://www.hathitrust.org/, 2011

Haycock, Kati and Danette Gerald. *Engines of Inequality*. Washington, DC: Education Trust, 2008.

Haycock, Kati. *Opportunity Adrift*. Washington, DC: Education Trust, 2010.

Holliday, Chad, chair. National Academies Committee on Research Universities. Research Universities and the Future of America: Ten Breakthrough Actions Vital to Our Nation's Prosperity and Security. Washington, D.C.: National Academy Press, 2012. (The complete report, summary, and videos of the press conference can be found on the National Academies website: http://sites.nationalacademies.org/PGA/bhew/researchuniversities/index.htm

Hollinger, David. "Academic Culture at Michigan". 50th Anniversary of Rackham School of Graduate Studies. Ann Arbor: Rackam School Publications, 1988.

Ito, M., *Hanging Out, Messing Around, and Geeking Out: Kids Living and Learning With New Media*. Cambridge: MIT Press, 2009.

ITS. "Trends in College Spending (ITS) On-Line". Delta Project on Postsecondary Education Costs, Productivity, and Accountatility, 2010.

Kane, Thomas J. and Peter R. Orzag. "Funding Restrictions at Public Universities: Effects and Policy Implications" (working paper, Brookings Institution, Washington, DC, September 2003).

Kelly, Kevin. "Scan This Book!". *New York Times Sunday Magazine*, May 14, 2006.

Kerr, Clark. *The Uses of the University*. Cambridge: Harvard University Press, 1963.

Kerr, Clark. *The Gold and the Blue: A Personal Memoir of the University of California, 1949-1967*. Volume One: Academic Triumphs. Berkeley, CA: University of California Press, pp. 172-190, 2001.

Kirkpatrick, David. The Facebook Effect: The Inside Story of the Company That Is Connecting the World. New York: Simon & Schuster, 2011.

Krug, Edward A., ed., *Charles W. Eliot and Popular Education*, Classics in Education, vol. 8 (New York: Teachers College, Columbia University, 1961).

Kuhn, Thomas S. *The Structure of Scientific Revolutions*. Chicago, IL: University of Chicago Press, 1963.

Kurashige, Scott, "The Diversity Gap at Michigan Flagship, Signs of a Lost Public Mission", Chronicle of Higher Education, March 3, 2014.

Kurzweil, Ray. *The Age of Spiritual Machines: When Computers Exceed Human Intelligence*. New York, NY: Viking, 1999.

Kurzweil, Ray. *The Singularity Is Near: When Humans Transcend Biology*. New York, NY: Viking Penguin, 2005.

Levy, Stephen. In the Plex: How Google Thinks, Works, and Shapes Our Lives. New York: Simon & Schuster, 2011.

Leonhardt, David, "If Affirmative Action is Doomed, What Is Next?", New York Times, June 17, 2014.

Lingenfelter, Paul E. "The Firing of Henry Philip Tappan, University Builder" (master's thesis, University of Michigan, 1970)

Longworth, Richard C. *Caught in the Middle: America's Heartland in the Age of Globalization*. New York, NY: Bloomsbury, 2008.

Lohmann, Susanne. Meeting of the National Academies IT Forum with the Provosts of the Association of American Universities, Beckman Center, Irvine, CA, September 9, 2003.

McPherson, Peter. *Assuring That Public Research Universities Remain Vital*. Washington: Association of Public and Land-Grant Universities, 2010.

McPherson, P., Shulenburger, D., Gobstein, H., and Keller, C. Competitiveness of Public Research Universities and Consequences for the Country: Recommendations for Change. Washington, D.C.: Association of Public and Land-Grant Universities, 2009.

Miller, Charles (chair). *A Test of Leadership: Charting the Future of U.S. Higher Education*. National Commission on the Future of Higher Education in America ("The Spellings Commission"). Washington, DC: Department of Education, 2006.

Mueller, Benjamin, "Officials' Pay at Public Colleges Rise Faster than at Private Ones", Chronicle of Higher Education, March 3, 2014

Moe, Michael. *The Knowledge Web: People Power– Fuel for the New Economy*. New York, NY: Merrill-Lynch, 2000.

National Intelligence Council. *Mapping the Global Future, Project 2020*. Washington, DC: Government Printing Office, 2004.

New York Times Editorial, "Keeping the Public Colleges Afloat". New York Times, 2004.

Newman, John Henry. *The Idea of a University* (New Haven, CT: Yale University Press, 1996; 1st ed., New York: Longman, Green, 1899)

Northwest Ordinance, Article 3., printed in F. N. Thorpe, ed. *The Federal and State Constitutions, Colonial Charters, and Other Organic Laws*. Washington, DC: U.S. Government Printing Office, pp. 957, 1909.

NRC, Committee on Developments in the Science of Learning. *How People Learn: Brain, Mind, Experience, and School*. National Research Council. Washington, DC: National Academy Press, 2000.

NRC. The Impact of Academic Research on Industrial Performance. National Research Council. Washington, D.C.: National Academies Press, 2003.

Obama, President Barack. State of the Union Address before the United States Congress, January 25, 2011.

Palmisano, Samuel J. "The Globally Integrated Enterprise". *Foreign Affairs*, May/June 2006.

Pancake, Cherry. Presentation to the Advisory Committee on Cyberinfrastructure, National Science Foundation, 2003

Peckham, Howard H. *The Making of the University of Michigan 1817–1992*, ed. and updated by Margaret L. Steneck and Nicholas H. Steneck (Ann Arbor: University of Michigan Bentley Historical Library, 1994)

Pensky, Marc. "Digital Natives, Digital Immigrants". NCB University Press, 9 (5), 2001.

Prahalad, C.K. and Gary Hamel. *Competing for the Future*. Cambridge, MA: Harvard Business School Press, 1994.

Price, Richard Rees. "The University of Michigan: Its Origin and Development," *Harvard Bulletin in Education* 3 (January 1923)

Raschke, Carl A. *The Digital Revolution and the Coming of the Postmodern University*. New York, NY: Routledge Falmer, 2003.

Reed, Dan. "Computing for the Future: Release 2016". Chapel Hill, NC: Renaissance Computing Institute, 2006.

Rhodes, Frank H. T. *The Creation of the Future: The Role of the American University*. Ithaca, NY: Cornell University Press, pp. 137-39, 2001.
Rhodes is the former president of the first of the nation's truly public-private hybrids, Cornell University.

Rudolph, Frederick. *The American College and University: A History* (Athens: University of Georgia Press, 1962)

Ruegg, Walter. *A History of the University in Europe*, Vol. I, Universities in the Middle Ages. Cambridge: Cambridge University Press, 1992.

Ruegg, Walter. *A History of the University in Europe*, Vol. II, Universities in Early Modern Europe. Cambridge: Cambridge University Press, 1996.

Ruegg, Walter. *A History of the University in Europe*, Vol. III, Universities in the 19th and Early 20th Centuries. Cambridge: Cambridge University Press, 2004.

Schmidt, Peter, "Supreme Court Upholds Bans on Racial Preference in College Admissions", Chronicle of Higher Education, April 22, 2014.

SHEEO. *State Higher Education Finance*. Washington, DC: State Higher Education Executive Officers, 2010.

Supiano, Beckie, "The Solution to the Student-Load 'Crisis'? Depends on How You Define it", Chronicle of Higher Education, June 24, 2014.

Tappan, Henry Philip. *University Education* (New York: George P. Putnam, 1851)

Thelin, John R. A History of American Higher Education. Baltimore: Johns Hopkins University Press, 2004.

Thomas, Douglas and John S. Brown, A New Culture of Learning. San Francisco: Douglas-Brown, 2010.

Thompson, Derek, "How America's Top Colleges Reflect (and Massively Distort) the Country's Racial

Evolution", The Atlantic, 2013.

Turner, James and Paul Bernard. "The Prussian Road to University", 50th Anniversary of Rackham School of Graduate Studies. Ann Arbor: Rackam School Publications, 1988.

UM Accreditation Report. *An Institution of Global Learning, Knowledge, and Engagement.* Ann Arbor: University of Michgan Regents, 2010.

UM Financial Reports, 2010, 2011, 2012, 2013

University of California, *A National Model for Providing Quality Educational Opportunity to Low-Income Students*, April, 2014.

Vest, Charles M. "Why MIT Decided to Give Away All Its Course Materials via the Internet". Chronicle of Higher Education, January 30, 2004.

Vest, Charles M. *Clark Kerr Lectures, The University of California, Berkeley.* Berkeley, CA: University of California Press, 2005.

Veysey, Lawrence R. *The Emergence of the American University.* Chicago: University of Chicago Press, 1965.

Waldrop, M. Mitchell. "Campus 2.0". Nature Vol. 495, March 14, 2013

Weber, Luc and James J. Duderstadt, eds. *The Globalization of Higher Education*, VI Glion Colloquium. Paris: Economica, 2007.

Weber, Luc and James J. Duderstadt, eds. *Innovation and University Research*, VII Glion Colloquium. Paris: Economica, 2009.

Wendler, C., Bridgeman, B., Cline, F., Millett, C., Rock, J., Bell, N., and McAllister, P. The Path Forward: The Future of Graduate Education in the United States. Princeton, NJ: Educational Testing Service, 2010.

Wiley, John. *Forward Thinking: The University and Wisconsin's Economic Recovery.* Chancellor's Report. Madison, WI: University of Wisconsin, 2003.

Wulf, William A. "Warning: Information Technology Will Tranform the University", *Issues in Science and Technology*, pp. 46-52, Summer, 1995.

Zarkaria, Fareed, "America's Higher Education Failings", New York Times, May 1, 2014.

Zemsky, Robert, William Massey and Gregory Wegner. *Remaking the American University: Market-Smart and Mission Centered.* New York, NY: 2005.

Zemsky, Robert. *Making Reform Work: The Case for Transforming American Higher Education.* Rutgers,

NJ: University of Rutgers Press, 2009.
See also Robert Zemsky, "Will Higher Education Ever Change as it Should?". *Chronicle of Higher Education Commentary*, August 3, 2009.

Made in the USA
Middletown, DE
05 March 2016